Indian Foreign Policy

The rise of India as a major power has generated new interest in understanding the drivers of its foreign policy. This book argues that focusing on the role that ideas and discourse play in producing India's state identity and shaping its foreign policy behaviour results in a more complete account of state action.

The book looks at Indian foreign policy from 1947 to 2004, and examines major moments of crisis such as the India–China war in 1962 and the conducting of nuclear tests in 1998, as well as the approach to international affairs of significant leaders like Jawaharlal Nehru. The analysis sheds new light on these key events and figures in India's history, and develops a strong analytical narrative around its foreign policy behaviour based on an understanding of India's post-colonial identity. It argues that a prominent facet of India's identity is that of a civilizational-state that brings to international affairs a tradition of morality and ethical conduct derived from its civilizational heritage and the legacy of its anti-colonial struggle.

This book provides an understanding of the motivations that will help to shape India's behaviour as a rising power by illuminating the conditions of possibility in which foreign policy is made.

Priya Chacko is Lecturer in International Politics in the School of History and Politics at the University of Adelaide, Australia. Her research interests include the normative basis of Indian foreign policy, non-Western thought in International Relations, and India's engagement with Africa and global governance.

Interventions
Edited by
Jenny Edkins
Aberystwyth University
and
Nick Vaughan-Williams
University of Warwick

As Michel Foucault has famously stated, 'knowledge is not made for under-standing; it is made for cutting.' In this spirit The Edkins – Vaughan-Williams Interventions series solicits cutting edge, critical works that challenge mainstream understandings in international relations. It is the best place to contribute post disciplinary works that think rather than merely recognize and affirm the world recycled in IR's traditional geopolitical imaginary

(Michael J. Shapiro, University of Hawai'i at Mãnoa, USA)

The series aims to advance understanding of the key areas in which scholars working within broad critical post-structural and post-colonial traditions have chosen to make their interventions, and to present innovative analyses of import-ant topics.

Titles in the series engage with critical thinkers in philosophy, sociology, pol-itics and other disciplines and provide situated historical, empirical and textual studies in international politics.

Critical Theorists and International Relations
Edited by Jenny Edkins and Nick Vaughan-Williams

Ethics as Foreign Policy
Britain, the EU and the other
Dan Bulley

Universality, Ethics and International Relations
A grammatical reading
Véronique Pin-Fat

The Time of the City
Politics, philosophy, and genre
Michael J. Shapiro

Politics and the Art of Commemoration
Memorials to struggle in Latin America and Spain
Katherine Hite

Indian Foreign Policy
The politics of postcolonial identity from 1947 to 2004
Priya Chacko

Politics of the Event
Time, movement, becoming
Tom Lundborg

Theorizing Post-Conflict Reconciliation
Agonism, restitution and repair
Edited by Alexander Keller Hirsch

Indian Foreign Policy

The politics of postcolonial identity from
1947 to 2004

Priya Chacko

Routledge
Taylor & Francis Group

LONDON AND NEW YORK

First published 2012
by Routledge
2 Park Square, Milton Park, Abingdon, Oxfordshire OX14 4RN

Simultaneously published in the USA and Canada
by Routledge
711 Third Avenue, New York, NY 10017

First issued in paperback 2014

Routledge is an imprint of the Taylor and Francis Group, an informa business

British Library Cataloguing in Publication Data
A catalogue record for this book is available from the British Library

Library of Congress Cataloging in Publication Data
Chacko, Priya.
Indian foreign policy: the politics of postcolonial identity from 1947–2004 /
Priya Chacko.
    p. cm. – (Interventions)
    Includes bibliographical references and index.
    1. India–Foreign relations–1947–1984. 2. India–Foreign relations–1984–
    3. National characteristics, East Indian. 4. Postcolonialism–India.
    I. Title.
    JZ1737.C47 2011
    327.54–dc23

                                                            2011025002

ISBN 978-0-415-66568-1 (hbk)
ISBN 978-1-138-84386-8 (pbk)
ISBN 978-0-203-14773-3 (ebk)

Typeset in Times New Roman
by Wearset Ltd, Boldon, Tyne and Wear

Contents

Acknowledgements

This book has its origins in a doctoral thesis written at the University of Adelaide, it was revised while I took up positions at universities in New Zealand and South Africa and finally, and fittingly, it was completed when I returned to Adelaide. I'd like to thank friends, colleagues and the administrative staff at the School of History and Politics at Adelaide, in particular, for providing a supportive and conducive research environment. My supervisors Anthony Burke, Juanita Elias and especially Peter Mayer offered unstinting encouragement and guidance and my fellow postgraduate students kept me in good spirits right to the end of the long haul.

A travelling fellowship and research abroad scholarship from the University of Adelaide funded my fieldwork in India and the Alexander family generously gave me a place to stay in Delhi. I'd like to thank Sanjay Chaturvedi for facilitating my attachment to the Centre for the Study of Geopolitics at Punjab University and a number of scholars at the School of International Studies at Jawaharlal Nehru University for useful conversations and for providing me with contacts for interviews. Many thanks to the editorial team at Routledge for their professionalism and enthusiasm for this project. Without Robbie Shilliam's urging I might never have sought to publish this book at all.

Finally, the support of my family, my mother Grace and brother Arun, has been invaluable and the inspiring memory of my late father, Elias Chacko guides me in everything I do. Thanks especially to Benny Thomas for his friendship and care and little Thabisa who happily kept me company during the late nights and early mornings when this book was being completed.

Permission Acknowledgement

Some of the material in this book, especially in chapters 2, 3 and 7 is drawn from 'The Internationalist Nationalist: Pursuing an Ethical Modernity with Jawaharlal Nehru', in Robbie Shilliam (ed.) *International Relations and Non-Western Thought: Imperialism, Colonialism and Investigations of Global Modernity*, London & New York: Routledge, copyright 2011, reproduced here by permission of the publisher, and 'The Search for a Scientific Temper: Nuclear Technology and the Ambivalence of India's Postcolonial Modernity', *Review of International Studies*, 37: 185–208, copyright 2011, reproduced here by permission of the publisher.

1 Introduction

'Emerging', 'rising', 'surging', 'blossoming' – these are just a few of the epithets that have become commonplace in discussions about contemporary India (Cohen 2001, 2006c, Di Lodovico *et al.* 2001, Walker 2006). In particular, there has been a preoccupation with the question of whether it will be – to borrow the title of the 2006 *Hindustan Times* Leadership Summit, an annual gathering of India's political and business elite – 'The Next Global Superpower?'. At this conference, Sonia Gandhi, the President of the Congress Party, which led India to its independence from Britain in 1947 and has been a prominent force in Indian politics ever since, said that she approved of the question mark affixed to the title because she was 'somewhat uneasy with the very word "Superpower"':

> For too many of us, it evokes images of hegemony, of aggression, of power politics, of military might, of division and conflict. But that is not what India has been all about through the centuries and it certainly is not what I would like to see India become. During long periods of our past, India exercised a profound influence on the course of world history, and it did so without exercising any kind of overt power. Consider, for instance, how Gandhiji, mocked as 'a half-naked fakir' by the British, took on the Superpower of the day through the mere force of his values and ideas. We Indians have always known our place in the world even when the world was treating us lightly … Why should we think of ourselves as a 'Global Superpower'? Why not instead work towards becoming a global force for Peace, Progress and Prosperity?
>
> (Gandhi 2006)

This account of India's exceptionalism – its ability to exercise influence without coercive power – is a narrative that has underpinned India's foreign policy discourse for the last six decades. Many recent discussions of Indian foreign policy, however, either ignore or dismiss this normative element of Indian foreign policy discourse. Indeed, a common assertion in recent studies of Indian foreign policy is that the shift in India's economic and political power is being accompanied by a shift from a foreign policy driven in part by 'idealism' to a foreign policy more narrowly anchored in 'realism'. Few of these studies, however, provide a considered theorization of Indian foreign policy, which would entail an examination of what 'idealism' and 'realism' mean in an Indian context or assess the relevance of these models of foreign policy analysis. Raja Mohan (2003: xix), for instance, argues that until the 1990s India viewed international and regional security issues through 'the prism of the Third World and anti-imperialism'. The end of the Cold War, however, forced it to 'not remain just a protesting leader of the Third World trade union' but to take an interest in managing the international system (Mohan 2003: xx–xxi). Underlying Mohan's analysis is the assumption that self-interested power politics is the natural and normal mode of behaviour for states. He writes of India's nuclear tests in 1998:

> For good or bad, and whether the world liked it or not, India decided to cross the nuclear Rubicon. Fifty years after Independence, India now wanted to become a normal nation – placing considerations of Realpolitik and national security above its recently dominant focus on liberal internationalism, morality and normative approaches to international politics.
>
> (Mohan 2003: 7)

Likewise, for Sumit Ganguly (2003/2004: 47), in the post-Cold War era, Indian foreign policy is 'growing up', shedding 'its ideological burden' of non-alignment and Third Worldism, and adopting 'more pragmatic policies at home and abroad' while for Ashok Kapur (2006: 5), since 1998, 'Indian statecraft was pursued on the basis of practical geopolitical considerations rather than the idealism of Nehru's peace policy'. Similarly, Jacques Hymans (2009) argues that while Nehruvian India sought to use 'soft idealism' to change the dynamics of international politics, this vision has been decisively abandoned. Yet even a cursory glance at speeches and statements by Indian leaders indicates that the vocabulary and practice of Indian foreign policy has not been dramatically altered. As Harsh Pant (2009) has noted, Indian leaders still express doubts about dominant conceptions of power, they still discuss the merits of the concept of non-alignment and promote the value of nuclear disarmament (see Gandhi 2006; Nath 2008). Moreover, as Amrita Narlikar (2006) points out, India continues to participate in anti-hegemonic coalitions in international organizations such as the World Trade Organisation (WTO).

Pant's (2009: 254) primary purpose is not to explain these continuities but to condemn them as 'irresponsible and dangerous' for, according to him, India is not behaving as rising powers should, by seeking 'to enhance their security by increasing their capabilities and their control over the external environment'. Narlikar's explanation for India's behaviour, on the other hand, is suggestive of another common approach to explaining India's foreign policy, which is to argue that it contains a combination of both 'idealism' and 'realism'. She suggests that a domestic political culture influenced by its colonial experience, and its mistrust of international regimes and great powers are the primary cause of its continued defensiveness (Narlikar 2006: 73). Stephen Cohen (2001: 308) likewise argues that India's foreign policy tradition combines elements of both idealism and realism and suggests that the gap between the two trends must be bridged in order to make Indian foreign policy more credible and predictable. Similarly, Kanti Bajpai (1998) claims that India's decision-makers adhere to a policy of 'modified structuralism' which, following Steven Krasner, he defines as the desire to maximize interests and power in a world of similarly-minded states, but also to transcend individual calculations of interest under certain conditions. India's modified structuralism, argues Bajpai (1998: 195), is driven by expediency and conviction – the former because of India's material weakness and the latter due to the 'Gandhian norms and principles of nonviolence' imbued during the nationalist struggle (See also Nayar and Paul 2004).

While these accounts go further in explaining the continuities in Indian foreign policy and its consistent use of language that defies the vocabulary of power politics, they theorize Indian thinking on international relations at a highly general level which, beyond a certain point, fails to be analytically illuminating. Bajpai for instance, does not detail what an 'idealism' shaped by 'Gandhian norms' entails at an epistemological or ontological level and nor does he offer an explanation as to why it has proven so resilient. Cohen (2001: 40) finds the source of India's 'idealism' in the political thought of Jawaharlal Nehru, India's first Prime Minister, who he labels a liberal internationalist without examining whether Nehru's thought can, in fact, be captured by this term. The circumstances, under which the 'realist' or 'idealist' strands of thinking come into play, moreover, are not made clear in these accounts.

This book seeks to move past an idealist/realist framework for understanding Indian foreign policy by reconceptualizing foreign policy as postcoloniality, which I define as a self-reflexive ethico-political project of identity construction that emerged in reaction to the colonial encounter. Specifically, I argue that in the post-independence period, under the government of Jawaharlal Nehru, foreign policy was established as a key site for the construction of an Indian postcolonial identity which is deeply ambivalent toward modernity because it at once embraces modernity, as the cure for the condition of backwardness that led to colonial subjugation, and repudiates modernity for its creation of an exploitative and violent colonial relationship in the first place. This ambivalence, however, gave rise to an ethico-political project based on the notion of India's 'civilizational exceptionalism' – the idea that India is equipped with unique moral qualities that will allow for the creation of an ethical modernity. While not all successive governments have subscribed to this ethico-political project in its entirety, I suggest that they have all grappled with aspects of it. Taking as points of departure key foreign policy events, issues and policies such as nuclear disarmament, non-alignment, intervention and conflicts with China and Pakistan during the period between 1947 and 2004, I trace the way in which narratives of India's civilizational past, inform the representations produced in India's foreign policy discourse and how they, in turn, enact a postcolonial identity for India.

Understanding India's postcolonial identity

'Indian civilization' and the colonial encounter

As the discussion above indicates, a number of scholars have touched on the role of India's colonial past in Indian foreign policy. However, most do not attempt to rigorously theorize it.[1] Some scholars (Banerjee 1994; Cohen 2001) have also noted the influence of the idea of an Indian civilization on India's foreign policy but, again, do not do so in a rigorous manner. Stephen Cohen (2001) for instance, argues that Indian nationalists came to define India as morally and spiritually superior which 'constructed (often in collaboration with Western scholars) a distinctive view of India's past that helped shape their vision of India's future' (Cohen 2001: 26). Thus 'Indian officials believe they are representing not just a state but a civilization' and 'contemporary Indian leaders also see India as playing a global, albeit benign, role' that is keeping with its intrinsic civilizational qualities (Cohen 2001: 52). While at some points Cohen (2001: 26) seems to suggest that the idea of an Indian civilization is socially constructed, in other places he appears to imply the prior existence of civilizational traditions which were simply revived during the nationalist struggle (Cohen 2001: 51).

Following Cohen, I argue in this book that a notion of India as a civilization constitutes a key aspect of India's postcolonial identity. Departing from Cohen, however, I explicitly treat this idea as a social construction. In particular, I analyse 'Indian civilization' as what Jean Francois Lyotard (1989: xxiii) calls a metanarrative or metadiscourse. Michel Foucault (1984b, 1984a) understood discourses as knowledge-power formations constituted by a system of rules that allow a bounded space in which some statements are made more meaningful than others. The system of rules that Foucault refers to is not a formalized, rigid structure but is a set of constraints, norms or conditions and these rules are enacted by discursive practices. A metanarrative or metadiscourse is a 'grand narrative' which gives rise to smaller narratives and provides them with cultural meaning, purpose and legitimacy. The metadiscourse of Indian civilization emerged as an outcome of the need to negotiate intercultural difference during the colonial encounter. This process of negotiation took place within a framework of Eurocentrism which was a key feature of the emergence of European modernity.[2] Central to this framework was the hierarchization of societies, according to which peoples were placed on a scale of development, beginning with 'savages' in a 'state of nature', proceeding to the 'barbarian' stage and then the 'civilized' stage, which was the pinnacle of social, political and economic development represented by Europe. The metadiscourse of Indian civilization was built into the edifice of this hierarchy of cultures, which became the basis of a theory of unequal political relations between societies.[3]

Most colonial writings granted India the right to call itself a civilization – that is, Indian society was thought to have experienced significant development since its emergence from the state of nature. However, it was a degraded and stagnant civilization that was far from the lofty heights of Western civilization. For

'Orientalist'[4] scholars such as Henry Colebrooke and William Jones, who established the first Indological institution, the Asiatic Society of Bengal in 1784, under the patronage of Warren Hastings, the English East India Company's first appointee to the position of Governor General of Bengal, India was a Hindu/Sanskritic civilization dominated by the caste system which had been in constant decline since its 'golden age' of the 'Vedic era' from the third to the seventh centuries AD (Jones 1788b: 421). Jones situated India within a European master narrative as a lost wing of European culture and Sanskrit literature, especially the *Vedas*, were depicted as documentary evidence of humans in their 'primitive' state (Trautmann 1997: 193; Jones 1788b: 425–6; Brimnes 2002: 252–3; Ali 1998: 99). While these scholars found India's current state to be 'degenerate', and used this assessment to justify colonial rule, they valorized its ancient past as being 'splendid in arts and arms, happy in government, wise in legislation and eminent in various knowledge' (Jones 1970: 712–13; Jones 1788b: 421).

The image of India as a stagnant civilization lost in time and in need of rescuing from cruel despots was particularly prominent in the writings of the Utilitarian thinkers of the nineteenth century. James Mill, an employee of the East India Company, who wrote a textbook on Indian history that remained hegemonic throughout the nineteenth century, saw no value in Indian culture, ancient or otherwise because it lacked rationalism and individualism, the qualities possessed by 'civilized' societies. Mill (1848a: 153) was unimpressed by the Orientalist valorization of ancient Indian culture, arguing that the state of India's arts, sciences, laws and institutions indicated 'but a few of the earliest steps in the progress to civilization'. Indeed, Indians were in a 'state of weak and profligate barbarism' with 'moral habits left in their minds by superstition and despotism' (Mill 1848a: 492; Mill 1848b: 576). Orientalist assumptions about the centrality of Hinduism and caste to Indian society were accepted by Mill who also argued that caste had disabled India's progress from the lower to higher stages of civilization.

Utilitarian discourses on Indian were dependent on the constant articulation of India's difference or radical Otherness, a preoccupation they shared with Romantic scholars like Friedrich von Schlegel. Romantics – through the interpretation of selected Sanskrit literature – established India as a land of mysticism, a fundamentally non-rational civilization. Concerned about an excessive focus on discipline and rationality due to the rapid industrialization of their societies, the Romantics constructed Asia, in general, and India, in particular, as a site of hope and fantasy – the source of an Oriental Renaissance, which would liberate Western scientific man from its obsession with rationalism (Schlegel 1889: 519–20). While the Romantics commended India's 'spirituality' as opposed to Europe's 'materialism' this did not entail full-fledged approval of what they saw as Indian values. Schlegel argued that if Western culture had gone to the one extreme of valuing rationalism over all else, then Indian culture was weighed down in superstition (Schlegel 1889: 471). Moreover, India's religious and cultural diversity bred disunity and it was particularly prone to foreign conquest (Schlegel 1889: 509, 10).

As this brief overview of Orientalist, Utilitarian and Romantic eighteenth and nineteenth century writings on India shows, the colonial encounter gave rise to a particular construction of Indian civilization with some consistent themes. While writers disagreed about the worth of Indian civilization, in general, they agreed that India was a Hindu civilization, dominated by religion and caste and riven by discord and, because of this, its current state was one of degeneracy. Rendering India a Hindu civilization, moreover, meant that India's Muslims were portrayed as belonging not just to a separate civilization, but to an invading and conquering civilization. This is a narrative which has been a trope in discourses of Indian civilization from the earliest published British accounts of Indian history (Metcalf 1994: 8–9, 138–9). As Thomas Blom Hansen (1999: 65) has argued, however, the 'Hindu religion', 'Hindu culture' and 'Hindu' as a distinct cultural category are all largely the result of the interventions by European scholars, missionaries and administrators since the eighteenth century. Prior to this, argues Romila Thapar (1989: 222), the notion of a uniform religious community which could be identified as Hindu was largely absent. Rather, in India's early history there existed multiple communities based around locality, language, caste, occupation and sect. The construction of India as a Hindu civilization was, however, indispensable in making it 'possible to identify the difference of the East from the West within a single conceptual grammar of civilizational order and hierarchy' (Hansen 1999: 66). Thus, the multitude of syncretistic religious practices found in India were given a previously unknown coherence and invented as a monolithic religion based around Sanskrit texts and a 'classical' Vedic high civilization.

Similarly, caste was never simply a static religious system that dominated the social and political order, as scholars such as Susan Bayly (1999), Nicholas Dirks (1987) and Niels Brimnes (2002) have shown. Rather, it was a highly politicized institution in which the positions of groups were changeable and varied according to the nature of local conditions (Bayly 1999: Ch.1). As Bayly (1999: Ch. 5), Dirks (1987: 9) and Brimnes (2002: 250) all point out, it was not until the nineteenth century displacement of indigenous political authorities that what we now call the caste system became a reified, Brahmin-centred hierarchy.

The colonial encounter, and the discourses of Indian civilization that it produced, led to a series of debates amongst the elite about why India was colonized, how it should become independent and the nature of the public good for a postcolonial India.[5]

The choice of Calcutta as the capital of British India gave rise, in the first half of the nineteenth century, to a movement championing reason and modernity in opposition to superstition and tradition and described 'with a profound imperialist irony' as the 'Bengali Renaissance' (Spivak 2001: 58). At the instigation of Bengal's land-owning and business elite, civic institutions such as the Hindu School, the Landholders Society and the British India Association were established and close collaboration with East India Company officials was encouraged, especially after the Asiatic Society of Bengal began accepting Indian members in 1829. Ram Mohan Roy and other members of the Bengali elite who were at the forefront of the 'Bengali Renaissance' were in agreement with the Orientalists that Indian civilization was essentially a Hindu one (Roosa 1995: 148). Their negotiation of an Indian identity was based on the Orientalist notion of a glorious but degraded Hindu civilization which was now inferior to Western civilization and therefore deserving of British rule. This conviviality however, did not survive. As Britain's economic exploitation of India increased and its colonial racism became entrenched, disillusionment with Western civilization replaced the previous sense of admiration (Roosa 1995: 148–9). Using the tools provided by European Romantic nationalism, early Indian nationalists set out to recover the 'authentic' cultural nation which, more often than not, involved a resort to the idea of Hindu superiority and exclusivity (Bhatt 2000: 23). In this view, while it was seen to be important to learn from the West, Indian/Hindu civilization remained vastly superior because it had reached a far more advanced level of philosophical and religious learning before its current state of degradation.

'Indian civilization' and the ambivalence of postcolonial modernity

These early debates laid the groundwork for later forms of anti-colonial nationalism, such as that of V.D. Savarkar who played a leading role in the anti-colonial, violent revolutionary nationalism which became influential in the wake of the first partition of Bengal in 1905, before Gandhian nationalism established its dominance in the 1920s. He was of the view that the ancient Hindus had laid the basis for a 'great and enduring civilization' long before the ancient Egyptians and Babylonians (Savarkar 1938: 7). Savarkar drew on the Orientalist conception of a Vedic, Sanskrit-based civilization built and maintained by upper-caste, North Indian Hindus (Savarkar 1938: 115). He argued that a sense of nationalism had been present in the subcontinent for more than 5,000 years in the 'Vedic nation' and that a cultural self-consciousness had developed through geographical interconnectedness (Savarkar 1938: 101–2). For Savarkar (1938: 54–6), India's current state of degeneracy was the result of the expansion of Buddhism, the subsequent decline of its military prowess and repeated invasions by Muslims.

He was particularly influenced by Herbert Spencer's evolutionary sociology, which stressed the 'natural law' of aggressive competition between nations, and the writings of Giuseppe Mazzini in whose work he found a blueprint for a nationalism that was strongly modernist and emphasized cultural exclusiveness and homogeneity (Bhatt 2001: 90). Hence, Savarkar's model for the nation-state tolerated no ambiguity of identity and Indian civilization was defined as strictly 'Hindu'. In his key text *Hindutva*, Savarkar (1938: 147) cites three main criteria for membership of the Hindu nation: territorially bounded descent, a bloodline that can be traced back to the Vedic nation and a common culture. Together these constituted a common race and civilization which were the basis of Hindutva or the feeling of Hinduness. Savarkar's Hindu nationalism has had an increasing influence on political and cultural life and foreign policy in postcolonial India through contemporary Hindu nationalist political parties and organizations such as the BJP and the Rashtriya Swayamsevak Sangh (RSS). In the immediate post-independence period, however, it was Nehru's views, which were influenced by the thought of Gandhi, which shaped the dominant construction of India's post-colonial identity.

Mohandas Karamchand Gandhi's meetings with revolutionary nationalists, including Savarkar, in London in the early twentieth century played an important role in the development of his political thought. Unlike Savarkar and the early nationalists, Gandhi did not consider India's status as a subject nation to be the result of its weakness, backwardness or stagnancy. Rather, India, had been seduced by the allure of materialism offered by modern civilization and that was why it had succumbed to British rule (Gandhi 1938: 38, 40). For Gandhi (1938: 61–2), the limitless urge for consumption inherent in modern social systems of production had been the moral downfall of the English and if India were to avoid a similar fate it had to look to its ancestors who 'set a limit to our indulgences'.

Key to his argument was a condemnation of 'modern civilization' which was contrasted to 'true civilization' or *sudharo* in his early tract, *Hind Swaraj*:

> Civilization is that mode of conduct which points out to man the path of duty. Performance of duty and observance of morality are convertible terms. To observe morality is to attain mastery over our mind and passions. So doing, we know ourselves. The Gujarati equivalent for civilization means 'good conduct'.
>
> (Gandhi 1938: 61)

Gandhi argued that while Western civilization was inclined toward the propagation of immorality, because it was beholden to modern civilization, 'the tendency of Indian civilization is to elevate the moral being' (Gandhi 1938: 61–3). It was the notion of Indian civilization having a distinct moral element that we also find in the writings of Jawaharlal Nehru. For Nehru, there was no doubting that India possessed a great civilization, but by abandoning 'a rational spirit of inquiry' and clinging to an atrophied caste system which created disunity, it had become backward (Nehru 1982 [1946]: 54; 2003: 33). Yet, although India had long been in a 'condition of mental stupor and physical weariness' something 'vital and living continues' and it possessed an 'essential unity had been so powerful that no political division, no disaster or catastrophe had been able to overcome it' (Nehru 1982 [1946]: 55, 9). It was this 'deep well of strength' that India would use to establish a modern, industrialized state and assume its 'proper station with others in the van of human civilization and progress' (Nehru 1982 [1946]: 55, 566).

Thus, for Nehru, the colonial encounter gave rise to a perception of India's backwardness and this in turn produced a desire to mimic modern Western governmental practices. Yet, like Gandhi, Nehru was also a critic of modernity who recognized its relationships with colonialism and imperialism and pointed to a tendency in Western modernity toward exploitation, violence and material betterment at the expense of the community's moral and cultural values. He was convinced that 'the world of to-day has achieved much, but for all its declared love for humanity, it has based itself far more on hatred and violence than on the virtues that make man human' (Nehru 1982 [1946]: 563). '[I]t would seem', he argued, 'that the kind of modern civilization that developed first in the west and spread elsewhere, and especially the metropolitan life that has been its chief feature, produces an unstable society which gradually loses its vitality' and he pinpointed the causes of this as emanating from the conditions created by modern industrialism and the capitalist structure of society as well as a 'a divorce from the soil' (Nehru 1982 [1946]: 554–5).

For Nehru, therefore, ambivalence lay at the core of his negotiation of the colonial encounter. Mimicry and ambivalence are both key concepts that have been used to understand the relationship between the colonized and the colon–izer. According to Homi Bhabha, for instance, both the colonizer and the colon–ized express a desire for mimicry and are constituted by ambivalence. For the colonizer, mimicry represents 'the desire for a reformed, recognizable Other, *as a subject of a difference that is almost the same, but not quite*' (Bhabha 1994: 86). Some sense of difference is also necessary, however, for the absence of difference would mean the elimination of their rationale for the colonial project. For the colonized, mimicry satisfies the urge to overcome the perception of backwardness that emerged in the colonial encounter while maintaining a critique of the suffering caused by the colonial enterprise, or as Bhabha (1994: 44) puts it, in Frantz Fanon-inspired prose: 'the fantasy of the native is precisely to occupy the master's place while keeping his place in the slave's avenging anger'.

As a split subject that is at once the subject and object of modernity, the colo-nized subject remains at risk of representing, as Dipesh Chakrabarty (2000: 40) argues, a 'sad figure of lack and failure'. Nonetheless, 'maneuvers are made within the space of the mimetic … to represent the "difference" and the "origin-ality" of the "Indian"', often within 'devices of collective memory' that are 'anti-historical' and 'non-modern' (Chakrabarty 2000: 40). In Nehru's national-ist project, this representation of difference comes in his comments on India's 'civilizational exceptionalism', which he describes at one point as its 'spirit of renunciation' and at another as a 'certain idealist and ethical background to the whole culture' (Nehru 1982 [1946]: 559, 95). This is not, however, simply an expression of 'avenging anger'. Rather, the ambivalence inherent in Nehru's response to the colonial encounter gave rise to an ethical project in which a par-ticular construction of India's past was a source of internal critique as well as a source of possibility for the future. In his reading, and in this he differed from Gandhi, the problems of modern industrial civilization were not inherent in modernity itself, but in its Western manifestation. Hence, while those factors that contributed to Indian civilization's decline could be overcome through a selec-tive appropriation of Western modernity, those that made it great, its 'civiliza-tional exceptionalism' could be used to fashion an ethical modernity as opposed to a modernity along Western lines. Moreover, Nehru's understanding of India's civilizational exceptionalism is not an exclusivist or communitarian idea for the source of India's 'spirit of renunciation' is not unique to Indian culture but is an ancient wisdom garnered through experience and present in all ancient civilizations whether in the 'Orient' or 'Occident'. Indeed the 'Orient/Occident' dichotomy was considered to be false since, despite their differences, ancient India, Greece and China 'all had the same broad tolerant, pagan outlook, joy in life and in the surprising beauty and infinite variety of nature, love of art, and the wisdom that comes from the accumulated experience of an old race' (Nehru 1982 [1946]: 151).

In understanding Nehru's nationalist project in this way, I am arguing against Partha Chatterjee's (1993) prominent reading of the hegemonic nationalist movement in India as being built upon a split between an inner and outer distinction. According to Chatterjee, nationalists sought to erase cultural difference from the outer or 'material' domain of the state which included statecraft, science and technology, while preserving it in the 'spiritual' domain, which constituted the 'true self' and was more important than the material domain, because here, the East was distinctive, superior and had nothing to learn from the West. Chatterjee (1986: 133, 227) argues that Nehru, in particular, represented nationalist thought 'at its moment of arrival' by giving primacy to the economic sphere and hence, placing 'the idea of the national state at its very heart'. However, Nehru's nationalist thought is far more ambivalent and ambiguous than Chatterjee allows for, as we have seen, Nehru, like Gandhi, was a critic of Western industrialism and Western modernity. These views are more clearly expressed in Nehru's *Discovery of India*, which was written in 1944–1945 when India was at the cusp of independence and contains critiques of modern science, the modern nation-state, industrialism and realist geopolitics and promotes a radical internationalist vision of a post-sovereign state 'One World', rather than his earlier *Autobiography*, on which Chatterjee mainly relies to make his argument (Nehru 1982 [1946]; 1980). While Chatterjee (1986: 75) rightly observes that the 'search for a postcolonial modernity has been tied, from its very birth, with its struggle against modernity', rather than aiming to 'make modernity consistent with the nationalist project', as Gyan Prakash (1999: 109) argues, the strand of nationalism represented by Nehru imagined postcolonial India as a 'culturally rooted moral community with a rational will to industrialize and achieve technological mastery'. Thus, India had to express itself in the language of modernity but its modern articulation had to be irreducibly different from its colonial expression (Prakash 1999: 109). Specifically, India's modernity would be an ethical modernity.

Foreign policy as postcoloniality

Postcoloniality, ethics and foreign policy

Dominant modes of industrialization and technological mastery were not the only focus of Nehru's critique of Western modernity – he was also sharply critical of way in which states interacted with one another in the modern international system. Indeed, foreign policy has been a key site for the enactment of Nehru's desire for an ethical modernity.

In arguing for a reading of foreign policy as postcoloniality, I wish to move past the analytical limits of both postcolonialism and conventional approaches to understanding foreign policy. 'Postcolonial', a term that has been attached to many societies following the formal end of colonial regimes, has been the subject of much controversy and debate regarding its meaning and implications (Harootunian 1999; McClintock 1992; Scott 1999). My particular concern here is postcolonialism's analytical limits for, as Srirupa Roy (2007: 23) has argued, much of the work on postcolonialism has focused on epistemology, on interrogating colonialism and on theorizing a modular, and often oppositional 'postcolonial condition', at the expense of paying attention to the 'political and institutional dynamics of postcolonialism as a historically specific, and contextually located, project of establishing a sovereign nation-state'. While Roy's focus is on the role of domestic political and institutional processes in the consolidation of state authority in postcolonial India, this book seeks to add to a small but growing body of literature that explicitly seeks to bring postcolonialism into dialogue with the discipline of International Relations (IR) in order to point out the latter's deep and limiting Eurocentrism and its failure to confront the colonial system and its legacies.[6]

In the case of foreign policy analysis, as Siba Grovogui (2003: 43) has argued, either by 'benign neglect or sheer intellectual hubris' the majority of theorists have 'forsaken the idea of an alternative conceptualization of foreign policy that might differ in both substance and ethos from that which emerged from modern Europe'.[7] In seeking to redefine foreign policy as postcoloniality I do not mean to imply the existence of a generalizable postcolonial foreign policy, but rather, a temporally and spatially bound process of identity formation that is the result of specific negotiations of the colonial encounter and the postcolonial, Western-dominated world order. Nonetheless it is possible to begin with the observation that, given its temporal specificity, the emergent postcolonial state was necessarily distinct from the early European state in its relation to modernity, subjectivity and power (Grovogui 2003: 43). If the emergence of the European state and its accompanying notions of subjectivity, were conditioned by disenchantment with the old regime, revolution and counter-revolution, then the postcolonial state was shaped by the cultural and political alienation and economic marginalization that were the product of colonialism and imperialism. As a consequence, many postcolonial entities 'generated antihegemonic discourses characterized by distinct ideological and cultural sensibilities as well as novel political and ethical bases as foundations for a different ethos of foreign policy and international relations' (Grovogui 2003: 43). They adopted, in other words, foreign policies with an ethical dimension that was conditioned by the experiences of colonialism and imperialism.

The term 'ethical foreign policy' has become prevalent in both the theory and practice of foreign policy in recent years although, as a political phenomenon, it is typically given a Western genealogy, beginning with Jimmy Carter's attempt to promote human rights in the 1970s and the idea of 'good international citizenship' in Australian foreign policy in the late 1980s and early 1990s (Wheeler and Dunn 1998: 848; Chandler 2003; Bulley 2009). Aside from the point that these accounts tend to overlook the fact that, as Dan Bulley (2009) argues, all foreign policies have an ethical dimension to the extent that foreign policy is essentially about how to constitute and relate to otherness, they also fail to acknowledge that prior to the 1970s many former colonial entities adopted foreign policies aimed at eradicating colonialism, inequality and injustice and they did so in the language of universality. Indeed, as Roland Burke (2010) has shown, in the 1950s it was newly decolonized Asian, African, Arab and Latin American states that were at the forefront of debates over establishing universal human rights norms. For instance, at the 1955 Bandung conference – a foundational moment for postcolonialism as an ideological and political position – endorsement of universal human rights was a prominent focus of many of the delegates and the final communiqué contains a reference to 'the Universal Declaration of Human Rights as a common standard of achievement for all peoples and all nations' (Burke 2006: 956; Young 2001: 191).

In the case of India specifically, in the immediate post-independence period, there was a broad perception that under Nehru's leadership, India had become, to quote the nationalist leader C. Rajagopalchari, 'the biggest moral power in the civilized world' (quoted in Guha 2007: 179). The term 'moral power' has parallels to contemporary discussions of the European Union as a 'normative power' and this shows that, as critics of the idea of 'normative power Europe' have argued, the notion is neither novel nor unique to the EU and needs to be seen, not as an objective category, but as a discursive practice that constructs European identity (Manners 2002; Diez 2005). The fashioning of India as a 'moral power' was aimed at both changing global norms and at the same time constructing a postcolonial Indian identity. It has at its core a desire to alter modern ways of conducting international relations, which were considered particularly violent and destructive. This was to be done by transforming the nature of the nation-state, through the promotion of an 'internationalist nationalism' and relations between nation-states, through a set of distinct foreign policies such as Panchsheel or peaceful coexistence, non-alignment, the rejection of collective defence pacts, disarmament and active involvement in the UN. It is my argument in this book that successive governments following Nehru's have had to grapple with the politico-ethical project and, therefore, that it has had a lasting impact on Indian foreign policy.

Identity and foreign policy

In examining the relationships between foreign policy, identity and ethics I treat foreign policy as a discursive practice and a social construction which is shaped by specific spatial and historical circumstances and experiences of modernity. I draw on the basic insight from constructive approaches in IR that foreign policy interests are constructed rather than pre-given and that identity forms the basis of interests. Conventional accounts of foreign policy assume the existence of an anarchic international system in which a state's foreign policy interests are primarily concerned with ensuring the state's survival through the accumulation of power and wealth. Constructivist critics of this understanding of a state's interests point to its vagueness and indeterminacy and the lack of clarity it provides as to what a state will or should do to ensure its survival and security (Weldes 1999: 6–7). Thus for instance, as I noted above, Harsh Pant (2009: 254–5) – who adopts a 'realist' framework, drawing on Robert Gilpin and Hans Morgenthau[8] – argues that India is not behaving as a rising state should because of its lack of an 'instinct for power', and he appears to equate power primarily with military strength. Precisely why India lacks an 'instinct for power' is not explained, however, and exactly how a greater emphasis on military power will make India more secure is not explicated, but, rather, treated as self-evident. Moreover, the idea of fixed and pre-given interests rests on a positivist epistemology, which assumes that policy makers can objectively assess an independent reality, and ignores the role of interpretation in comprehending a reality. By contrast, a constructivist reading of foreign policy argues that before policy makers can direct state action, they engage in a process of interpretation and then representation, in order to make sense of the situation they are faced with (Weldes 1999: 6–7).

Constructivist understandings of foreign policy therefore move away from asking *why* particular foreign policy decisions are made, toward an approach that asks *how* the 'reality' that policy makers function in is produced and maintained and how this, in turn, makes decisions possible (Doty 1993: 303). As Roxanne Doty (1993: 297–8) has noted, conventional approaches to foreign policy analysis are limited because in asking *why* certain courses of action are taken they unproblematically assume the pre-existence of subjects, meanings and interpretive dispositions that make certain decisions possible. In contrast, asking *how* policy decisions are made entails an examination of the processes by which subjects, meanings and interpretative dispositions are materialized. *How* questions, therefore, pay attention to power as productive of subjects rather than treating power as something just wielded by subjects.

Constructivist approaches vary in their understanding of how the identities that shape interpretations of situations are formed. 'Conventional constructivism' assumes that state behaviour is shaped by certain pre-existing 'basic interests' and sets of social rules which have come about because of the dominance of a particular shared meaning system that has narrowed the ways in which actors understand the world (Wendt 1992, Jepperson *et al.* 1996). This approach emphasizes the impact of the interaction between states in the construction of identities and interests. 'Critical constructivists' assumes that the policy makers who act in the name of the state are not blank canvases prior to interstate interaction but, rather, usually have an elaborate understanding of the world and their state's place in it. Further, this understanding is partly developed in, and constrained by, domestic political, historical and cultural contexts (Weldes 1999: 9). Thus, critical approaches to foreign policy analysis not only ask different questions but also broaden the scope of analysis. David Campbell (1992: 75–7), for instance, makes a distinction between 'foreign policy' and 'Foreign Policy' whereby the former refers to all societal practices of differentiation or modes of exclusion which provide the 'discursive economy or conventional matrix of interpretations' in which the state-based practice of Foreign Policy operates (Campbell 1992: 76). Foreign policy therefore is not something that emerges after the establishment of the state, but is essential to its development 'as a cultural artifact implicated in the intensification of power in the state' while Foreign Policy 'serves to reproduce the constitution of identity made possible by 'foreign policy' and to contain challenges to the identity which results' (Campbell 1992: 76)

Drawing on this approach I argue that Indian policy makers continue to produce a representation of postcolonial India based on collective meanings which emerged during the anti-colonial negotiation of the colonial encounter. This postcolonial 'social imaginary', which following Castoriadis (1998: 128) can be defined as 'an original investment by society of the world and itself with meaning', is the basis of India's 'foreign policy' and gives rise to Foreign Policy interests, such as, for instance, an aversion to alliances and an attraction to anti-hegemonic coalitions that often appear to be counterintuitive to conventional readings of foreign policy. This book analyses the writings of the Orientalist, Utilitarian and Romantic scholars discussed above and the writings of anti-colonial nationalist leaders and their negotiation of the colonial encounter, in addition to analysing the 'Foreign Policy' pronouncements found in speeches, cables, press conferences, White papers and interviews, which as Cynthia Weber (1998: 92) argues, 'are often moments when states traumatically confront the impossibility of 'being' sovereign and thus insist upon their sovereign subjectivity all the more'. Foreign policy statements, particularly those that make ethical claims are often dismissed as rhetorical masks that cover up a state's 'real' self-interested motivations. Rather than speculating about 'real' motivations, however, my analysis is based on the post-positivist assumption that 'reality' can only be known through its representation in discourse. Thus, foreign policy actions can only be accessed through their textual representation and they can only be understood by accounting for the context that makes a representation possible.

This book focuses on analysing several moments of 'crisis' in Indian foreign policy such as the 1962 India–China war, the 1971 war with Pakistan, the 1974 'Peaceful Nuclear Explosion' and the 1998 nuclear tests. It treats these instances of 'crisis' as 'political acts, not facts' that do not simply threaten states but are 'social constructions forged by state officials in the course of producing and reproducing state identity' (Weldes 1999: 219). Hence, my focus is on understanding how particular situations and events come to be constructed as a 'crisis', how policies are developed to deal with the 'crisis', how the 'crisis' is linked to, or enabled by, India's state identity and/or whether it succeeds in reproducing this state identity. This last point is key, because constructivist approaches have been critiqued for their tendency to emphasize the persistence of state identities over long periods, even while they acknowledge that identity is inherently unstable and incomplete (Laffey 2000). As Mark Laffey (2000) points out, however, while states attempt to reproduce their identity, this process can have unforeseen consequences which produce shifts in the social landscape, thereby empowering other groups and competing discourses. This can have significant implications, leading to the transformations of identities.

Most constructivist approaches tend to emphasize the role of the creation of foreign enemies and the clear demarcation between an ordered domestic sphere and an anarchical international sphere in the process of identity production. Campbell (1992: 8) for instance, argues that the 'constitution of identity is achieved through the inscription of boundaries which serve to demarcate an "inside" from an "outside", a "self" from an "other", a "domestic" from a "foreign"'. My analysis of Indian foreign policy and identity, however, indicates the extent to which internal critiques of the national Self can also be crucial in the constitution of identity. As I noted above, the construction of postcolonial India's state identity depends on narratives of its civilizational past. While some of these narratives promoted the idea of India's civilizational exceptionalism by glorifying Indian civilization's apparently superior qualities, others were narratives of 'backwardness' that sought to explain India's colonial subjugation and provided a rationale for the (partial) mimicry of Western modernity. India's postcolonial identity therefore, is constituted in significant ways by what Thomas Diez (2004) has called 'temporal Othering', a process that was central to the colonial encounter.

My argument also draws on the constructivist insight that, 'foreign policy performative moments that affect sovereign states are themselves hopelessly crossed with sex, sexuality, and gender performances' (Weber 1998: 93). Rather than accepting the conventional IR understanding of states as female and feminine in the domestic arena and male and masculine in the international arena, Weber (1998: 94, f.n.77) makes the observation that arguments about sex, sexuality and gender codings of a specific state cannot be generalized to other states or across time. Rather, Weber argues in favour of an approach that investigates how 'various particular, historically-bounded sex and gender codings participate in affecting the state and sovereignty' (Weber 1998: 93). In India's case, the colonial encounter produced a racially gendered hierarchy of feminized or effeminized, non-white Others against a masculine, white Europe as well as a anti-colonial nationalist discourse on the resilience and virtues of 'Mother India', a representation of India which initially emerged in colonial Bengal but eventually became a key symbol of Indian nationalism and was appropriated by nationalists of all ideological hues. The narratives of India's civilizational past are therefore gendered in highly specific ways, and I argue that these gender codings affect the production of India's state identity and the ethico-political project that lies at its core.

Outline of the book

The first part of the book spans the period between 1947, when India became an independent nation-state to 1964, the year that marked the death of India's first Prime Minister, Jawaharlal Nehru. This period, which is often called the Nehruvian era of Indian foreign policy because of the dominance exercised by Nehru in the foreign policy arena, marks the formative years of the production of India as a postcolonial subject and as a 'moral power'. Chapter 2 examines the emergence of India's contradictory nuclear policies (promoting nuclear disarmament while developing nuclear technology) in Nehru's foreign policy. It argues that these policies need to be understood in the context about the Indian negotiations of gendered and racialized colonial narratives about the mental and physical weakness of Indians. While some Indian leaders negotiated these colonial narratives in ways that led to a focus on physical regeneration and the creation of an indigenous scientific tradition, Nehru was more critical about the uses of science and violence in Western modernity. It was in this context that nuclear disarmament, as a marker of India's postcolonial difference as a nation-state that is pursuing an ethical modernity, became central to his foreign policy. This chapter and those following it are also aimed at showing how gendered colonial narratives produced gendered narratives of anti-colonial resistance and, in turn, a uniquely gendered state identity in which resistance is expressed in a feminized semiotic.

Chapters 2 and 3 both focus on tracing the development of Nehru's international thought. In Chapter 2, I argue that his 'internationalist nationalism' is formulated from insights drawn from Buddhist philosophy, Marxism and the thought of Gandhi and Rabindranath Tagore while in Chapter 3 I analyse Nehru's policies of non-alignment and Panchsheel (peaceful coexistence) as constituting an international politics of friendship which also bears the influence of Gandhian and Buddhist thought. Nehru's attraction to internationalism was also, I argue, informed by a reading of India's past, according to which, the dynamism of Indian civilization occurred when it was actively engaged with the world while backwardness set in during times of isolation. Both chapters also argue that Nehru regarded psychology and emotion as central to understanding political action. For Nehru the possibilities for transforming the way in which states interacted with one another depended on the amelioration of fear and the affects of trauma in their social relations. Building friendship and cultivating trust through universal nuclear disarmament were important steps in this direction.

In Chapters 3 and 4, I examine Nehru's attempts to operationalize this politics of friendship in India's relations with countries in Asia and South Asia. Chapter 3 focuses on his attempt to build a collective identity based on friendship through a discourse on 'Asianism'. However, Nehru's desire not to project India as a leader but to build relationships based on equality proved to be a difficult path to navigate. In relation to the countries in India's immediate vicinity, now collectively known as South Asia, Nehru often slipped into a disover equality and stymied his ability to achieve his aims. This chapter also explores Nehru's approach to Pakistan, which was excluded from both a politics of friendship and a politics of fraternity. Pakistan was instead approached in a discourse of rejected fraternity in which its form of nation-building, based on what Nehru regarded as a 'narrow nationalism', was represented as the antithesis of the ethical modernity being pursued by India. Finally, the chapter considers the alternative conceptualizations of political friendship by Gandhi and the nationalist leader C. Rajagopalchari and suggests that near the end of his life, Nehru moved toward endorsing their advocacy of unilateral measures of goodwill and generosity to build friendship across hierarchy and difference in relation to Pakistan.

The policy of Panchsheel was first outlined in 1954 in an agreement with China, which was a particular focus of Nehru's politics of friendship. Chapter 4 explores the trajectory of Nehru's approach to China from his anti-colonial declaration of India and China's civilizational affinities, a belief that was shared by other nationalists, to the culmination of the border war in 1962. Nehru's role in the development of the border conflict is usually interpreted as one of extreme naivety regarding China's intentions (Khilnani 1999: 40) or, paradoxically, a single-minded realpolitik disregard for negotiation with China (Noorani 2004). I argue, however, that the war was the result of a more complex postcolonial politics. Nehru's approach toward China was informed by a desire to repudiate the imperial geopolitics of British India, in which China was viewed as a threat, even though he accepted the gendered colonial narrative of India's vulnerability to invasion and conquest. By focusing on India's resilience in the face of aggression he sought to transform this narrative into one of civilizational exceptionalism and rejected imperial geopolitics for a politics of friendship. The latter came undone, however, when India's 'customary borders', which were in dispute with China, were rendered into a symbol of India's resilience as a civilization and discourses of honour, humiliation and self-respect came to the fore. The war and its aftermath undermined Nehru's policies of Panchsheel and non-alignment, his politics of friendship and his ethico-political project. In general, however, I argue in the second part of the book that successive governments have continued to grapple with Nehru's conceptualization of India's identity and the role that foreign policy would play in it.

Chapter 5 focuses on the two major foreign policy incidents of the 1970s, India's 1971 intervention in Pakistan's civil war, which led to the creation of Bangladesh, and the nuclear test of 1974. The chapter argues that the 1971 'crisis' worked to both consolidate and undermine the dominant conception of India's postcolonial identity and that this identity also placed constraints on the actions that India could take. The Indian leadership's assertion of humanitarian reasons for intervening in Pakistan's civil war reiterated the representation of Pakistan within a discourse of 'rejected fraternity' which buttressed India's self-identity as a state pursuing an ethical modernity while its other legitimating reason of 'refugee aggression', according to which, India, while tolerant and welcoming, was also too politically and socially fragile to cope with the influx of refugees from East Pakistan, invoked narratives of India's backwardness. The chapter also details the ways in which the international and domestic reactions to India's military action undermined the reproduction of India's self-identity.

In Chapter 6 I analyse India's military and political intervention in Sri Lanka's civil war in the 1980s, which I argue should be seen in the shifting context of India's domestic political environment and leadership. India's intervention is often interpreted in terms of a desire to establish India as the regional hegemon (Krishna 1999; DeVotta 2003). Its legitimating reasons – that it acted out of humanitarian concern for Sri Lanka's Tamil minority and concerns about India's domestic stability, since it was claimed that Indian Tamils shared close bonds with their Sri Lankan brethren – are usually dismissed or subordinated to its apparent desire for hegemony. I argue, however, that taking India's legitimating reasons seriously reveals a great deal about the circumstances that made it possible for it to undertake its intervention during the 1980s, but not before, in the 1970s when the conflict started, or later, in 2000 when Sri Lanka specifically asked for help.

I continue to analyse developments in India's approach to South Asia and its nuclear policies in Chapter 7, which focuses on the period between the late 1990s and 2004. This period marked the rise of the Hindu nationalist Bharatiya Janata Party (BJP) and the chapter pays particular attention to the ways in which Hindu nationalist conceptions of strength and identity were constituted during the colonial encounter, and came to the fore during this time in the BJP's attempt to refashion India's foreign policy and identity. In particular, I argue that the 1998 nuclear tests were an attempt to mark a distinct break from the Nehruvian legacy in Indian foreign policy by articulating a new, militaristic approach inspired by an aggressively modernist Hindu nationalist ideology. I show, however, that this was not wholly successful for the BJP reiterated certain discourses of India's 'ethical modernity', despite its stated ambition to overhaul Indian foreign policy.

In sum, as I conclude in Chapter 8, the ethico-political project established in the post-independence period has proved remarkably resilient and an approach that reconceptualizes foreign policy as postcoloniality helps us understand why this has been the case. This approach, moreover, assists in gaining a better understanding of the ideational basis of India's foreign policy behaviour in the past and in the present as it negotiates its rise as a major power.

Part I

India as a 'moral power'

1947–1964

2 Nuclear technology, disarmament and the ambivalence of postcolonial identity

In 1996 the Indian government submitted a Memorial to the International Court of Justice on the legality of the threat or use of nuclear weapons. In this carefully argued Memorial, India concluded that the use of nuclear weapons in a first attack or even as retaliation would be illegal under international law (India 1998a: 72). Further, the Memorial stated that India considered the theory of nuclear deterrence 'abhorrent' since it implied that the 'keeping of peace or prevention of war is to be made dependent on the threat of horrific indiscriminate destruction' and because it justified the stockpiling of weapons of mass destruction 'at an enormous expense' (India 1998a: 73). Finally, it argued that if it is the case that the use of nuclear weapons is against international law, then, as with biological and chemical weapons, the manufacture of nuclear weapons itself must be considered illegal (India 1998a: 74). Yet, just two years later India conducted nuclear tests and declared itself a nuclear weapons state. In March 2006 India reached an agreement on civil nuclear energy cooperation with the United States which, in the words of Prime Minister Manmohan Singh (2006b), 'offered the possibility of decades-old restrictions being set aside to create space for India's emergence as a full member of a new nuclear world order'. On the same day that Singh was heralding the global acceptance of India's nuclear weapons, Jayant Prasad, India's Permanent Representative at the Conference on Disarmament in Geneva reiterated India's belief that the 'very existence of nuclear weapons, and of their possible use or threat of their use, poses a threat to humanity' and that India 'remained committed to the goal of a nuclear-weapon free world, to be achieved through global, verifiable and non-discriminatory nuclear disarmament' (Prasad 2006). As these two examples illustrate, India has an ambivalent, contradictory relationship with nuclear technology. It would be easy to dismiss India's advocacy of disarmament as a superficial mask for its realpolitik pursuit of nuclear weapons. In his discussion of India's refusal to sign the Nuclear Non-Proliferation Treaty (NPT) on the grounds that it did not require the declared nuclear powers to commit to time-bound nuclear disarmament, Sumit Ganguly (1999: 158) argues that '[a]lthough India's argument was couched in moral terms, a more pragmatic consideration – namely keeping its nuclear weapons option open – guided its decision not to sign the treaty'. Disarmament, however, is a long-standing and consistent feature of India's foreign policy discourse that governments of all hues have upheld and dismissing it as superficial rhetoric does not explain why this has been the case. Even in 2006, as we saw above, when India believed it was on the cusp of being recognized as a nuclear weapons state it still felt obliged to engage in a discourse of disarmament that reiterates a self-image of morality and ethical conduct. Alternatively, an English school or conventional constructivist explanation would focus on the impact of international norms and structures against the proliferation of nuclear weapons in compelling India to validate its nuclear transgressions by raising the issue of disarmament. Yet, the international discourse of non-proliferation is one that has enjoyed little legitimacy in India and has long been identified with a discriminatory world order and labelled 'nuclear apartheid'.

In this chapter I argue that tracing the origins of India's contradictory nuclear policies produces important insights into India's postcolonial identity and a more complete understanding of the motivations behind its foreign policy. Specifically, I argue that taking India's discourse on disarmament seriously reveals the ambivalent nature of India's postcolonial identity. This ambivalence is the product of a critique of Western modernity, which emerged during the anti-colonial era, and the widespread acceptance of the idea among nationalists that India's failure to become modern was the reason for it succumbing to colonial rule. In particular, a widely-held conviction in nationalist discourse was that Indian civilization's inability to develop a scientific outlook and modern technology contributed to civilizational backwardness which, in turn, led to colonial subjugation. Given this perception of civilizational backwardness, nuclear technology in postcolonial India took on a special significance as an explicit example of both the promise and the violence of Western modernity. The production of nuclear technology would instil in India what Nehru referred to as a 'scientific temper' to provide a cheap source of power for India's economic development and foster scientific cooperation which, in turn, would facilitate an internationalist ethic that was vital for the construction of an ethical modernity. Yet, nationalist discourse also produced significant critiques of the destructive nature of Western modernity and this meant that the outright adoption of a technology with the capacity to unleash an unprecedented level of violence was untenable. The discourse of disarmament is an attempt to resolve this dilemma by recourse to India's moral strength, which is seen as an innate attribute of Indian civilization.

To begin this examination of the significance of nuclear technology and nuclear disarmament in postcolonial India, I take as my point of departure a comment from Bal Thackeray, the leader of the militant Hindu nationalist Shiv Sena party, who declared his support for the 1998 nuclear tests on the grounds that 'we have to prove that we are not eunuchs' (1998b). Several authors have commented on the gendered nature of discourses on nuclear weapons (See for example, Cohn 1987). In the Indian context, Runa Das (2002, 2006) has analysed the representations of masculinity and femininity that underpin Hindu nationalist ideology and which, she argues, are used to justify its pro-nuclear policies. One purpose of this chapter is to introduce the colonial origins of the gendered discourses that contemporary Hindu nationalists like Thackeray perpetuate. I further explore Hindu nationalist discourse on nuclear weapons in Chapter 7. In this chapter my aim is to show that the Hindu nationalist linkage of masculinity and nuclear weapons was only one particular negotiation of the complex, competing and gendered narratives regarding modernity and progress that emerged as a reaction to a perception of India's civilizational backwardness among the Indian elite during the colonial encounter. Other nationalist leaders, like Nehru, negotiated these narratives differently and this negotiation, I argue in this chapter, led to the prioritization of nuclear disarmament instead of the production of nuclear weapons.

The first section of this chapter examines the gendered narratives of India's scientific backwardness and moral superiority that emerged during the colonial era. I pay particular attention to Nehru's negotiations of these narratives and his construction of a (gendered) civilizational identity for India. The second part of the chapter focuses on how Nehru's understanding of Indian civilization's flaws and attributes made possible post-independence policies that prioritized the development of nuclear energy alongside a championing of nuclear disarmament.

Science, violence and Indian civilization

Colonial masculinity and native effeminacy

By invoking the figure of the eunuch to describe India's pre-nuclear character, Thackeray was drawing on what Nandy (1983: 4) calls the 'language of the homology between sexual and political dominance' that saturated colonial discourse from the middle of the nineteenth century. This discourse constructed a gendered and racialized hierarchy of effeminized, non-white Indians against masculine, white Europeans. The stereotype of the effeminate Hindu draws on hegemonic codings of both race and gender and can be traced back to the beginnings of colonial rule in the eighteenth century. Since masculinity is frequently constructed as a cornerstone of modernity and white Europeans were thought to be at the pinnacle of modernity the pathologizing of the Indian male as effeminate, due to both mental and physical weakness, became an integral part of the ideology of the British civilizing mission and was used extensively in nineteenth and twentieth century writings on India (Krishnaswamy 1998; Sinha 1995).

Romantic scholars, like Friedrich Schlegel, and Orientalists, like William Jones, were heavily reliant on the language of effeminacy in their writings on India. For Schlegel, the Indian mind was dominated by the faculty of imagination rather than reason while Jones described Indians as 'soft and voluptuous' (Inden 1990: 94; Krishnaswamy 1998: 94). Utilitarian discourse drew on this as evidence of England's moral superiority since the English language and English literature were thought to be rational, energetic and masculine (Krishnaswamy 1998: 21–3). According to James Mill (1848a: 465) 'Hindus possessed a feminine softness both in their persons and in their address'. For Mill (1848a: 517) 'the Hindu, like the Eunuch, excels in the qualities of a slave'. By contrast, 'the Mohammedan is more manly, more vigorous' (Mill 1848a: 517). Mill (1848a: 150) admitted the existence of Indian scientific learning only to dismiss it because, according to him, Indians had cultivated their understanding of the astronomical and mathematical sciences 'exclusively for the purposes of astrology; one of the most irrational of all imaginable pursuits; and one of those which most infallibly denote a nation barbarous'.

Likewise, for Thomas Macaulay (Macaulay 1870: 517, 611) 'there never perhaps existed a people so thoroughly fitted for a foreign yoke' because,

> the physical organisation of the Bengalee is feeble even to effeminacy ... During many ages he has been trampled upon by men of bolder and more hardy breeds. Courage, independence, veracity are qualities to which his constitution and his situation are equally unfavourable.
>
> (Macaulay 1870: 517, 611)

Moreover, '[h]is mind bears a singular analogy to his body. It is weak even to helplessness for purposes of manly resistance...' (Macaulay 1870: 611).

While all Hindu men were thought to show signs of effeminacy, by the nineteenth century the label came to be applied most often to the men of Bengal – the capital of British India and the site of the most extensive contact between the British and the 'natives'. The late-nineteenth century construct of the effeminate Bengali *babu* referred specifically to the elite, Hindu, Bengali man who had a Western education. The Bengali *babu* was set apart not only from the manly Englishman but was also distinguished from the so-called 'martial' races, such as the Gurkhas, Marathas, Rajputs and Sikhs. The martial race theory – the notion that some communities are more biologically and culturally suited to military occupations than others – emerged at a time when colonial rule came under increasing challenge by the same section of the Indian middle class population that had once mediated between the British colonial administration and the wider Indian population. The colonial classification of martial and non-martial Indian races had a long history in the colonial practice of favouring certain sections of the Indian elite over others and, as Sinha (1995: 8) suggests, was based on peculiarly colonial understandings of the Indian caste system and 'the ways in which certain attributes of masculinity were supposedly distributed in traditional Indian society'. It was only fully developed, however, in the period of heightened agitation after the Indian army mutiny in 1857 when it became necessary to justify the selective recruitment of officers to the army (Sinha 1995: Ch.2).

The martial race theory gained credence from its association with nineteenth century European race science. Among the explanations that scholars devised to explain Indian effeminacy were the hot climate, the Indian diet and the early age of marriage and motherhood. According to Macaulay (1870: 517), for instance, Bengalis were a 'race ... enervated by a soft climate and accustomed to peaceful employments'. These explanations drew on nineteenth century 'scientific' theories of race as based in biology. Colonial administrator and anthropologist

Herbert Risley (1999) did the most to apply the 'scientific methods' of the time – anthropometry and craniology – to build a race-based ethnography of Indian society. These ideas on the physicality of race pervaded colonial institutions including in the recruitment to, and the management of, the army and the police (Arnold 2004: 261–2). Risley was particularly concerned with aligning caste with race and, for him, the structures of caste reflected the effeminate nature of the 'Indian intellect':

> It is clear that the growth of the caste instinct must have been greatly pro-
> moted and stimulated by certain characteristic peculiarities of the Indian
> intellect – its lax hold of facts, its indifference to action, its absorption in
> dreams, its exaggerated reverence for tradition, its passion for endless divi-
> sions and sub-division, its acute sense of minute technical distinctions, its
> pedantic tendency to press a principle to its furthest logical conclusion, and
> its remarkable capacity for imitating and adapting social ideas and usages of
> whatever origin.
>
> (Risley 1999: 275–6)

The effeminate Indian 'mimic man' was a trope that was deeply unsettling to the colonial imagination because of its ability to transgress gender roles and, in its 'capacity for imitating', to threaten the boundary between colonizer/colonized. Thus, for all of Macaulay's (1870: 611) bluster, his prose is riven with contradic-tion and the effeminate Bengali ultimately emerges as a figure of threat: 'With all his softness the Bengalee is by no means placable in his enmities, or prone to pity … Nor does he lack a certain kind of courage which is often wanting in his masters'. As we shall see, it was this element of threat that some Indian national-ists tried to exploit in their engagement with the trope of effeminacy.

Reclaiming martial valour

The colonial construct of the effeminate Bengali was a product of what Nandy calls the hypermasculinity of British culture during the colonial period – a culture that:

> de-emphasized speculation, intellection and *caritas* as feminine, and justi-
> fied a limited cultural role for women – and femininity – by holding that the
> softer side of human nature was irrelevant to the public sphere. It openly
> sanctified – in the name of such values as competition, achievement, control
> and productivity – new forms of institutionalized violence and ruthless
> social Darwinism.
>
> (Nandy 1983: 32)

Bengali leaders and intellectuals did not so much refute the effeminate *babu* tag as internalize it and try to find ways to overcome it by resorting to a hypermas-culinity of their own – hyper-Kshatriyahood – an exaggeration of a sub-tradition of Indian masculinity that emphasized martial valour (Nandy 1983: 52). The figure of the Kshatriya warrior was linked to India's supposed original conquerors, the Aryans from Central Asia, as well as the more recent 'martial' Rajputs and it was thought that only a recovery of these values would rehabilitate Indians from their current state of weakness (Chakravarti 1990: 48–9). The Bengali intellectual, Bankim Chandra Chatterjee, argued that India's subject status was due to Indians being weak and effeminate. Hence, he advocated the development of a strong, militant, unified nation and the restoration of pride through a recreation of the past that recovered the Hindu 'warrior' (Chakravarti 1990: 49). Another leading figure, Sarala Debi sought to reclaim a heroic martial history akin to that of the Marathas, Sikhs and Rajputs for the humiliated Bengalis who, she argued, had been robbed of their national heritage by foreigners (Chowdhury-Sengupta 1995: 301–2). Likewise, Swami Vivekananda's attempt to reform Hinduism was based on the understanding that contemporary Hindu emasculation was due to the move away from textual Brahmanism and Kshatriya values, which had taken Hindu society away from the Aryan qualities they originally shared with the West. Thus, he instructed his followers: 'No more weeping, but stand on your feet and be men. It is a man-making religion I want. I want the strength, manhood, *kshatravirya* or the virility of a warrior' (Quote in Krishnaswamy 1998: 44). Vivekananda and Bankim's exhortations did not go unheard. Police raids in the early twentieth century on the hideouts of Bengali revolutionaries committed to violent insurrection against the British often discovered copies of Vivekananda's speeches and Bankim's *Anandamath* along with biographies of the Italian revolutionary nationalist Guiseppi Mazzini (Heehs 1993: 25–6).

Bengali writers also contrasted the image of the effeminate *babu* against an image of ideal Aryan womanhood which was militant, courageous and capable of mothering fearless sons. In particular, the figure of the medieval Rajput heroine who took up arms and preferred death to surrender came to embody this ideal of heroic Aryan womanhood in late nineteenth century Bengali writings (Chowdhury-Sengupta 1995: 291–3). This was not, however, intended to challenge dominant gender roles. Sangeeta Ray's reading of Bankim Chandra Chatterjee's two novels *Anandamath* and *Devi Chaudurani*, for instance, shows that ultimately the female rebels in these novels represent '"woman" as the metonymic ideal of the disembodied feminine that helps generate a particular Hindu masculinity, while marking "woman" as the signifier of a sacrosanct traditional domesticity' (Ray 2000: 49).

The preoccupation of Bengali elites with physical regeneration culminated in their leadership of the national volunteer movement in 1885. This movement demanded the extension of membership to the Volunteer Force – which was established after the 1857 Indian rebellion to suppress internal dissension – to Indians. These demands were rejected by the colonial authorities on the basis of fears that such a Volunteer Force would consist primarily of effeminate *babus* who were eager for political power rather than the 'warlike races' who were already permitted into the regular army. This led to the claim that it was the colonial authorities who were now responsible for emasculating Bengali men (Sinha 1995: 93). As Sinha (1995: 94) and Nandy (1983: 8–11) have argued, however, this critique of colonial policies had little to offer by way of a radical challenge to colonial rule for it was thoroughly invested in the politics of colonial masculinity.

Rediscovering Hindu science

As noted earlier, nineteenth century race science was employed to give the martial race theory scientific credence and the politics of colonial masculinity was therefore legitimized through the authority of science. It was also the authority of science, however, that was behind the drive to 'rediscover' an indigenous 'Hindu science' – a movement that I argue should also be seen as a response to the labelling of Hindu men as effeminate.

One of the consequences of the cultural authority invested in science as a vehicle of freedom, power and progress was the emergence in the middle of the nineteenth century of a number of organizations run by Western-educated, upper-caste Indian men aimed at encouraging the development of a scientific culture. After originally appearing in Bengal, this movement quickly spread to different regions of India and was taken up by religious leaders, literary figures, philosophers and scientists alike. Bankim Chandra Chatterjee, for example, wrote numerous essays, novels and satires expressing his belief in the superiority of scientific reason and using the language of science and rationality to interpret and defend Hinduism against the colonial assault (Prakash 1999: 57–8). Aurobindo Ghose – for whom the Bengali 'race' had a 'boundless intellect' but 'a frail constitution and a temper mild to the point of passivity' – tied together the need for physical and cultural regeneration when he argued that India could only regain her former glory by worshipping the mother goddess as 'the Shakti [strength] of war, the Shakti of wealth, the Shakti of science' for these 'are a thousand times more prolific in resources, weapons and instruments than ever before in recorded history' (Quoted in Heehs 1993: 20, 66).

By the late nineteenth century the push for a scientific disposition became widespread in the emerging middle class culture centred on the Hindi language and literature and religious revivalism in north India. Key to this was the re-examination of ancient Indian texts and traditions, which were now identified as 'Hindu', with the goal of finding within them a body of indigenous scientific knowledge. In doing this, members of this elite were building on the work of European Orientalist scholars who had long held that India had once flourished in field of scientific endeavour. Dayananda Sarasvati, the leader of the Hindu revivalist organization, the Arya Samaj, argued in his numerous writings and speeches that only a return to the timeless and scientific truths of the Vedic Hinduism of the ancient Aryans would help Indian civilization overcome such corruptions as the caste system and idol worship (Prakash 1999: 92). The ancient Aryans of the Vedic age thus represented a masculine ideal not just because they were physically strong, but also because they possessed the capacity for scientific reasoning. Showing ancient texts like the *Vedas* to be scientific provided proof of Indian civilization's basis in universal, timeless laws. As Prakash (1999: 89) argues, 'Hindu' texts could be 'projected as the basis for a unitary modern community of Indians, while the contemporary division of Indians into different religions, sects and cults could be seen as corruptions introduced by the passage of time'. Thus, Hindu science gave Indian civilization an ontological unity that was crucial for justifying nationalist claims to independent, modern nationhood. As we shall see, nuclear science was similarly linked to modernity and nationalism in postcolonial India and understanding the links between science, masculinity, modernity and nationalism is, thus, crucial to making sense of India's nuclear politics.

Gandhian nationalism and maternal moral strength

Not all nationalists, however, subscribed to the politics of colonial masculinity. Under the influence of Gandhian movements in the 1920s the charge of effeminacy against Indian men took on a new and disruptive meaning. One of Gandhi's (1938: 44) major points in *Hind Swaraj* was that 'Strength lies in absence of fear, not in the quantity of flesh and muscle we may have on our bodies'. In this book Gandhi appears to connect weakness, cowardice and a lack of self-control with emasculation, unmanliness and effeminacy. Writing about the British suppression of the mounted marauders, the Pindaris, he says, 'It is ... better to suffer the Pindari peril than that someone else should protect us from it and thus render us effeminate' (Gandhi 1938: 43). In the original Gujarati, the word used was *abada*, meaning 'without strength' and also at the time a word for women (Skaria 2006: 5068). Gandhi, however, distinguished between different forms of femininity, in particular, weak femininity and strong femininity and it was the former that he referred to on the rare occasions when he used the conventional language of effeminacy.[1] Indeed, Gandhi sought to separate courage and activism from aggression by recognizing its compatibility with strong femininity, which he associated with motherhood. This was a move that contained truly radical potential to disrupt the authority of colonial rule (Nandy 1983: 54). Thus, to return to his remarks on Pindaris, for Gandhi it was the job of Indians to win over the marauders, not by physical coercion, but through friendship and fearlessness.

In associating courage with femininity Gandhi was drawing on a cultural tradition inspired by the Bhakti religious tradition which emphasized positive androgyny and dynamic womanhood to articulate an alternative model of masculinity (Krishnaswamy 1998: 45). Thus, as Krishnaswamy (1998: 19) suggests, the notion of the effeminate Indian man was not just a false, colonial stereotype but a 'misvalued and distorted recognition of something real in Indian culture'. Similarly, Ashis Nandy (1983: 48) argues that by preserving something of India's 'androgynous cosmology and style' Gandhi was able to produce a 'transcultural protest against the hyper-masculine world view of colonialism'. To borrow Leela Gandhi's (Gandhi 1996–1997: 110) words, Gandhi sought to ground resistance within a 'feminized semiotic'. However, the androgyny that Gandhi extolled did not involve a transcendence of the gender dichotomy or an equal focus on both femininity and masculinity. Rather, he sought to give men access to an essentialized understanding of femininity that would liberate them from an activism wedded to violence and aggression.

Gandhi's understanding of femininity followed from his view that women possessed moral power far in excess of men: 'Has she not greater intuition, is she not more self-sacrificing, has she not greater powers of endurance, has she not greater courage?' (Gandhi 1999n: 57). Thus, if for the early Bengali nationalists the true patriotic defenders of Mother India consisted of a select group of elite, Hindu men (revolutionary militants and world-renouncing holy leaders), for Gandhi the true patriots of Indian civilization were women and peasants. Both were thought to possess the life-affirming qualities of motherhood – women because of their biology and peasants because of the nature of their labour (Sarkar 2001: 258). Furthermore, it was women, for Gandhi (1999n: 9), who were most suited to his brand of non-violent resistance for women were 'the very embodiment of renunciation and compassion'. A man, he stated, 'understands the dharma of non-violence through his intellect whereas a woman has imbibed it even before her birth' (Gandhi 1999n: 9).

Thus, while Gandhi did not speak of devotion to an abstract Mother India or an Aryan ideal of womanhood, he too put an emphasis on women's roles as mothers, albeit as activist mothers who were directly involved in the nationalist movement rather than as just inspirational symbols. Urging women to join the boycott of foreign cloth in 1921, for instance, Gandhi wrote:

> The economic and the moral salvation of India thus rests mainly with you. The future of India lies on your knees, for your [sic] will nurture the future generation … The destiny of India is far safer in your hands than in the hands of a Government that has so exploited India's resources that she has lost faith in herself.
>
> (Gandhi 1999o: 78)

Given the superior qualities of women, Gandhi implored men to feminize themselves so as to gain the courage and moral strength that women possessed (Fox 1996: 42). As Leela Gandhi (1996–1997: 112) argues, 'by disassociating the sign of positive femininity from the home and relocating it in the world' Gandhi was able to accommodate and mobilize a variety of women – those who 'stand in some structural or temporal relationship to the institution of marriage', as well as those who remained unmarried, in favour of political activism. Hence, the assumption of leadership by women in the salt marches of 1930 – a protest against the colonial regime's tax on salt – despite Gandhi's disapproval on the basis that 'they were destined to do greater work in this struggle than merely breaking salt laws' (Gandhi 1999n: 58).

Yet, although he made a space for women in the nationalist movement and wrote in favour of the need for legal and social equality between men and women, Gandhi's own essentialist assumptions were rarely challenged by his followers or his critics. In contrast, other aspects of his political thought and praxis were contested from various perspectives – such as, for example, from the Marxist and Dalit standpoints – and this resulted in him on occasion changing his positions (Hardiman 2003: 116). In the absence of a feminist challenge, Gandhi employed an essentialized notion of femininity which held the maternal, nonsexual woman to be the paragon of non-violence and morality to fashion a morally superior counter-model of Indian masculinity in which the feminine would be absorbed by the male. As Krishnaswamy (1998: 46) argues, 'in Gandhian nationalism, as in various forms of Hindu militancy and subaltern insurgence, femininity, particularly maternity, serves as an important discursive site for the mobilization of male interests and aspirations'. Thus, even though women and femininity had a major role to play in Gandhian nationalism ultimately it was men (by embodying a maternal masculinity) who were responsible for redeeming Indian civilization since, as he wrote in *Hind Swaraj*, it was 'Because the sons of India were found wanting, its civilization had been placed in jeopardy' (Gandhi 1938: 39).

Keeping science in its place

If Gandhi did not follow the early nationalists by seeking national regeneration through a hypermasculine search for martial valour, he also departed from them in his attitude to scientific reason and modern technology. For Gandhi, valuing scientific reason above all else would hinder the achievement of non-violence because a technological frame of mind fosters an abstract view of the world and relies on an understanding of truth as cognitive rather than as lived, moral experience (Bilgrami 2003: 4164). He lamented in a speech in 1938:

> Nowadays I am relying solely on my intellect. But mere intellect makes one insane or unmanly.... My innermost urge is for pure non-violence. My weakness is that I do not know how to make it work. I use my intellect to overcome that weakness. If this intellectual cleverness loses the support of truth, it will blur my vision of non-violence, for is not non-violence the same as truth? Mere practical sense is the covering for truth.... The reasoning faculty will raise a thousand issues. Only one thing will save us from these and that is faith.
>
> (Gandhi 1999k: 63)

Yet a common misunderstanding, Gandhi (1986b: 310) noted, was that he was opposed to science whereas in fact he thought that 'we cannot live without science, if we keep it in its right place'. Keeping science in its right place meant a rejection of what Nandy (1987: 136) calls 'scientism' and 'technicism', the former for its promotion of hard materialism and its reduction of human rationality to a narrow objectivity and objectivism and the latter for its instrumental use of technology and its hierarchization of the relationship between nature and humans and between those that possess technology and those that do not. Nandy (1987: 137–8, 160) argues that Gandhi promoted a plural vision of science and technology that did not privilege its modern forms and denounced any technology, including aspects of traditional technology – which he considered ethically and cognitively superior to modern technology – that were alienating or dehumanizing.

It was for this reason that in *Hind Swaraj* Gandhi (1938: 93–5) condemned machinery such as cotton mills as a modern technology that was used to impoverish India and had begun to 'desolate' both Europe and India. Instead he celebrated the *charka* or spinning wheel, which he considered a morally superior and non-dehumanizing traditional technology that could be used to resist colonialism. Given that Gandhi (1999n: 92) considered the spinning wheel an exemplary type of traditional technology and regarded spinning to be the natural domain of women, it could be argued that Gandhi's understanding of ideal technology aligned it with the feminine and was thereby another key part of his radical challenge to the model of colonial masculinity.[2]

The inevitability of science

Gandhi's views on science and technology initially won little sympathy from the man he had anointed his political heir. In his *Autobiography*, which was written in the 1930s, Nehru wrote of how Gandhi bewildered him:

> Gandhiji … was a very difficult person to understand, sometimes his language was almost incomprehensible to an average modern … Often we [members of the Congress] discussed his fads and peculiarities among ourselves and said, half-humorously, that when Swaraj [self-rule] came these fads must not be encouraged.
>
> (Nehru 1980: 73)

Among such 'fads' were Gandhi's thoughts on machinery and modern civilization which were dismissed as old ideas that could not be applied to modern conditions (Nehru 1980: 77). By the time he wrote *Discovery of India* in the late 1940s, however, Nehru was more circumspect about the promise of modern science. His 'early approach to life's problems had been more or less scientific, with something of the easy optimism of the science of the nineteenth and early twentieth century' whereas, religion 'did not attract me' (Nehru 1982 [1946]: 26). He had come to the realization, however, that religion dealt with 'regions of human experience' which were 'uncharted … by the scientific positive knowledge of the day' (Nehru 1982 [1946]:, 26). Moreover he had become increasingly aware that it was not tenable to advance an outright mimicry of the colonial oppressor he was trying to cast out. Contemporary India, he wrote, 'swings between a blind adherence to her old customs and slavish imitation of foreign ways' but, 'there can be no real cultural or spiritual growth based on imitation' (Nehru 1982 [1946]: 564).

While Nehru still thought that some of Gandhi's criticisms of modern civilization in *Hind Swaraj* were 'completely unreal' he agreed with Gandhi that a large part of the world 'appears to be bent on committing suicide' and that this may be 'an inevitable development of an evil seed in civilization that has grown' (Nehru 1981: 556). Unlike Gandhi, Nehru (1982 [1946]: 511) did not identify modern science as being at the root of this 'evil' but he did critique it for ignoring 'the ultimate purposes' and looking 'at fact alone'. He argued that for all science had achieved in building up a glittering civilization 'there was some essential lack and some vital element was missing' for 'science had told us nothing about any purpose in life' (Nehru 1982 [1946]: 511). Moreover, he worried that

> the very progress of science, unconnected with and isolated from moral discipline and ethical considerations, will lead to the concentration of power and the terrible instruments of destruction which it has made, in the hands of evil and selfish men, seeking the domination of others – and thus to the destruction of its own great achievements.
>
> (Nehru 1982 [1946]: 511)

It was precisely this problem that the West was now grappling with: 'Something of this kind [of destruction] we see happening now, and behind this war there lies this internal conflict of the spirit of man' (Nehru 1982 [1946]: 33). Thus, while India 'must learn from the West, for the modern West has much to teach, and the spirit of the age is represented by the West', it was clear that the West 'is also obviously in need of learning much' for 'with all its great and manifold achievements' conflict 'is inherent in it and periodically it indulges in self-destruction on a colossal scale' (Nehru 1982 [1946]: 506–7).

Nonetheless, Nehru still attached enormous significance to the 'scientific temper'. For him, '[t]he scientific temper points out the way along which man should travel. It is the temper of a free man' (Nehru 1982 [1946]: 512). Humankind's ultimate purposes were to gain knowledge, realize truth and appreciate goodness and beauty – science was considered indispensable for all of these (Nehru 1982 [1946]: 513). Advancing his critique of India's backwardness, Nehru argued that its 'progressive deterioration during the centuries' could be seen in its loss of a 'rational spirit of inquiry' that was 'so evident in earlier times, which might well have led to the further growth of science' but was 'replaced by irrationalism and a blind idolatry of the past' (Nehru 1982 [1946]: 54). Expounding on this theme in 1955, he said:

> Often our people fail to realize what the modern world is all about. How did Europe and the US advance? Why were they able to conquer us? It is because they had science through which their wealth and economic and military strength grew. Now they have even produced the atom bomb. All these things stem from science and if India is to progress and become a strong nation, second to none, we must build up our science.
>
> (Nehru 2001a: 31)

As for why India experienced this 'progressive deterioration', Nehru's explanation pointed to Indian civilization's failure in the past to recognize the importance of interdependence and instead, turn inward. In *Glimpses of World History*, Nehru (1996 [1934–1935]: 61–7, 305–11) located what he considered the greatest moments of Indian history – the reign of Ashoka and the Mughal emperor Akbar, for instance – during times of cultural mixing and conscious efforts to engage with the world. Searching for the sources of India's 'deterioration and decay' in *Discovery*, Nehru found that the 'urge to adventure and the overflowing of life which led to vast schemes of distant colonization and the transplantation of Indian culture in far lands' had faded away 'and a narrow orthodoxy taboos even the crossing of the high seas' (Nehru 1982 [1946]: 54). 'So long as India kept her mind open and gave of her riches to others, and received from them what she lacked', Nehru wrote, 'she remained fresh and strong and vital', but, 'the more she withdrew into her shell, intent on preserving herself, uncontaminated by external influences, the more she lost that inspiration and her life became increasingly a dull round of meaningless activities all centred in the dead past' (Nehru 1982 [1946]: 209). A mastery of modern science, in part, by learning from the West was vital if India was to once again become dynamic and strong for '[i]n the present context of the world we cannot even advance culturally without a strong background of scientific research in every department' (Nehru 1972: 555).

So, despite 'realising these limitations of reason and scientific method' Nehru concluded, 'we have to hold on to them with all our strength, for without that firm basis and background we can have no grip on any kind of truth or reality' (Nehru 1982 [1946]: 512). Indeed, the real problem was that 'the west is still far from having developed the real temper of science. It has still to bring the spirit and the flesh into creative harmony' (Nehru 1982 [1946]: 514). According to Nehru, India was uniquely placed to develop this 'real temper of science' by which he meant a combination of what he considered the highest ideals of the modern age: humanism and the scientific spirit (Nehru 1982 [1946]: 558). As he explained:

> In India in many obvious ways we have a greater distance to travel. And yet there may be fewer major obstructions on our way, for the essential basis of Indian thought for ages past, though not its later manifestations, fits in with the scientific temper and approach, as well as with internationalism. It is based on a fearless search for truth, on the solidarity of man, even on the divinity of everything living, and on the free and co-operative development of the individual and the species, ever to greater freedom and higher stages of human growth.
>
> (Nehru 1982 [1946]: 514–15)

At the same time, although for Nehru (1980: 432) 'the West brings science', this did not mean that India had to mimic the West to reap the benefits of science and technology because it had its own tradition of scientific inquiry which meant that it was already a part of the global history of scientific endeavour. His portrayal of India's scientific past, however, is more subtle than those of his predecessors and only goes as far as pointing out that 'it is interesting to compare some of the latest conclusions of science with the fundamental ideas underlying the Advaita Vedantic theory' such as 'that the universe is made of one substance whose form is perpetually changing, and further that the sum-total of energies remains the same' (Nehru 1982 [1946]: 32).

In this way, science could be used as a tool with which to reconcile India to a modernity in which the West was seen as the standard of material development without inviting the charge of mimicry. Nehru sought to draw on India's moral and cultural traditions to create a modern, scientific world-view that was distinctly Indian. This, however, was a significant departure from Gandhi – a traditionalist who borrowed elements from modernity and fit them into a traditional world-view (Nandy 1987: 161) Whereas Gandhi subordinated science and technology within a world-view that promoted an alternative model of masculinity in which the feminine was a source of moral power, Nehru was too desperate to hold on to modern notions of reason and science to be in a position to pose a radical challenge to the colonial ideology of progress or its attendant politics of masculinity. Instead, Nehru sought to draw on India's traditions in order to fit them into a modern world-view which valorized modern science and technology at the expense of non-'expert' thinking and local knowledges.

As a consequence, Nehru displayed a profound ambivalence toward the feminine, which can be seen in his treatment of the nationalist symbol of Mother India in his writings. Initially, in *Autobiography*, Nehru (1980: 429) invokes an image of Mother India as a victim: 'woeful accumulations of superstition and degrading custom' had 'borne her down'. In his later *Discovery of India* an anxiety emerges that she is not so much a victim as an unruly woman who refuses to be tamed by modernity. Hence, he wrote:

> About her there is the elusive quality of a legend of long ago; some enchantment seems to have held her mind ... There are terrifying glimpses of dark corridors which seem to lead back to primeval night, but also there is the fullness and warmth of the day about her.
>
> (Nehru 1982 [1946]: 563)

As the last part of the sentence in the passage above indicates, however, while Nehru's Mother India possessed some dangerous non-modern elements she was also possessed traits that would prevent India's postcolonial modernity from going down the violent path of Western modernity:

> I was eager and anxious to give her the garb of modernity. And yet doubts arose within me. Did I know India? – I who presumed to scrap much of her past heritage? There was a great deal that had to be scrapped, that must be scrapped; but surely India could not have been what she undoubtedly was, and could not have continued a cultured existence for thousands of years, if

she had not possessed something very vital and enduring, something that was worthwhile. What was this something?

(Nehru 1982 [1946]: 50)

Nehru never seemed to come to a conclusive answer as to the nature of this 'something' but he came close when he later discussed the establishment of a 'certain idealist and ethical background to the whole culture' by the ancient 'Indo-Aryans' which 'persisted and still persists' and helped those 'at the top' to 'help together the social fabric and repeatedly rehabilitated it when it threatened to go to pieces' (Nehru 1982 [1946]: 95). Elsewhere he described it as the 'spirit of renunciation with which India has been so familiar' (Nehru 1982 [1946]: 559). Putting it more poetically in *Autobiography*, he wrote: '[b]ehind and within her battered body one could still glimpse a majesty of soul' and now as 'India puts on her new garment, as she must, for the old is torn and tattered, she will have it cut in this fashion, so as to make it conform both to present conditions and her old thought' (Nehru 1980: 432). Hence, '[t]hough her attire may change, she will continue as of old, and her store of wisdom will help her to hold on to what is true and beautiful and good in this harsh, vindictive, and grasping world' (Nehru 1982 [1946]: 563). Like Gandhi then, but to a lesser degree, Nehru grounded resistance, which he identified with an ethic derived from Indian civilization, in a feminized semiotic.

My reading of gender in Nehru's writings differs from that of both Partha Chatterjee and Gyan Prakash. Chatterjee (1986: 147) suggests that while for Bankim and Tagore, Mother India carried a passionate, utopian meaning, for later nationalist figures like Nehru, Mother India was 'just another political slogan' that was used simply because it had become part of the language which 'the masses' spoke at political meetings. Yet, the representation of the nation as mother occurred throughout both Nehru's *Autobiography* as well as *The Discovery of India*, both of which were texts that were written for those of his ilk rather than 'the masses'. Furthermore, Nehru continued to use the expression even though he was aware that it did not concur with his rationalist vocabulary of politics. He says at one point in his *Autobiography*:

It is curious how one cannot resist the tendency to give an anthropomorphic form to a country. Such is the force of habit and early associations. India becomes *Bharat Mata*, Mother India, a beautiful lady, very old but ever youthful in appearance, sad-eyed and forlorn, cruelly treated by aliens and outsiders, and calling upon her children to protect her ... And yet India is in the main the peasant and the worker, not beautiful to look at, for poverty is not beautiful ... We seek to cover truth by the creatures of our imaginations and endeavour to escape from reality to a world of dreams.

(Nehru 1980: 431)

Prakash (1999: 207–8) has argued that '[i]t would be a mistake to conclude that Nehru had defined the nation as feminine, as tradition and home, and opposed it to the masculine, the modern and the world' for 'the latter were already implicit in the former, the masculinist and the modern already complicit and emergent in the feminization of the nation ... the 'lady with a past' was a masculine figure in disguise'. I would suggest, however, that Nehru attached more value on India's non-modern past than either Chatterjee or Prakash allow. Indeed, Nehru was unable to break his 'habit' of representing India as *Bharat Mata* because it facilitated the construction of a postcolonial modernity that desired to be at once derivative of, and distinct from, Western modernity. In Nehru's writings, therefore, India's postcolonial identity emerges as a woman in drag – a mother that needed to be disciplined into wearing the distinctly masculine garb of modernity while retaining the moral, feminine spirit that is the guarantee that she does not succumb to copying the hypermasculine modernity of the West.

Nuclear technology, disarmament and postcolonial modernity

Nuclear technology, development and internationalism

The adoption of a scientific outlook was central to India's project of postcolonial modernity but it was one type of technology – nuclear technology – that was particularly acclaimed as 'a symbol of the modern times' (Nehru 2003: 40). In the Constituent Assembly debates on nuclear energy in 1948 Nehru elaborated on the importance he attached to it:

> Consider the past few hundred years of human history; the world developed a new source of power, that is steam – the steam engine and the like – and the industrial age came in. India with all her many virtues, did not develop that source of power. It became a backward country in that sense; it became a slave country because of that. The steam age and the industrial age were followed by the electrical age which gradually crept in, and most of us were hardly aware of the change. But enormous new power came in. Now we are facing the atomic age; we are on the verge of it. And this is obviously something infinitely more powerful than either steam or electricity.
>
> (Nehru 1987: 427)

Hence, the lack of a scientific temper meant that Indian civilization had missed the steam age, the industrial age and the electrical age and Nehru was adamant that modern India was not going to miss the atomic age. As Itty Abraham (1998: 20) has argued, the nuclear reactor – along with the dam, the steel mill, and new planned cities like the Le Corbusier-designed city of Chandigarh – was a 'technological artefact' which the postcolonial state hoped would 'transform traditional landscapes through their sheer power'. Nuclear technology thus emerged as a 'theatrical science' used to 'create the illusion of spectacular development' (Nandy 1988).

As well as being a means of material betterment and nationalist self-reliance, Nehru saw nuclear technology as a tool for fostering international cooperation and breaking down cultural, political and geographical barriers. In 1960, for instance, Nehru hailed India's collaboration with Canada on its second nuclear reactor as a symbol of the power of modern technology to make the world smaller (Nehru 2003: 204). As we saw above, according to Nehru, India had fallen behind on the development of science and had therefore suffered material backwardness, in part, because it had withdrawn 'into her shell'. Global interdependence also had ethical value for Nehru for he was in agreement with H.G. Wells that, 'we shall have to put an end to the national state and devise a collectivism which neither degrades nor enslaves' (Nehru 1982 [1946]: 531). Thus, he sought to ground postcolonial India's foreign policy in an internationalist nationalism rather than a 'narrow nationalism'.

The intellectual genealogy of this internationalist ethic can be traced to what he once called, 'a strange medley' of 'Buddha-Marx-Gandhi' (Nehru 1974: 367). Nehru's participation, as the Indian National Congress representative, in the Congress of Oppressed Nationalities in Brussels during his visit to Europe in 1926–1927 led to an attraction to a Marxist understanding of anti-imperialism as a global struggle linked to rejecting the acquisitiveness of capitalism and narrow and intense nationalism. His comments in *Autobiography* indicate that at the end of the conference there had developed a strong connection in Nehru's mind between social democracy and internationalism, on the one hand, and capitalism, imperialism and nationalism, on the other:

> My outlook was wider and nationalism by itself seemed to me definitely a narrow and insufficient creed. Political freedom, independence, were no doubt essential, but they were steps only in the right direction; without social freedom and a socialistic structure of society and the State, neither the country nor the individual could develop much.
>
> (Nehru 1942 [1936]: 166)

From Marxism he gained an awareness of the exploitative and interlinked nature of certain forms of economic and political relations: '[t]he capitalist organisation of industry and civilization led inevitably to this imperialism. Capitalism also led to an intensification of the feeling of nationalism' which 'was not merely a love of one's own country, but hatred of all others' (Nehru 1996: 399). This was because the 'competitive and acquisitive characteristics of modern capitalist society, the enthronement of wealth above everything else, the continuous strain and the lack of security for many, add to the ill-health of the mind and produce neurotic states' (Nehru 1982 [1946]: 556). Thus, Nehru's frequent assertions that a country's internal policy and external policy affect each other and should be integrated are important normative statements (Nehru 1961: 83). For instance, when he said in a speech in 1947, '[u]ltimately, foreign policy is the outcome of economic policy' he meant something more than just that material capabilities will shape foreign policy (Nehru 1986: 596). Rather, he was arguing that the way in which material interests were pursued would determine how India would relate to the world. To this end, cooperation in science and technology as a tool of economic policy would facilitate an internationalist ethic and buttress Nehru's project for an ethical modernity.

While Marxism offered a rationale for interdependence, it 'did not satisfy me completely' for Nehru did not like frequent divorce between action and the 'basic urges or principles' of a moral approach to life (Nehru 1982 [1946]: 29–30). Moreover, the example of an increasingly nationalistic Soviet Union had proven that the internationalist orientation of socialism had proven fragile in practice (Nehru 1982 [1946]: 515). Hence, in search of a moral approach, Nehru turned to Buddhist thought. 'Of all of the great men of the past' Nehru (1974: 371) wrote in a letter to his daughter, Indira, in 1935, 'the Buddha attracts me more and more'. The Buddha, he wrote in *Discovery*, was the product of India's 'deep reserves of wisdom and inner strength' and in Buddhist thought Nehru found a deeper explanation for why the problems Marx identified occurs and a rationale for an ethic of interdependence (Nehru 1982 [1946]: 130). In Nehru's interpretation, Buddhist thought was grounded in a reasoned morality because it relied 'on reason and logic and experience' and encouraged the deployment of rationality away from self-interest and toward the cultivation of a moral life (Nehru 1982 [1946]: 128). The Buddha's method, Nehru wrote, invoking the authority of science and indeed, once again pre-figuring modern scientific insights in ancient India, 'was one of psychological analysis and ... it is surprising to find how deep was his insight into this latest of modern sciences' (Nehru 1982 [1946]: 129). On the idea of the non-permanent Self:

> [r]eality is not something that is, permanent and unchanging, but rather a kind of radiant energy ... We cannot say that one thing is the cause of something else for there is no core of permanent being which changes ... In a sense we are dying all the time and being reborn and this give the appearance of an unbroken identity.
>
> (Nehru 1982 [1946]: 129)

Thus, the 'essence of a thing is its immanent law of relation to other so-called things' (Nehru 1982 [1946]: 129`). Given the knowledge of this interdependence, Buddhist thought recognized that 'ethical relations have a definite value in our finite world. So in our lives and in our human relations we have to conform to ethics and live the good life' and to 'that life and to this phenomenal world we can and should apply reason and knowledge and experience' (Nehru 1982 [1946]: 174). Buddhist thought, therefore, provided a morally reasoned rationale for an ethic of interdependence.

For Gandhi: '[t]hat nationalism, which is based upon pure selfishness and the exploitation of other nations, is indeed an evil. But I cannot conceive of internationalism without a healthy and desirable national spirit' (Gandhi 1999l: 216). A nationalism based on selfishness and exploitation, according to Gandhi, was the product of understanding truth as a cognitive notion which gives rise to the treatment of reality as something to be mastered and conquered (Bilgrami 2003: 4164). This type of nationalism would, therefore, only produce an abstract and potentially destructive internationalism. Gandhian nationalism, on the other hand, was based on a notion of truth as a product of moral experience and a nationalism based on this understanding necessarily gives rise to an internationalism rooted in moral, non-violent action. Nehru did not necessarily subscribe to the philosophical underpinnings of Gandhian nationalism for he did believe in the cognitive value of truth and he placed great importance on scientific reason. However, as we have seen, he was aware of the limitations of the latter and this made him more open to Gandhi's emphasis on ethics in political praxis.

Apart from 'Buddha-Marx-Gandhi', Nehru's writings on internationalism bear the influence of the thought of Rabindranath Tagore (2002), who was a strident critic of modern nationalism who distinguished between the nation as a community and the nation as a mechanical organization of power. Tagore argued that it was the latter which underpinned modern nationalism while India had traditionally held to a concept of the nation as community with porous cultural boundaries and a sense of cultural and social hospitality (Nandy 2006). Modern nationalism, therefore, was explicitly anti-Indian in its denial of porous cultural boundaries, its negation of cultural and social hospitality and its organization of society according to an instrumental, bureaucratic rationality. From Tagore, then, Nehru drew an understanding of the nation as a community that is wholly consistent an internationalist ethic. The result was a normative project that attempted to combine an open, non-essentialist nationalism with a rooted internationalism which was unthreatened by political or cultural attachments. 'Nationalism is a narrowing creed', Nehru wrote in *Discovery*, 'and nationalism in conflict with a dominating imperialism produces all manner of frustrations and complexes' but it was 'Tagore's immense service to India, as it has been Gandhi's in a different plane, that he forced the people in some measure out of their narrow grooves of thought and made them think of broader issues affecting humanity' (Nehru 2002 [1946]: 340). Gandhi, a man of 'concentrated and ceaseless activity' contributed an ethical doctrine which emphasized the equivalence of ends and means and had shown how to apply this doctrine to large-scale public activity and, Tagore, who was 'primarily a man of thought' – had 'been India's internationalist par excellence, believing and working for international cooperation'. Yet, from Tagore he had learned that a commitment to universalism did not have to conflict with a commitment to a national community for 'with all his internationalism, his feet have always been planted firmly on India's soil and his mind has been saturated with the wisdom of the Upanishads' (Nehru 2002 [1946]: 340).

Hence, for Nehru there was no inconsistency between advocating science as a tool of internationalism but, on the other hand, promoting India's ability to master modern science on its own as an important element of India's independence and self-reliance. As Raja Ramanna, one of India's leading nuclear scientists put it:

It was a spirit of self-reliance which guided the scientific programmes in India in the years that followed [independence]. Although we were prepared to receive assistance and advice from all friendly countries … we were not to take orders from anybody in the choice of our programmes nor undermine our capability of tackling problems in-house.

(Ramanna 1991: 61)

Despite his enthusiasm for nuclear technology as a means of facilitating greater interdependence, however, Nehru was also wary of efforts to institutionalize control over nuclear technology in international organizations. In a speech in the Lok Sabha in 1954, Nehru expressed his unease over American proposals to establish an organization for the 'so-called international control' of nuclear energy. He feared that any such organization would be dominated by certain countries, and that 'it may be to the advantage of countries which have adequate power resources to restrain and restrict the use of atomic energy' at the expense of 'power-starved' countries like India, thereby reinforcing global hierarchies and endangering India's future as an modern nation-state (India 1988b: 38–9). In referring to the 'so-called international control' of nuclear energy Nehru was effectively raising questions about the notion of the 'international community' and the neo-colonial hierarchies that this concept conceals – hierarchies which would come in the way of achieving an ethical modernity since, as he put it in *Discovery*, 'true internationalism' can only flourish on 'a basis of freedom and equality' (Nehru 1982 [1946]: 565).

His concerns about the control of nuclear technology came to the fore in 1956 when India protested against the safeguards proposed for the statute of the planned International Atomic Energy Agency on the grounds that they would place a large part of the world under certain controls which other parts would be free from (Mirchandani 1968: 229). In this way, it was Nehru who established the basis of the dimension in India's nuclear discourse that opposed a neo-colonial hierarchical and discriminatory global order, a dimension that in the 1960s would come to be known as 'nuclear apartheid'.

Disarmament and postcolonial difference

While his speeches on nuclear energy maintained a conviction that it would be the future vehicle of material progress, independence and internationalism, Nehru's words also revealed an anxiety about the uses of nuclear technology. The enormous destructive capacity of nuclear technology, as displayed in Japan in 1945, preyed heavily on Nehru's mind. Indeed, he regarded the struggle between the evil represented by the atom bomb and the 'spirit of humanity' as the defining conflict facing the modern world (Mirchandani 1968: 3–4). Still, as he made clear in a speech to the National Physical Laboratory in 1947, this could not be allowed to hinder India's pursuit of nuclear energy. India, he noted,

may have to follow other countries in having a great atomic energy research institute also, not to make bombs, I hope, but nevertheless I do not see how we can lag behind in this very important matter, because atomic energy is going to play a vast and dominating part, I suppose, in the future shape of things.

(Nehru 1984a: 377–8)

The tensions inherent in the promotion of nuclear technology for peaceful uses became apparent in the 1948 Constituent Assembly debates on nuclear energy. When questioned by S.V. Krishnamurthy Rao on what he regarded to be the excessive secrecy provisions of the proposed Atomic Energy Act for a peaceful nuclear program, Nehru would admit that he did not know how to distinguish between the peaceful and military uses of atomic energy when the science used in both were almost identical (Nehru 1987: 426). At this early moment, as Abraham (1998: 50–1) notes, Nehru was forced to come to terms with the fact that he could not divorce India's nuclear energy program from its military implications simply by proclaiming the program to be peaceful.

Abraham, however, tends to underplay Nehru's critique of science and technology in favour of a reading of Nehru as a straightforward statist developmentalist when, in fact, Nehru's speeches and writings reveal someone grappling with a discursive dilemma. How could a potentially violent product of modernity be neutralized into a benign instrument for the development of postcolonial India? How could the hypermasculine garb of nuclear technology not weigh down Mother India and upset postcolonial India's carefully crafted gender ambiguity – its maternal masculinity? Fortunately, he still had India's civilizational heritage to fall back on. India would draw on its heritage – an 'ancient belief' in an 'inner, spiritual strength' and the lesson learnt 'during the Gandhian era not to base our policies on fear' – to use a potentially violent technology for peaceful purposes (Nehru 2003: 42, 1961: 83). In a speech on non-violence and modern India in 1956, he noted that nuclear technology 'can bring complete ruin upon the world or contribute to progress. It depends on how it is used. But more important, is ultimately the kind of human beings who will use it' (Nehru 2003: 40). An attempt to produce India and Indians as the 'right kind of human beings' to have nuclear technology was made in India's foreign policy discourse through the strong advocacy of global nuclear disarmament, which was presented as the product of the ethical values inherent in India's civilizational heritage and anti-colonial struggle.

The issues raised in a speech given just after Independence in 1948 titled 'A Crisis of Spirit' were a precursor to the enduring themes of Nehru's foreign policy speeches as Prime Minister. 'We live in an age of crisis', he said in this speech, but Gandhi had showed the world how to apply 'moral values to political action and pointed out that ends and means can never be separated' (Nehru 1961: 182). Hence, 'so long as we do not recognize the supremacy of moral law in our national and international relations we shall have no enduring peace' (Nehru 1961: 183). This speech also contained a passage that bore the influence of the emphasis in Buddhist and Gandhian thought on interdependence and the need to willingly give up rights to affirm the rights of others. There had been 'far too much emphasis', Nehru (1961: 183) said, on the rights of individuals and nations 'and far too little on obligations'. If 'obligations were undertaken, rights would naturally flow from them. This meant an approach of life different from the competitive and acquisitive approach of today'. In this speech, Nehru (1961: 183) also challenged the notion that fear was the only emotion that could govern relations with other nations for even though '[t]oday fear consumes us all – fear of the future, fear of war, fear of the people of the nations we dislike and who dislike us', fear 'is an ignoble emotion and leads to blind strife'. Ridding the world of this fear and basing 'our thoughts and actions on what is essentially right and moral' was the way, he said, to build 'a world order based on freedom'. Together with the policies of nonalignment and Panchsheel, which I will discuss in more detail in the following chapters, disarmament was an important plank in the realization of this vision in Nehru's postcolonial India. At the core of this vision was essentially an attempt to fashion an ethical modernity – an alternative way of discursively and practically constructing the international system and India's place within it. If disarmament was a means by which to free the world from fear, then making incremental steps toward this at the UN and inculcating a sense of obligation and cooperation, more generally, was the means by which disarmament could be normalized.

He touched on these themes in a speech in the UN General Assembly in 1960. Every country, he said, had to 'shoulder its responsibility' to work towards disarmament although, 'the United Nations should be closely associated with such efforts' (Nehru 1961: 220). He was not, however, under any illusion as to what could be achieved: 'disarmament should take place in such stages as to maintain broadly the balance of armed power. It is only on this basis that success can be achieved and this pervading sense of fear countered' (Nehru 1961: 220). Ultimately, he said, 'it is necessary to bring about the change in our minds and to remove fears and apprehensions, hatreds and suspicions. Disarmament is a part of this process, for it will create an atmosphere of co-operation' (Nehru 1961: 219). But, 'it is only a step towards our objective, a part of the larger efforts to rid the world of war and the causes of war' (Nehru 1961: 219).

Hence, India was among the first countries to propose the major non-proliferation regimes in existence today. Among India's initiatives under Nehru's leadership was the formation of the Disarmament Sub-Committee in the UN in 1953 and the 'Standstill' proposal of 1954 for the suspension of nuclear tests, which at one point he condemned as 'a crime against humanity' given their potential to endanger present and future generations (Nehru 1961: 212). In establishing India's moral authority to speak on the issue, Nehru was careful to note in a speech at the Carnegie Endowment in 1956 that he did not mean 'to imply that people in India are more virtuous than others' (India 1988b: 58). Rather, drawing on a narrative of India's civilizational exceptionalism which ascribed to India a legacy of ethical behaviour, he argued that: 'the capacity for big scale vice is not with them. And therefore, therefore we can moralize more easily than others can' (India 1988b: 58).

With the beginning of the Cold War, disarmament became even more vital for it offered a way out of the 'mental military bloc' of Cold War politics (Nehru 1961: 11). For Nehru (1961: 205), the Cold War's significance did not lie in ideological struggle but because it represented 'the approach of fear and anger, the approach of not being made to appear that one is weak'. Nehru ridiculed the idea of nuclear deterrence which arose from this thinking: '[i]f the hydrogen bomb is thus elevated to the level of being the custodian of peace, the inter-war nuclear race would claim that it stands justified as a peace agent' (India 1988b: 75). More generally, he criticized the notion of security based on a system of instrumental reason which underpinned the Cold War:

> [i]t is a strange way to ensure security by adding to every conceivable danger … in the name of security all kinds of terrible weapons should be evolved; and in the name of security each party slangs the other and thereby creates an atmosphere where the danger becomes more acute.
>
> (Nehru 1961: 204)

At this point in this speech, which was given in 1957, Nehru articulated his understanding of security in terms that reveal that anti-colonialism was still at the core of India's self-identity: '[n]o country and no government can risk its future, or can accept a position when another country can impose its will upon it'. However, a postcolonial logic of difference was also evident, for he added that: 'if in order to ensure security, measures are to be taken which really endanger it still further, then we fail in getting that security' (Nehru 1961: 204).

Nehru's analysis of the Cold War was the product of his attraction to psychology for understanding political action. The language of psychology suffused two of his major pre-independence works, *Discovery of India* and *Autobiography*, his admiration for Gandhi and the Buddha stemmed from his view of them as, first and foremost, exemplary psychologists. His critique of British colonialism was also grounded in the language of trauma (Majeed 2007: 33–5). 'Alien rule' he wrote in *Discovery* 'is inevitably cut off from the creative energies of the people it dominates … and leads to spiritual and cultural starvation of the subject peoples' (Nehru 1982 [1946]: 508). It was precisely because of the psychological damage which would be incurred that Nehru was so keen, as I discussed earlier, to avoid any semblance of simply mimicking the colonial oppressor: 'there can be no real cultural or spiritual growth based on imitation' (Nehru 1982 [1946]: 564). While he was well-read in the psychological/philosophical theories of Sigmund Freud, William James and John Dewey, Nehru did not appear to adhere to their biological or naturalist conceptions of emotion and he avoided any 'totalising narrative of psychology and psychoanalysis which might yet again render Indians objects open to distant scrutiny' (Majeed 2007: 35). Nehru did not regard fear as having a 'natural' or inevitable presence in social relations because he rejected the idea of an unchanging human nature shaped by fear and selfishness as a notion that 'takes refuge in irrationalism, superstition, and unreasonable and inequitable social prejudices and practices' (Nehru 1982 [1946]: 30). Instead, he argued 'that there is nothing so changeable as human nature and society', a position consistent with the understanding of the Self in Buddhist thought as a process without an essence (Nehru 1982 [1946]: 540–1). At the same time, his approach did not treat emotions as deviations from rationality. Rather, he took a cognitive approach to emotion and drew from the books of ancient India as well as Gandhi's political praxis in equating an absence of fear with moral strength and security. It was what he saw as the psychological aspect of Gandhi's mode of anti-colonial resistance which attracted him the most:

> [t]he essence of his teaching was fearlessness and truth, and action allied to these ... The greatest gift for an individual or a nation, so we had been told in our ancient books, was *abhaya* (fearlessness), not merely bodily courage but the absence of fear from the mind. Janaka and Yajnavalka had said, at the dawn of our history, that it was the function of the leaders of a people to make them fearless. But the dominant impulse in India under British rule was that of fear – pervasive, oppressing, strangling fear ... It was against this all-pervading fear that Gandhi's quiet and determined voice was raised...
>
> ...It was a psychological change, almost as if some expert in psychoanalytical methods had probed deep into the patient's past, found out the origins of his complexes, exposed them to his view, and thus rid him of that burden.
>
> (Nehru 1982 [1946]: 358–9)

It was a psychological change that Nehru also hoped to bring about with policies like disarmament, through which he sought to inject a different set of emotions into world politics.

Conclusion

I have argued in this chapter that understanding postcolonial India's nuclear policies requires an appreciation of India's colonial experience and the narratives of civilizational backwardness and civilizational exceptionalism that it produced. While the narratives of backwardness constituted internal critiques of India's failure to master modern technology and its tendency in the past to turn inward, a conviction that India possessed a unique ability to use science in moral ways produced a narrative of civilizational exceptionalism. In postcolonial India during the Nehru era, nuclear technology signified modern scientific development, and the potential for global interdependence and cooperation, but it also implied the dangers of science without moral restraints. The result was a pursuit of a nuclear energy program that would work to make India modern, alongside the consistent promotion of disarmament, which would shape Indian modernity as an ethical project.

In examining Nehru's approach to nuclear weapons and disarmament, what this chapter has also revealed is a conception of postcolonial identity that is deeply ambivalent about modernity and gendered in ways that produce this ambivalence. In particular, since Nehru's nationalist discourse grounded his ethic of postcolonial difference in a feminized semiotic, India's postcolonial identity, which conceived India as a civilizational-state, was produced as female, feminine and masculine at the same time, for its mimicry of a masculine, modernizing state is balanced by a femininely coded civilizational morality. This challenges the usual gendered reading of IR in which states are female and feminine in the domestic arena and male and masculine in the international realm and points to the unique intertwining of gender and ethics in the dominant mode of Indian nationalist thought.

This chapter has also pointed out aspects of Nehru's international thought that make it difficult to characterize him as a liberal internationalist or a realist. In particular, Nehru rejected the liberal ontology of the individual and the nation-state as self-interested, autonomy-seeking entities and instead, influenced by Gandhian and Buddhist thought, understood both the individual and the nation as interdependent, relational entities. Thus, he connected both nuclear technology and disarmament to an internationalism which, by encouraging cooperative relations and ameliorating fear, would one day culminate in a post-sovereign state world order. As we shall see in the next chapter, by rejecting the dominant ontology of IR, Nehru was also able to include in his international thought a conception of friendship.

3 Rejecting the 'fear complex'

Constructing an international politics of friendship

Friendship has long been marginalized in a discipline in which both critical and conventional approaches have assumed that fear, enemies and 'threatening others' are the most important factors governing relations between states. Nehru too recognized fear as a driver of world politics, but he was convinced that this was not inevitable but could be changed. Indeed, Nehru saw the amelioration of fear, as the emotion governing social relations both within and between nations, as a key part of both the anti-colonial struggle and his post-independence attempt to construct an ethical modernity which could overcome the destructiveness of modern inter-state relations. Moreover, by engaging in a politics of friendship, modern India would be able to overcome an important source of India's civilizational backwardness. Looking into India's past, Nehru found evidence of a dynamic Indian civilization aware of its interdependence with, rather than isolation from, other societies. Looking at India's colonial present, however, Nehru came to the conclusion that it was precisely because India had turned inward that it had become a stagnant, backward civilization. The outward outlook of Western states was therefore something to be emulated, but Nehru's international politics of friendship went further by encompassing policies, namely nonalignment and Panchsheel (peaceful coexistence), whose history he traced back to ancient India, that would challenge the 'fear complex' that Western modernity had produced and which, he suggested to a newspaper in 1933, was the 'cause of half the troubles of the world' (Nehru 1973: 509). When he expressed these sentiments in 1933, Nehru's preoccupation was the prospect of another devastating world war. However, as we will see in this chapter, the psychology of fear amongst states remained central to his analysis of conflict well into his tenure as Prime Minister.

In suggesting that nonalignment and Panchsheel be read in terms of a politics of friendship I am arguing against more typical readings of these policies. The idea that policies like nonalignment constituted an Indian Monroe Doctrine-style bid for regional hegemony, for instance, has been suggested by several authors. Devin Hagerty (1991: 363), for instance, argues that 'although it was never enunciated explicitly or officially, successive Indian governments have systematically pursued an active policy of denial in South Asia similar to that applied to the Western Hemisphere by the United States in the nineteenth century'. Bharat

Karnad (2002b: 66–162) argues that Nehru's opposition to regional defence pacts such as the South-East Asia Treaty Organisation (SEATO), was not the result of deeply-held moral convictions, but reflected a desire for regional dominance. A.Z. Hilali (2001) argues that regional dominance has been India's ongoing motivation since 1947 and claims that the Indian leadership, beginning with Nehru, have seen themselves as the successors to the British Raj and have adopted colonial strategic concerns as their own. Raja Mohan (2003: 238–9, 2007: 101) also attributes Monroe doctrine-style ambitions to Nehru and describes nonalignment as 'a means to protect India's newly won freedom to conduct its own independent foreign policy and to maximize India's relative gains in the bipolar system'. The interpretation of nonalignment in realist terms, however, requires a sustained disregard for Nehru's copious writings which display a consistent critique of the assumptions and outcomes of realist policies. Moreover, it overlooks the fact that the normative origins of policies like nonalignment and the rejection of collective defence pacts can be found in writings penned well before the beginning of the Cold War or the creation of Pakistan.

A more common interpretation of Nehru's policies places them within a framework of liberal internationalism or classical idealism (Mitra 2001: 362). A.P. Rana (1969: 311), for instance, traces the roots of nonalignment to Gandhi's influence on Nehru but argues that he lacked Gandhi's more transformational sensibility and 'firmly linked his non-aligned policy to the maintenance of the structure of international society and continually manoeuvred towards this end'. Kanti Bajpai (2003: 242) characterizes Nehru's position as 'Westphalia plus nonalignment' because while accepting basic Westphalian assumptions, Nehru challenged the idea that order and stability in the international system was dependent on the great powers and argued that the non-aligned would be the most positive force in world politics. Bajpai does not, however, explain why Nehru arrived at this conclusion and does not question whether this should complicate the portrayal of him as a liberal internationalist. Indeed, he is dismissive of Nehru's frequent comments on the inevitability of a 'world government' or 'world federation' suggesting that they should not be read literally because he 'was probably suggesting that states would increasingly collaborate in propagating international law and organisations' (Bajpai 2003: 240).

Gopal Krishna (1984: 272, 4, 85–6) on the other hand, calls Nehru a 'pragmatic idealist' who tried, and failed, to 'promote the transformation of world order' by pursuing a foreign policy based on securing autonomy without power while Srinath Raghavan (2010: 14) has argued that Nehru was a liberal realist because like 'many liberals he abhorred war for its inherently illiberal effects and consequences' but 'unlike the liberals Nehru also held that conflict was an endemic feature of politics; for all national and social groups were inevitably moved by self-interest'. Yet, as will be discussed, Nehru did not seek to rid international relations of power but rather, envisioned these policies as a means of exercising power in moral ways. Moreover, as I argued in the last chapter and will further elaborate on in this chapter, Nehru did not believe in any unchanging conception of human nature that makes conflict among collectivities inevitable.

Amitav Acharya's constructivist reading portrays Nehru's policies as contributing to norm-building in ways that buttressed existing structures. Specifically, he argues that ideas like nonalignment 'infused and strengthened the legal norms of state sovereignty prevailing at the international level' (Acharya 2005: 21). However, although Nehru was committed to the principle of moral equality between nations and rejected coercive interference by one country into the affairs of another, his comments on world government indicate that he was not wedded to a legalistic notion of absolute sovereignty. Rather, I would suggest that instead of being policies aimed at disengagement or strengthening state sovereignty, nonalignment and Panchsheel were intended to further his radical internationalist vision through a conception of security that did not depend on generating insecurity in others. At the same time, they would promote an understanding of national autonomy that resisted interactions with individual countries and groups that were inherently unequal.

Jacques Hymans (2009: 248) argues for a reading of Nehru's foreign policy as a 'soft power strategy' which 'aimed not to ingratiate India with the masters of the world, but rather – somewhat paralleling Gandhi's strategy in the freedom struggle – to perplex, anger, shame, and ultimately transform them'. Hymans, however, is unclear as to the intellectual underpinnings of Nehru's soft power strategy or its relationship with Gandhi's thought or praxis. I would argue that rather than seeking to perplex, anger and shame, nonalignment and Panchsheel constituted a rejection of the idea that fear is necessarily the driver of world politics. I would suggest that friendship, a concept that implies trust, equality and goodwill, is the appropriate framework in which to analyse Panchsheel and nonalignment and to elucidate the fundamental ways in which Nehru mobilized a particular ontology of truth and being to challenge dominant conceptions of world politics and formulate his own unique normative project.

The first section of this chapter examines the absence of the study of friendship and emotion in IR and recent attempts to remedy this. It then goes on to examine the role of friendship in Nehru's international thought and traces the origins of non-alignment and Panchsheel. The second section analyses Nehru's pre-independence writings and post-independence speeches in order to examine why it was the countries of Asia and South Asia, in particular, which were the focus of Nehru's international praxis of friendship. This section also assesses the successes and failures of Nehru's politics of friendship in Asia and examines the alternatives offered by Gandhi and his 'conscience keeper', the nationalist leader, C. Rajagopalchari.

Fear and friendship in world politics

Fear and friendship in international relations

The assumption in realist approaches that the international system is akin to a state of nature, and that the nation-state is a self-interested actor concerned primarily with survival, mitigates against any serious consideration of friendship between states for, as Neta Crawford (2000) has argued, fear and hate are taken to be the emotions that fuel world politics (See Waltz 1979: 118). Although liberal and English School approaches promote interdependence as a way of overcoming the climate of distrust that they assume pervades the international system, the relationships produced between states in these approaches, based as they are on some sort of contract, falls far short of friendship. Moreover, while there has been a revival in IR of Carl Schmitt and his understanding of politics as the opposition between friend and enemy (Odysseos and Petito 2007), given Schmitt's main argument that politics is essentially about conflict and the creation of the friend-enemy boundary, this has also failed to produce any focus on the idea of friendship or the category of the friend.

The 'conventional' constructivist scholarship of Alexander Wendt (1999) does suggest a need for a theory of friendship and envisages the possibility of a 'Kantian culture' in world politics in which states have internalized the role of friend and have built collective identities. However, Wendt concurs with the idea that survival is a state's primary motive and the master variables he identifies as necessary for collective identity formation, interdependence, common fate, homogeneity and self-restraint do not take us very far in theorizing friendship as a particular relationship of intimacy (Wendt 1999: 356). Critical constructivist approaches, influenced by Foucauldian understandings of discipline and order, emphasize the construction of state identities as contingent on the identification of dangerous Others. David Campbell (1992: 99) suggests, for instance, that '[a]lthough it has been argued that the representation of difference does not functionally necessitate a negative figuration, it has historically more often than not been the case…'.

Janice Bially Mattern (2005) comes closer to theorizing something akin to friendship in world politics in her discussion of the socio-linguistic construction of attraction between states and her analysis of 'special relationships' and their impact on international order. Her argument, however, is based on the idea that attraction often rests on coercion by way of a representationally forceful narrative which pressurizes Others with threats to their subjectivity unless the force-wielder's representation of reality and, thus, its self-identity is acknowledged. In a similar vein, the ontological security approaches of Brent Steele and Jennifer Mitzen emphasize that states seek ontological security as well as physical security and that the 'anxiety which engulfs the Self does not necessarily have to originate from the Other' (Steele 2007: 32). Nonetheless, neither Steele nor Mitzen consider positive identification as a means of ontological security-seeking. Instead, drawing on Anthony Giddens, Mitzen (2006) focuses on how states can become 'routinized' into perpetuating conflict because it serves to fulfil ontological security needs. Steele (2007: 148) leaves more room for state agency and suggests that states may engage 'other-help' behaviour if it fulfils self-identity needs. His focus, however, is on the internal logic of ontological security, as expressed in concepts such as honour and shame, rather than the role of Others, whether defined positively or negatively.

Felix Berenskoetter (2007) on the other hand, does address positive identification among states in one of the few contributions to IR to explicitly attempt to theorize the concept of friendship in world politics. Berenskoetter (2007: 654–5) argues that theorizing friendship in IR is only possible by employing an alternative to the Hobbesian understanding of the human condition as marked by a fear about survival, which leads to a lack of trust between individuals and states. Drawing on Heidegger's understanding of the human condition as characterized by a lack of certainty rather than a fear of death – since humans can only fear what they have experienced – he suggests that anxiety and not fear is the most important element of being. Like Steele and Mitzen, Berenskoetter (2007: 656, 63) also draws on Giddens to argue that 'anxiety-controlling' mechanisms are necessary to gain ontological security. In addition, however, he draws on Louiza Odysseos's reading of Heidegger and employs Charles Taylor's notion of authenticity to suggest that one way of controlling anxiety, and the desire for authenticity that this anxiety generates, is by seeking companionship with Others who can help to sustain a sense of Self. Berenskoetter (2007: 664) then goes on to draw on Aristotle to theorize the content of a particular form of companionship, friendship, reading Aristotle's view of friendship as necessary for individual happiness within a framework of dealing with anxiety (Berenskoetter 2007: 664). Aristotle's notion of 'true' friendship, Berenskoetter (2007: 666–8) argues, had as its purpose the achievement of happiness through moral fulfilment, is based on reciprocated goodwill and is necessarily a relationship between equals. Applying this to IR, he argues that neither geographic proximity, trade, membership in institutions, similarity in political systems or religious commonality are sufficient for friendship because none of these factors by themselves generate the type of emotional attachment associated with mutual moral fulfillment. Rather, '[f]riendship designates an intimate relationship between states voluntarily bonded by a shared moral space (sense of virtue) grown out of significant experiences and translated into a genuine commitment to a common project which lends significance to the future. In short, friendship, as an evolving relationship, is a process of building a 'common world' to which states become emotionally attached' (Berenskoetter 2007: 670).

Nehru, friendship and international relations

Nehru's policies of non-alignment and Panchsheel have some similarities with this Aristotelian-inspired conception of friendship in world politics, for moral fulfillment, goodwill, equality and dialogue to build a 'common world' are all key aspects. On the other hand, Nehru's metaphysical and historical assumptions and the intellectual framework he employs are distinctly the product of the particular context of Indian anti-colonialism.

Non-alignment was officially launched at the Bandung Conference in 1955 and Panchsheel was first articulated in 1954, but the intellectual roots of both policies can be traced back to the anti-colonial struggle and Nehru's pre-independence writings which critiqued the dominant conceptualizations of world politics for being based on fear and an incorrect assessment of human nature as unchanging and selfish. These were notions, he argued, that take 'refuge in irrationalism, superstition, and unreasonable and inequitable social prejudices and practices' and were being used to justify self-interest based on narrow, aggressive nationalism (Nehru 1982 [1946]: 30). In *Discovery*, for instance, he argued that European balance-of-power policies were responsible for sowing the seeds of distrust and fear and 'that fear has led to aggression and torturous intrigues' (Nehru 1982 [1946]: 539). While 'self-interest itself should drive every nation to … wider co-operation in order to escape disaster in the future and build its own free life on the basis of others', the

> self-interest of the 'realist' is far too limited by past myths and dogmas, and regards ideas and social forms, suited to one age, as immutable and as unchanging parts of human nature and society, forgetting that there is nothing so changeable as human nature and society … war is considered a biological necessity, empire and expansion as the prerogatives of a dynamic and progressive people, the profit motive as the central fact dominating human relations, and ethnocentrism, a belief in racial superiority, becomes an article of faith … Some of these ideas were common to the civilizations of east and west; many of them form the back-ground of modern western civilization out of which fascism and nazism grew.
>
> (Nehru 1982 [1946]: 540–1)

Friendship is explicitly mentioned in one of the concluding passages of *Discovery*:

> It was India's way in the past to welcome and absorb other cultures. That is much more necessary to-day, for we march to the one world of to-morrow where national cultures will be intermingled with the international culture of the human race. We shall therefore seek wisdom and knowledge and friendship and comradeship wherever we can find them, and co-operate with others in common task, but we are no supplicants for others' favours and patronage. Thus we shall remain true Indians and Asiatics, and become at the same time good internationalists and world citizens.
>
> (Nehru 1982 [1946]: 566)

Friendship was important, Nehru claimed in this passage, because it was a part of the best traditions of Indian civilization and because interdependence is a desirable goal. Nonetheless, he was aware of the novelty of this notion in the context of international politics and for the potential for it to be reduced to superficial rhetoric. 'Our general policy' he said in a speech in 1949,

> was to cultivate friendly relations with all countries, but that is something which anyone can say. It is not a very helpful thought. It is almost outside, if I may say so, of politics. It may be just a verbal statement or a moral urge. It is hardly a political urge. Nevertheless, something can be said for it even on the political plane.
>
> (Nehru 1961: 45)

The 'normal foreign policy of a country', he went on to note, was to be very friendly with some and hostile to others, but since India had not inherited any past hostility to any country, '[w]hy should we then start this train of hostility now with any country? ... our friendship with other countries should not, as far as possible be such as brings us into conflict with some other country'. Some, he acknowledged, would call this hedging, a 'middle of the road policy' but he insisted that, 'it is nothing of the kind ... It is a positive, constructive policy deliberately aiming at something and deliberately trying to avoid hostility to other countries...' (Nehru 1961: 45).

One of the post-independence policies that these convictions produced, nonalignment, was articulated in opposition to membership in Cold War blocs and collective defence pacts like the South East Asian Treaty Organisation (SEATO) which, Nehru argued,

> is inclined dangerously in the direction of spheres of influence to be exercised by powerful countries ... it is the big and powerful countries that will decide matters and not the two or three weak and small Asian countries that may be allied to them.
>
> (Nehru 1961: 89)

While '[c]ountries in Asia as well as outside may have certain justifiable fears' the 'approach of this Treaty is wrong and may antagonize a great part of Asia. Are you going to have peace and security by creating more conflicts and antagonisms?' (Nehru 1961: 89). A Congress resolution in 1957 invoked the links between military alliances, fear and insecurity and the need for new approaches:

> The Congress realizes that fear and suspicion have led to competition in armaments and to the maintenance of foreign armed forces and bases in a large number of countries.... And yet this very policy of reliance on armed force and military pacts has led to an increase of that fear and to a greater lack of security and the world moves in a vicious circle seeking a way out, and finding none. It has become essential, therefore, for new policies to be framed and for new approaches to be made with courage.
>
> (Nehru 2005: 278)

Nehru's disavowal of military alliances, however, was not a rejection of supranational cooperation for 'I think the world is too small now for any few countries, including the Asian countries, to say that nobody else can interfere with an area and that that area is their sole concern' (Nehru 1961: 90). Indeed, as the following quote on nonalignment indicates, rather than being a way to create a third way or a third bloc in the Cold War, Nehru viewed it as a means of creating an environment in which dialogue with all parties was possible while not compromising on working to bring about political equality:

> We have tried to work together with other countries on the basis of comradeship and we have done so without breaking our friendly ties with other

countries. But it would be a wrong approach to gather together a number of like countries which, like us, are militarily weak, and raise our voice in hostility to the great powers. We have therefore, opposed the idea of a Third Force. The moment we talk in these terms, we adopt to some extent the cold war approach and language of hostility.

(Nehru 1961: 78)

Dialogue was a central feature of the anti-colonial movement and Nehru's thoughts on the matter, as expressed in *Discovery*, indicate the influence of Gandhi's moral philosophy, which drew on the Jain doctrines of *anekantavada* that regards reality to be multi-dimensional and *syadvada*, which holds that truth can only ever be known in the plural:

There is an endless variety of men's minds. Each one sees the truth in his own way and is often unable to appreciate another's viewpoint. Out of this comes conflict. Out of this interaction also a fuller and more integrated truth emerges. For we have to realize that truth is many-sided and is not the monopoly of any group or nation.

(Nehru 1982 [1946]: 560)

These beliefs underpinned Nehru's post-independence foreign policies as he made clear in a speech to the Indian Council of World Affairs in 1949 when he justified nonalignment in the following terms: '... we should not align ourselves with power blocs' because '[w]e can be of far more service without doing so and I think there is just a possibility ... that at a moment of crisis our peaceful and friendly efforts might make a difference and avert that crisis' (Nehru 1961: 47). Hence, it was not,

a question of our remaining isolated or cut off from the rest of the world ... We wish to have the closest contacts, because we do from the beginning firmly believe in the world coming closer together and ultimately realizing the ideal of what is now being called One World.

(Nehru 1961: 47–8)

Nehru's alternative to military alliances in Asia was part of a broader policy of friendship:

Every country's foreign policy, first of all, is concerned with its own security and with protecting its own progress. Security can be obtained in many ways. The normal idea is that security is protected by armies. That is only partly true; it is equally true that security is protected by policies. A deliberate policy of friendship with other countries goes farther in gaining security than almost anything else.

(Nehru 1961: 79)

The doctrine of Panchsheel was another part of Nehru's policy of 'security through friendship' and an analysis of the origins of this doctrine gives a clearer idea of its ontological assumptions. Panchsheel was first enunciated in an agreement with China in 1954 and consisted of (i) mutual respect for each other's territorial integrity and sovereignty, (ii) mutual non-aggression, (iii) mutual non-interference in each other's internal affairs, (iv) equality and mutual benefit and, (v) peaceful coexistence (Nehru 1961: 99). According to Nehru, these five principles were 'the result of a long correspondence between the Government of India and the Government of China' and, therefore, the product of a dialogue rather than the inspiration of any individual leader (Quoted in Fifield 1958: 505). Whereas the Chinese tended to refer to the agreement as the 'Five Principles of Peaceful Coexistence', however, Nehru adopted a term derived from Sanskrit, Panchsheel, after he heard it used in Indonesia to refer to the basic principles of government: '... it struck me immediately that this was a suitable description of the five principles of international behaviour to which we had subscribed' (Quoted in Fifield 1958: 505). This was particularly the case because the expression had 'been used from ancient times to describe the five moral precepts of Buddhism relating to personal behaviour' (Quoted in Fifield 1958: 505). He again explicitly linked his understanding of Panchsheel to Buddhist ethics in a speech in which he noted that the Mauryan emperor Ashoka, who adopted Buddhist practices after witnessing the horrors of a particularly bloody war, had set the precedent for adapting these moral precepts into the principles of government when he set forth five principles of Buddhist politics in his stone-carved edicts (Nehru 1961: 101–2).[1] Numerous other speeches also made the link between the ethics of individual behaviour in Buddhist thought and the ethics of state behaviour encompassed in Panchsheel, including one given in Washington in 1956 in which Nehru argued that the true test of friendship was learning to deal with differences of opinion. Panchsheel, he claimed in this speech,

> is a very old concept which has been prevalent in India for over two thousand years, from the time of the Buddha ... in those days it used to refer to the character of human beings. Now we are using it in the political field, to lay down a code of conduct for the countries of the world. That too involves a question of character – the character of nations.
>
> (Nehru 2005: 473)

In Buddhist thought, individuals are driven not by a fear of death or a fear of uncertainty but, rather, *trishna* or craving to achieve a new state of being and permanence. Craving is the result of impulses that produce the desire for things like power and status, combined with ignorance of the nature of the Self as impermanent and lacking an essence. Driven by craving, individuals seek happiness in the affirmation of an illusory Self in an impermanent world and consequently experience only frustration and suffering. This could be remedied, however, by individuals following the eightfold path which includes recognizing the impermanence of reality, acting with benevolence and compassion and rejecting selfishness, violence and emotional states such as anger and greed. Taitso Unno argues that since there is no conception of the isolated, unchanging Self in Buddhist thought,

> the recognition of rights is not a static but a dynamic fact which makes it imperative that as we affirm our own individual rights we must also be willing to give up ourselves in order to affirm the rights of others. When, however, we affirm only our own rights at the expense of the rights of others – including the rights of humanity over nature, one nation or race over another, one belief or view over others – we become tyrannical and oppressive.
>
> (Unno 1988: 140)

Nehru's interpretation of Panchsheel as consistent with Buddhist philosophy and his reading of the Buddha's method as 'one of psychological analysis' (Nehru 1982 [1946]: 128) implies that he did not mean it to be a doctrine aimed at strengthening an absolutist understanding of state sovereignty – a form of self-affirmation which would lead to the proliferation of destructive desires in an interdependent, non-permanent world. Rather, applying a Buddhist-inspired ethic of interdependence to international relations means that nation-states are treated as social entities capable of forming emotional attachments with one another. Moreover, it means that assertions of sovereign rights are seen to contribute to a just world community of equals only when there is an understanding of an interdependent reality and an expression of responsibility, compassion and benevolence to others. This is the context in which Nehru's enthusiasm for Panchsheel as an ideal should be interpreted. Combined with an understanding of nonalignment as a means of facilitating dialogue, moreover, a politics of friendship – understood as a voluntary emotional attachment which grows from recognition of interdependence and translates into a commitment to a common project – becomes visible. However, Nehru's politics of friendship does not limit amity to a small circle of friends, necessitate the creation of enemies or rely on the creation of formal institutions to create loyalty and trust. Rather, Panchsheel and nonalignment were to work together to facilitate the creation of a common identity and common values, which would, in turn, facilitate the emergence of a broader internationalist ethic. They are thus a means of empowerment that offer the possibility of moral transformation in world politics.

Asia, India and friendship

Cultural and psychological affinities

Panchsheel and nonalignment were most actively promoted in Nehru's foreign discourse on Asia, if only as a first step toward global cooperation. 'Asianism', Nehru (1999a: 559) said in a speech in 1953 was 'not a very beautiful word' and to put the diverse countries of Asia 'into one basket and call it 'Asianism' has no meaning to me'. However, 'it has a certain meaning to me when I think along different lines' for,

> apart from geography which brings these countries nearer to each other ... [it is] cultural and other association, sometimes extending to two or three thousand years or more, which naturally has brought us nearer to each other and made to us some extent understand each other, there is the major fact of common experience for a long period of time for these countries of Asia – common experience, common suffering, being subject to domination for a long period.
>
> (Nehru 1999a: 559)

As a result, 'we have drawn mentally, you might say psychologically and morally, nearer to one another' (Nehru 1999a: 559). 'Asianism' therefore had meaning for Nehru as a normative idea for although he 'did not mean to say that we in Asia are in any way superior, ethically or morally to the people of Europe', there was 'a legacy of conflict in Europe' which Asia lacked, despite 'quarrels with their neighbours here and there' (Nehru 1961: 22–3). Hence, an experience of common suffering, cultural ties and the lack of a legacy of European-style conflict meant that Asia was particularly suited to an international relations defined by friendship.

Nehru's understanding of Asia's thousand-year-old cultural interaction was first explicated in *Discovery*, in which he drew on the work of the French Indologist Sylvain Levi and the notion of 'Greater India'. Levi and other French Indologists like Jules Bloch, Jean Pryzluski and George Coedes used their work on Hindu or Hindu-Buddhist monuments in Cambodia and Java and Sanskrit and Pali texts and inscriptions found in various locations in South East Asia to draw parallels between the French *mission civilisatrice* – which they contrasted to what they saw as the narrow and racist imperial ideology of the British – and ancient India's civilizing dynamic in Asia. For Levi, the far East was ancient India's Mediterranean (Bayly 2004: 713–15). This idea was enthusiastically promoted by a group of scholars in Calcutta who in 1927, on the eve of the Bengali poet Rabindranath Tagore's voyage to Southeast Asia, formed the Greater India Society. One of Tagore's travelling companions, the philologist Suniti Kumar Chatterji, became a key figure in the Greater India Society and Tagore himself was listed in the Society's publications as its honorary *Purodha* (spiritual head) (Bose 2006: 245; Bayly 2004: 710). Tagore took pride in India's transcendence of its boundaries but sought to downplay instances of Indian military aggression against Southeast Asia and emphasized the idea of cultural exchange while depicting Southeast Asians as active historical agents. He made no effort to hierarchize Indian culture as a superior or purer cultural source and rather than treating India as a monolith, Tagore highlighted the role of certain regions in the spread of cultural influence. His purpose, therefore, was not to buttress a territorially-bounded vision of an Indian nation-state with a sense of historical achievement (Bose 2006: 259–60). The aims and ideas of Tagore's followers in the Greater India Society, among them Kumar Chatterji, R.C. Majumdar, P.C. Bagchi and Kalidas Nag, however, were more narrowly nationalist and India-centric. Like Tagore these scholars emphasized India's cultural expansion rather than its military conquests and they were uninterested in authoritarian state power like the movements for a Greater Germany or a Greater Syria. Yet, rather than highlighting cultural interchange, their interest lay in presenting India as a civilizing force diffused through an ancient cultural colonialism that stretched into Burma, Java, Cambodia, Bali, Vietnam, and societies in the Pacific and the Buddhist world including Ceylon, Tibet, central Asia and Japan (Bayly 2004: 713). They did so to repudiate the image of Indians, and Bengalis in particular, as effeminate, other-worldly dreamers and instead represent them as men of action. At the same time, however, they sought to distinguish India's benign cultural colonialism from the armed conquest of the British and the Muslims (Bayly 2004: 721). According to Phanindranath Bose:

> the real charm of Indian history does not consist in these aspirants after universal power, but in its peaceful and benevolent Imperialism – a unique thing in the history of mankind. The colonizers of India did not go with sword and fire in their hands; they used ... the weapons of their superior culture and religion [to bring] the world under their sway. Wherever they went, they conquered the world through their culture.
>
> (Quoted in Bayly 2004: 712)

Bose's major concern was highlighting Hinduism's proselytizing initiatives and showing that the diffusion of 'Hindu' culture continued even after the 'coming of the Moslems' which, according some Orientalist scholarship, was when India began to stagnate (Bayly 2004: 724–6). His vision of Greater India, therefore, was an especially Hindu supremacist one and later inspired proponents of Hindu nationalism like Savarkar who declared in his key text, *Hindutva*:

> Let our colonists continue unabated their labours of founding a Greater India, a Mahabharat, to the best of their capacities and contribute all that is best in our civilization to the upbuilding of Humanity ... The only geographical limits of Hindutva are the limits of our earth!
>
> (Savarkar 1938: 152–3)

Nehru rejected this understanding of Greater India in both his pre-independence writings and his post-independence foreign policy. In *Discovery*, his notion of Greater India echoes Tagore's emphasis on cultural exchange and his concern is to naturalize an identity for India which was not narrow and isolated but formed in interdependence with others (Nehru 1982 [1946]: 201–2). He argued that an examination of ancient records showed Indian civilization,

> bubbling over with energy and spreading out far and wide, carrying not only her thought but her other ideals, her art, her trade, her language and literature,

and her methods of government. She was not stagnant or standing aloof, or isolated and cut off by barriers and perilous seas.

(Nehru 1982 [1946]: 207)

Like Tagore and the Greater India scholars, Nehru was cautious not to over-emphasize the military nature of India's expansionism. While the 'early colonizing ventures of the Indian people' were driven by 'trade and adventure and the urge for expansion' these 'early colonists settled down, more followed and thus a peaceful penetration went on. There was a fusion of the Indians with the races they found there and also the evolution of a mixed culture' (Nehru 1982 [1946]: 203).

Sylvain Levi's influence on Nehru's thinking on Greater India was evident. 'Just as Hellenism spread from Greece to the countries of the Mediterranean and in Western Asia', Nehru wrote, 'India's cultural influence spread to many countries and left its powerful impress on them'. Like Kalidas Nag before him he quoted Levi approvingly:

'From Persia to the Chinese Sea,' writes Sylvain Levi, 'from the icy regions of Siberia to the islands of Java and Borneo, from Oceania to Socotra, India has propagated her beliefs, her tales and her civilization. She has left indelible imprints on one-fourth of the human race in the course of a long succession of centuries. She has the right to reclaim in universal history the rank that ignorance has refused her for a long time and to hold her place amongst the great nations summarising and symbolising the spirit of Humanity'.

(Nehru 1982 [1946]: 210)

Unlike Nag, who described a rather one-sided process of 'Indianization' (Bayly 2004: 722–3), however, Nehru emphasized the agency of the recipients of India's 'cultural colonization' and the shifting nature of the identities produced. Writing about the expansion of Indian culture and art, for instance, he argued that, '[i]n each of these countries, Indian art encounters a different racial genius, a different local environment, and under their modifying influence it takes on a different garb' (Nehru 1982 [1946]: 210). The key aim of Nehru's (1982 [1946]: 209–10) account of Greater India, however, is its contemporary relevance for the creation of a new world order and his desire to re-establish links that had been broken by colonialism:

[t]hen came the British and they barred all the doors and stopped all the routes that connected us with our neighbours in Asia … This sudden isolation from the rest of Asia has been one of the most remarkable and unfortunate consequences of British rule in India.

(Nehru 1982 [1946]: 149)

Now, however,

[e]verywhere an intense and narrow nationalism has grown, looking to itself and distrustful of others; there is fear and hatred of European domination and

yet a desire to emulate Europe and America; there is often some contempt for India because of her dependent condition; and yet behind all this there is a feeling of respect and friendship for India, for old memories endure and people have not forgotten that there was a time when India was a mother country to these and nourished them with rich fare from her own treasure-house.

(Nehru 1982 [1946]: 149)

British colonialism, however, was not the sole cause of India's recent isolationism for, as discussed in the previous chapter, a part of Nehru's narrative of India's civilizational decline was an internal critique of the fading away of the 'urge to adventure and the overflowing of life' (Nehru 1982 [1946]: 54). This critique lay in the background of a speech he gave in the United States in 1949 in which he said: 'India, in Southern, Western and South-Eastern Asia, has to play a distinctive and important role. If she is not capable of playing it properly, then she will just fade out' (Nehru 1961: 595). Negotiating this 'distinctive and important role' in such a way that did not cast India in a hierarchical leadership role that would impact negatively on a politics of friendship was, however, a delicate balancing act which was not always successful.

Asianism, nonalignment and Panchsheel

According to A. Appadorai 'the first (ever) expression of an Asian sentiment' can be 'traced to August 1926 when the Asian delegations to the non-official International Conference for Peace held at Bierville declared in a memorandum that Asia must have its rightful place in the consideration of world problems' (Quoted in Chakrabarty 2005: 4814). The idea took further shape at the first Asian Relations Conference held in New Delhi in March 1947 and at the Asian-African Conference at Bandung in 1955. In his address to the Asian Relations Conference, Nehru defined Asia broadly, including Egypt and the Arab countries of West Asia, Iran, and the countries of Southeast Asia as well as Afghanistan, Tibet, Nepal, Bhutan, Burma and Sri Lanka (Nehru 1961: 249). His later speeches seek to construct a common identity based on experiences of suffering under colonialism, resistance to potential neo-colonialism and a future project of renewal:

> Far too long have we of Asia have been petitioners in Western courts and chancelleries. That story must now belong to the past. We propose to stand on our own legs and to co-operate with all others who are prepared to co-operate with us. We do not intend to be the playthings of others.
>
> (Nehru 1961: 251)

Asia, Nehru argued, had been lost in time but was now striving toward modernity:

> In Asia we have been kept down and are now trying to catch up with others who are ahead of us. We have been engrossed in things of the past and time

has passed us by. We have not been able to keep pace with it and so we must run now.

(Nehru 1961: 264)

Asia's common psychological state, which was more conducive to an international politics of amity and friendship, was a key part of the common identity Nehru sought to construct. There was a 'basic difference' he asserted, '... in the European approach to problems and the Asian approach' for Asia had comparatively less of the 'fear complex' that was driving European power politics (Nehru 1961: 262). Thus, he claimed in a speech in the Lok Sabha in 1955, 'the Panchsila [Panchsheel] are a challenge of Asia to the rest of the world' (Nehru 2001a: 314).

The pinnacle of Panchsheel's influence in Asia came shortly after it was enunciated in 1954 during India's involvement in the Geneva Conference which was convened to find a resolution to the first Indochina war. India was elected to lead the International Supervisory Commissions charged with the task of implementing the Geneva agreements. On the one hand, for Nehru (1961: 401) the Geneva Conference was another reminder of the 'territorial, racial and political imbalance in the modern world' since, even though they were concerned with the countries and peoples of Asia, the main participants were non-Asian states. On the other hand, 'the historic role of this conference was that it was the alternative or the deterrent to what threatened to lead to the third world war' (Nehru 1961: 402). The influence of Panchsheel was evident for:

It is a notable feature of the Indo-China settlement that it provides for the establishment of the independence of the three States – Viet-Nam, Laos and Cambodia – and seeks to safeguard their sovereignty on the pledges of mutual respect of each other's territorial integrity, freedom from interference in each other's internal affairs, and the undertaking not to enter into military alliances with other States. Thus, the Indo-China States bid fair to find a place in collective peace rather than in war blocs.

(Nehru 1961: 403)

Nehru often stressed the equal status of all countries in Asia and, in his speech at the Asian Relations Conference in 1947, emphasized that India had no desire for leadership. Nevertheless, he still gave India a central position in this Asian identity:

In this Conference and in this work there are no leaders and no followers ... Apart from the fact that India herself is emerging into freedom and independence, she is the natural centre and focal point of the many forces at work in Asia. Geography is a compelling factor, and geographically she is so situated as to be the meeting point of Western and Northern and Eastern and South-East Asia.

(Nehru 1961: 250)

Reiterating these sentiments two years later in 1949 in a speech to the Constituent Assembly, he argued that India 'inevitably has to play a very important part in Asia' but 'not because of any ambition of hers, but because of geography, because of history and because of so many other things' (Nehru 1961: 22). Thus, although it was foolish to suggest that India assume the leadership of Asia, 'a certain special responsibility is cast on India. India realizes it, and other countries realize it also. The responsibility is not necessarily for leadership, but for taking the initiative sometimes and helping others to co-operate' (Nehru 1961: 44). Nehru, therefore, cast India in a maternal, nurturing role, rather than a paternal, disciplinarian role and a private note outlining how independent India should behave in the UN General Assembly reveals that this careful inscription of India as a facilitator was made with an awareness that any mention of Indian leadership 'does not help us in any way and merely irritates others and creates suspicion' (Nehru 1988: 611). Nevertheless, Nehru (1988: 611) states in this note that he regarded India as 'the natural leader of South East Asia[2] if not of some other parts of Asia also' for 'there is at present no other possible leadership in Asia and any foreign leadership will not be tolerated'. The difficulty of maintaining this subtle distinction between taking responsibility for facilitating dialogue and assuming leadership came to the fore at the Bandung Conference in 1955. According to the representative of the Philippines Carlos Romulo, Nehru's 'pronounced propensity to be dogmatic, impatient, irascible, and unyielding ... alienated the goodwill of many delegates [at Bandung]' (Quoted in Chakrabarty 2005: 4813). For him, Nehru typified 'the affectations of cultural superiority induced by a conscious identification with an ancient civilization which has come to be the hallmark of Indian representatives to international conferences' (Quoted in Chakrabarty 2005: 4813).

Nehru's closing remarks at the Bandung Conference came with the acknowledgment that, despite cultural ties and a common experience of colonialism, reaching a consensus on a common vision on which to consolidate a politics of friendship was far from a straightforward endeavour: '...we wrestled with one another these seven days because we wanted to arrive at a common opinion and common outlook. Obviously, the world looks different according to the angle from which you look at it' (Nehru 1961: 269–70). Among the most contentious issues were pro-US collective defence pacts of which states like Thailand and the Philippines were members. Carlos Romulo for instance, argued that the needs of small countries were different from large countries, and that the Manilla Pact, which later became SEATO, was a defensive pact that was in conformity with the UN Charter (Abraham 2008: 207).

Ultimately, however, SEATO failed to take root. In an attempt to explain this outcome, Acharya has attributed Nehru's ideas on non-alignment and the rejection of the pact by the four of the 'Colombo' Powers,[3] India, Sri Lanka, Burma and Indonesia – countries whose involvement were thought vital to the success of SEATO – with consolidating in Asia an international norm of non-intervention which in turn led to the creation 'a normative injunction against participation in collective defence pacts in Asia that would prove resilient' (Acharya

2005: 26, 34–5). According to Acharya, this normative injunction 'continued to influence the nature and purpose of subsequent Asian regional organizations', in particular, the Association of South East Asian Nations (ASEAN) which was formed in 1967 with a focus on the economic, social, cultural, technical, scientific and administrative fields rather than collective defence (Acharya 2005: 39–40). It could be argued, therefore, that Nehru's politics of friendship had an important, if indirect, impact on the contemporary international order for, as Acharya (2005: 43–4) goes on to note, despite several initiatives such as the ASEAN Regional Forum and the Pacific Security Community, multilateral security cooperation in Asia has been limited to intelligence-sharing and capacity building activities.

On the other hand, ASEAN would have been far from what Nehru hoped would be the outcome of his politics of friendship for he expressed little interest in formal regional institution building and, indeed, argued that regionalism would come in the way of a long-term ideal of a world federation. Nehru's ideas on nonalignment, moreover, should not be conflated with non-intervention and a rigid conception of state sovereignty for he consistently and actively sought to entrench a vision of an independent India in a radically internationalist framework: 'When we talked of the independence of India' he wrote in *Discovery*, 'it was not in terms of isolation' for '[w]e realized, perhaps more than many other countries, that the old type of complete national independence was doomed, and there must be a new era of world cooperation' (Nehru 1982 [1946]: 421). Hence, '... we were perfectly agreeable to limit that independence in common with other nations, within some international framework' which 'should preferably cover the world or as large a part of it as possible, or be regional' (Nehru 1982 [1946]: 421). But, 'I have no liking for a division of the world into a few huge supra-national areas, unless these are tied together by some strong world bond' (Nehru 1982 [1946]: 536). Indeed, the appearance of regionalism would be a failure of imagination: 'if people are foolish enough to avoid world unity and some world organization, then these vast supra-national regions, each functioning as one huge state but with local autonomy, are very likely to take shape' (Nehru 1982 [1946]: 536).

His ideal of a 'world federation of free nations' was clearly outlined in the Congress's 'Quit India' Resolution of the 8th of August, 1942. The 'Quit India' Resolution, which was drafted by Nehru, demanded immediate recognition of India's independence 'both for the sake of India and for the success of the cause of the United Nations' and outlined plans for a provisional government that would 'defend India and resist aggression with all the armed as well as the non-violent forces at its command, together with its allied powers' (Nehru 1982 [1946]: 477). It also, however, detailed rather radical objectives for a future federation which would replace the system of sovereign nation-states:

> While the A. I. C. C. must primarily be concerned with the independence and defence of India in this hour of danger, the Committee is of the opinion that the future peace, security and ordered progress of the world demand a

world federation of free nations, and on no other basis can the problems of the modern world be solved. Such a world federation would ensure the freedom of its constituent nations, the prevention of aggression and exploitation by one nation over another, the protection of national minorities, the advancement of all backward areas and peoples, and the pooling of the world's resources for the common good of all. On the establishment of such a world federation, disarmament would be practicable in all countries, national armies, navies and air forces would no longer be necessary, and a world federal defence force would keep the world peace and prevent aggression.

(Gandhi 1942: 453)

Manu Bhagavan has argued that it is the 'Quit India' Resolution that most clearly sets out Nehru's vision for the UN and that it was this vision which he and his sister, Vijaya Laxmi Pandit, who led the Indian delegation at the UN, attempted to make a reality in the post-independence period, in particular through the establishment of the Human Rights Commission (HRC) (Bhagavan 2008: 8–9). Bhagavan (2008: 19) has convincingly argued that Nehru saw in the HRC the first step toward developing the UN into a supra-national global body. India's representative to the HRC, Hansa Mehta, together with the Indian Permanent Representative to the UN, Rajeshwar Dayal, were among the most forceful supporters of the right of individuals to petition the HRC in the 1940s and 1950s in the face of resistance from Western and Soviet representatives (Burke 2010: Ch. 3) and Nehru himself indicated his support for the subordination of state sovereignty to individual human rights in February 1947:

Today the Human Rights Commission is meeting in New York. Our representatives are there. The conception is that there are common individual rights which should be guaranteed all the world over.
...What is the UNO? It is developing into a world republic in which all States, independent States are represented and to which they may be answerable on occasions, for instance South Africa over the South Africa Indians' question, even though this was a domestic question because Indians are South African citizens.

(Nehru 1984b: 216–17)

That this vision was still very much on Nehru's mind after he assumed the Prime Ministership is clear from his comments on the Bandung conference in the Indian parliament where he emphasized its importance in fostering the ideal of a 'world community':

We did not permit our sense of unity or our success to drive us into isolation and egocentricity. Each major decision of the Conference happily refers to the United Nations and to world problems and ideals. We believe that from Bandung our great organization, the United Nations has derived strength.

This means in turn that Asia and Africa must play an increasing role in the conduct and destiny of the world organization.

(Nehru 1961: 279)

A more direct outcome of Nehru's politics of friendship for international order, and perhaps one more in keeping with Nehru's vision for a world community, concerns the activities of the Non-Aligned Movement (NAM) which was founded in 1961. Despite being recognized as a co-founder of the NAM with Tito and Nasser, Nehru was initially hesitant about the creation of a 'movement' that could be construed as a third bloc and damage the purpose of nonalignment as a means of facilitating dialogue with all (Gopal 1984: 185). Nonetheless, some of the achievements of NAM were entirely in keeping with Nehru's politics of friendship as a means of achieving greater global interdependence for, despite the political and economic diversity of NAM members, there have been instances in which it articulated a common project and achieved concrete results with important consequences for international norm-building. Take, for instance, the sanctions regime against apartheid South Africa. It was an Indian resolution censuring South Africa at the first session of the UN which won a two-thirds majority in the General Assembly and according to Henri Laugier, the Assistant Secretary-General for Social Affairs at the HRC, served to establish a 'precedent of fundamental significance in the field of international action ... out of these debates the general impression had arisen that no violation of human rights should be covered up by the principle of national sovereignty' (Quoted in Bhagavan 2008: 13). Building on this, in 1952 India put forward the first motion censuring South Africa specifically on apartheid and racial discrimination and from the 1960s worked with other NAM countries to entrench a norm of racial equality in world politics despite resistance from the 'great powers'. The NAM grouping in the UN General Assembly also played a key role in the evolution of the Palestinian cause from 1967 by introducing a number of resolutions related to the rights of Palestinians despite resistance from the United States and Europe. For instance, compliance with UN Security Council Resolution 446, which grew out of NAM's advocacy in the General Assembly and declared Israeli settlement activity on occupied territories to be illegal has since become recognized by the 'international community' as essential for a negotiated settlement to the conflict (Morphet 2004: 526–7).

Beyond friendship

As difficult as fashioning a politics of friendship in Asia was, it proved even more difficult with the countries in India's immediate vicinity, Sri Lanka, Pakistan, Nepal and Bhutan. Commonly referred to today as constituting the region of 'South Asia', together with India and Bangladesh, these countries were not considered a distinctive subordinate system during the Nehru era (Brecher 1968: 329–30). Indeed although the term 'South Asia' occasionally occurred in Indian foreign policy discourse in the 1950s, it only gained meaning and popularity in the 1980s, long after the terms 'South-east Asia', 'West Asia' and 'Central Asia' became commonplace. Yet, Nehru's (2005: 713) response in 1960 to a question on the possibility of a subcontinental federation of India, Pakistan, Burma and Sri Lanka implies that he did expect a confederation of India and its neighbours to be the first step toward the world federation he outlined in the 'Quit India' resolution of 8 August, 1942. Had the question been asked fifteen or twenty years ago, Nehru replied, 'I would have said that certainly ... some kind of confederation ... of independent states with common defence and economic policies' should have been a 'normal development – something that would have come about this century ... Just at the beginning of the war I drafted the Congress resolution hinting at just this'. But, 'the difficulty in our way now is if we talk about it, this upsets our neighbours because of course, we are so much bigger'. Nevertheless, for Nehru, a confederation was still 'the logical future path' (Nehru 2005: 713).

In the years between his articulation of a 'world federation' in 1942 and his 1960 interview, Nehru's attempts at overcoming the barriers posed by the inequalities in size between the countries of the subcontinent resulted in a politics of friendship that occasionally slipped into the language of fraternity and a discourse of love and closeness. Yet, as Hannah Arendt has argued, fraternity, with its naturalistic or organic connotations can fail to accommodate the diversity and plurality of the world (Chiba 1995: 514–15). Nehru's slippage into a discourse of fraternity, thus, often proved counter-productive, producing not reassurance but a desire for greater distance.

'Mountain-girl Nepal, daughter of the Himalayas, young sister of India, I have come here at last' Nehru (1961: 437–8) declared on the eve of his departure from Kathmandu after his first visit in 1951. In 1950 India had signed a Treaty of Peace and Friendship with Nepal because '[n]aturally' Nehru (1961: 439) argued at the time, 'our relations should be closer and our ties stronger with those countries which are our old friends, companions and neighbours'. Moreover, 'it is necessary that our hearts should be clear, that we should look at each other with the eyes of love, and trust each other'. He explained India's motivation for pursuing close relations with Nepal in the following terms:

> India has no designs on Nepal's independence and seeks no special advantage for herself. But neither India nor Nepal can escape geography or resist the forces of modern political trends. All that India seeks is to ensure Nepal's security and her own by timely and wise adjustment of old institutions and usages to new needs.
>
> (Nehru 1993: 381)

He wrote in another letter in 1950 that, '[o]n the advent of independence in India, many people in Nepal and many Nepalese in India naturally looked towards India and thought that our advice would result in substantial changes there' (Nehru 1993: 365). By 1960, Nehru was still articulating a discourse of fraternity: '[t]he relationship between Nepal and India is age-old, based on geography, religion, culture, customs ... It is there like the relationship between brothers. The bond of love between them is inviolable' (Nehru 1961: 439). Private notes, however, indicate an unravelling of the political relationship between Nepal and India which could not be prevented by assertions of brotherhood and love. India's request to the Nepalese government that 'any treaty of Nepal with a foreign country should be considered in cooperation with us and after reference to us' was repeatedly ignored as Nepal proceeded to establish friendship treaties with a number of countries including the Soviet Union and China (Nehru 1999b: 462–3; Nehru 1956: 390; Dutt 1956: 388–9). A letter written in 1950 argued that although the Nepali government was at first apprehensive about India, once they 'realized that we would confine ourselves to advice only, they lost that feeling of apprehension and ignored what we told them' (Nehru 1993: 365).

In 1956, Nehru wrote to the Indian Ambassador in Nepal confirming that he had decided to, 'reconsider our attitude towards Nepal' for, '[t]hey have not only bypassed us and practically ignored us, but have done so with discourtesy. This is obviously a deliberate attitude to emphasize their own complete independence from us' (Nehru 1956: 390). He went on to note that,

> the policy of thrusting help in the hope of winning goodwill is always unsafe and sometimes leads to harmful reactions. The other country thinks that we are trying to buy their goodwill. Instead we get their ill will. Anyhow, we can neither afford to help them much nor do we desire to do so in existing circumstances. They are perfectly free to go their own way and we shall go our own way.
>
> (Nehru 1956: 390)

Like Nepal, Bhutan was said to share 'a special tie, personal tie' with India for 'we are all the children of the Himalayas (Nehru 1999a: 592). In 1949 India and Bhutan signed the Treaty of Friendship and Cooperation according to which Bhutan was to be guided by India's advice in its foreign relations in exchange for India's non-interference in its internal affairs. In a speech in New Delhi at a banquet for the Maharaja and Maharani of Bhutan in 1954, Nehru (1999a: 592) sought to reassure them that as a 'large country' and an 'ancient land' that had in the past 'always extended the hand of friendship out to neighbouring countries' India would always be there to help 'not only materially but to help you with affection and understanding of your problems'. In this case, however, there appeared to be, at least initially, a desire for something other than friendship with Bhutan. Nehru wrote to the Indian Ambassador to Nepal in 1949:

> ... in the international sense Bhutan is subordinate to India, because she can have no foreign relations and cannot declare war or peace. As a matter of fact Bhutan remains autonomous only because we choose to allow it to remain so. Even financially it is dependent upon us and it can carry on only because of the subsidy we give.
>
> (Nehru 1949: 80)

India's demand for a resident Political Agent in Bhutan, however, was resisted because it evoked memories of the British method of exercising indirect colonial rule and despite his own abhorrence of colonialism Nehru (1999a: 594) could not understand Bhutan's sensitivities:

> I did not understand why the Maharaja or his Government should be apprehensive in this matter. That showed a certain lack of confidence in us. We should proceed on a basis of accepting each other's *bona fides* and having confidence in each other.
>
> (Nehru 1999a: 594)

The idea was later given up in favour of maintaining India's self-representation as a non-coercive nation-state and resulted in a reversion to a politics of friendship over hegemony. Nehru (2001b: 313) thus instructed that instead of asking for closer political contacts India 'should lay greater emphasis on the social and economic side. Even there, there should be no attempt at any imposition. Help should be given when asked for and not thrust upon Bhutan'.

On the eve of Sri Lanka's independence Nehru (1987: 534) delivered a message in New Delhi heralding Sri Lanka's impending freedom which indicated that friendship and fraternity were to be the basis of India's foreign policy: 'No country can rejoice more at this change than India which has been and is like an elder brother to Lanka. Geography, tradition, culture, religion and economic interest all combine to bring Lanka and India close to one another'. Continuing with this theme in a cable to D.S. Senanayake, Nehru (1987: 534) based the India–Sri Lanka relationship on fraternity, anti-colonialism and 'world peace':

> I send you fraternal greetings on the attainment by Ceylon[4] of independence. Simhala Dweep is once again sovereign and free India looks forward to even closer cooperation than in the past with her kin and neighbour in tasks of mutual interest and in common endeavour, with other friendly nations, for emancipation of people still struggling for their liberties and for establishment of enduring world peace.
>
> (Nehru 1987: 534)

Yet, India's relations with Sri Lanka quickly became dominated by the latter's unwillingness to grant citizenship rights to people of Indian descent living in Sri Lanka despite their long presence in the country. For Nehru, no immutable link existed between diasporas and the lands of their ancestors and he sought to deal with the problem of populations displaced by colonialism by arguing that states defer to the authority of a meta-national body which would be entrusted to protect the rights of minority populations (Bhagavan 2008: 31–2). In the case of Sri Lanka, despite his conviction that people of Indian descent there were 'not our nationals' and could not be asked to 'walk across to India' when they had been born in Sri Lanka and had lived there for generations, he recognized that

'the real difficulty was the fear of the Ceylonese that India might absorb them' –
a fear that 'was wholly unjustified' (Nehru 1961: 301, 298). Still:

> we have always to remember this fear of the Ceylonese. Any so-called pres-
> sure tactics on our part tend to increase this fear, and therefore, make the
> solution a little more difficult. They begin to look away from India in
> matters of trade etc. and rely on some distant country like England or, it
> may be, even Australia rather than India. And yet, every interest of theirs,
> including their basic cultural outlook, draws them to India, if but this fear
> was absent.
>
> (Nehru 1999b: 557)

'Hence', he added, 'it is necessary for us not to say or do anything which adds to
this fear complex'.

In a note written in 1955 Nehru (2001a: 275) pointed out that while India
'used to have problems with Burma ... they were all resolved, and there was the
greatest friendship between India and Burma'. 'Why', he asked 'could we not
achieve that friendship between India and Ceylon?' The Sri Lankan High Commissioner offered an appealing explanation in an unofficial discussion which
Nehru summarized in the note:

> The High Commissioner then said that the background in Ceylon was dif-
> ferent from that of India. India had gone through a great struggle, while
> Ceylon had no such experience.[5] I agreed and pointed out how a struggle
> conditions a people as it had done in India, as to some extent it had done in
> Burma though their struggle started in wartime. In Pakistan, the people cer-
> tainly were partly conditioned by the Indian struggle for freedom, but not so
> the leaders. In fact, they had opposed that struggle.
>
> (Nehru 2001a: 276)

In the case of Sri Lanka and India then, a crucial element of what was to sustain
friendship – an experience of common suffering and struggle – was missing.
However, the central problem in India's relationship with Sri Lanka, and with
the other countries in its vicinity, as Nehru seemed to recognize, was the material inequality that was the product of the size differential between the two
countries.

The caution with which Nehru approached Nepal, Bhutan and Sri Lanka was
missing in his discourse on Pakistan and reflects the legacy of the politics which
led up to the partition of British India in 1947 and the dispute over Kashmir.
The approach to Pakistan was not, however, simply a case of declaring it an
enemy Other. Rather relations between India and Pakistan were characterized
by the construction of a deep and ultimately damaging intimacy. Nehru's critique of Pakistan rested on the latter's desire to seek security not in the interdependent internationalist nationalism consistent with an ethical modernity but in
a self-interested, fearful, narrow nationalism. This was a continuation of what

was depicted in *Discovery* as a fraternal divide that emerged in the colonial era: 'the difference of a generation or more in the development of the Hindu and Moslem middle classes' had produced a 'psychology of fear' among Muslims. However,

> Pakistan, the proposal to divide India, however, much it may appeal emotionally to some, is of course no solution for this backwardness, and it is much more likely to strengthen the hold of feudal elements for some time longer and delay the economic progress of the Moslems.
>
> (Nehru 1982 [1946]: 351–2)

Whereas the Congress Party, 'undoubtedly represents the historic process of growth toward these new ideas and institutions, though it tries to adapt these to some of the old foundations', on the Muslim side, 'feudal elements have continued to be strong and have usually succeeded in imposing their leadership on their masses' (Nehru 1982 [1946]: 351–2).

He explained his understanding of the difference between India and Pakistan in the postcolonial era in a debate in Parliament in 1951:

> We wanted a peaceful solution of our internal problems and a joint effort to win our freedom. We hoped we could live together in that freedom. The supporters of Pakistan had a different gospel. They were not for unity but disunity, not for construction but for destruction, not for peace but for discord, if not war. I do not think that the people of Pakistan are any better or any worse than the people of India. But fortunately, a certain ideal was before us in this country during the last twenty or thirty years which naturally affected our thinking and action. And in spite of everything that ideal continues to be our guiding star. That is the major difference between our policies today and those of Pakistan.
>
> (Nehru 1961: 469)

The 'ideal' that Nehru mentions above was, of course, secularism, which for him was an essential part of an ethical modernity. For Nehru, Indian civilization was always predominantly secular and secularism in postcolonial India was not just a modern appendage but simply a modern manifestation of a traditional orientation. Modern secularism, defined as tolerance for all religions, was prefigured in Indian civilization and therefore constituted a component of India's exceptionalism. He wrote in *Discovery of India* for instance:

> …the whole history of India was witness of the toleration and even encouragement of minorities and of different racial groups. There is nothing in Indian history to compare with the bitter religious feuds and persecutions that prevailed in Europe. So we did not have to go abroad for ideas of religious and cultural toleration: these were inherent in Indian life.
>
> (Nehru 1982 [1946]: 382)

In adopting a 'different gospel', therefore, the supporters of the Pakistan movement were both anti-modern and betraying the tradition of tolerance inherent in Indian civilization. He said at a public meeting in 1951 for example:

> no modern civilized state can be other than a secular State. It is a sign of going back, to some hundreds of years back, to the Middle Ages of Europe, if you can think of anything but a secular State. Apart from that it is the only civilized way to solve the State's problems.
>
> (Nehru 1994: 314)

Accordingly, Pakistan, which had been 'built on a communal theory',

> was bound to suffer, as every country must suffer that follows that kind of policy. That is to say the country suffers not because of the inability, it suffers because of the internal forces that it creates in its own land ... Because it is an out-of-date, and fantastically wrong basis for a nation to progress, a country that adopts that cannot go ahead (Nehru 1994: 315).

Pakistan's participation in SEATO and its growing military relationship with the United States consolidated this representation of Pakistan as a misguided, failed version of India's postcolonial Self. For Nehru (1961: 471; 1999b: 423), since 'one of the symbols of freedom has been the withdrawal of foreign armed forces', by inviting foreign troops back to Asia, Pakistan had become 'practically a colony of the US'. In response to similar criticisms made at the Bandung Conference, Pakistani Prime Minister, Mohammad Ali unrepentantly replied that as 'an independent sovereign nation' following its 'national interest', he did not feel it 'necessary for us to justify our actions to anybody except to ourselves' (Quoted in Acharya 2005: 1).

Ayesha Jalal (1998, 1985) has detailed the process by which the articulation of Muslim difference in colonial India became rendered as 'religious communalism' and opposed to 'secular nationalism' in the 1930s and, from the 1940s, asserted as Muslim nationhood. Ultimately, she claims, the Partition of India was the result of the Congress's unwillingness to accommodate the desire for the confederal structure of governance that accompanied this understanding of Muslim nationhood. She argues, moreover, that the existence of Muslim difference did not inevitably lead to the expression of Muslim identity and then unavoidably to Partition, but rather, that the denial of difference and the space this created for the mobilization of identity along religious lines, was key. Nehru recognized a 'psychology of fear' as being central to Muslim mobilization but in focusing on a materialist explanation for this fear, and with his belief in centralized planning as necessary for India's economic modernization, he continued espousing a nationalism that dealt with difference through the imposition of secular tolerance and a state structure that was strongly centralized. In fact, despite voting for Partition, it seems that Nehru expected the division to be temporary, both because of the artificial nature of the two-nation theory and because 'as the world shrinks and its problems overlap', only a large united India would be able to cope with the pressures of a world of internationalized activities and 'give them scope for development' (Nehru 1982 [1946]: 532–3). He wrote in *Discovery* that the sentiment for Partition 'has been artificially created and has no roots in the Moslem mind' although 'even a temporary sentiment may be strong enough to influence events and create a new situation' (Nehru 1982 [1946]: 530). Thus, '[i]t may be that some division of India is enforced' but '[e]ven if this happens, I am convinced that the basic feeling of unity and world developments will later bring the divided parts nearer to each other and result in a real unity' (Nehru 1982 [1946]: 530). In an interview in 1960, moreover, he told the historian Leonard Mosley that 'we expected that a partition would be temporary, that Pakistan was bound to come back to us. None of us guessed how much the killings and the crisis in Kashmir would embitter relations' (Mosley 1961: 248). Indeed, after the violence that accompanied Partition, the Kashmir crisis, Mohammad Ali Jinnah's untimely death and the rise of the military in Pakistani politics, it soon became clear that no reunion with India would be imminent and Pakistan was approached not within a politics of friendship in which differences were respected and dialogue encouraged, but within a discourse of rejected fraternity. Nehru was well aware of the dangers of passionate prejudice but he was less attuned to the passions that underpinned the totalizing discourse of fraternity and secularism directed at Pakistan and at Muslims in pre-partition India, paradoxically in the interests of a tolerant ethical modernity. His subsequent inability to deal with the difference represented by Pakistan came at the expense of long-term relations with Pakistan and Kashmir and to the detriment of Nehru's ethical modernity.

The issue of Kashmir was referred to the UN Security Council after the Pakistan-backed incursion and ensuing war in 1947 as 'an act of faith, because we believe in the progressive realization of a world order and a world government' (Nehru 1961: 451). The handling of the issue in the Security Council, however, did not involve an unequivocal condemnation of Pakistani aggression as India expected and, therefore, created the perception that India and Pakistan were being morally equated. The perception of the Security Council's, and particularly Britain's, bias toward Pakistan led to the loss of the UN's credibility as a neutral arbiter in the eyes of the Indian leadership. Thus, against his own conviction that the rights of minorities be protected by the subordination of state sovereignty to a supra-national organization, Nehru subsequently refused to uphold its commitment to hold a plebiscite, which has resulted in lasting ill-will from both Pakistanis and Kashmiris (Behera 2006: 34–7, 210–13). Nehru also presided over the progressive whittling away of Kashmir's constitutionally-guaranteed autonomy. This contributed to a breakdown in his close relationship with Sheikh Mohammad Abdullah, the secular leader of the National Conference, the only mass-based political organization in Kashmir. Abdullah had favoured accession to India over Pakistan but by 1953 he had started to publicly call for Kashmiri independence, which resulted in the dismissal of his government and his arrest and detention without trial. All of this occurred with Nehru's complicity, although his remorse drove him to write sympathetic letters to Abdullah in prison while paying for his son to attend medical school in

London and spend his vacations in his home (Zachariah 2004: 213; Crocker 1966: 146).

Near the end of his life Nehru became increasingly preoccupied by the memories and the ideals of the anti-colonial struggle and he was troubled that he had not lived up to Gandhi's expectations (Nehru 1965: vii–viii). In 1962 while speaking to a *Washington Post* reporter he suggested a confederal solution for India and Kashmir and for West and East Pakistan, since relations between the two parts of Pakistan had grown increasingly contentious. Eventually, he hoped that a larger confederation of India and Pakistan could be created:

> Confederation remains our ultimate goal. Look at Europe, at the Common Market. This is the urge everywhere. There are no two peoples anywhere nearer than those of India and Pakistan, though if we say it, they get alarmed and think we want to swallow them.
>
> (Quoted in Gopal 1984: 261–2)

He broached this idea again in 1964, in one of his final speeches in the Lok Sabha in which the language of friendship finally made its appearance. 'I have often thought these days of Gandhiji, how he would have dealt with our existing problems, specially those with Pakistan' he said in this speech, concluding that a Gandhian approach would mean solving the conflict 'on a basis of friends who have fallen out coming together, of not agreeing with each other, of approving of each other occasionally but nevertheless remaining friends and co-operating'. This involved admitting wrongdoing on India's part for 'I am afraid, we are growing very self-righteous', undertaking unilateral measures of goodwill and setting an example of good behaviour to 'psychologically' remove the 'hatred and fear complex' that lay at the heart of the conflict (1964: 10719, 10721, 10711). Prior to this speech, and following his first stroke in January, Nehru had facilitated the release from prison of Sheik Abdullah who was then sent to Pakistan for talks with President Ayub Khan. Nehru suffered a second stroke in May which took his life, so we will never know what the consequences of this change of approach may have been. Nonetheless, in the next section I will consider what a Gandhian approach to a politics of friendship may have entailed.

Friendship across hierarchy

The most significant problem faced by Nehru in his politics of friendship concerned the challenge of building friendship in the context of hierarchy. India's size, its perception of itself and by others as an ancient and resurgent civilization all contributed to a lack of recognition of equality often considered vital for friendship. This was particularly the case with India's dealings with the countries in its immediate vicinity. The possibility of friendship across hierarchy is something that Aristotle grappled with but, according to Berenskoetter (2007: 667), did not entirely resolve. Aristotle suggested that friendship was possible in a relationship of hierarchy if there was sufficient similarity in virtue and mutual love. However, he also argued that true friendship was near impossible where inequalities of wealth and power were significant and capable of corrupting the logic of reciprocity which, for him, was vital for friendship. In contrast to Aristotle's ambiguous stance on the possibility of friendship where some form of inequality exists, building friendship across hierarchy was at the centre of Gandhi's conception of political friendship as neighbourly love, which could also be seen as a counterpoint to Arendt's conviction that a politics of friendship can only be based on a dispassionate commitment to the well-being of the world and the 'dignity of man' (Arendt 1963: 84; Chiba 1995: 532).

Arendt's opinion that love is harmful to the political world rested on her understanding of it as a sentiment tending toward emotional bias and passionate outburst (Chiba 1995: 511). She wrote in *The Human Condition*:

> Love, in distinction from friendship, is killed, or rather extinguished, the moment it is displayed in public ... Because of its inherent worldlessness, love can only become false and perverted when it is used for political purposes such as the change or salvation of the world.
>
> (Arendt 1958: 51–2)

In contrast, love played an essential role in Gandhi's moral philosophy without the totalizing effects feared by Arendt. Love was understood by Gandhi not as a sentiment of affection or as compassion, which are both unpredictable, but as *ahimsa*: 'The only force of universal application can ... be that of ahimsa or love' (Gandhi 1999i: 340). *Ahimsa* is often literally translated as 'non-violence' but is better understood as a means toward cultivating 'neighbourliness', and therefore, 'friendship' (Gandhi 1999j: 190; Skaria 2002: 957).

At first glance Gandhi may not appear to be the best proponent of friendship given his propensity to use the language of brotherhood. Prakash (1999: 223) has argued, for instance, that Gandhi is guilty of imposing a 'stifling organic unity of love and kinship on difference'. However, as Faisal Devji (2005: 97) has argued, the idea of brotherhood that Gandhi used was one specific to the Gujarati language, in which the terms brother and sister (*bhai* and *ben*) are attached to all names, whether they belong to relatives or strangers. Brotherhood in the Gujarati usage thus has no naturalist or nationalist connotations. Rather, Gandhi's understanding of kinship rested on a radical inclusiveness rather than the exclusionary commonality of sentiment that underpins a liberal conception of kinship (Skaria 2002: 974; Devji 2005: 93):

> Real ahimsa or love originates in one's heart and is known by one's conduct even as gold is known by its qualities. A man who is full of love never forgets that the world is full of life like his and takes great care that he does not harm any living thing. He sees his love reflected in the eyes of those whom he meets. He is the friend of all.
>
> (Gandhi 1999g: 148)

Hence, Gandhi's kinship was not exclusionary but neighbourly (Skaria 2002: 975). Moreover, friendship was not to be given in affection or agreement but, rather, was invited, or 'cultivated' to use Gandhi's word, by a willingness to personally suffer for, '[l]ove does not burn others, it burns itself' (Gandhi 1999i: 340; Devji 2005: 94–5). Thus, Devji argues that for Gandhi, friendship is not an attempt to pre-empt enmity but rather, enmity is seen as 'friendship's very condition of possibility' because, after all, 'ethical life in general can only reveal itself in the face of enmity, not that of inclination' (Devji 2005: 97–8). A friendship based on intimacy, therefore, was to be discouraged given that it would produce a blurring of boundaries between friends. A politics of friendship, however, was based on equality and where equality existed, friendship was to be cultivated through the willingness to unconditionally and disinterestedly share in the suffering of the neighbour. 'The test of friendship, Gandhi wrote, 'is a spirit of love and sacrifice independent of expectation of any return' (Gandhi 1999b: 119). Where inequality existed, neighbourliness could either take the form of *seva* (service), which is to be carried out by the dominant and involves devotion and sacrifice to bridge the gulf between the dominant and the subordinate, or *satyagraha* (truth force or soul force) which would be employed by the subordinate to show the dominant that it was the cooperation of the subordinate that made their authority possible, thus, highlighting the basic kinship and equality between the dominant and the subordinate (Skaria 2002: 979–80).

Gandhi's politics of friendship was developed in colonial India through his efforts to cultivate friendship between Hindus and Muslims, *harijans* ('untouchables') and Hindus and, Indians and the British. In the postcolonial era, political friendship was no less relevant for Gandhi who sought to forge friendship between India and Pakistan by resorting to a fast, 'the last weapon in the armoury of the votary of ahimsa' which was 'addressed to the conscience of all' in response to the violence suffered by Delhi's Muslims and to India's decision to withhold funds to Pakistan after the Kashmir incursion (Gandhi 1999h: 21; Gandhi 1999m: 233). After the Indian government and Hindu and Sikh leaders met Gandhi's conditions, he ended what turned out to be his last fast. His aim of cultivating friendship, however, remained unfulfilled at the time of his assassination in 1948.

Yet, a Gandhian-style attempt to cultivate friendship was not entirely missing from Indian foreign policy in the post-independence era for it can be detected in the politics of C. Rajagopalchari, a leading Congress anti-colonial leader whom Gandhi (1999d: 86) referred to as the 'keeper of my conscience'. Rajaji, as he was known, out-lived Gandhi by more than two decades and in that time served as Governor of West Bengal, India's first Governor General, Home Minister, Chief Minister of Madras, and founded the Swatantra Party as an opposition to what he saw as flaws of the Congress Party's statist socialism. He is better known today, however, for his renderings of the *Mahabharata* and the *Ramayana*, which he interpreted as a source of 'practical wisdom' and the moral virtues of courage, tolerance and friendship – the indispensable virtue of a good life in these epics (Srinivasan 2009: 222). In Rajaji's understanding, a lack of equality or virtue was not a barrier to friendship and the best way to build lasting friendship was unsolicited generosity (Srinivasan 2009: 224–5). Applying this to foreign policy, he became a strong proponent of unilateral initiatives toward both Pakistan and Kashmir. After initially agreeing with Nehru's reluctance to go ahead with a plebiscite in Kashmir, in the 1960s Rajaji came to see a plebiscite as the only way to 'ensure the contentment of the people of Kashmir' (Quoted in Srinivasan 2009: 167; Gandhi 1984b: 324–5). On Pakistan he advocated unilateral measures by India to facilitate friendship through trade and tourism and emphasized the value of taking risks to build friendship instead of relying on bargains and negotiations (Srinivasan 2009: 173–4). None of these positions made him a popular figure in postcolonial India, where opposition to any dialogue or compromise was resisted by factions in the Congress and the Hindu nationalist opposition. Yet, it was to Rajaji that Sheik Abdullah turned before embarking on his trip to Pakistan to seek a way forward on the issue of Kashmir and, as Nehru recognized too late, his espousal of disinterested friendship may have been exactly what was required for the alternative international relations that Nehru was trying to construct.[6]

Conclusion

I have argued in this chapter for a reinterpretation of Nehru's policies of nonalignment and Panchsheel as a politics of friendship aimed at ameliorating the psychology of fear that, Nehru argued, dominated world politics. As components of a politics of friendship, nonalignment and Panchsheel were part of Nehru's broader internationalist ethic which, while promoting the anti-colonial tenets of political equality and non-interference, also advocated the voluntary subordination of state sovereignty to a supra-national world body. Nonalignment, by creating an environment in which dialogue with all was possible, and Panchsheel, by providing an alternative to the pursuit of security through military means, were to be the first steps toward Nehru's ideal of a post-sovereign 'One World'. In tracing the intellectual origins of Nehru's politics of friendship, I suggested that he drew on a particular understanding of the human condition drawn from Buddhist thought that understands individuals (and nations) as prone to suffering, and causing suffering, if they seek happiness in self-affirmation instead of recognizing the interdependent, impermanent nature of the Self. An important internal critique also played a role in Nehru's turn to friendship. In India's past, he found evidence of a dynamic but benign and largely peaceful Indian civilization precisely during times when it was actively engaged with the world and stagnancy and backwardness when Indian civilization was isolated and inward-looking.

Although nonalignment and Panchsheel were seen as a means toward creating an environment conducive to the ultimate emergence of a world federation, friendship was initially promoted with the countries of Asia. Nehru assumed certain cultural and psychological affinities between the countries of Asia, given their common experience of suffering under colonialism and imperialism, their long history of cultural interchange and the lack of a legacy of violent and enduring

European-style conflict. Nehru's attempts to facilitate friendship, however, were often interpreted as a desire for the leadership of Asia and it soon became clear that he had not taken into account the 'fear complex' generated by India's size, particularly to the smaller countries in its immediate vicinity. Friendship across material inequality, Nehru eventually recognized, is difficult to sustain and his slippage into a discourse of fraternity with India's neighbours proved equally problematic. The exemption of Pakistan from Nehru's politics of friendship in favour of a discourse of rejected fraternity, meanwhile, was an ethical and practical failure that Nehru acknowledged too late.

As we shall see in chapters to come, the question of how to relate to the countries in India's immediate vicinity continued to flummox Indian leaders, who have invoked everything from Rajagopalchari-esque gestures of unilateral goodwill to attempts to position India as a consensual regional hegemon. As for the rest of Asia, Panchsheel, a key part of Nehru's politics of friendship, suffered a heavy blow in the India–China war in 1962 from which it never fully recovered. It is to this foreign policy/identity crisis that we now turn.

4 From friendship to 'betrayal'

The India–China war

In 1962, India and China went to war over Aksai Chin, a mostly unpopulated high altitude desert along the western sector of the Himalayan border between India and China and the North East Frontier Agency (NEFA), now known as the state of Arunachal Pradesh in India and South Tibet in China, along the eastern sector of the Himalayan border. The conflict resulted in an overwhelming military victory for China which declared a unilateral cease-fire and claimed control of Aksai Chin but withdrew from NEFA. The origins of the India–China war are difficult to fathom from conventional IR perspectives. Both NEFA and Aksai Chin were resource poor, sparsely populated and located well away from major population centres. While Aksai Chin provided access to Tibet and might, therefore, have had 'strategic' value for the Chinese, no such argument is adequate in explaining India's claim. While NEFA has been integrated into the Indian Union as the state of Arunachal Pradesh, it did not hold this significance in 1962 and there are clear indications that China was willing to renounce its claim to the region on the basis of a new border agreement.

The most comprehensive attempts to analyse the motivations of India and China in 1962 are Neville Maxwell's 'revisionist' *India's China War* and Stephen Hoffmann's 'post-revisionist' *India and the China Crisis*. Refuting the dominant international understanding at the time of the war as an unprovoked aggression by China against India, Maxwell (1972) argued that China was committed to a conciliatory approach to the problem of converting ambiguously defined borders into the boundaries of modern nation-states. By contrast, Nehru, according to Maxwell, had from the outset followed a policy of non-negotiation with regard to the India–China border and was implicitly committed to the use of force to impose India's territorial claims. In a more recent article, Maxwell argues that India effectively forced war on China through expansionist and irrational behaviour which, he speculates, was 'perhaps traceable to the psychological wound inflicted on Nehru and his generation by the sundering of India to create Pakistan, which imparted mystical or religious significance to territorial issues' (Maxwell 2006: 3877).

Hoffmann's study is guided by the International Crisis Behaviour (ICB) theoretical model which focuses on the link between perceptions and war and relies on 'objective behavioural data about conflictual interaction in the international system'. Hoffmann (1990: 265) argues that 'Indian decision-making in many ways followed what might be called 'normal' practices, found in governments elsewhere ... India's 1962 tragedy came about not just from practices that are peculiar to India but also from behaviours that may be quite usual in international affairs'. These 'behaviours' are the consequence of the threat perceptions and worldviews of key decision-makers and their semi-permanent images of international and domestic realities. As the threat perception changes, so do worldviews and images. He argues that due to a number of incidents during the 1950s, both India and China hardened their stances toward their border claims and soon the 'conflict spiral possessed a momentum of its own and culminated in the Indian-Chinese border war' (Hoffmann 2006: 183). Hoffmann (2006: 25–8) goes beyond the ICB model in pointing to the importance of Indian nationalism in the border conflict. The Indian leadership, he suggests, was wedded to the idea that India was demarcated by historical borders which existed long before the British established their state structure. Hence, both Hoffmann and Maxwell touch on the role of identity and nationalism in understanding India's motivations in the India–China conflict, without fully developing this argument. Instead they employ conventional problem-solving approaches to analysing crises as objective facts that are the product of pre-existing sets of dispositions and world-views. In keeping with an approach that asks *how* rather than *why* particular foreign policy decisions are made, this chapter analyses the border 'crisis' as a social construction which was produced by policy-makers who drew on representations that were the product of particular understandings of India's past and desired present and future. We have seen that Nehru's construction of India's postcolonial identity was anchored in a desire to construct an ethical modernity in which an internationalist nationalism, rather than a territorial nationalism, was key. In analysing the India–China war therefore, we are analysing not simply a foreign policy crisis but a significant moment in the production of identity.

I begin by exploring British India's imperial geopolitics and the ways in which Nehru attempted to deal with this legacy. Nehru, I argue, generally accepted a narrative which emerged during the colonial encounter and presented Indian civilization as being perpetually vulnerable to invasion and conquest. This narrative contributed to the perception of India's backwardness among the Indian elite. Despite accepting this narrative, however, Nehru was also a critic of realist and imperial geopolitics and he was determined to engage China in ways that departed from the geopolitical reasoning of British India. In particular, there was an attempt to establish India–China relations along the lines of friendship. This relationship, therefore, constituted an important element of India's postcolonial identity as a part of Nehru's attempt to construct an international politics of friendship.

Through an examination of the correspondence on border issues between India and China, the chapter analyses how a dispute over borders emerged and overwhelmed the discourse of friendship by being constructed as a crisis linked to identity. I suggest that the introduction of discourses of humiliation, honour and self-respect were key to this process. How India dealt with the aftermath of the war is explored by analysing speeches and government statements. Many of these sustained a discourse of betrayal which was an attempt to minimize the damage to India's self-identity, for it contained possibilities for resistance and renewal. Finally I evaluate the identity costs of India's war with China and the damage done to Nehru's vision of India's postcolonial identity.

Rejecting imperial geopolitics

Imperial geopolitics

The imperial geopolitics of British India consisted of two important dimensions that John Agnew and Gearoid O Tuathail have described as 'practical geopolitical reasoning' and 'formal geopolitical reasoning'. According to Agnew and O Tuathail (1992: 191) 'it is through discourse that leaders act, through the mobilization of certain simple geographical understandings that foreign-policy actions are explained and through ready-made geographically-infused reasoning that wars are rendered meaningful'. They make a distinction between practical geopolitical reasoning – the 'common-sense' type of reasoning that is dependent on the 'narratives and binary distinctions found in societal mythologies' – and the formal geopolitical reasoning of strategic thinkers who 'produce a highly codified system of ideas and principles to guide the conduct of statecraft' (O Tuathail and Agnew 1992: 194). Both types of geopolitical reasoning are inherently reductionist for they work by whittling down the complex geographical realities of the world into geopolitical abstractions that can be controlled and manipulated (O Tuathail and Agnew 1992: 195).

Practical geopolitical reasoning

The practical geopolitical reasoning of British India's policy-makers derives from a long-standing narrative of Indian civilization's vulnerability to invasion. It is generally accepted that the cultures and societies of pre-modern India were in part shaped by a series of migrations, particularly from central Asia. Western narratives, however, have tended to frame these migrations in terms of invasion and conquest. According to Orientalist scholars, for instance, Indian civilization began with invasion and conquest. William Jones (1790: 58–9; 1788b: 422) argued that civilization was brought to India by invading peoples from Persia who practiced a 'primeval religion' that provided the basis of the caste system and spoke a language which was the ancestral forebear of Sanskrit (Jones 1788a). Jones described these peoples as a 'race' of conquerors or 'the Hindu race', although the term 'race' at this time was conceived of as a cultural and linguistic category rather than a biological classification. He also formulated the concept of an 'Indo-European' language family (later termed Aryan[1] by the Orientalist scholar Friedrich Max Muller) after his discovery of the link between Sanskrit, Greek and Latin.

This philological theory of race, which implied kinship between Indians and Europeans, was an affront to the civilizational logic of nineteenth century race science which equated race with civilization and assumed a vast difference between the dark-skinned and light-skinned human-beings (Trautmann 1997: 162). The racial theory of Indian civilization rests on the idea that the constitutive event through which it came into existence was the clash between an invading 'race' of fair-skinned, civilized, Sanskrit-speaking Aryans from the northwest and the dark-skinned, barbarous aboriginal inhabitants of the sub-continent called *Dasas* or *Dasyus*. The identity of the latter was much debated, but upon the discovery of a distinct language group in 1816, the 'Dravidian'[2] speakers of South India were commonly assumed to be the descendents of the original inhabitants of the subcontinent (Ali 1998: 108–9; Philip 2003: 195).

The feminization of colonized territory and the metaphor of rape have been enduring tropes in discussions of colonial relations. Yet, the trope of rape which underlaid the Aryan invasion theory somewhat unconventionally reversed the masculine conqueror/feminine victim binary, for early Aryans were thought to have possessed a 'manly independence' that was overwhelmed by the 'overheated female matter of India' (Sinha 1995: 20; Inden 1990: 119–20). Hence, while the emasculation of Indian men was the central concern in the gendered discourse of Aryan invasion, this was achieved by highlighting the influence of women and femininity in Indian culture. As we shall see below, the notion of India's immutability despite being repeatedly conquered was a common theme in Western and Indian nationalist discourses and complicates the depiction of India as a submissive object of desire for male conquerors. Instead, the female characterization of India emerges as a source of threat and anxiety – India was ultimately untameable even to the bearers of a superior European rationality.

This narrative of invasion and conquest was reproduced in the work of a number of other thinkers. Hegel, for example, reprised a representation of India as a land of fabulous wealth and wisdom which was prominent in medieval European thought (Le Goff 1980; Hamilton 1996; Uebel 2000; Hegel 1956: 142). India's wealth made it the 'Land of Desire' and consequently it had been repeatedly conquered: 'there is scarcely any great nation of the East, nor of the Modern European West, that has not gained for itself a smaller or larger portion of it' (Hegel 1956: 142). For James Mill, 'it appears that the people of Hindustan have at all times been subject to incursions and conquest, by nations contiguous to them on the north-west' (Mill 1848a: 234; 1848c: 209). He found that this was due to the 'simple, and rude' character of the 'Hindu' military system but he also blamed India's inherent political disunity, which he attributed to the caste system (Mill 1848c: 209; 1975: 240). It was the inability to unite different states under a common power 'which has rendered India so easy a conquest to all invaders; and enables us to retain, so easily, that dominion over it which we have acquired' (Mill 1848a: 200). Likewise, for Friedrich Schlegel (1889: 509) India's cultural diversity had bred disunity and as a result 'the history of India since the time of Alexander the Great certainly presents little more than a series of foreign conquests and internal revolutions...'.

Alexander the Great was a common figure in early Western depictions of Indian history even though there was no mention of his supposedly momentous incursion in 332 BCE in Indian texts until 1 CE (Lal 2003: 272). Nonetheless, this event was thought so important that the historian Vincent Smith (1924) devoted an entire chapter to the episode in his *The Early History of India* which replaced Mill's *History of British India* in 1904 as the hegemonic text on Indian history. The story of Alexander's Indian foray allowed Western scholars to situate India within a singular vision of European history, to bring India into a global frame of reference and to emphases its need for the guiding hand of European rationalism. Mill, for example, argued that, 'the people of Hindustan and the ancient nations of Europe came in contact at a single point. The expedition of Alexander the Great began, and in some sort ended, their connexion' because ever since India had stagnated (Mill 1848c: 168–70). Similarly, for Hegel (1956: 142), 'Alexander the Great was the first to penetrate by land to India' and as such, the episode is presented as the precursor to India's 'necessary fate ... to be subjected to Europeans'.

Formal geopolitical reasoning

Perhaps the first word regarding British India's formal geopolitical reasoning should go to its much-despised, geopolitically-minded former viceroy Lord Curzon who described India's strategic position as follows:

> She is like a fortress with the vast moat of the sea on two of her faces, and with mountains for her walls on the remainder. But beyond those walls, which are sometimes of by no means insuperable height and admit of being easily penetrated, extends a glacis of varying breadth and dimensions. We do not want to occupy it, but we also cannot afford to see it occupied by our foes. We are quite content to let it remain in the hands of our allies and friends: but if rival and unfriendly influences creep up to it, and lodge themselves right under our walls, we are compelled to intervene, because a danger would there by grow up that might one day menace our security. This is the secret of the whole position in Arabia, Persia, Afghanistan, Tibet, and as far eastwards as Siam. He would be a short-sighted commander who merely manned his ramparts in India and did not look out beyond; and the whole of our policy during the past five years has been directed towards maintaining our predominant influence and to preventing the expansion of hostile agencies on this area which I have described.
>
> (Curzon and Raleigh 1906: 130–1)

Curzon's views on India's defence often varied markedly from his contemporaries, but the passage above encapsulates the importance of India to the security of the British Empire and to the shaping of British strategic culture in the nineteenth and early twentieth centuries. Moreover, it is a good example of how India came to be rendered as a unified geographical entity in colonial discourse.[3]

In Curzon's gendered narrative, India is a geopolitical space of desire. She is easily conquered and in her permissiveness, poses a threat to her British master. This is the sort of 'geopolitical sighting' that O Tuathail (1994: 270) has called 'pornographic voyeurism' – 'an obscene will to see [and, therefore, control] everything' alongside 'a systematic refusal to see the real'. Curzon's geopolitics operates here as 'ego-politics', securing his identity as a rational and hard-headed realist (O Tuathail 1994: 270).

The main point of British India's vulnerability had long been identified as the north-west frontier. It was here that the British were most militarily vulnerable and it was also where India had faced invasions in the past from Afghanistan and Persia (Dawson 1923: 72). Thus, the colonial narrative on India's vulnerability came to constitute an important part of British policy, giving it an air of geopolitical destiny and 'common sense' that put it above critical scrutiny. In the pre-colonial period, however, the north-west frontier was not a frontier at all but the centre of an Indo-Persian and Indo-Islamic economic, cultural and political zone that had stretched between Afghanistan and Punjab for two thousand years. The linear demarcation of a north-west frontier by the British in the nineteenth century was thus an entirely new innovation that destroyed traditional historical links (Bose 2002: 56).

In the nineteenth century neither the Shah of Persia nor the Amir of Afghanistan appeared to pose much direct threat. Rather, Persia and Afghanistan's relations with Russia were considered crucial to India's security since, from early in the nineteenth century, Britain's main preoccupation was the threat posed by Russia. It was thought that if Persia and Afghanistan were weak and amenable to Russia this would pose a serious danger to the integrity of India's borders. For this reason the British attempted to keep both Persia and Afghanistan friendly and independent, even intervening militarily when the opportunity arose, as it did in 1856 when the Shah of Persia sought to gain control of Herat in Afghanistan (Mahajan 2002: 21–2).

As rival hegemons of the post-1815 world Britain and Russia saw themselves as enemies primarily because of Britain's perception of Russia's threat to its Indian Empire – the possession of which qualified it for the status of a great power (Mahajan 2002: 11–12). This Anglo-Russian rivalry was played out in central Asia and was famously termed 'the Great Game' by Rudyard Kipling (1987) in *Kim*, a fictional story inspired by Kipling's own experiences as a journalist in the North-West Provinces.[4] The frontier in Kipling's *Kim*, emerges as a barrier between the civilized and the barbarous – a masculine, homosocial space in which both Indian and British men would fight to defend a benevolent empire. As such, the frontier was a marked contrast to the urban centres where British rule was coming under heightened challenge (Krishnaswamy 1998: 128). Hence, not only did the 'Russian threat' turn India into an object of geopolitical desire, it also served to perpetuate the politics of colonial masculinity and helped to keep alive the myth of Britain's civilizing mission.

While the Great Game was being played out in Central Asia, back in Great Britain, the 'founding father' of the discipline of geopolitics, Halford Mackinder, was busy trying to fulfil the Royal Geographical Society's (RGS) goal of turning a collection of practices (geography) into a coherent, scientific, academic discipline (Geography). The RGS was driven in this regard by the actions of the Prussian and French states to establish academic geography in universities and schools as a way of disciplining students into official understandings of national territory. Geographical education in Britain came to be seen as vital to giving the British empire territorial and commercial meaning (O Tuathail 1996: 84–5). Mackinder became a key figure in the RGS's campaign after the success of his lecture tours of Britain on 'the New Geography', which he undertook in 1885 and 1886 as part of the adult education programs provided by the Oxford University Extension movement in provincial England.

Meanwhile, a similar educational operation was underway in India, aimed at trying to inculcate the 'irrational Hindu mind' with pedagogical geography's 'correct' 'scientific' view of the earth (Edney 1997). The scientific map and the terrestrial globe – which by the twentieth century had become the ultimate symbol of geopolitical power and mastery – acquired unparalleled status, both in and out of the classroom, as the tool with which to wean the 'natives' away from their myths about India's central position in the wider world toward an understanding of India as simply one of many bounded territorial entities to span the face of the earth (Ramaswamy 2002: 156–7).[5]

The spatialization of India and the articulation of its strategic importance to Britain formed an important part of Mackinder's theories. In his first address to the RGS in 1887 on 'The Scope and Methods of Geography', Mackinder (1951) used India ostensibly as a special illustration of the explanatory power of geography in trying to account for why Delhi and Calcutta were chosen as the old and new capitals of India. In doing so, however, he was also implicitly arguing for the importance of geographical knowledge to the maintenance of the British Empire. He argued that India's existence as a 'wealthy civilized community' and its appeal to 'the conqueror' was due to its geography. Moreover, there were two kinds of conquerors, 'land-wolves and sea-wolves' and it was because of geography that some succeeded and some failed. For instance, Alexander the Great (a land wolf) could not conquer India because he took a wrong turn that led him away from the route that is the only path to Delhi. With its position 'at the head of the Jumna-Ganges navigation, the place of transshipment from land to water carriage' Delhi was the 'natural centre of commerce' and the 'natural base of operations for the Asiatic conqueror', while, Calcutta, because of its position at the 'junction of river and sea shipping', was the 'natural basis of operations for the conquerors from over the sea', such as Britain (Mackinder 1951: 28). Thus, according to Mackinder, the deciphering of India's geography had the ability to decide its fate and that of its would-be conquerors.

In his 1904 address to the RGS, which was entitled 'The Geographical Pivot of History', Mackinder argued that 'Euro-Asia' was the strategic pivot on which world history has turned. While it was once controlled by the Mongol Empire, this pivot area, which he later called the Heartland, was now in Russia's grasp (Mackinder 1951: 41–2). The Anglo-Russian rivalry now became an inevitable clash of sea power and land power and the British colonial occupation of India – which was a haphazard and highly contingent phenomenon at best – was imparted with a sense of destiny and intentionality. Britain, he argued, was 'compelled to make a steady advance in India' in order to fend off the Russian advance which was 'knocking at the landward gates of the Indies' (Mackinder 1962: 134). India's strategic function in the British Empire was thus to act as a 'bridgehead' in Britain's military front against Russia. In this way, Mackinder provided the theoretical, 'scientific' support for the ideas of his friend and patron Lord Curzon who argued that India's geographical position would 'push her into the forefront of international politics' as 'the strategical frontier of the British Empire' (Curzon and Raleigh 1906: 130). Underlying the discourses of both Curzon and Mackinder however, was a sense of the fragility of Britain's hold on India and, hence, the vulnerability of its place in the world.

In the late nineteenth century and early twentieth century, Curzon's anxieties about the Russian threat to the British Empire led him to refocus 'the Great Game' on Tibet where he was certain the Russians were trying to establish a presence (Lamb 1960: 259). In 1901, in a letter to George Hamilton, the Secretary of State for India, he raised the prospect of turning Tibet into a buffer state between the Indian and Russian empires. However, Curzon's views were considered alarmist and it was not until 1912 that his desire for a buffer became British policy (Lamb 1966b: 10; 1960: 260). By 1910, Russia was considered less of a danger and, despite the lack of supporting evidence, China's expansionism, its influence in Nepal and Bhutan and the potential for Chinese incitement of Indian nationalist agitation were greater concerns (Lamb 1966b: 229–30; 1966a: 279). In 1912, the British took advantage of the collapse of Chinese authority in Lhasa to attempt to turn both Tibet, and the area known then as Assam Himalaya (later NEFA) into buffers between China and the north-eastern Indian region of Assam (Lamb 1964: 143). In 1914, after meetings between Chinese, Tibetan and British officials, the Assam Himalayan buffer area was demarcated by a boundary which came to be known as the McMahon Line after a top British official, Henry McMahon. The McMahon Line, however, was negotiated only by Tibetan and British representatives and the Chinese rejected the proposed Convention for dealing with the China–Tibetan frontier that finally emerged from the meetings (Lamb 1964: 142–3).

The Aksai Chin demarcation was also implicated in British paranoia in the late nineteenth century about the Russian threat to India's northern frontier due to the undefined boundaries of Afghanistan, the Chinese-held territory of Sinkiang and north-western Kashmir. It was feared that Russian contact with the population of British India could lead to political destabilization or demands for concessions in other parts of the British empire of interest to Russia (Lamb 1964: 89–90). In attempting to counter the Russian threat the British used several strategies including direct negotiations with the Russians, the demarcation of Afghanistan's borders and the provision of support to the Chinese in Sinkiang (known today as Xingjian) in order to establish a buffer. Following China's defeat by Japan in 1895 the British administration attempted to settle the boundary between a weakened China and Kashmir in a way that would confer British sovereignty over Aksai Chin as a defence against Russian advance (Lamb 1964: 98–109). Curzon adopted the Ardagh Line, named after the head of British military intelligence in 1896–1897, which included Aksai Chin as a part of British India, over the McCartney-Macdonald Line proposed by the British representatives to China, George McCartney and Claude Macdonald, which divided Aksai Chin between China and India. The Ardagh Line remained British doctrine until 1927 by which time Britain's geopolitical preoccupations had changed, leaving Aksai Chin unadministered and mostly devoid of human presence (Lamb 1964: 112). Both Aksai Chin and the McMahon Line therefore, were deeply implicated in imperial geopolitics and how India and China chose to deal with these legacies would come to have momentous and unforseen consequences.

Critiquing imperial geopolitics

The historical narrative of India's vulnerability to invasion and conquest constituted a component of the perception of backwardness which emerged among the Indian elite as a result of the colonial encounter. The theory of Aryan invasion figured prominently, for instance, in Savarkar's Hindu nationalist discourse. Savarkar was adamant that Hindus were a race – the product of the welding of the invading Aryans and indigenous non-Aryans – and that India's unity was based on a racial unity: 'the Hindus are … united not only by the bonds of the love they bear to a common motherland but also by the bonds of a common blood' (Savarkar 1938: 17, 94, 105). For Savarkar there was no question of the manly Aryan being overwhelmed by the feminine indigenous non-Aryans. Rather, Vedic blood had flowed

> down from the altitudes of the subline [sic] Vedic heights to the plains of our modern history fertilizing much, incorporating many a noble stream and purifying many a lost soul, increasing in volume and depth and richness.
>
> (Savarkar 1938: 107)

The idea of Aryan invasion was eventually discarded by later Hindu nationalists who could not countenance a theory that suggested that Aryans were initially foreign to India and that Hinduism had hybrid, syncretic origins (Bhatt 2001: 587). Nonetheless, India's invasion by 'foreign races', particularly Muslims, continued to play an important role in Hindu nationalist discourse. Savarkar writes that after 'the Mohamedans' opened the floodgates, India was deluged by 'nearly all of Asia, quickly to be followed by nearly all Europe'. Still, despite centuries of this 'ghastly conflict … India single-handed kept the fight morally and militarily' (Savarkar 1938: 55–6). And, importantly, it was because of 'this prolonged furious conflict' that 'our people became intensely conscious of ourselves as Hindus and were welded into a nation to an extent un-known in our history' (Savarkar 1938: 56–7). For Savarkar then, it took these repeated episodes of invasion to give form to the primordial sense of nationalism which he argued had been present in India for five thousand years.

The narrative of India's vulnerability to invasion and conquest also served a productive role for Nehru who interpreted the story of Alexander the Great as one of resistance:

> Alexander's invasion of India in the fourth century B.C. was, from a military point of view a minor affair. It was more of a raid across the border, and not a very successful raid for him. He met with such stout resistance ... that the contemplated advance into the heart of India had to be reconsidered.
>
> (Nehru 1982 [1946]: 114)

Likewise, for Gandhi (1999a: 1) it was in India 'that Alexander the Great, though victorious, for the first time met a foe, under King Porus, who shattered his dream of a world-wide dominion'. He argued that while 'India certainly has not proved unconquerable', the 'wonder of all wonders seems to be that the Indians ... are irrepressible in spite of centuries of oppression and bondage' (Gandhi 1999e: 306). Unlike his fellow nationalists, however, Gandhi placed little contemporary political value in historical awareness of the past since '[h]istory is really a record of every interruption of the even working of the force of love or the force of soul' and therefore an inaccurate record of the past (Gandhi 1938: 77–9).

Nehru did not share Gandhi's scepticism of history, and even employed a stereotypical metaphor of rape to depict India's colonial relationship with Britain. He wrote in *Autobiography*:

> They seized her body and possessed her, but it was the possession of violence. They did not know her or try to know her. They never looked into her eyes, for theirs were averted and hers downcast through shame and humiliation.
>
> (Nehru 1980: 429)

Nehru's invocation of this trope, however, did not end here. In his later *Discovery of India*, he used the trope of heterosexual rape to depict a more general historical narrative of India's vulnerability to invasion and conquest. In this narrative, the nation-mother becomes less a victim and more an uncontrollable woman: 'Shameful and repellent she is occasionally, perverse and obstinate, sometimes even a little hysteric, this lady with a past' (Nehru 1982 [1946]: 563). Despite being 'overwhelmed again and again, her spirit was never conquered, and to-day when she appears to be the plaything of a proud conqueror, she remains unsubdued and unconquered' (Nehru 1982 [1946]: 563). This 'lady with a past', *Bharat Mata*, was also key to his ethical framework, as we saw in Chapter 2, because it was 'her store of wisdom' that would help modern India 'hold on to what is true and beautiful and good in this harsh, vindictive, and grasping world' (Nehru 1982 [1946]: 592). Thus, Nehru transformed the trope of rape from a sign of victimization to a sign of the resilience of Indian civilization's 'spirit' – the same spirit which for him could make postcolonial India into a different sort of nation-state, one that would use science ethically and would have the courage to overcome fear and narrow nationalism. This intertwining of gender and ethics worked to transform a memory of victimization into a normative politics of resistance against the dominant but destructive ways of fashioning national Selves.

Nehru's transformation of the narrative of India's vulnerability to conquest was marked by a refusal to promote a sense of victimhood and mimicry and entailed the rejection of the geopolitical theories of Halford Mackinder and his colleagues. Indeed, he devoted an entire section, titled, 'Realism and Geopolitics. World Conquest or World Association. The USA and the USSR' in *Discovery* to a critique of realism and geopolitics:

> Whatever the mass of the people may think foreign policy remains a preserve for the experts in charge of it and they are usually wedded to a continuation of old tradition … but it is a curious realism that sticks to the empty shell of the past and ignores or refuses to understand the hard facts of the present, which are not only political and economic but also include the feelings and urges of vast numbers of people. Such realism is more imaginative and divorced from to-day's and to-morrow's problems than much of the so-called idealism of many people.
>
> (Nehru 1982 [1946]: 539)

Moreover,

> [g]eopolitics has now become the anchor of the realist and its jargon of 'heartland' and 'rimland' is supposed to throw light on the mystery of national growth and decay. Originating in England (or was it Scotland?), it became the guiding light of the nazis, fed their dreams and ambitions of world domination, and led them to disaster.
>
> (Nehru 1982 [1946]: 539)

The geopolitical theories of Mackinder and Nicholas Spykman, another 'founding father' of the discipline, looked 'very clever and realistic' but were actually 'supremely foolish' for they were 'based on the old policy of expansion and empire and the balance of power, which inevitably leads to conflict and war' (Nehru 1982 [1946]: 540). In fact, '[s]elf-interest' Nehru (1982 [1946]: 540) wrote, 'should drive every nation to … co-operation in order to escape disaster in the future and build its own free life on the basis of others' freedom'. However,

> the self-interest of the 'realist' is far too limited by past myths and dogmas, and regards ideas and social forms, suited to one age, as immutable and as unchanging parts of human nature and society, forgetting that there is

nothing so changeable as human nature and society ... war is considered a biological necessity, empire and expansion as the prerogatives of a dynamic and progressive people, the profit motive as the central fact dominating human relations, and ethnocentrism, a belief in racial superiority, becomes an article of faith ... Some of these ideas were common to the civilizations of east and west; many of them form the back-ground of modern western civilization out of which fascism and Nazism grew.

(Nehru 1982 [1946]: 540–1)

This is not to say that geography and the physical territory of India were completely unimportant in Nehru's imagining of India. The Himalayas played an important role in Nehru's construction of India's identity as one of 'unity in diversity':

the accidents of geography have had a powerful effect on determining national character and history. The fact that India was cut off by the tremendous barrier of the Himalayas and by the sea produced a sense of unity in this wide area ... within that unity geography again produced diversity.

(Nehru 1982 [1946]: 452)

Moreover, like Mackinder, Nehru sought to find geographical explanations for India's political history: '... the Mughal Empire was broken up, among other causes, by the Marathas ... from the hilly tracts of the Deccan' who 'had preserved some spirit of independence when the great majority of the dwellers on the northern plains had grown servile and submissive' and the 'British had an easy victory in Bengal' because 'the people of the fertile plains there submitted with extraordinary docility' (Nehru 1982 [1946]: 452). In the modern era, although '[g]eography counts still and must count in the future' Nehru was convinced that:

other factors play a more important role now. Mountains and seas are no longer barriers, but they still determine a people's character and a country's political and economic position. They cannot be ignored in considering new schemes of division, partition or re-merging, *unless the planning is on a world scale.*

(Nehru 1982 [1946]: 452) (emphasis added)

We have seen that in Nehru's vision of an ethical modernity, the organization of nations would indeed be undertaken on a world scale within a world federation. Thus, geography and territory do not play a major role in Nehru's internationalist nationalism and while he may have subscribed to the narrative on India's vulnerability to conquest, he did not accept the relevance or ethical legitimacy of British India's formal geopolitical reasoning for modern India. Rather, his narrative on invasion emphasized India's un-conquered, irrepressible spirit and he would come to rely on this in the wake of the India–China war. In the absence of

British India's geopolitical reasoning he was convinced that India 'will always be in favour of peace and co-operation and against aggression' and he firmly anchored India's postcolonial identity in a framework of friendship with China (Nehru 1982 [1946]: 536). Given his focus on internationalism rather than territorial nationalism, moreover, dealing with questions related to India's borders with China was accorded low priority (Brown 2003: 317).

Befriending China, fearing China

As far back as the 1927 Congress of Oppressed Nationalities in Brussels, representatives of India and China highlighted a civilizational friendship. A joint India–China declaration at the Congress, which was co-authored by Nehru, asserted that 'for more than three thousand years the people of India and China' had been united 'by the most intimate cultural ties' (Keenleyside 1982: 212–13). Writing about these ancient cultural links, Nehru (1982 [1946]: 199, 518) emphasized the thousands of years of trade, the diffusion of Buddhism into China and also lamented that India did not learn more from China's 'reason and commonsense' which could have checked its 'extravagant fancies'.

Expressions of India–China solidarity went beyond rhetoric. The first links between Indian and Chinese nationalists were established in the early 1900s when revolutionaries from both countries travelled to Japan, buoyed by its defeat of Russia (Saklani 1999). The Chinese scholar Tan Yun-Shan undertook three visits to India in the 1930s and other Chinese scholars and religious leaders made a number of war-time goodwill missions to India (Keenleyside 1982: 213). In 1938, during the Sino-Japanese War, the Congress party sent a medical team to China, set up a China relief fund and called for a boycott of Japanese goods (Keenleyside 1982: 217–18). In 1935, the Sino-Indian Cultural Society was founded, Nehru went to China in 1939 and Chiang Kai-shek reciprocated in 1942 (Keenleyside 1982: 213).

For both Nehru and Gandhi, India and China were vital to the maintenance of peace in Asia. Gandhi's politics of neighbourliness assumed a radical inclusiveness that meant that every human and animal, whether located nearby or faraway should be considered neighbours. This did not, however, entail serving an abstract humanity for 'I am so constructed that I can only serve my immediate neighbours' and it would be sheer 'conceit' and 'attempting the impossible' to 'pretend to have discovered that I must with my body serve every individual in the universe' (Gandhi 1999c: 269–70). As immediate neighbours then, friendship between India and China was vital for: '[p]eace in Asia depends on India and China. These two countries are large. And if they build their edifices on the foundation of *ahimsa* they will become known among the great countries of the world' (Gandhi 1999f: 249).

For Nehru, China and India were predisposed to peace and cooperation: 'Ancient societies like India and China ... tended to concentrate on the cultivation of those virtues which made the individual less self-centred and willing to cooperate – tact, poise, balance were essential' (Quoted in Jaffrelot 2003: 64). Although he had previously expressed admiration for Chiang Kai-shek and had a well-known antipathy toward the Indian Communist Party, under his leadership, India became one of the first countries in the world to recognize the communist government of the People's Republic of China and even took to championing its case for recognition by the UN. Nehru reasoned that the rise to power of the Chinese Communists was less a victory for communism than a win for Chinese nationalism and Asia's resurgence and although he condemned the Communist world's reliance on 'force and the hydrogen bomb' he argued that it was 'a little wiser in its approach. It does not forget how human beings react and takes full advantage of the passionate dislike in Asia and Africa of colonialism and racialism' (Quoted in Boquerat 2005: 217). It would be going too far to argue, as Sunil Khilnani (1999: 40) does, that Nehru saw conflict between India and China as an historical impossibility. Nehru did, however, reason that just as the wisdom and understanding of human behaviour garnered during its thousand-year old civilizational history would prevent India from going down the violent path of Western modernity, China's ancient civilization would eventually temper its Marxist dogma, making conflict unlikely.

China's invasion of Tibet in 1950 was the first incident to produce unease within the Indian government and provoke public demonstrations against China. Nehru too was initially adamant that China's claim to Tibet was limited to suzerainty (Nehru 1961: 302–3). However, despite facing domestic criticism from parties sympathetic to the Tibetans, from those who wanted to continue the British policy of using Tibet as a buffer state and from elements who saw this as the first indication of the looming threat of Chinese expansionism, Nehru eventually sought to understand China's behaviour as the result of a history of suffering the trauma of oppression. In a speech in 1951 he employed a psychoanalytic understanding of trauma, in which emotional wounds that remain unhealed can lead to 'acting out' to argue that, 'China in her new found strength has acted sometimes in a manner which I deeply regret', but it had to be remembered that this was in reaction to '...the long period of struggle and frustration, the insolent treatment that they have received from the imperial Powers, and the latter's refusal to deal with them in terms of equality' (Nehru 1993: 475). In this context, the reassurance provided by a relationship rooted in friendship was vital, not just for India and China, but for Asia, in general, because a conflict between the two, Nehru assumed, would have catastrophic effects. Reiterating the civilizational friendship narrative in a speech, Nehru said:

> We in India have two thousand years of friendship with China. We have differences of opinion and even small conflicts ... when we hark back to that long past something of the wisdom of that past also helps us to understand each other. And so, we endeavour to maintain friendly relations with this great neighbour of ours, for the peace of Asia depends upon these relations.
>
> (Nehru 1961: 186)

The trade agreement in which Panchsheel first appeared was one that implicitly recognized Chinese sovereignty in Tibet (Nehru 1961: 302–3). His insistence on including Panchsheel in this agreement and his push for UN recognition of the Chinese communist government were a way of creating an environment that would steer China away from a narrow nationalism, foster within it an ethic of internationalism and thus, provide long-term protection for the Tibetans who would be protected as a minority in China under a system of international law. Responding to debate in the Lok Sabha over the agreement, Nehru argued that India had little choice but to accept China's actions for,

> where did we come into the picture unless we wanted to assume an aggressive role of interfering with other countries? Many things happen in the world which we do not like and which we would wish were rather different … we put up with these things because we would be, without making any difference, merely getting into trouble.
>
> (Nehru 1961: 304)

A politics of friendship, then, was another way of coming into the picture, by drawing on a common experience of imperial oppression and ancient civilizational bonds to construct a modern relationship based on amity and goodwill. What was important for Nehru was highlighting the commonalities between India and China and this entailed downgrading the invasion of Tibet to a difference of opinion. Thus, during Chou En-lai's visit to India in June 1954, the focus of Nehru's public speeches was the two thousand years of 'peaceful commerce of ideas, of religion and of art and culture'. According to Nehru (1961: 306), even though India and China 'each has her own special cultural inheritance' and are different in many ways, 'we have been good neighbours and friends and have not come into conflict with each other during the millennia of history'. This was 'the witness of the past, and as we stand on the fine edge of the present in this turbulent world of ours, we can learn a lesson from that past, which will help us in the present and in the future'.

Nehru's views on China, however, were not universally accepted among others in the Indian leadership. The Home Minister and Deputy Prime Minister, Sardar Vallabai Patel, and the director of the Intelligence Bureau (IB), B.N. Mullik, for example, were adamant about China's expansionist tendencies. For Patel, China's communist imperialism was 'ten times more dangerous' than the imperialism of the Western powers due to its 'cloak of ideology' which conceals 'racial, national and historical claims'. He wrote in a letter to Nehru in 1950 that a strong, united Communist China posed a threat to India's north and north-east frontiers as well as to parts of Assam and Burma (Quoted in Mullik 1971: 117–18). According to Mullik (1971: 109), the Chinese would not stop with overrunning Tibet but would 'come right up to the borders of India and also claim those parts of northern India, Bhutan, northern Burma etc. which had been shown in Chinese maps as coming under the jurisdiction of the Chinese Emperors'. Further, the Chinese presence on the frontier 'would open up for the Communists of India to build bases on the frontier of Tibet and thus they would be able to get all forms of material and moral assistance from the Chinese' (Mullik 1971: 109).

Mullik has claimed that Nehru shared some of these concerns and recounts in his memoir a conversation in 1952 in which the latter described China as a country that had displayed an aggressive streak throughout its history and was now being governed by aggressive leaders and an aggressive political philosophy (Mullik 1972: 78–80; 1971: 84–5). Whatever suspicions Nehru may have had of China's aggressive tendencies, however, he rejected the idea that they would be directed against India. In a private memo written in 1953 to members of his staff, for instance, he dismissed the concerns of S. Sinha, an Officer on Special Duty in the Ministry of External Affairs, who had written him a note titled 'Chinese Designs on the North East Frontier'. He admonished Sinha for lacking objectivity, being too imaginative and not understanding India's broader foreign policy, by which he presumably meant the advocacy of friendship and cooperation over a posture driven by fear and insecurity (Nehru 1999a: 594–6). Nehru further added that India's frontier borders were settled and not open to discussion except for 'minor tracts here and there'. He wrote that although he could not read the 'Chinese mind' he felt that 'it is completely impracticable for the Chinese Government to think of anything in the nature of invasion of India. Therefore I rule it out'.

The 1954 agreement was seen by Nehru as a new starting point on India's relations with China and Tibet and he assumed that the agreement meant that the China–India boundary was settled (Maxwell 1972: 74). He came away from his talks with Chou En-lai in 1956 with a similar impression, reporting to External Affairs officials that although Chou thought that the McMahon Line had been unfairly established by British imperialists, it was an accomplished fact and should be recognized (Nehru 2005: 614). While Aksai Chin was not specifically discussed, Nehru reported that,

> apart from the McMahon Line, there were certain very minor border problems between India and Tibet. These should be settled soon to put an end to these petty controversies ... The settlement should be based on established practice and custom as well as the watershed if there was any such thing there. In these small border problems very small pieces of uninhabited territory in the mountains were involved. They had no importance and the border should be a geographical one as far as possible. Premier Chou agreed that these should be settled soon on this basis.
>
> (Nehru 2005: 614–15)

An examination of the transcript of the talks, however, has Chou answering '[y]es, the question can be solved and we think it should be settled early', which indicates that Nehru's assumption of a consensus on border issues was an overstatement (Nehru 2005: 601). Moreover, although Chou explicitly states a willingness to accept the McMahon Line, Neville Maxwell (1972: 89–90) argues that what he did not make clear to Nehru was that while China was willing to accept the boundary alignment, this should be done on the basis of a new treaty negotiated between equals. Chou's failure to raise the issue of

Aksai Chin, moreover, as Maxwell (1972: 90) points out, would have damaging consequences because it would become clear in future correspondence on border issues that the Chinese considered Aksai Chin to have always been under Chinese jurisdiction.

Customary borders, honour and self-respect

By September 1959, there was a marked shift in the tone of the correspondence between China and India[6] due to several incidents: the Indian discovery of China's construction of a highway from Tibet to Sinkiang running across Aksai Chin in 1958, the Tibetan revolt in March 1959 and the decision by the Indian government to grant asylum to the Dalai Lama, the alleged mistreatment of Indian nationals in Tibet and mutual accusations of territorial encroachment.

Opinion on the highway was divided. According to Mullik (1971: 204–5, 40), the Chief of Army Staff, K.S. Thimayya, regarded the road to be of little importance for India while the Foreign Secretary, Subimal Dutt, regarded the territory to be disputed, of little use to India and simply an improvement of the old silk route which was an international trading route. Both rejected Mullik's assessment that the road could be used to threaten eastern Ladakh and his suggestion that India respond by establishing army posts near Aksai Chin. Such an action, they argued, would be perceived as threatening and this was an assessment Nehru concurred with, although he later allowed a compromise whereby several posts were established in positions less provocative than Mullik desired (Mullik 1971: 204). Nonetheless, an informal note was dispatched to the Chinese government claiming that the road ran across territory that had been 'part of the Ladakh region of India for centuries' and that it was a 'matter of surprise and regret that the Chinese Government should have constructed a road through indisputably Indian territory without first obtaining the permission of the Government of India and without even informing the Government of India' (India 1954–1959: 26).

An indication of the significance of Tibet in Chinese calculations can be gleaned from Chou En-lai's interview with the American journalist Edgar Snow in 1960 in which he said that the boundary dispute only 'came to the fore' after 'the Dalai Lama had run away and democratic reforms were started in Tibet' (Snow 1963: 762). India, Chou claimed, wanted to turn Tibet into a 'buffer zone ... and to maintain in Tibet the former system of serfdom' (Snow 1963: 762). In 1959, the issue led to a letter in which China accused India of interfering in its internal affairs by playing 'encouraging the Tibetan rebels' (India 1954–1959: 74). The letter then exclaimed:

> Our Indian friends! What is your mind? Will you be agreeing to our thinking regarding the view that China can only concentrate its main attention eastward of China, but not south-westward of China, nor is it necessary for it to do so ... Friends? It seems to us that you too cannot have two fronts.
>
> (India 1954 1959: 76)

This letter further escalated tensions and India's reply, which was written in the name of the Foreign Secretary but drafted by Nehru, said that the Indian government had found the Chinese letter, 'not only not in consonance with certain facts but ... wholly out of keeping with diplomatic usage and courtesies due to friendly countries' (India 1954–1959: 78). The statement went on to say that India did not 'consider or treat any other country as an enemy country, however-somuch it may differ from it' (India 1954–1959: 78). India had 'endeavoured to cultivate the friendship of the Chinese people and Government in spite of differences of opinion' and has 'avoided interference with China's internal affairs', but that this did not mean that it would 'discard or vary any of their own policies under any pressure from outside' (India 1954–1959: 78).

In a speech in the Lok Sabha in early September 1959, Nehru spoke of inequality creeping into the India–China relationship and began linking 'national dignity' with national territory:

> Friendship cannot exist between the weak and the strong, between a country that is trying to bully and the other which agrees to be bullied. It is only when people are more or less equal, and when they respect each other, that they can be friends. This is true of nations also.... In petty disputes it seems to me absurd for two great countries to rush at each other's throat and decide whether two miles of territory are on this side or on that side. *But where national prestige is involved, it is not the two miles of territory that matter, but the nation's dignity and self-respect.*
>
> (Nehru 1961: 344) (emphasis added)

Tensions came to a head when a few days later, Chou En-lai made what were seen as vast claims on Indian territory in a letter in which he reiterated the illegality of the McMahon Line and claimed that according to the customary boundary alignment, Aksai Chin was Chinese territory. In their early correspondence on the border issue during the 1950s, Chou En-lai continued to hold to the position he took in his 1956 talks with Nehru. He rejected the McMahon Line as an imperial border which was the product of British aggression and Chinese powerlessness but since it had been established as the effective boundary, he was prepared 'to take a more or less realistic attitude towards the McMahon Line' (India 1954–1959: 53). Although China 'cannot but act with prudence and needs time to deal with this matter', it was confident of reaching a 'friendly settlement' (India 1954–1959: 53). As for Aksai Chin, however, this had 'always been under Chinese jurisdiction. Patrol duties have continually been carried out in that area by the border guards of the Chinese Government' (India 1954–1959: 53). The letter of September 1959 was less conciliatory in tone and explicitly claimed both Aksai Chin and much of the territory demarcated by the McMahon Line as belonging to China by way of customary boundary alignments. China also claimed that India was following the policies of the British instead of adopting a sympathetic attitude to a fellow victim of imperial aggression (India 1959: 27).

India's position in the border correspondence on the McMahon Line was that it was a correct representation of the customary border that had been accepted for centuries and in 1954, when Nehru issued a directive ordering India's borders to be precisely marked on maps, the Line was given as a full international border despite the fact that it was yet to be demarcated on the ground (Maxwell 1972: 68, 77). The status of Aksai Chin was considered to be more ambiguous because as Nehru noted in a speech in the Lok Sabha:

> The actual boundary of Ladakh with Tibet was not very carefully defined. It was defined to some extent by British officers who went there. But I rather doubt if they did any careful survey. They marked the line. It has been marked all along in our maps. As people do not live there, by and large, it did not make any difference. But the question of the border has now arisen. We are prepared to sit down and discuss these minor things.
>
> (Nehru 1961: 345)

In his response to Chou En-lai's September 1959 letter, Nehru expressed 'surprise' and 'distress' and reiterated that the boundaries of India were 'settled for centuries by history, geography, custom and tradition' for the McMahon Line 'correctly represents the customary boundary in this area' (India 1959: 34). The water-parting formed by the crest of the Himalayas is the natural frontier which was 'accepted for centuries as the boundary by the peoples on both sides' and the McMahon Line had simply 'formalized the natural, traditional ethnic and administrative boundary in the area' (India 1959: 39–40). Moreover, he argued that the British did not always reinforce customary boundaries because of their incomplete knowledge of Indian geography (Hoffmann 1990: 25–6). If, then, an Indian claim departed from British historical records, as the Chinese would later argue, it could be put down to this reason. The Aksai Chin claim was a case in point. Chou En-Lai had argued in his letter that early British maps by John Walker corresponded closely to Chinese maps but were later changed to put Aksai Chin into Indian territory (India 1959: 28–9). Nehru responded that Walker had been using information from Henry Strachey, an army captain who 'knew little or nothing about Aksai Chin' and drew the natural boundary erroneously (India 1959: 36–7). It was true, he wrote that the 'British occupied and ruled the Indian sub-continent against the wishes of the Indian people' but the 'boundaries of India were settled for centuries by history, geography, custom and tradition' (India 1959: 34).

Later, in a speech to the Lok Sabha as Nehru detailed the contents of Chou's letter he began articulating a new discourse on the gulf that separated India and China which encompassed the themes of betrayal, moral superiority and resistance. He spoke of China's lack of understanding of India, how it valued Indian friendship to a 'very small extent', and how China had forgotten 'that India is not a country which can be ignored even though she may speak in a gentler language' (Nehru 1961: 346–58). Nonetheless, at this stage there was still uncertainty in Nehru's mind about India's claim on Aksai Chin as he admitted in a speech in Parliament:

The Aksai Chin area is in our maps, undoubtedly. But it is a matter for argument as to what part of it belongs to us and what part of it belongs to somebody else. I have frankly to tell the house that the matter has been challenged for a hundred years. There has never been any delimitation there.

(Nehru 1961: 354)

The Kongka Pass incident of October 1959 – in which a small detachment of Indian police officers became involved in a shooting incident with Chinese troops – consolidated this perception of China hostility. The skirmish resulted in the deaths of several Indian officers and one Chinese soldier and there were wounded personnel on both sides. Moreover, several Indian officers were captured and held by the Chinese for almost one month. Chinese and Indian accounts of what transpired at Konga Pass are contradictory, with each side accusing the other of shooting first. For the Chinese, the Kongka Pass in Aksai Chin was a boundary feature on which they had legitimately established a post. The patrolling Indians were therefore trespassing on Chinese territory and their actions indicated their intent to capture the Chinese post (India 1959–1960: 29–34). The Indian side, on the other hand, argued that the Kongka Pass was in Indian territory, that the Chinese troops were the trespassers and that the purpose of the patrol was to locate a scouting party that had set out the previous day and had not returned (India 1959–1960: 10–22).[7]

The Chinese version of events was given little credibility in India due to accounts from the released officers of their mistreatment at the hands of the Chinese forces and Nehru now explicitly began to employ a historical narrative that portrayed China as an expansionist power. History and the idea of traditional borders, moreover, were given a heightened significance from this point. The ambiguity surrounding Aksai Chin disappeared in November following advice from Sarvapelli Gopal, the director of the Historical Division of the Ministry of External Affairs, that the archival documents on India's northern frontiers indicated that its claim to Aksai Chin was stronger than China's (Maxwell 1972: 118). Nehru had earlier argued during his talks with Chou that '[h]istorical knowledge is not important but is useful as background information. History is gone', which implied that a historical approach was not necessarily seen as the best way of resolving disputes (Nehru 2005: 599). Nehru's Defence Minister, Krishna Menon, and others in his Cabinet apparently continued maintain this stance but, although they expressed their misgivings to Gopal, Nehru was not reproached. Nehru's willingness to now use 'historical evidence' in making the case for India's claim to Aksai Chin suggests an important shift which was verbalized in a speech in November 1959. He argued that China's recent behaviour was a result of the 'semi-isolation in which revolutionary China has grown up in the last ten years' and that it had developed a 'one-track mind' whereby it sought to achieve its national interests at the expense of everything else (Nehru 1961: 367). Looking through history, he said, China had an '... inherent tendency to be expansive when she is strong'. Given China's growing strength and the 'abnormal state of mind' created by the revolution, China posed a definite danger to India. Indeed, he doubted there was 'any country in the world which cares less for peace that China today' (Nehru 1961: 369–70).

In another speech in November Nehru argued that China had developed a 'sensation of greatness' early on and thought it natural 'that other countries should pay tribute to them' (Nehru 1961: 362). He vowed to keep seeking a peaceful solution but India's 'honour' and the 'integrity of its territory' was at stake and 'you cannot barter your self-respect and honour' (Nehru 1961: 363). Still, he was aware of the dangers of this type of rhetoric, for he added that in standing up for one's honour and self-respect,

> if you take some action which puts the same dilemma before the other country and the other country thinks that its honour is being attacked and its self-respect brought down, you shut all the doors to any kind of peaceful solution.
>
> (Nehru 1961: 363)

Nevertheless, Nehru ended the speech not by moderating this line of argument but by linking India's 'self-respect and honour' to its Himalayan frontier:

> I wish the Chinese Government and indeed other countries would try to understand. The Himalayas are something much more to us and more intimately tied up with India's history, tradition, faith, religion, beliefs, literature, and culture … they are part of ourselves … this question affects our innermost being.
>
> (Nehru 1961: 364)

This linking of honour with territorial nationalism was a key turning point, not just in India's relationship with China but in Nehru's discursive construction of India's postcolonial identity. Before examining the significance of this discursive shift, however, I will briefly turn to the issue of honour in international relations.

Richard Ned Lebow has pointed out the importance of honour in modern international relations. Drawing on classical Greek thought, Lebow (2006: 431) argues that three psychic drivers, appetite, spirit and reason underlie human motives. Modern thought, however, has privileged individual appetite and instrumental reason to the extent that the spirit, which is associated with honour and victory, has disappeared from view. Lebow aims to show that the drive for honour continues to be prominent in modern societies in various cultural forms but particularly through national standing and reputation. Standing and reputation, for instance, dominated both Soviet and American calculations during the Cold War, in particular, during the Cuban missile crisis (Lebow 2006: 432–3). Although the individual psyche is Lebow's starting point, in moving away from the modern focus on individual appetite and instrumental reason and because the 'the spirit can express itself only in society', his focus is on external honour as a social construction which at present is predominantly measured by material factors and recognition by others (Lebow 2006: 432).

Brent Steele (2008: 245), on the hand, argues that neither honour nor its inverse, shame, is dependent only on public judgement but also involves introspective reflection and evaluation. He thus focuses on the role of internal honour as a disciplinary mechanism in securing a state's identity. He argues that in the case of the United States, for instance, this internal honour is linked to the discursive construction of American exceptionalism – the idea that democracy, geographical separation from arenas of conflict and multiculturalism set the United States apart from other world powers – and notions of 'strength', 'will' and 'manhood' (Steele 2008: 248). 'Shame', 'humiliation' and 'honour' are therefore interlinked in these conceptualizations of world politics, as they were in Nehru's thought in a rather different manner which drew on a Buddhist-inspired social ontology and Gandhi's rejection of a politics of victimhood.

For Nehru, as we saw above, the shame and humiliation experienced by India was associated with colonial violence and subjugation. Yet, dwelling on shame and humiliation and focusing on reclaiming honour would reduce Indians to mere victimhood and risked reproducing a colonial modernity focused on instrumental reason and self-interest, which amounted to an ultimately damaging mimicry. Instead, India remained 'unsubdued and unconquered', and Nehru's alternative ethical modernity conceived of state identity in terms of a relational ontology that formed the basis of his politics of friendship. Nehru's adoption of the language of humiliation from 1959 and his reliance on 'history' to resolve the border dispute, therefore, marks a significant shift which destabilized the dominant construction of India's postcolonial identity.

How did such a dramatic shift occur? In 1959, the border dispute had become public knowledge and at the request of opposition members, Nehru had authorized the release of White Papers consisting of correspondence between India and China on the border issue, a move which Maxwell (1972: 134) argues 'effectively surrendered to the legislature the executive's power and responsibility to conduct the country's foreign relations'. Indeed, from 1959 Nehru was faced with persistent attacks on his China policy from members of the Hindu nationalist Jana Sangh, the Socialist parties, the Swatantra Party and from factions in his own party (Guha 2007: 315–16, 26–7; Brown 2003: 319–21). More generally, several commentators and biographers have suggested that Nehru's political ideals were often constrained by his susceptibility to the pressures of domestic politics (Gopal 1984: 299; Zachariah 2004: 251, 9). On the conflict with China, Benjamin Zachariah (2004: 242, 3, 64) argues that Nehru found himself 'trapped by the increasingly hysterical nationalism surrounding the border issue (not so much a popular sentiment as one among the 'political classes')' and pushed 'into a more and more aggressive posture' which led 'away from his principles into a disastrous war, and saw his policies collapse around him'. Judith Brown (2003: 320) argues that although Nehru had more autonomy in foreign policy than in domestic policy, once the border dispute became public knowledge, his dominance over foreign policy was quickly compromised and his 'policies could not be insulated from the nation's major forum of educated public opinion'.

Although these insights have some validity, in the context of the India–China war, as Maxwell (1972: 135) argues, the collision course was set – by both sides, contrary to Maxwell who tends to blame only India – long before the dispute became public knowledge. This suggests that in order to understand Nehru's shift toward territorial nationalism, we need to look beyond the pressures of public opinion and domestic politics. Specifically, to understand the emotions expressed in Nehru's speeches in relation to the idea of 'customary' borders we must take heed of the practical geopolitical imagining of India as a country that has faced continual invasion and conquest – a narrative perpetuated by both the British colonial regime and Indian anti-colonial leaders, including Nehru.

I noted above that Nehru's historical narrative of India's vulnerability to invasion was invoked primarily as a narrative of resistance rather than as a narrative of humiliation or shame linked to the loss of territory. While Nehru's *Bharat Mata* in *Autobiography* was subjected to humiliation and shame, in the ethical framework he develops in *Discovery* she becomes unsubdued and unconquered because the physical possession of territory (*Bharat Mata's* geo-body) was recognized as less important than her 'spirit' which remained free. Moreover, as we saw in the previous section, in the vision of an ethical modernity that Nehru sets out, which was buttressed by internationalism and global political structures, a focus on geography and territory were much less relevant and even counterproductive. For Nehru, then, moving away from a discourse of humiliation was vital for the construction of an ethical postcolonial modernity. Yet, underpinning the latter was a narrative of civilizational resilience and longevity and during the correspondence with China this manifested into a preoccupation with 'customary borders'.

On the other hand, China's insistence on drawing new border treaties with India can be understood by taking into account the narrative of national humiliation that underpins the hegemonic discourse of Chinese national identity. 'National humiliation' holds that foreign imperialism encouraged by domestic corruption led to China's downfall and William Callahan (2004: 205–6) argues that this narrative is used to construct another narrative of 'national salvation'. This narrative, Callahan argues, has been used to inspire everything from economic reforms to military action to the reclamation of territory lost in the 'century of national humiliation' during which China suffered invasions, occupations, wars, looting and unequal treaties, in particular, at the hands of the British and Japanese. Overcoming national humiliation was clearly a factor in China's position in the border dispute with India since it regarded parts of the India–China border to be the product of unequal treaties.

Yet, what was for China a symbol of national humiliation was for India a symbol of its resistance and longevity in the face of British colonialism. In the reconstructed nationalist narrative of invasion and conquest, the British, like other foreign rulers, had failed to destroy India's 'spirit', which was symbolized at least in part by 'customary borders' negotiated during thousands of years of its existence as a civilization. For China, abolishing all 'unequal' treaties and starting afresh with new boundary agreements, even if these would reaffirm the status quo, was essential for national salvation. For India, abrogating established treaties would mean threatening the autonomy and affirmation garnered in the achievement of independence from Britain. Thus, it was to the narrative of shame and humiliation we encounter in *Autobiography* that Nehru reverted with his invocation of India's customary borders and territorial integrity. The *Bharat Mata* of *Discovery*, and the ethical vision it represented, would return only in the aftermath of war.

War and betrayal

The 'forward policy' and the border war

The abandonment of a politics of friendship in favour of a politics of reclaiming honour led to what has been called a 'forward policy' of preventing further Chinese advance and establishing an Indian presence in Aksai Chin through the establishment of posts and patrols. Krishna Menon later refuted the idea that this constituted a forward policy and B.N. Mullik denied that Nehru had ever referred to it as such (Mullik 1971: 318). According to Menon, 'a forward policy means trying to get into someone else's territory like Lord Curzon tried to do ... Establishing posts in an area which belongs to us cannot be called a forward policy' (Quoted in Mullik 1971: 319). Still, despite the differences in motivation and ideology, given the similarity of the emotional drivers behind the border policies of British India and postcolonial India – both were driven by fear, vulnerability and honour – the term 'forward policy' does not seem entirely inappropriate.

The 'forward policy' was developed after Chou En-lai's visit to India in April 1960 during which he offered a 'package deal' whereby the status quo would be accepted in both the eastern and western sectors. India would give up its claim to Aksai Chin and the McMahon Line was to be the subject of a new India–China agreement but would remain fundamentally unchanged (Hoffmann 2006: 182). The tone of the 1960 talks, however, was similar to that of the 1959 correspondence and therefore proved unconducive to compromise. Nehru expressed hurt at China's infringement of India's frontiers after his efforts to facilitate the entry of China at the UN and to ensure a positive welcome for Chou at the Bandung conference, while Chou again raised the issue of Tibet and the activities of the Dalai Lama as a political refugee in India as belying the friendship that India had professed for China (Guha 2007: 317). Ultimately, India rejected the Chinese proposal on the basis that Aksai Chin had been illegally occupied by China and could not be equated with India's legal possession of the territory demarcated by the McMahon Line. The McMahon Line could not be subjected to negotiation, moreover, because India did not accept that China had any legal or customary claim to this territory (Hoffmann 2006: 185).

In 1961, as pressure bore down on Nehru from the opposition parties and members of the Congress, a new leadership took control of the Indian Army.

This leadership, according to Mullik (1971: 310) was more alert and responsive 'to the strong feelings in the country against making any more concessions to the Chinese' resulting in a 'more resolute handling of the frontier situation'. Mullik (1971: 314) dates the beginning of the 'forward policy' to November 1961 after he warned Nehru and his Ministers of China's deepening 'penetration into our territories'. While it was decided that the Indian Army would maintain a presence across the entire frontier from NEFA to Ladakh, Indian troops were ordered not to fire except in self-defence. The Ministry of External Affairs and the IB were confident that India's military activity would not lead to an escalation in conflict because in past incidents Chinese troops had refrained from confrontation with their Indian counterparts when they had come into contact. Although there were also examples of the Chinese reacting with gunfire to Indian activity at the Konga Pass and at Longju in August 1959, these were treated as exceptions. Chinese actions in the early stages of the forward policy also implied an unwillingness to carry through with an attack. The lesson learned from this was that if Indian troops held firm to their positions, the Chinese would back down. Moreover, there was a genuine conviction among civilian officials that even if China were to react with force to India's forward moves, the army would be able to cope with it. This was despite the indications to the contrary from military personnel who had warned Nehru of the numerical, logistical and tactical problems involved in executing the 'forward policy' (Hoffmann 1990: 98–100).

The belief that India was in full control of the situation on the Sino-Indian border was shattered on 10 October, 1962 when a Chinese assault unit of about 800 troops supported by mortar fire confronted an Indian platoon of about 50 men near Tseng Jong in NEFA. The Indian patrol managed a retreat but not before suffering casualties. Six officers were killed and eleven were wounded while five remained unaccounted for (Hoffmann 1990: 152–3). On 20 October, the Chinese began their full assault, attacking various Indian posts in NEFA and in Ladakh with the goal of taking all that India had gained through its 'forward policy' while pushing Indian troops back to China's 1960 claim line, which was considerably further behind the 1959 actual line of control.

On 24 October the Chinese halted their military advance and Nehru received a letter from Chou En-lai that proposed to reopen negotiations for '[o]ur two peoples' common interests in their struggle against imperialism outweigh by far all the differences between our two countries' (India 1963: 1). For Nehru, however, the potential for friendship had well and truly passed and his response was full of aggrieved emotion:

> Nothing in my long political career has hurt me more and grieved me more than the fact that the hopes and aspirations for peaceful and friendly neighbourly relations which we entertained and to promote ... worked so hard ... should have been shattered by the hostile and unfriendly twist given India–China relations during the past few years.
>
> (India 1963: 4)

'Only on the basis of decency, dignity and self-respect and not under threat of military might', he went on to add, could India resolve its differences with China (India 1963: 6).

China's offer of a cease-fire thus came to nothing and it resumed its military offensive on 15 November, making gains across NEFA and edging toward the Indian state of Assam. On 21 November, however, China unexpectedly announced a cease-fire and on 1 December began withdrawing their troops to positions they held before the war.[8] China's ceasefire plan was tacitly agreed to by India and although it refused to accept China's demarcation of the line of control it was forced to tolerate it. China later refused to agree to proposals put forward at the Colombo conference which had been organized by Sri Lanka and several other non-aligned states[9] to discuss the India–China situation. The Colombo proposals called on China to give up territory occupied after 8 September 1959 which, to China, was seen as legitimizing India's earlier 'forward policy'. Likewise, for India, the Chinese line of control did not align with either a customary boundary or the pre-war administrative reality (Hoffmann 1990: 226–8). Without the means or inclination to challenge it, however, India has mostly abided by the Chinese line of control since 1962 with relatively few major incidents, with the exceptions of clashes during the 1965 Indo-Pakistan war and at Nathula Pass on the Sikkim-Tibet border in 1967. Troop build-up also occurred in 1986–1987 following the establishment of rival posts in the disputed Sumdorong Chu Valley and in 1986 after India moved to make the NEFA (or Arunachal Pradesh as it had been known since 1972) an official state of the Indian union (Hoffmann 1990: 231).

Betrayal

India's defeat in 1962 is usually described as 'humiliating' by analysts and indeed, the idea that China was seeking to humiliate India was often raised. During a debate in the Lok Sabha on 14 November 1962, for instance, many speakers made reference to history repeating itself, thus invoking the narrative of invasion and conquest which was popularized during the colonial era. According to S.N. Chaturvedi, for instance:

> We have failed to learn lessons from our failures, for history has repeated itself ... The hoards of Central Asia are again on the march and we are confronted with the organised might of a dictatorship based on terror and reeking with blood.
>
> (1962: 1643)

Other speakers approvingly pointed to Nehru's statement at a press conference held during the war in October 1962 in which he seemed to admit the failure of his fundamental foreign policy beliefs: 'we were getting out of touch with reality in the modern world and we were living in an artificial atmosphere of our own creation. We have been shocked out of it, all of us' (Quoted in Gopal 1984: 223).

Yet, the predominant emotion expressed by the Indian government and members of Parliament during, and in the aftermath of the war was not humiliation but 'betrayal', an emotion distinct from 'humiliation' because it assumes the prior existence of a relationship of trust. As we saw above, in his correspondence and discussions with Chou En-Lai Nehru regularly expressed 'shock', 'surprise' and 'regret' at China's claims and actions, given India's attempts to build friendship. According to Krishna Menon, even as late as October 1962 neither he nor Nehru foresaw China initiating a major war against India (Brecher 1968: 148). In the wake of the war, claims of betrayal were common. In the MEA's background paper on the conflict, for instance, which was published in November 1962 and titled *China's Betrayal of India*, the India–China relationship is depicted in seven stages from '2000 years of goodwill' – the period in which trust and friendship was established – to a retroactive reading of the Tibetan situation in 1959 as 'the first rebuff' – when trust started to erode – followed by successive episodes of growing animosity leading up to the final 'naked aggression' in 1962 (India 1962).

On 8 November, Nehru moved a resolution in the Lok Sabha proclaiming: 'deep regret that in spite of the uniform gestures of goodwill and friendship ... China has betrayed this goodwill and friendship and the principles of Panchsheel...' (1962: 106). This betrayal, moreover, was linked to a new imperialism (1962: 110). 'It is sad to think', he went on to say, 'that we in India who have ... sought the friendship of China and treated them with courtesy and consideration and pleaded their cause in the councils of the world should now ourselves be victims of new imperialism and expansionism' (1962: 109). In response to the discourse of humiliation and the accompanying exhortations from various members of Parliament that India 'brutalize' itself in response to China's aggression, Nehru sought to reassert his vision of an ethical modernity underpinned by a Buddhist social ontology and Gandhian ethics:

> By becoming brutal and thinking in those brutal ways we lose our souls and that is a tremendous loss. I hope that India which is essentially a gentle and peace-loving country will retain that mind even though it may have to carry on war with all its consequences to the utmost ... Brutality and hatred and the offspring of these things do degrade a nation and the people ... I hope, no such emotion will rise in our country and, if it does rise, it will be discouraged.
>
> (1962: 1647–8)

The resilient *Bharat Mata* which symbolized his ethical modernity also reappeared. China's actions Nehru said, had

> suddenly lifted a veil from the face of India. During the last three weeks or a little more we have had a glimpse of the strength of the serene face of India, strong and yet calm and determined, that face, an ancient face which is ever young and vibrant.
>
> (1962: 1645)

The discourse of betrayal therefore, served an important function in Nehru's attempt to secure India's identity in the face of a war-induced identity crisis because, unlike humiliation which leaves open to the victim a form of agency that only acknowledges the victor's superior material power and seeks to better it, betrayal is accompanied by a form of agency in which the victim retains superior moral power. 'Betrayal' thus prevented any radical break in India's postcolonial identity. Nonetheless, the war severely damaged several aspects of Nehru's effort to ground India's postcolonial identity in an ethical modernity.

Identity costs

While Nehru sought to keep his ethical project intact in the wake of the war, China was no longer a part of this ethical vision and his conviction that Asia was uniquely positioned to develop a new international relations lay shattered. Edgar Snow quotes Nehru as arguing in a 1959 interview that the basic cause of the dispute was that both India and China were newly independent nations under 'dynamic nationalistic leaderships' which were 'meeting at their frontiers for the first time in history ... In the past India was a colony and China a semicolony. The boundary was not so clear and for the administrative needs of the time the boundary did not particularly have to be clearly delineated' (Quoted in Snow 1963: 592). Yet, Mullik writes in his memoir that in early 1963 Nehru argued in a briefing to the IB that the cause of the border war was a 'basic eternal conflict between China and India' and that 'the two civilizations had fought each other over centuries and none had so far been able to overcome the other'. India 'had to be humiliated' because it would not accept China's leadership or follow its political example: 'So it became necessary for China to remove this obstruction – remove in the psychological sense – to show other countries that though India might be very big on the map, yet India was no match against China' (Quoted in Mullik 1971: 454–5).

This was a striking departure from Nehru's earlier historical rendering of the India–China relationship even though his analysis of the causes of the conflict – fear, China's desire to humiliate India in order to strengthen its sense of Self – are consistent with his tendency toward understanding international relations in psychological terms. Hence, while his ontological assumptions may not have changed, the historical narrative – of India and China being especially well-placed to avoid a politics of fear because they were both ancient societies that 'tended to concentrate on the cultivation of those virtues which made the individual less self-centred and willing to cooperate' – that buttressed Nehru's politics of friendship had been dramatically destroyed (Quoted in Jaffrelot 2003: 64).

The war also produced criticisms of nonalignment, with many speakers during parliamentary debates in November 1962 arguing that it should be abandoned (1962). As one Member of Parliament put it:

I want to ask the Prime Minister whether he is in time or out of time when he repeats all the time the formula of non-alignment. It may be that every human being becomes out of date; and it is the context that changes.

(1962: 439)

Faced with what was perceived as a 'massive invasion' (1962: 111) by China and with a war many predicted would last not just for days or months but years, on 9 November, Nehru did indeed make a request for arms to the United States, which responded positively and, at India's insistence, with the understanding that the arms sale did not amount to a military alliance. In one of his final parliamentary speeches in April 1964 Nehru mounted a defence of nonalignment on the grounds that given the changing world situation – improved Soviet-US relations, the Soviet-China split, decolonization and the emergence of a number of new nonaligned countries – the policy had both succeeded and was all the more relevant. 'Non-alignment', Nehru reiterated, 'is not merely not joining a military bloc, but it affects economic and other policies. It is especially psychological' (1964: 10707).

Nonalignment remained official government policy, but the debate generated by the war constituted the first time that nonalignment as a central facet of foreign policy and identity came under serious and sustained challenge. Moreover, the steep rise in defence expenditure in the wake of the war[10] meant that one of the intended 'psychological' effects of nonalignment – creating a climate in which fear and paranoia would not dominate world politics, thus freeing the government to focus on economic problems and social justice – would be increasingly difficult to achieve.

Another serious casualty of the India–China war was Nehru's internationalist nationalism. The comments of one member of Parliament on 12 November were typical of the anti-Chinese feeling that emerged during the war:

I would like to give a time-limit and tell the Chinese that if this is going to continue, we shall deport every Chinese from this country, be he the cook, be it a man who makes shoes, because I think these Chinamen in India are spies who must be conveying every news [sic] to their country...

(1962: 1010)

Nehru criticized such sentiments in his speech on 14 November:

...we must always distinguish between people of any country – much more so of a great country, great in size, great in history – and its government and not transfer somehow our anger and bitterness ... I have not liked some poor Chinese shopkeepers, some restaurant-keepers being attacked in Delhi or elsewhere as if they were the symbols of the attack on us ... it brutalizes us and give us a bad name.

(1962: 1648–9)

Nonetheless, as the conflict ensued, the incidence of 'narrow nationalism' across India increased and the long-settled Chinese community in India became the target of new ordinances and laws that infringed on their civil liberties. More than 2000 people of Chinese descent, 900 of them Indian citizens, were interned in Rajasthan while others were ordered to leave India or were imprisoned. By 1963, more than 1600 of those interned and their dependents had been forcibly deported to China and 7500 people of Chinese descent voluntarily emigrated to other countries between 1962 and 1967 (Banerjee 2007: 447–8).

Conclusion

This chapter has attempted to understand how Nehru, the internationalist nationalist, became embroiled in a war over territorial boundaries and how this, in turn, affected the construction of India's postcolonial identity. Understanding how this 'petty dispute' as Nehru often referred to it in the 1950s was transformed into a full-blown war is possible, I have argued, by paying attention to the role of 'humiliation', 'honour' and 'self-respect' in India's foreign policy discourse. To this end, I examined the narrative of India's susceptibility to invasion and conquest that emerged during the colonial encounter. In Nehru's construction of India's postcolonial identity, this narrative was re-worked into one of resistance by emphasizing Indian civilization's resilience in the face of aggression. In this way, Nehru was able to fashion an internationalist nationalism that rejected imperial geopolitics for a politics of friendship. As the border dispute with China gained momentum, however, and India's 'customary borders' became a symbol of India's civilizational resilience, the language of honour and humiliation came to the fore and China was re-presented as a civilizational enemy instead of a civilizational friend.

Although in the aftermath of the war Nehru attempted to minimize the cost to his ethical project, the loss of China as a partner in his politics of friendship, the rise in 'narrow nationalism' and the questioning of nonalignment all served to produce a significant challenge to the place of Nehru's ethical modernity in India's postcolonial identity. Responding to heckles during Nehru's speech in the Indian Parliament on the Colombo Conference proposals in 1963, a member of his Congress Party, Joachim Alva, interjected: 'May I submit that the foreign affairs debates have been conducted by us with great dignity in the past? It is not quite fair to interrupt the hon. Prime Minister in this fashion' (1963: 5998). Alva's interjection is indicative of the fact that by 1963, Nehru's days of dominating the construction of foreign policy/identity discourse had ended. Nonetheless, as we shall see in the chapters to come, the ethical project that Nehru placed at the centre of India's postcolonial identity continues to linger in India's foreign policy/identity discourse. Precisely how successive governments grappled with Nehru's legacies will be the focus of the remaining chapters.

Part II

Grappling with postcoloniality

1964–2004

5 Interventions and explosions
Whither an ethical modernity?

In this and the next chapter I explore the period in Indian foreign policy following the end of the Nehru era, during which the Congress Party's dominance of Indian politics came under heightened challenge. This chapter examines two significant events during this period, India's involvement in the creation of Bangladesh in 1971 and the exploding of a nuclear device in 1974. Both the intervention and the nuclear explosion were undertaken by the administration led by Indira Gandhi who dominated Indian politics unlike any other Prime Minister, except for her father, and is remembered by many as the leader that rid Indian foreign policy of its Nehruvian idealism (Dixit 2004, Mansingh 1984). Yet, the tendency to focus on the differences between foreign policy in the Nehru era and the Indira Gandhi era means that significant continuities are overlooked. Indira Gandhi employed much the same language of Nehruvian foreign policy and nonalignment, friendship, the rejection of balance of power politics, disarmament were all fixtures of her foreign policy discourse. I would argue that this was not a meaningless parroting of Nehru's normative discourse. Rather, Nehru's normative project continued to play a defining role in the construction of India's postcolonial identity and, therefore, placed limits on the options available for state action and made certain courses of action possible.

The first section of this chapter is concerned with India's military and political involvement in the creation of Bangladesh. It begins by charting the rise of Indira Gandhi in Indian politics and examining the discursive continuities in the construction of state identity under her leadership. I then look at the lead-up to the war, which established Bangladesh, and the war itself focusing, in particular, on the mutual constitution of foreign policy discourse, identity and interests. I analyse how the conditions for intervening in Pakistan's civil conflict were brought about and the limits that were placed on India's actions. I focus specifically on India's legitimating reasons for its intervention and its reiteration of discourses, which emerged in the Nehru era, on India's ethical but fragile modernity, Pakistan's flawed model of nation-building and South Asia as a space of kinship. Finally, I examine the aftermath of the war and the consequences of the military intervention for India's state identity. The second section seeks to understand developments in India's nuclear program and the manifestation of tensions, which also emerged in the Nehru era, between the desire to promote international norms against nuclear weapons and to resist norms considered to be perpetuating a global hierarchy. To this end, I address India's rejection of the Nuclear Non-Proliferation Treaty (NPT) in 1969 and its 'Peaceful Nuclear Explosion' in 1974.

'Rescuing' East Bengal

The rise of Indira Gandhi

Despite predictions to the contrary (see Guha 2007: 344), Nehru's death was not followed by the collapse of democracy, the spread of communism, military dictatorship or a general state of anarchy. Instead, although the Congress Party's authority had diminished following the India–China war and the rise of regional political parties, it remained in power under the leadership of Lal Bahadur Shastri, a trusted advisor to Nehru who had held several Cabinet positions prior to his elevation. Shastri's tenure, though eventful due to the 1965 India–Pakistan war, was short-lived. He died suddenly of a heart attack in January 1966, the day after signing the Tashkent peace declaration with the Pakistani President Ayub Khan. Spurred by India's defeat in 1962, the re-arrest of Sheik Abdullah and Pakistan's gains in a skirmish over the Rann of Kutch, a disputed salt marsh in April 1965, Ayub had precipitated the war by ordering Pakistani infiltration into Indian-held Kashmir with the intention of sparking a mass uprising against Indian rule. This was unsuccessful and India, seeking to relieve pressure on its troops in Kashmir, responded by sending tanks and infantry over the international border that divided the Punjab toward Lahore. The war was brought to end by a UN-mediated ceasefire in September 1965 and with the fighting at a stalemate and both sides suffering a comparable number of casualties, there was no outright winner. The Tashkent Agreement, which was mediated by the Soviet Premier Alexei Kosygin, enforced a troop withdrawal to positions held before the war, the transfer of prisoners, the recommencement of diplomatic relations and a commitment against the use of military force in future disputes. While there was some resentment at the pressure exerted on India to give up the territory it had gained during the war, the Agreement was represented as a victory. Hailed as a 'remarkable achievement' by the External Affairs Minister Swaran Singh, the Agreement endorsed key principles of Indian foreign policy – peaceful coexistence, friendship and the non-use of force to resolve disputes – despite Pakistan's protestations that none of this was possible before the Kashmir question had been resolved (Singh 1966: 10–11). China's condemnation of the Tashkent Declaration, on the grounds that Pakistan had been compelled to sign it, also contributed to the sense of an Indian victory and consolidated the emerging perception of China and Pakistan as a conjoined threat. According to Swaran Singh, China's condemnation was designed to convince Pakistan that the Chinese were the 'sole saviours of Pakistan' and was in line with the 'central philosophy of China's way of thinking these days'. That is, 'the theory that there cannot be peaceful co-existence' and 'the principle that war is inevitable' (Singh 1966: 58).

It was in this triumphant climate that Indira Gandhi rose to power with help from the 'Syndicate', a group of regional Congress Chief Ministers and the members of the Congress Working Committee, which promoted her despite her lack of administrative experience because they thought she was weak and ideologically indistinct enough to be controlled (Kaviraj 1986: 1697). But Indira Gandhi proved to be something altogether different and in 1969 she began a process of centralizing political power that would cause long-term damage to India's democracy. Although Nehru had dominated Indian politics throughout his time in office he was able to see the importance of institution building (Nandy 1980: 122). Indira Gandhi, on the other hand, thought that the institutions India had inherited from the colonial era were unfit to lead it into the post-colonial modern era:

> I am not afraid to say that the Congress Party has become moribund. It has scarcely a single leader with a modern mind … The trouble is that Congress has never succeeded in evolving into a modern political party. Sometimes I feel that even our parliamentary system is moribund. Everything is debated and nothing gets done.
>
> (Quoted in Mehta 1970: 501)

Her personalized style of politics was evident as far back as the Congress's successful 1967 election campaign that legitimized her political elevation, during which she portrayed herself as Mother Indira/India:

> My family is not confined to a few individuals. It consists of crores of people … my burden is manifold because crores of my family members are poverty-stricken and I have to look after them … sometimes they fight among themselves, and I have to intervene, especially to look after the weaker members of my family, so that the stronger ones do not take advantage of them.
>
> (Quoted in Frank 2001: 303)

This was reinforced by the 1971 campaign which she contested, and decisively won as the leader of the new Congress (R) party. Her campaign was run with the slogan 'Garibi Hatao' ('end poverty') and set a precedent by focusing almost exclusively on her as an individual candidate. Katherine Frank (2001: 303) has suggested that Indira Gandhi's relationship to 'the masses' was both maternal and paternal which implies some parallels with the politics of that other Gandhi, the Mahatma. While Gandhi's mix of femininity and masculinity produced a politics of feminized masculinity, however, Indira Gandhi's politics was one of masculinized femininity. Not only was she committed to draping Mother India in her masculine garb of modernity, she also saw herself as Mother India personified. As a result, she was convinced of her commitment to morality, democracy and pluralism but was also certain that only she could put India on the path to modernity. India's postcolonial identity thus became inextricably tied up with the individual personality of Indira Gandhi and, as we shall see, this was reiterated in her foreign policy discourse on the Bangladesh war.

Unlike her father, Indira Gandhi did not write prolifically and she gave little indication prior to her ascent to the position of Prime Minister of her views on India's role in the world. Indeed, she is often described as 'non-ideological' and foreign policy during her tenure is said to have been marked by a radical change from 'idealism' to 'realism' (Dixit 2004). Surjit Mansingh (1984: 24) describes 'flexibility and pragmatism' and 'her concern for the tangible over the moral' as her hallmarks. Nevertheless, her foreign policy speeches as Prime Minister did not depart significantly from Nehru's. Her critique of the notion of 'spheres of influence' was articulated in a 1970 speech:

> Most of these super-powers would like to have spheres of influence. Although we are very friendly with them we do not agree with this attitude of theirs and we are certainly not going to help them to have this kind of sphere of influence. The only sphere of influence we want is one of friendship and of mutual help.
>
> (Gandhi 1975a: 140)

A speech in Kathmandu laid out her commitment to the policy of Panchsheel and she too linked the policy to India's civilizational traditions:

> India does not covet others' territory. Nor does it seek to impose its ways or will on any nation. We accept the freedom of nations to choose their own destiny; we do not seek to interfere in the affairs of others. Our belief in peaceful co-existence is not a matter of expediency. It is rooted in our tradition and way of life.
>
> (Gandhi 1971c: 404)

As in the Nehru era, there was little inclination in the first phase of Indira Gandhi's leadership (1966–1977) to demarcate the South Asian region as a particular area of foreign policy concern and her foreign policy discourse on Nepal, Sri Lanka and Bhutan continued to emphasize a friendship bordering on kinship. Speaking in December 1972 on an agreement with Bhutan on postal services, India's Communications Minister H.N. Bahuguna (1972: 379) talked of the 'impregnable bond of friendship and brotherhood between our two people'. Likewise, Sri Lanka was 'a respected sister nation for which we have great affection, regard and friendship' (Gandhi 1971c: 397). The rancour over the issue of people of Indian origin in Sri Lanka had subsided after an agreement in 1964 in which India agreed to grant citizenship to about two-thirds of the stateless tea plantation workers of Indian origin while Sri Lanka granted citizenship to the remaining one-third. Speaking in Colombo in 1967 Indira Gandhi (1971c: 397) used the resolution of this issue – which affected almost one million people, none of whom were consulted in the negotiations leading to the 1964 pact – to emphasize the familial nature of the relationship between India and Sri Lanka:

'Our relations are too close for either of us to allow minor matters to interfere with our traditional friendship'. Her speeches on Nepal also contained a familial discourse:

> Nepal and India are two independent and sovereign countries but both children of the Himalayas. They follow independent policies of peace and non-alignment and co-existence and friendship. These policies are characterized by a deep sense of shared history and common aspirations and a basic sense of kinship between our peoples which is, perhaps, unparalleled elsewhere in the world.
>
> (Gandhi 1966: 112)

I argued in Chapter 3 that Nehru's foreign policy toward Pakistan was dominated by a discourse of 'rejected fraternity' although he later sought to move to a politics of friendship. Indira Gandhi's foreign policy discourse on Pakistan reverted to a 'rejected fraternity' and followed Nehru's inclination toward separating the Pakistani people from the Pakistani government thus de-legitimizing Pakistani sovereignty and asserting the superiority of India's project of postcolonial modernity (Gandhi 1971a: 34–5). This strategy would become essential during India's intervention in the Bangladesh war.

Intervention and identity

Of the scholarly works that attempt to explain the war that led to the creation of Bangladesh, Richard Sisson and Leo Rose's *War and Secession: Pakistan, India, and the Creation of Bangladesh* is perhaps the most comprehensive (See also Ayoob and Subrahmanyam 1972; Palit 1972; Kumar 1975). The authors have drawn on extensive interviews with 'political leaders, their principal advisers and associates' to understand and reconstruct the 'decisional structures and processes' that characterized the war and to gain insight into the 'relations between motivation, calculation, and context' in order to explain why the war was 'fought when at the outset the principals neither anticipated nor wanted them' (Sisson and Rose 1990: ix, 1). As Abraham (1995: 23) has pointed out in his critique, however, the evidence that Sisson and Rose produce in the book is at variance with this initial assumption that the war was an outcome that neither side wanted. In particular, they argue that the Indian leadership had begun to prepare for the possibility of war as early as March or April and consistently rejected overtures from third-party mediators, in the latter half of 1971, to assist in finding a peaceful settlement (Sisson and Rose 1990: Ch. 9). Abraham (1995: 25–6) attributes this disjuncture to the authors' desire to construct a consistent narrative and to discover the 'essential truth' of why the war occurred. This meant eliminating the varying interpretations gleaned from multiple interviews and prioritizing particular strands of information.

By contrast, my analysis of the Indo-Pakistan war of 1971 does not rest on the hypothesis that there is only one story to be told and my concern is not to arrive at a penultimate explanation for the war. Instead, I look specifically at how India constituted the events of 1971 into a crisis, the possibilities this created for foreign policy action and how this was linked to India's postcolonial identity. I argue that representing the region as a family, delegitimizing Pakistan's sovereign authority and the authority of the 'international community' as a moral actor, and constructing the conflict in East Pakistan as both a threat to, and as validation of, India's project of postcolonial modernity helped to create the political space necessary for the intervention to occur. In this respect, foreign policy in the Indira Gandhi era drew on legacies from the Nehru era but added a willingness to use overt and covert coercion which was previously absent.

Nonetheless, I argue against the idea that India's humanitarian justifications were a mere smokescreen for its real 'strategic' reasons. This is the position taken by Zaglul Haider (2009) in a recent article revisiting the Bangladesh war in which he argues that India's two main justifications for its intervention, the instability caused by the refugee flight across the India–East Pakistan border and humanitarian concerns were merely justifications that masked India's 'hidden agenda' to 'dismember its main enemy' and 'to integrate the economy of Bangladesh with the economy of eastern India' (Haider 2009: 543). These assertions are not, however, substantiated with new evidence and without access to the archives from this period, the precise considerations contemplated by Indira Gandhi and her advisors are difficult to ascertain. Moreover, in light of the difficulties faced by India in imposing its influence on its smaller neighbours in the region, Haider's (2009: 544) suggestion that Indian policy makers thought that a liberated Bangladesh, 'together with Nepal and Bhutan, would go under the security system of India' seems unlikely, particularly given Indira Gandhi's reservations about certain leaders in the Awami League – the party that led the secessionist struggle – and the Awami League's hard-line position on the sharing of water from the Ganges River, an issue that acutely affected East Pakistan (Sisson and Rose 1990: 135). In any case 'strategic' reasoning itself is a social construction and what constitutes a strategic action is dependent on the social imaginary from which it emerges. What would lead India to seek economic and security integration on the subcontinent and why it would regard Pakistan as an 'enemy' to be 'dismembered' must be explained rather simply asserted.

The idea that the Indian leadership was more than happy to see the weakening of Pakistan is more plausible and partly substantiated by the contents of a letter written by D.P. Dhar, the head of policy planning in the Ministry of External Affairs, to the head of Indira Gandhi's private secretariat, P.N. Haksar. Dhar and Haksar were two of the most important advisors to Indira Gandhi in 1971 and in the letter, which was written in April, Dhar advises against following the path advocated by Indian analysts like K. Subrahmanyam, who were calling for immediate military action and even the seizure of parts of East Pakistan and the establishment of an Indian Army-protected provisional government of Bangladesh (Guha 2007: 453; Sisson and Rose 1990: 149–50). Rather than 'policies and programmes of impetuosity', Dhar wrote, what was required was 'not an immediate defeat of the highly trained army of West Pakistan' but the creation of 'the whole of East Bengal into a bottomless ditch which will suck the strength and resources of West Pakistan. Let us think in terms of a year of two, not in terms of a week or two' (Quoted in Guha 2007: 453). The direct intervention that Dhar seemed to be suggesting was indeed a new approach to dealing with Pakistan and the ontological challenge it posed to India. Yet, Dhar also writes of his satisfaction that India was succeeding in its propaganda war against Pakistan by providing support to those fleeing the violence in the East (Guha 2007: 453). This implies that presenting India as a 'moral power', particularly in relation to Pakistan, remained as important for the Indian leadership in the 1970s as it did during the Nehru era and, as an enabling factor in the 1971 intervention, it cannot be dismissed. It is a fundamental error to posit the separation of words and deeds and 'rhetoric' and 'truth' for, in the construction of social worlds, the two are inextricable. As Nicholas Wheeler (2000: 287) argues, the 'legitimating reasons employed by governments are crucial because they enable and constrain action' and as Weldes (1999: 115) suggests, even the most exaggerated statements provide us with insight into the 'structures of meaning on which concrete national interests depend'.

As noted above, in 1971, India justified its intervention into Pakistan's civil war primarily in terms of self-defence against the threat of instability posed by the refugee influx into West Bengal, and as an act of humanitarian intervention to prevent what was described as the Pakistan army's genocidal actions in the East. Both of these arguments were novel at the time. Article 51 of the UN Charter specifies that states have a right to self-defence to protect their territorial integrity when faced with armed attack and, as the negative reaction of the Security Council to India's arguments shows, humanitarian considerations were not considered legitimate grounds for intervention during the Cold War (UN Security Council 1971). While India did not succeed in changing the norms of intervention in 1971, Jean-Pierre L. Fonteyne (1973–1974: 230), writing in 1973, noted that India's actions 'revived the debate among scholars on the question of the legality of unilateral humanitarian intervention under the UN Charter'. Similarly, Thomas M. Franck and Nigel S. Rodley (1973: 303), writing in the same year, argued that the 'Bangladesh case is an instance, by far the most important in our times, of the unilateral use of military force justified *inter alia*, on human rights grounds ... Perhaps India's example, by its success, has already entered into the nations' conscious expectations of future conduct'.

In fact, it was not until the end of the Cold War that the concept of humanitarian intervention became central to debates in International Relations and an attempt at promulgating a new international norm based on the 'Responsibility to Protect' (R2P) was made. As set out in the 2005 World Summit Outcome statement, R2P is based on the idea that the 'international community' working through the UN has the responsibility to take collective action on a 'case-by-case basis and in cooperation with relevant regional organizations as appropriate, should peaceful means be inadequate and national authorities are manifestly failing to protect their populations from genocide, war crimes, ethnic cleansing and crimes against humanity' (Assembly 2005: 31). In his contribution to the renewed debate, Nicholas Wheeler (2000: 75) in *Saving Strangers* cited India's role in the creation of Bangladesh as a legitimate case of humanitarian intervention 'because (in addition to meeting the requirements of necessity and proportionality) the security reasons that led it to intervene and the means employed did not undermine the humanitarian benefits of the intervention'. As Wheeler (2000: 288–9) notes, India challenged significant international norms to undertake its military actions, norms that he argues were only successfully undermined in the 1990s due to the efforts of Western governments which, in turn, were acting because of pressure from their domestic populations who were shocked by the carnage produced by conflict in Northern Iraq and Somalia. In this reading, normative change at a domestic level forced normative change in the international sphere. Since Wheeler ties humanitarian actions and justifications so closely to changes at the international normative level, his analysis is limited in its explanation of why India chose, in part, to frame its intervention in 1971 in humanitarian terms. He argues that although India's intervention counts as humanitarian, it 'was not motivated by primarily humanitarian reasons' (Wheeler 2000: 75). He suggests that a combination of weakening Pakistan and the negative public reaction to the refugee inflow and declining electoral fortunes were India's primary reasons for intervention (Wheeler 2000: 62). What is important for Wheeler is that India chose to raise humanitarian arguments at all and for him this points to the power of human rights norms in the UN Charter and the Genocide Convention, without which 'India would have lacked the normative language to name Pakistan's repression as a 'shock to the conscience of mankind'' (Wheeler 2000: 74).

However, contrary to Wheeler's suggestion that electoral imperatives were a factor in India's decision to intervene, Sisson and Rose (Sisson and Rose 1990: 151) argue that while public views on the events in East Pakistan were not ignored, the Indian government 'handled all suggestions and criticisms calmly, rarely rejecting anything out of hand, but also rarely, if ever, revising policies to suit'. Indeed, Indira Gandhi had achieved a decisive victory in the March 1971 election with her Congress (R) party, she was little-inclined to follow her father's coalitionist style of politics, and faced little opposition from within her party or from the decimated opposition in the Parliament. While some Hindu nationalist and pro-Soviet newspapers were in favour of immediate action, most of the mainstream Indian media were cautious in their response to the developments in East Pakistan (Sisson and Rose 1990: 149). As Sisson and Rose (1990: 140–1) point out, moreover, her core group of policy advisors were largely united on major policy issues. Thus, although there was some criticism from a few newspapers, analysts like Subrahmanyam and members of the opposition that the government should undertake more decisive action, unlike in the lead-up to the India–China war, the government was firmly at the helm of policy-making during the conflict in East Pakistan. This is not to say that domestic political considerations resulting from the refugee inflow were not important in India's response. However, the public reaction to the domestic challenges caused by the influx of refugees was not strong enough to be labelled a significant driving force behind policy decisions.

Moreover, while India fully recognized the challenge its engagement in Pakistan's civil war posed to international norms against intervention, as the following statement by Indira Gandhi in March 1971 in the Lok Sabha indicates, its leadership consciously persisted in using humanitarian language:

> It is not merely a suppression of a movement but it is meeting an unarmed people with tanks. We are fully alive to the situation and we shall keep constantly in touch with what is happening and what we need to do. We must not take a merely theoretical view. At the same time we have to follow proper international norms.
>
> (Gandhi 1971b: 669)

Against Wheeler, I will argue in this chapter that India's continued invocation of humanitarianism was not simply an instrumental use of international normative language for, as I have argued in previous chapters, attempting to shape human rights norms at the UN was a long-standing part of Indian foreign policy and an integral feature of the internationalist nationalist identity that Nehru sought to craft for postcolonial India. Equally important was the normative condemnation, which was inherent in India's humanitarian discourse, of Pakistan's prioritizing of narrow nationalism and religion over secularism and internationalism. India's humanitarian arguments in 1971 made sense at a domestic level, therefore, because they reiterated long-standing discourses of state identity and the same is true, as we shall see below, of the arguments about 'refugee aggression'.

Setting the scene (March–December 2)

The first period of the Indian government's discourse on the issue extended from March to April 1971. In Pakistan's first democratic elections in December 1970 the Awami League, led by Mujibur Rahman – who had campaigned on a platform of autonomy for East Pakistan which had long been dominated, and discriminated against, by West Pakistan – won a sweeping victory in East Pakistan, winning 160 out of the 162 seats it was allotted. The opposing Pakistan People's Party, led by Zulfikar Ali Bhutto, won 81 out of the 138 seats allotted to West Pakistan (Mansingh 1984: 214). Mujibur Rahman, as the leader of the majority party, had expected the Prime Ministership but faced resistance both from Bhutto and the Pakistani army – whose financial base and political power was threatened by the Awami League's demand for the equitable division of resources and revenue between East and West Pakistan (Marwah 1979: 559). Upon the failure of talks in March 1971 between Mujibur, Bhutto and General Yahya Khan to resolve the constitutional issue of autonomy, the Pakistani army took over in East Pakistan, with a wave of brutal repression against anyone deemed to be opponents of the military regime (Mansingh 1984: 214–15). India's initial reaction to the aftermath of Pakistan's election was to issue statements of support for the Awami League and regret at the abrogation of democracy (Gandhi 1972: 11–13). At this stage, however, Indira Gandhi and other government spokesmen implied that the issue was still an internal matter for Pakistan to deal with. She stated that India's support for the Awami League was 'not because we wanted any interference in another country's affairs, but because these were values ... for which we have always stood and for which we have always spoken out' (Gandhi 1971b: 669). This soon changed, however, to revert to an older familial narrative.

In this narrative of a family drama there were three main characters: the 'Benevolent Mother' – India; the 'Long-Suffering Daughter' – the people of East Pakistan; and the 'Bastard Son' – Pakistan, which having been, as Ashis Nandy (1997: 911) puts it, the 'product of the conspiracy between India's erstwhile British rulers pursuing a 'divide and rule' policy and the religion-based parties in the region' was seen to be 'the illegitimate child of the West'. The Long-Suffering Daughter had been torn from its twin, West Bengal by the British at the turn of the century and had opted for life with the Bastard Son upon the partition of India in 1947. After many years of abuse and neglect, however, the Long-Suffering Daughter rebelled against the Bastard Son and expressed her desire for freedom from repression. 'The people of East Bengal are being sought to be suppressed by the naked use of force, by bayonets, machine guns, tanks, artillery and aircraft' Indira Gandhi said in a speech (Gandhi 1972: 13). India had 'always desired and hoped for peaceful, normal and fraternal relations with Pakistan' but, 'situated as India is and bound as the peoples of the sub-continent are by centuries-old ties of history, culture and tradition, this House cannot remain indifferent to the macabre tragedy being enacted so close to our border' (Gandhi 1972: 13).

While Indira Gandhi invoked a narrative of civilizational fraternity to explain India's concern about events in East Pakistan, a note to the UN Secretary General U Thant from India's Representative to the UN, Samar Sen, invoked India's internationalist identity to express India's interest in the issue:

> India has perhaps been one of the most active countries to take part in a large number of civilized documents and instruments that we have adopted. We are proud of our participation, but we do think that all these instruments, all these principles, all these codes of morality, must be taken together and not be torn piecemeal to serve the temporary purpose of this country or that ... the scale of human sufferings is such that it ceases to be a matter of domestic concern of Pakistan alone.
>
> (Sen 1971b: 495)

In April, there were important discursive shifts in India's discourse on events in East Pakistan. Indira Gandhi told an All-India Congress Committee meeting that the issue was not simply an internal matter for Pakistan (Sisson and Rose 1990: 296 n.24). What was previously 'East Bengal' or 'East Pakistan' in Indian discourse was now increasingly 'Bangla Desh' and, as refugees began pouring across the border into Western India, the situation was re-presented as a crisis concerning domestic security. Although India was proud of her 'tradition of tolerance' the burden of caring for three and half million 'victims of war who have sought refuge from the military terror' was heavy (Gandhi 1972: 15, 7). Besides this, India was busy with its own problems – the garb of modernity she had been trying to dress herself in since 1947 was proving difficult to wear. In particular, West Bengal, into which the refugees were streaming, was riddled with political instability thanks to a Maoist insurgency, weak coalition governments and the repeated imposition of central government rule in the state in the name of re-establishing stability. Refugees also added to the pressure on West Bengal's over-crowded labour market. Thus, India was facing a 'new kind of aggression' from Pakistan for the entry of millions of refugees into India threatened to alter eastern India's religious and social demography making it weak and unstable (Gandhi 1972: 50). Millions of people had 'been terrorized and persecuted by the military rulers of Pakistan, and have been pushed inside our territory, jeopardizing our normal life and our plans for the future' (Gandhi 1972: 50). Hence,

> what was the problem of another country has now been deliberately converted into a problem for India. This is not just an economic question. It has deep political and social overtones and is a real threat to our security and stability.
>
> (Gandhi 1972: 50)

Indeed, the refugee influx threatened to tear the garb of modernity from Mother India's battered body, for what was at stake was the very essence of the postcolonial modern – the secularism of the society. Most of the refugees that had initially left East Pakistan were Hindu and the government was concerned that Indian Muslims would bear the brunt of their misgivings:

> The main question today is that communal tension has grown and the policy of those across our border is to do everything possible to increase it. It is therefore, a heavy responsibility on the people of all parties here to see that Pakistan's rulers do not succeed in this nefarious intention.
>
> (Gandhi 1972: 32)

In this way, the government tied the notion of 'refugee aggression', which would lie at the core of India's justification for the use of force in December, not just to India's political and economic stability, but to long-standing discourses of identity.

India's humanitarian justifications were also tied to its identity discourses in ways that sought to distinguish it from both the 'international community' and Pakistan, which were both gradually delegitimized as moral actors. Indira Gandhi conducted two tours of foreign capitals in 1971 to put forward India's views on East Pakistan and to convince the US, in particular, to help facilitate the release of the now-imprisoned Mujibur Rahman and open a dialogue with the Awami League. She gained little other than expressions of sympathy, however, and the behaviour of the US was described as 'extremely callous' (Singh 1971: 102). The US President Richard Nixon had a poor relationship with Indira Gandhi and a fondness for the Pakistani leadership. Moreover, he was seeking rapprochement with China and considered Pakistan to be an indispensable go-between (Kissinger 1979: 842–18).[1] Consequently, the Nixon Administration continued to supply arms to Pakistan and rejected suggestions from State Department officials to put pressure on Yahya Khan to exercise restraint and make political concessions in East Pakistan (Van Hollen 1980: 340–1).[2] On a visit to Germany, Indira Gandhi held this alliance responsible for Pakistan's lack of democracy, and therefore indirectly responsible for the situation in East Pakistan:

> ...unfortunately, all these years, Pakistan has had a very strong Western support and this is what has encouraged them to continue in this [undemocratic] manner. I personally think that this is what is leading to disruption and the weakness of Pakistan. Otherwise, by now, I think, it could have been a strong and unified country such as we are.
>
> (Gandhi 1972: 96)

Sisson and Rose (1990: 188–9) note that there was an inherent contradiction between India's attempt to internationalize the conflict and its refusal to accept the characterization of the events on the subcontinent as an India–Pakistan dispute. By June, they observe, India became increasingly unwilling to allow UN involvement in the issue, either through direct mediation by U Thant or by the posting of UN observers in refugee camps or on either side of the India–Pakistan border (Sisson and Rose 1990: 189–90). An offer of $70 million from the US government to alleviate the cost of the refugee influx and tentative efforts to mediate between the Awami League and the Pakistani military regime of Yahya Khan were also rejected by India which reacted by discouraging contact between the Bangladesh government in-exile and American government officials (1971c). India perceived these efforts as morally equating India and Pakistan and as propping up the Pakistani government without seeking real concessions (Sisson and Rose 1990: 191–2). Henry Kissinger's secret visit to China via Pakistan further alienated the Indian leadership from the US.

As noted above, these observations complicate Sisson and Rose's main argument that the Bangladesh war was unforseen and unwanted by India, but neither can they be treated as proof that India sought to deliberately dismember Pakistan. Rather, I would argue that its contradictory approach to the 'international community' in the lead-up to war is an indicator of the role that identity played as an enabling factor for India's eventual military intervention. Third-party mediation in the conflict came with the implication of equivalence between India and Pakistan, which was an unacceptable identity cost for India. This, and the US's support for Pakistan, made it possible to delegitimize the moral authority of the 'international community' and, in June, to step up its covert military support to the armed East Pakistani resistance group, the Mukti Bahini, with the

aim of putting further pressure on the Pakistani military regime to make concessions to the Awami League (Sisson and Rose 1990: 184).

The internationalist aspect of India's postcolonial identity was still important,
however, and this was evident in the leadership's attempt to garner support for
its position through the conclusion of a Treaty of Peace, Friendship and Cooperation with the Soviet Union. The Soviet Union had previously offered a friendship treaty to Nehru in 1956 and to his daughter in 1969 (Dutt 1956: 389,
Mansingh 1984: 140). The reasoning behind Nehru's rejection of the offer in
1956 was explained in a cable sent by the Foreign Secretary, Subimal Dutt to the
Indian Ambassador in Moscow:

> ...while there was no objection to such a treaty as it would actually repre-
> sent our present relations, there appeared to be no special need for it. Indeed,
> it might have some adverse reactions and create misunderstandings in some
> countries. India was anxious not only for friendship with the Soviet Union
> but also to help in removing barriers to peace and understanding in the
> world. Anything that might come in the way of India's role in this respect,
> would not be helpful.
>
> (Dutt 1956: 389)

In 1969 Indira Gandhi was more open to a friendship treaty due to the change in
the Soviet Union's approach to the subcontinent. In 1966, in a shift from its
policy of providing support to India only, the Soviet Union strengthened its economic aid to Pakistan and offered it military aid. In 1969, the Soviet Union indicated that ending its military aid to Pakistan depended on India engaging in
negotiations with the Soviet Union about a friendship treaty as a first step toward
Brezhnev's plan for an Asian collective security system. Concern about the
Indian public's receptivity to what could been seen as a major shift from the
policy of nonalignment, however, delayed the signing of the treaty until 1971
when, as the conventional argument goes, a deterrent was needed to ward off
Chinese or American threats to India in the advent of war against Pakistan
(Chandrasekhar Rao 1973). On the basis of interviews, however, Sisson and
Rose (1990: 198) conclude that the government did not in fact fear a Chinese or
American attack, because it had obtained correspondence between the Chinese
and Pakistani regimes stating that China would not support Pakistan militarily in
the advent of conflict with India. Indeed, the treaty was successfully concluded
on the basis of India's reassurance that it was not seeking a formal or secret
commitment of military assistance in the advent of Chinese intervention – an
indication that no such development was envisaged (Sisson and Rose 1990:
242). The China factor was apparently of such little concern to the Indian leadership that orders were given in July to transfer half of the six army divisions from
the north-eastern Sino-Indian border region to the East-Pakistani front (Sisson
and Rose 1990: 199). Given the US's ongoing military entanglement in the
Vietnam war and the nascent status of the US-China relationship, the Indian
leadership was also unconcerned about a US–China–Pakistan axis against India

or a US military intervention against India. Instead, Sisson and Rose (1990: 198–200) argue that the signing of the treaty in 1971 was driven more by the desire to finally put an end to Soviet military support to Pakistan – which was reflected in the addition of a new clause requiring both signatories to refrain from providing assistance to any third country that engages in conflict with either of the signatories – and, importantly, to 'bolster the morale of the Indian bureaucracy' which was flagging because of India's inability to attract international support for its cause'. In this way, it could be argued that the imperative of reiterating a particular aspect of its state identity, internationalism, was a key factor in India's decision to sign the friendship treaty with the Soviet Union.

Yet, the fact that the Indian leadership promoted the idea that the treaty was a response to threats from the United States, China and Pakistan is also significant. This argument helped to further delegitimize those internationalist actors that were most vocal in their opposition to India and to consolidate the construction of a crisis to which India had to respond with extraordinary measures. Indira Gandhi referred to an emerging China–US–Pakistan triangle in an interview in August 1971:

> International relations have entered an era of rapid change, the range and direction of which is not predicable. Nations are seeking new ties and are cutting across old rigidities. This is a welcome trend. But some countries are taking advantage of these changes to embark upon opportunistic adventures.
>
> (Gandhi 1972: 40)

In light of this, '[w]e are convinced that the present Treaty will discourage such adventurism on the part of countries which have shown a pathological hostility towards us' (Gandhi 1972: 40). More specifically, 'the Treaty will act as a deterrent against any rash adventurism on the part of Islamabad' (Gandhi 1972: 41).

The treaty, however, threatened another aspect of state identity, nonalignment, and because of this, India's approach was inherently contradictory. Although Indira Gandhi portrayed the treaty as a deterrent, Article Four specified the Soviet Union's respect for India's policy of non-alignment and the treaty avoids mentioning military cooperation, committing the parties only to 'mutual consultations' in the case of a threat or attack (Mansingh 1984: 388–9). Moreover, while presenting the treaty as a response to US and Chinese threats, the Indian leadership also insisted that it was a part of normal diplomatic practice rather than a novel development:

> We have not signed a defence pact with the Soviet Union, it is merely a Treaty of Friendship, Cooperation and Peace. We can have discussions with them but it is not a military treaty in any sense of the word ... whatever we now have got from them is all in the normal course, which we would have taken from any country, and which had been agreed to earlier. We certainly hope that should we be in trouble, not only the Soviet Union but other countries also will like to help us.
>
> (Gandhi 1972: 92–3)

In November, Indira Gandhi undertook a second tour of world capitals to seek support for India's position on the situation in East Pakistan after having decided that unless there was a major breakthrough in finding a political solution, India would seek a military solution (Sisson and Rose 1990: 210). Without the United States or the rest of the 'international community' willing to exert the pressure necessary for a political solution to occur, however, a breakthrough was always unlikely and by the end of the tour there were further discursive shifts. Firstly, Indira Gandhi (1972: 105) completed the delegitimization of the 'international community' by revoking its legitimacy as an arbiter of foundational meanings like sovereignty, intervention and 'the people', and installing India in its place: 'we cannot depend on the international community ... to solve our problems for us ... the brunt of the burden has to be borne by us and by the people of Bangla Desh...'. Secondly, Bangladesh's independence from Pakistan was now presented as inevitable and Indira Gandhi expressed her public support for the Mukti Bahini, which had proven that it had a mass following in East Pakistan and could fight the Pakistani military without heavy Indian support. She presented the Mukti Bahni and the Awami league as the legitimate bearers of sovereign authority in the Indian Parliament by acknowledging them as the rightful representatives of the East Pakistani people (Gandhi 1972: 120).

At the same time, it was important that India's self-image as a non-aggressive nation-state stayed intact. Hence, Indira Gandhi's (1972: 106) speeches reiterated India's 'self-restraint' and its 'urge for peace, freedom and justice'. India had 'kept quiet, patiently listening to the abuses hurled at us, and watching the growing threat to our security' she asserted, but '[i]f there is to be war, it is not we who have taken the initiative or threatened anyone' (Gandhi 1972: 113). The conflict was also an opportunity for a reiteration of the politics of Partition and the key narratives that underpinned India's postcolonial identity. Pakistan's civil war showed that: 'When the sub-continent of India was partitioned into India and Pakistan it was an unnatural partition. We knew it was bound to create problems, but we accepted it because it seemed to be the price for freedom.' (Gandhi 1972: 77). The world was now, however, 'realizing the truth of all that we had said not only about Pakistan but about our own country as well. Difference in religion, language, dress and ways of living are not important for national unity' (Gandhi 1972: 114).

The period between March and December prior to the advent of war on the subcontinent was crucial for the construction of the events in East Pakistan as a crisis. This process of crisis construction was social and cultural and invoked dominant discourses of India's postcolonial identity related to its moral authority to intervene on behalf of East Pakistanis such as, its commitment to human rights, the superiority of its model of nation-building and the fraternal nature of its relationships with its neighbours. The fragility and vulnerability of India's postcolonial modernity, the threat posed by unstable neighbours, the danger of reverting to a prior condition of backwardness and division and the chance to diminish the normative, ontological and military challenge posed by Pakistan were all also vital in enabling it to consider foreign policy actions that were counter to international norms as well as its own objections to the use of force in international politics. As we shall see in the next section, however, the threat this posed to the dominant rendering of India's postcolonial identity placed limitations on how India could proceed with its military intervention.

The intervention

On 3 December, Indira Gandhi (1972: 122–3) addressed a rally in Calcutta in which she explained what she saw as the fundamental difference between India and Pakistan: 'In India, the freedom fighters won elections and formed government. But in Pakistan, they remained behind prison walls, and power was usurped by those who had cooperated with the British rulers during the struggle for freedom' (Gandhi 1972: 122–3). Pakistan, the 'Bastard Son', was indulged by its irresponsible sponsors: 'When they committed aggression against us, no one told them that it was bad and that they should desist from it. This encouraged them to persist in their folly' (Gandhi 1972: 122–3). During the speech, she was handed a note with the news that Pakistan had launched an attack on Indian airfields. She ended the speech without publicly announcing the start of hostilities but is reported to have said privately to those with her, '[t]hank God they've attacked us' because, despite not wanting to be seen as the aggressor, she had apparently approved plans for a military assault on Dhaka for 4 December (Frank 2001: 338).

Indira Gandhi's official announcement proclaimed that, 'today the war in Bangla Desh has become a war on India' (Gandhi 1972: 128). The Mukti Bahini were a 'courageous band of freedom fighters' who 'have been staking their all in defence of the values for which we also have struggled, and which are basic to our way of life' (Gandhi 1972: 128). On 6 December, India granted official recognition to Bangladesh which, Indira Gandhi assured the Indian Parliament, was to be led by a government that had 'proclaimed their basic principles of State policy to be democracy, socialism, secularism' and which would 'follow a policy of non-alignment, peaceful co-existence and opposition to colonialism, racialism and imperialism...' (Gandhi 1972: 134).

While Indira Gandhi spoke of self-defence and the victory of India's model of postcolonial modernity, at the UN Samar, Sen responded to the debate, much of it critical of India, by citing Pakistan's 'refugee aggression' and 'military aggression' and also by invoking India's internationalist identity and positioning India as a rescuer:

> we shall not be a party to any solution that will mean continuation of the oppression of East Pakistani people ... So long as we have any light of civilized behaviour left in us, we shall protect them ... We are glad that we have, on this particular occasion, absolutely nothing but the purest of motives and the purest of intentions: to rescue the people of East Bengal from what they are suffering.

> (Sen 1971c: 429, 31)

In another speech on 6 December he argued:

> Now, several principles have been quoted by various Delegations: sover-
> eignty, territorial integrity, non-interference in other peoples' affairs and so
> on. But I wonder why we should be shy about speaking of Human Rights?
> What happened to all the other social rights and conventions which you
> have so solemnly accepted? Are we, therefore, to be selective in serving
> what is known as the motto of our era – peace, progress and justice? What
> happened to the justice part?
>
> (Sen 1971a: 483)

Sen (1971b: 497) further argued that had the UN recognized the root causes of
the conflict 'it would have been able to influence the development of the present
crisis, but the concept of domestic jurisdiction, non-interference in internal
matters and territorial integrity, was successfully advanced to inhibit this'. While
these 'concepts were of fundamental importance' it was not recognized that the
'savage repression applied by the Pakistan Army against the people of Bangla
Desh was of such magnitude, so genocidal, and so designed to annihilate a
people that is was beyond the scope of normal standard of reasoning and judgement'. As Wheeler argues, India did not formally invoke the principle of humanitarian intervention at the United Nations and it failed to attain legitimation for
its claim to be 'rescuing' the 'people of East Bengal' from the Security Council.
Nonetheless, Wheeler's (2000: 74) statement that 'after the attempt to present its
action as a 'rescue' had failed to secure any legitimacy from other members of
the Security Council, India never mentioned it again' is not entirely accurate for
while it may be true that Samar Sen tempered his assertions of India's 'purest
motives', humanitarian rescue and the need to uphold human rights norms continued to find expression in the speeches of Indian leaders[3] who were determined
to reiterate India's claims to an ethical modernity while it undertook military
action. Indira Gandhi's speech to a public rally on 12 December, for instance,
did not primarily invoke 'national security' to justify India's military engagement but rather cited the impossibility of India, a 'great civilization' with a
history of having experienced oppression, standing by 'as a mere onlooker when
lakhs [hundreds of thousands] of people were being butchered in a neighbouring
country … (Gandhi 1972: 138). 'We are fighting not only for India' she said 'not
only for our own principles, but for all those who have been suppressed for centuries' (Gandhi 1972: 138).

India's humanitarian discourse also, however, limited the extent of its military action. Both Pakistan and the United States were convinced that India
intended to continue its military operations in East Pakistan into the Western
sector. At the Security Council, Pakistan's Representative to the UN, Agha
Shahi (1971: 420) cited K. Subrahmanyam's writings as proof of India's aggressive intentions and according to Henry Kissinger: '[t]hey're going to move their
forces from East Pakistan to the west. They will then smash the Pakistan land
forces and air forces, annex the part of Kashmir that is in Pakistan and then call

it off' (1971d). This assessment led the Nixon administration to encourage China to undertake a military build-up along the India–China border and to send a detachment of the US Seventh Fleet to the Bay of Bengal because as Nixon put it, '[t]he Indians have got to get a little scared' (1971d). This was a high-risk geopolitical strategy, given the possible Russian reaction, as Kissinger realized when he cautioned Nixon: 'Mr President, if our bluff is called, we'll be in trouble' (1971d). China, however, had no intention of becoming militarily embroiled in a conflict on the subcontinent – something that India was well-aware of – and since, as Nixon noted, 'we can't do this without the Chinese helping us', US attempts to intimidate India achieved little (Sisson and Rose 1990: 216, 305 f.n. 21; 1971d). Sisson and Rose's interviews with Indian officials in the Defence Ministry and in Indira Gandhi's inner circle at the time reveal that the Indian leadership were not concerned that the US fleet would intervene in the conflict or that it would cause India any problems in that sector of the Indian Ocean and instead viewed the dispatch as a symbolic move (Sisson and Rose 1990: 217).

If Pakistani and American officials were convinced that India would extend its military action, then some Indian analysts still question why it did not do so. J.N. Dixit, (2004: 134), for instance, has asked '[w]hy did India not continue the military operations to recapture the whole of Jammu and Kashmir and to destroy the military power structure of Pakistan completely?' (Dixit 2004: 134). Indeed, if the primary motivation for its military intervention in East Pakistan was security-seeking and was aimed at diminishing Pakistan's capacity to exert pressure on Kashmir, then a serious consideration of extending its military action into the Western sector would be expected. Yet, although the issue was raised by the Defence Minister Jagjivan Ram on 4 December in a meeting of the Political Action Committee, Indira Gandhi and her key advisors had already made the decision to undertake limited strikes in West Pakistan. These were aimed at reclaiming small sections of the Kashmir cease-fire line that had been won in the 1965 war but relinquished in the Tashkent Agreement, and at deterring Pakistani action in Kashmir, Punjab and Rajasthan (Sisson and Rose 1990: 215). Why this decision was been made is not clear without access to archival material.[4] However, if we accept that there was more at stake in the 1971 war for India than security, and that issues of identity were key, then it is highly unlikely that India would launch a war of outright aggression which would so dramatically challenge its self-identity.

The aftermath

Following a military campaign that involved the enforcement of air superiority to prevent combat in the western sector, a naval blockade in both the West and East which was capable of stopping Pakistani reinforcements in East Pakistan, the bombing of the Karachi port to prevent the departure of Pakistani ships and the provision of military support to the Mukti Bahini where necessary, Indira Gandhi announced the unconditional surrender of West Pakistan forces on 16

December (Gandhi 1972: 152–3; Mansingh 1984: 224–5). The next day she declared that India wanted to fashion its relations with the people of Pakistan on the basis of friendship and understanding and that it was 'this sincere desire which prompted us last evening to instruct our Army, Navy and Air Force to cease operations from 20.00 hours today on all fronts in the West' (Gandhi, 1972: 152–3).

In international relations, intervention is defined as the violation of one state's sovereignty by an uninvited intruder. As Cynthia Weber (1999: 94) argues, it is considered rape on an international scale. Indeed, the 'rape of an ally' is exactly how Henry Kissinger referred to India's actions in his conversations with Richard Nixon, while Pakistan's decision to declare war was apparently 'influenced by the caustic advocacy of [Pakistani Foreign Minister] Bhutto who in a meeting with Yahya at the end of November reportedly described in rather graphic and primitive detail what Mrs. Gandhi was doing to the military leaders of Pakistan' (1971d; Sisson and Rose 1990: 230). Yet by limiting its actions to gaining control of East Pakistan and preventing further Pakistani penetration into its territory, India's intervention was not a conventional one, for it utilized a defensive employment of the strategies of encirclement and entrapment, which Weber (1998: 99) argues 'are the modalities of female rape of a male' and which carry with them the threat of symbolic castration. The declaration of a ceasefire in the Western sector, however, meant that the threat of 'symbolic castration' remained incomplete and India avoided a hypermasculine subjectivity by re-gendering itself as feminine. Yet the feminine gendering of India – the Bharat Mata of the Nehru era – and the relationship between ethics and foreign policy that this represents, was altered by India's resort to force, as an interviewer's comments to Indira Gandhi following the ceasefire indicates: '...a brilliant victory has been scored by India over Pakistan and you are being hailed as Empress of India, Bharat Mata and Durga...' (Gandhi 1972: 166). The war produced the melding of Indira Gandhi with Bharat Mata and her incarnation into an aggressive symbol of female energy, Durga, which infused Indian foreign policy with a willingness to use covert and overt force that had not been seen before.

In the wake of the war, India and Bangladesh signed a Treaty of Friendship, Co-operation and Peace which endorsed non-alignment, peaceful co-existence and mutual consultations in the event of a threat or attack on either party. The Treaty officially brought Bangladesh into the ambit of a politics of friendship that, as with other countries in South Asia tended to border on fraternity. According to Indira Gandhi's (1975b: 622) parliamentary statement, the Treaty '...solemnizes the close ties of friendship between our two countries and peoples cemented through blood and sacrifice'.

Negotiations toward a settlement with Pakistan began in April 1972, after Zulfikar Ali Bhutto had secured his position as President of Pakistan, and culminated in the Simla Agreement on 2 July. Like the Tashkent Declaration, the Simla Agreement endorsed the principles of peaceful coexistence and, hence, again sought to reiterate the superiority of India's postcolonial modernity. However, unlike the Tashkent Declaration there was no reference to the 1948

UN mediated cease-fire line. Instead, the cease-fire line resulting from the 1971 war, which was more favourable to India, was recognized as the new line of control. The Simla Agreement, moreover, endorsed India's desire to deal with the conflict with Pakistan on a bilateral basis and excluded UN involvement in maintaining peace along the Line of Control (LoC) (Mansingh 1984: 229). Aside from this, however, India's position during the negotiations was conciliatory – something that was quite contrary to predictions. For instance, a memorandum written by members of the National Security Council and sent to Henry Kissinger in 1972 prior to the Simla talks claimed that,

> Mrs Gandhi clearly wants to exploit Pakistan's crushing defeat to resolve problems far beyond those directly connected with the fighting – agreement on a Western frontier, settlement of the Kashmir dispute in India's favour, ending the arms race … even if peace talks begin soon, the road to settlement will be long and arduous and Mrs Gandhi will not be inclined to magnanimity.

> (Saunders and Hoskinson 1972: 2)

Yet, India did not demand to keep the territory gained in the western sector, failed to seek monetary compensation for the care of refugees and refused to take advantage of Pakistan's internal political woes to reinforce India's bargaining position (Mansingh 1984: 633). Such was the sensitivity to being labelled an occupying force that even the request from Bangladesh's new leader Sheikh Mujibur Rehman for Indian troops to remain in the country for six to eight months after the ceasefire was turned down and Indira Gandhi (1975b: 628–35) used interviews to downplay India's military and political pre-eminence in the region (Dixit 2004: 135). This 'soft approach', according to P.N. Dhar (2000: 205) was intended to dispel any fears on the part of India's other neighbours, in particular Nepal and Sri Lanka, of 'the emergence of Indian hegemony'.

Yet, India's inability to garner support at the UN – where a General Assembly vote on 7 December on a resolution calling for an immediate cease-fire resulted in 104 votes in favour and only 11 against (Marwah 1979: 578) – in addition to its treaty with the Soviet Union and the support given to Pakistan by the United States, all posed fundamental challenges to the dominant construction of India's self-identity, based as it was on concepts such as internationalism and non-alignment. It was a challenge India approached head on, before, during and after the war by drawing on the marginalized 'justice part' of the UN Charter, by continuing to reiterate its adherence to nonalignment and attempting, and sometimes succeeding, in controlling the narrative in the international media (Sisson and Rose 1990: 217). Anthony Lewis of the *New York Times* wrote, for instance, that,

> correspondents who have dealt with the leading Indian Generals have found them a sober group, with an understanding and even sympathy for

the Pakistanis and no desire to crush their country. Very few armies have fought a war under such difficult emotional circumstances with so much control.

(1971a: 596)

Yet, many journalists also consistently interpreted the war as producing a change in the balance of power on the subcontinent that made India the regional hegemon. Indian officials were also taken aback by the US's labelling of the war as one of 'aggression', and the unusually fast and one-sided nature of the vote against India at the UN (1971b). In response, the government sought to delegiti-mize the support given to Pakistan by raising an older anti-colonial narrative of 'divide and rule': '[j]ust as in the earlier days when the colonial power had used religious sentiments to blunt the nationalist drive in India, some powers sought to use Pakistan to offset India' (Gandhi 1975a: 207–8). While a confidential memorandum to Kissinger reveals that there was some understanding within the US government that the Indo-Soviet treaty did not amount to an alliance, despite India's efforts to argue this point, the Indo-Soviet treaty was, in general, treated as heralding an Indian tilt toward the Soviet Union (Saunders and Hoskinson 1972: 4).

On the other hand, India's humanitarian discourse, its military restraint and magnanimity following the war reiterated key narratives that underpinned its self-identity. The use of force against Pakistan and the covert aid to Mukti Bahini meant that the war did imply a significant shift in India's dealings with its neighbours but to argue, as Sankaran Krishna (1999: 22, 107) does, that 1971 was a 'critical rupture' which turned India's self-construction from a pacifist nation to regional hegemon as 'the rightful legatee of the Raj's role as the strategic centre of South Asia', is overstating matters. As the Hindu nation-alist politician Jaswant Singh (1999: 184) notes, despite achieving a significant military victory in 1971, it was '[m]any years after the event [that] the Indian Defence Ministry, almost as an afterthought, has lately begun to observe 16 December as 'Vijay Divas' (Victory Day)'. As I have sought to argue, India's self-identity has been anchored in narratives that generated a desire to prove that postcolonial Indians were, not simply on par with, but *better* than their former colonial masters, in particular, because India's postcolonial modernity is marked by a rejection of domination and aggression. Thus, the government's discourse in the aftermath of the war consistently side-lined India's military victory for the humanitarian and moral victories that resulted from, as Indira Gandhi put it, having 'spoken up not just for the people of Bangladesh, not just for the cause of India but against oppression of people all over the world' (Gandhi 1975b: 775). She was insistent, moreover, that military victory had not changed India's fundamental character: 'we are not tied to the traditional concepts of a foreign policy designed to safe-guard overseas possessions, investments and the carving out of spheres of influence and the erection of *cordons sanitaires*. We are not interested in exporting ideologies' (Gandhi 1975a: 206).

The 'peaceful nuclear explosion' and beyond: nuclear policy from 1965 to 1998

In 1972, Indira Gandhi was asked by an interviewer whether, since Pakistan had been supported by two nuclear powers, the US and China, this meant that India was reviewing its nuclear policies and planned to produce a nuclear deterrent (Gandhi 1972: 173). Although she replied to this question in the negative, her decision to conduct a 'peaceful nuclear explosion' (PNE) two years later, suggests that there had indeed been a shift. This shift did not, however, come about as a result of the 1971 war, during which, as we have seen, concerns about the US and China were not a high priority. Rather, the change in nuclear policy began in 1968 when India refused to sign the Nuclear Non-Proliferation Treaty (NPT).

The discourse of non-proliferation

A common explanation for India's rejection of the NPT comes from the perspective of structural realism. Baldev Raj Nayar and T.V. Paul (2004: 77) argue for instance, that the 'Indian opposition to the NPT regime has always been couched in normative goals ... However, the fundamental, though unstated, reason has been structural'. The 'real' reason that India did not sign the NPT, according these authors, was because the treaty 'did nothing to allay India's security concerns vis-a-vis China, and later, Pakistan' and because 'by subscribing to this treaty, India would have perpetually forfeited its claim to major-power status' (Nayar and Paul 2004: 77). Yet, the authors do cite any archival evidence to support their claims that their interpretation reflects the 'real' intentions of India's policy-makers and they fail to explain why India has been so reluctant to make known these 'real' concerns, instead choosing to cite normative objections. Hence, the authors overlook the opportunity to analyse the role of something tangible – political discourse – in the making of foreign policy for, even if archival evidence did support structural realist explanations, the very fact that India chose legitimating reasons that were normative rather than power- or security-focused gives us an important insight into the constraints and enabling factors that drive foreign policy. In other words, India's decision not to support the NPT was the product of the construction of a particular social world and within this world, the discourse of non-proliferation has long been treated with suspicion, not because it posed a threat to India's physical security, but because it undermined India's self-identity as a postcolonial nation-state pursuing an ethical modernity that could only flourish within an international order which was not unequal and discriminatory.

As we saw in Chapter 2, despite his commitment to disarmament, Nehru expressed anxiety that the restriction of nuclear technology could reinforce global hierarchies and endanger India's future. The discourse of non-proliferation came to dominate the issue of nuclear technology after 1964 – the year that China conducted its first nuclear test. Coming just two years after the India–China war,

China's nuclear tests generated enough anxiety in India to spark a debate over whether India should seek out a nuclear umbrella or develop nuclear weapons of its own. The secretary of the Congress Party, K.C. Pant, urged the government in 1966 to follow China and give up its policy of 'nuclear celibacy' (Mirchandani 1968: 48). Such a move would be in keeping with realist precepts which suggest that China's nuclearization would heighten India's insecurity and lead it to seek out nuclear protection either from an ally or from a nuclear weapons program of its own. There is evidence that Nehru's successor as Prime Minister, Lal Bahadur Shastri, secretly broached the idea of seeking nuclear protection from the United States (Abraham 1998: 125). He had little support for this from members of his government, however, and ultimately stuck to the original disarmament script, stating that India 'will try to eliminate the threat and terror of nuclear weapons rather than enter into competition with other countries to make or produce atom bombs here' (Noorani 1967; Quoted in Mirchandani 1968: 29). At the end of 1964, India submitted a memorandum to the UN proposing 'A Treaty To Prevent the Proliferation of Nuclear Weapons' which included steps to curb the spread of nuclear weapons and binding commitments toward nuclear disarmament (India 1988a: 26–32). As a study conducted by Ashis Nandy revealed, this position had broad support among the 'strategic elite' – political leaders, their political opponents, government scientists, opinion leaders, academics and analysts specializing in international relations, strategic studies and military affairs. Nandy (1974: 967) found that between 1969 and 1970, 58 per cent of these elite were against India developing a nuclear bomb while 38 per cent were in favour.

The same study found an overwhelming rejection by the strategic elite of the NPT, not because of the threats posed by China or Pakistan, but due to the unequal nature of the treaty, its inability to prevent the vertical proliferation of nuclear weapons and its potential to limit research into atomic energy (Nandy 1974: 967). There was no correlation, the study found, between the view that China and Pakistan were immediate threats to India, which was a widespread opinion, and the view that India needed nuclear weapons to protect itself (Nandy 1974: 969). Nor was there a correlation between those who were pessimistic about India's future and a desire for nuclear weapons. This indicates that Nayar and Paul's assumption that Indian elites in the 1960s and 1970s made a clear connection between nuclear weapons and security is not necessarily correct (Nandy 1974: 970).

The focus on inequality and hierarchy among the respondents in Nandy's study is reflective of the fact that from its beginnings, the discourse of nuclear non-proliferation was expressed in ways that were perceived to perpetuate a racially hierarchical global order. Two days after China's test, the President of the United States, Lyndon Johnson, declared that '[n]uclear spread is dangerous to all mankind' and, four months later, Vice-President Humphrey voiced his opinion that a more pressing issue than curtailing the nuclear arms race with the Soviet Union was 'the prevention of further proliferation of nuclear weapons in Asia' because the presence of nuclear weapons in Asia would result in major political and economic instability (Quoted in Mirchandani 1968: 115). Humphrey's patronizing suggestion that Asia was less-equipped to deal with advanced weaponry reinstated a colonial world order in which some continued to remain the objects rather than the subjects of history. Needless to say such a colonizing act was not well received in India. As Mirchandani (1968: 121) in his contemporary account of this debate put it, '...talk of non-proliferation to non-nuclear powers comes with ill-grace from nuclear powers who themselves continue feverishly to proliferate weapons of mass destruction'. India's official response to the Western discourse of non-proliferation emerged in the negotiations for an NPT which began in 1967.

The NPT committed signatories to 'seek to achieve the discontinuance of all test explosions of nuclear weapons for all time and to continue negotiations to this end'. Further, it aimed to:

> facilitate the cessation of the manufacture of nuclear weapons, the liquidation of all their existing stockpiles, and the elimination from national arsenals of nuclear weapons and the means of their delivery pursuant to a Treaty on general and complete disarmament under strict and effective international control.
>
> (1968)

India refused to sign the treaty on the basis that it failed to seek a binding commitment from the five declared nuclear powers to complete disarmament, did not contain a clear ban on the use of nuclear weapons and lacked a specific clause for negotiations on a comprehensive test ban. Although the NPT permitted countries to develop nuclear energy and to seek help to do so, India's representative to the UN, V.C. Trivedi argued at the 1967 Eighteen Nation Disarmament Commission that the treaty simply legitimized the vertical proliferation of the five declared nuclear powers while insisting on the 'renunciation of the sovereign right of unrestricted development of energy by some countries only' (Trivedi 1967: 234). This was unacceptable to Trivedi, who declared that the 'civil nuclear Powers can tolerate a nuclear weapon apartheid but not an atomic apartheid in their economic and peaceful development' (Trivedi 1967: 234). Following Nehru, he went on to say that '[i]t is completely wrong to deduce that what is evil is science and technology, skill and progress' and although the

> Indian delegation does not deny that the technology involved in the production of a nuclear weapon is the same as the technology which produces a peaceful nuclear device ... That does not mean, therefore that only the poor and developing nations should be denied all technology for fear they may use it for military purposes.
>
> (Trivedi 1967: 234)

Azim Hussain, a member of the Indian delegation to the UN, reiterated this discourse linking racial discrimination and development when he raised the spectre of neo-colonialism in a statement on non-proliferation in May 1968:

the proposed treaty creates a juridical discrimination between States according to whether they possess nuclear weapons or not, regardless of the fact
that it is unwise to divide the world into a few 'haves' and a lot of 'have-
nots', who would become dependent on the goodwill of the 'haves' in
regard to development in the vital area of nuclear energy, thereby making
them subject to pressures.

(Husain 1968: 332)

Indira Gandhi's statement on the matter also highlighted the issue of discrimination and tapped into fears of a continuing colonial global order: '[w]e shall continue our efforts for nuclear disarmament because it is only through nuclear
disarmament that discrimination would be eliminated and equality between
nations re-established' (India 1988b: 177). For Gandhi, resistance to the NPT
was framed along the lines of anti-colonialism. Resisting the NPT thus meant
producing a unified, independent and resurgent India:

not signing the treaty may bring the nation many difficulties. It may mean
the stoppage of aid and the stoppage of help. Since we are taking this
decision together, we must all be together in facing its consequences. I personally think that although it may involve sacrifice and hardship, it will be
the first step towards building the real strength of this country and we will
be able to go ahead on the road to self-sufficiency.

(India 1988b: 178)

The addition of the language of nuclear apartheid reveals India's disarmament
discourse as a split discourse signifying the desire for both sameness and difference. Ostensibly it is an assertion of resistance against the continued dominance
of the colonial impulse and its attendant politics of racial hierarchy. Yet, India's
quest for nuclear energy is the outcome of its acceptance of a model of techno-
scientific development derived from the very Western frameworks India purports
to be resisting.

The 'peaceful nuclear explosion'

During the negotiations for an NPT it emerged that India would be staunchly
opposed to a treaty that banned 'peaceful' nuclear explosions (PNEs) for nuclear
energy programs despite having signed the Partial Test Ban Treaty (PTBT) in
1963. The PTBT prohibited all types of nuclear testing except underground
testing and thus, like the NPT, was aimed more at stopping the emergence of
new nuclear powers rather than preventing vertical proliferation. Nonetheless,
Nehru viewed the signing of the PTBT in the context of his belief that it was
possible to work toward disarmament and internationalism through incremental
normative change. 'A partial agreement', he argued, 'does not rule out a comprehensive agreement; it is a step towards that; it produces an atmosphere of
confidence to go further' (quoted in Narlikar 2006).

There is little separating PNEs from their military counterparts other than the question of intent but given that both the US and the Soviet Union had extensive PNE programs, they had long enjoyed a degree of international legitimacy. It was on this basis that Lal Bahadur Shastri first sanctioned work toward a PNE program and, on 18 May 1974, India conducted its first nuclear test at Pokhran in the Rajasthan desert. Yet, what might have been construed as a major shift in Indian foreign policy was not even acknowledged as an act of foreign policy. The statement announcing the explosion was released by the Atomic Energy Commission (AEC) and emphasized that the test had been undertaken for reasons of technological development, particularly in the area of mining and earth moving operations, and reiterated that India had no intention of producing nuclear weapons and remained strongly opposed to military uses of nuclear explosions (India 1974: 146). Official government statements were not provided until three days after the event on 21 May. Echoing the AEC statement, India's Minister for External Affairs called the test an experiment that was 'an important landmark in the development of nuclear technology for peaceful and economic uses' and maintained that India had 'no intention of developing nuclear weapons' (Singh 1974: 147). Indira Gandhi's statement emphasized that 'India is not a 'nuclear weapons' country, as we do not have any bombs and we do not intend to use nuclear knowledge or nuclear power for any other than peaceful purposes' (1974f: 7). Countering claims of economic profligacy and highlighting the indigenously-produced nature of the technology used in the test, Gandhi emphasized that the test had been conducted with '[n]o new budgetary provision ... there was no foreign exchange expenditure and no dependence on any other country' (1974f: 7).

As the negative international reaction grew – Japan, Canada, Sweden, the United States all released statements to the Conference of the Committee on Disarmament (CCD) indicating that they considered India's nuclear test to be contradictory to efforts to hinder nuclear weapons proliferation – the Indian political leadership made more statements insisting on the peaceful nature of the nuclear explosion (1974d: 150–5). On 23 March India's representative to the CCD, B.C. Mishra said that since the Indian government had made clear that the nuclear explosion was carried out for peaceful purposes 'we do not understand how we are accused of contributing to the proliferation of nuclear weapons' because

[a]s the whole world knows, India has been in a position to manufacture nuclear weapons, if it so desired for several years now. It is out of a sense of responsibility and commitment to a principle that the Government has consistently maintained a policy of not using nuclear technology for weapons purposes.

(Mishra 1974: 171–2)

An official government press note issued on 24 May repeatedly stressed that the nuclear test was a triumph of Indian science for peaceful purposes. Not only was it a 'hundred per cent Indian effort' but it marked the first time in history that a country had tested its first nuclear device underground (1974e: 8).

As for the timing of the test, the Indian political leadership left this unexplained and there still remains no archival evidence that may be drawn on to account for this. India's technical ability to conduct a nuclear explosion prior to 1974 is not in doubt. In a speech in London in 1964 Homi Bhabha, the founder of the Indian nuclear program, declared that India had the capacity to carry out a nuclear explosion within eighteen months of a decision to do so (Ramana 2003: 225). Various scholars have speculated that the test was an attempt to divert attention away from mounting domestic problems and the US government also held this view (Ganguly 1999: 160; 1974a). The test was conducted at a time when a nation-wide railway strike was reaching its pinnacle and inflation was increasing by as much as 20 per cent following the global oil price rise in 1973 and the shortage of wheat due to the failure of the monsoons. Yet, this overlooks the fact that the decision to undertake preparations for the test had been made three years prior at the peak of Indira Gandhi's popularity after her sweeping electoral victory and India's defeat of Pakistan in the Bangladesh war (Nandy 1974: 966). Moreover, signs that Pakistan was attempting to procure the means to produce nuclear weapons only became evident after 1974 in reaction to India's nuclear test (Perkovich 1999: 192).

This suggests that the test should be seen in a broader context – as an attempt to enact India's postcolonial identity – rather than as an opportunistic decision based on domestic political expediency. According to Raja Ramanna, who was one of the scientists involved in the test, despite facing opposition from some of her advisors up to the last moment, 'Mrs Gandhi decreed that the experiment should be carried out on schedule for the simple reason that India required such a demonstration' (Ramanna 1991: 89). The military leadership was notably absent from the select group of men privy to the test, which consisted wholly of scientific and political advisors. This was clearly meant to be demonstration of India's techno-scientific ability rather than its military might. Yet, it is significant that Indira Gandhi made her first comments several days after the tests, and not in an announcement to the nation but in an interview with an American newsmagazine. This indicates that while the political leadership initially intended the test as a self-explanatory demonstration of Indian science, the adverse international reaction, which linked the explosion to military ends, meant that it instead marked a critical foreign policy moment in which India's self-representation as a distinctly different, modern postcolonial state was in danger of failing. In the belated pronouncements of the Indian political leadership we see the Indian state confronting the impossibility of enacting its postcolonial difference and, therefore, insisting on its postcolonial subjectivity all the more.

Conclusion

This chapter has sought to understand the continuities and changes in India's foreign policy/postcolonial identity in the late 1960s and early 1970s by focusing on a moment of 'crisis', India's 1971 military intervention, and by examining the developments in its nuclear policy. I have argued that the legitimating reasons given by India to justify its military intervention in 1971, its humanitarian concerns for East Pakistanis and the threat posed to India by 'refugee aggression', should not be dismissed, given the co-constitutive nature of foreign policy discourse, identity and interests. Both of India's legitimating reasons drew on representations which are the product of a particular postcolonial social imaginary and formed the basis of the dominant conception of India's postcolonial identity. Pakistan posed a challenge to India's postcolonial Self, not primarily because it threatened India's physical security, but because it chose a path to modernity that rejected secularism, democracy and nonalignment. India's humanitarian discourse, which was a consistent feature of India's response to the East Pakistan situation, reiterated this representation of Pakistan and, in the process, affirmed India's self-identity as grounded in an ethical modernity. India's second legitimating reason, 'refugee aggression' was not just raised at the UN after the war had begun as a 'self-defence' justification, but was an integral part of India's response to the events in East Pakistan from as early as April. This discourse focused on the threat posed by refugees to India's unity and communal harmony rather than the financial costs of the refugee influx and it was given meaning in the Indian context because it resonated with the narratives of backwardness and exceptionalism, such as India's political and social fragility and its tradition of tolerance, that inform India's postcolonial social imaginary. While India's postcolonial imaginary made possible its military intervention, it also placed limits on its military actions for there is little evidence that, despite the potential territorial and 'strategic' gains, the Indian leadership ever contemplated a more extensive military assault against Pakistan.

While India's foreign policy discourse in 1971 reproduced certain facets of its self-identity, its actions also undermined this identity, particularly because its arguments were so poorly received internationally. The US's objections were ameliorated by representing it as a neo-colonial Other but the lack of support for India at the UN posed a more serious identity threat given that institution's position in Nehru's vision for an ethical modernity. The friendship treaty concluded with the Soviet Union was an attempt to mitigate India's international isolation. Yet, the danger of diluting its claims to nonalignment meant that India attempted to portray the treaty both as a defensive move against threats from the US and China and as a normal part of diplomatic practice. Above all, in order to reproduce India's postcolonial identity it was necessary to present its actions as both humanitarian and defensive. Controlling the signification of its actions, however, proved highly problematic particularly because of the antagonistic international climate created by the Cold War and since humanitarian intervention lacked international legitimacy. Whatever the intentions of the political leadership moreover, the use of military force empowered those in the Indian community who favoured a more militaristic foreign policy. Thus, at the end of the conflict, the universalist internationalism that underpinned Nehru's politics of friendship had certainly been eroded, if not altogether abandoned. The reproduction of identity in this case led to a shift in the social landscape in favour of competing discourses.

This chapter has also examined the development of India's nuclear policy, beginning with the rejection of the NPT in 1968 which brought to the fore the tensions in India's postcolonial imaginary between the desire for an ethical modernity that promoted disarmament and non-proliferation and the need to resist the perpetuation of neo-colonial hierarchies at the global level. Nehru resolved this tension in favour of the former by signing the Partial Test Ban Treaty, but his departure from the Indian leadership, the challenges to the legitimacy of his ethical project after the 1962 war, the rise of a (small) pro-bomb lobby following China's nuclear test and the emergence of a discourse of non-proliferation which was perceived to be hypocritical and patronizing meant that the impetus to put aside concerns about 'nuclear apartheid' in the interests of eventual disarmament had diminished. India's 'peaceful nuclear explosion', I have argued, was supposed to be a communication of its techno-scientific achievements; however, it garnered the unintended consequence of widespread international condemnation which challenged India's self-understanding as a state pursuing an ethical modernity and, as we shall see in Chapter 7, played a role in discouraging future governments to conduct further nuclear tests. The next chapter further explores how successive Indian governments grappled with the ambivalent politics of postcolonial identity by addressing its relations with the countries of South Asia during the mid-1970s to the late-1990s and, in particular, examining another significant political and military intervention, this time in Sri Lanka's civil war.

6 India in South Asia

Danger, desire, friendship and fraternity

India's political and military intervention in Sri Lanka in the 1980s resulted in its longest-running and most expensive war, lasting 32 months, from October 1987 to March 1990 with the loss of 1,155 soldiers and at an estimated cost of Rs. 5 crores (Rs. 50 million) a day (Gunaratna 1993: 315). As we saw in Chapter 3, India and Sri Lanka had a difficult relationship in the immediate post-independence period. Nehru's attempts to build a relationship grounded in friendship were undermined because, as he saw it, the Sri Lankan leadership and its people were not 'conditioned' by the same anti-colonial solidarity that cemented India's relationships with its other neighbours. Nonetheless, friendship and fraternity continued to be the basis of India's foreign policy discourse on Sri Lanka. Indira Gandhi (1971c: 397), for instance, described Sri Lanka as 'a respected sister nation' and by the 1970s India–Sri Lanka relations were mostly conciliatory. The contentious issue of the repatriation of people of Indian origin in Sri Lanka had been resolved in 1964 and during the 1970s India moved to resolve the boundary dispute in the Palk Strait and gave up its claim to the island of Kachchativu. Even as Sri Lanka's civil conflict escalated during the 1970s India was careful not to interfere with Sri Lanka's internal politics. Why then, did India make involvement in Sri Lanka's civil conflict such an imperative in the 1980s?

This chapter argues that understanding how it became possible for India to undertake such a substantial diplomatic and military intervention in Sri Lanka in the 1980s requires an understanding of India's perceptions of the South Asian region in general and this, in turn, depends on understanding the domestic and international political contexts and their impact on India's state identity.

The 1980s was the period in which the term 'South Asia', which is usually taken to refer to India, Pakistan, Sri Lanka, Nepal, Bangladesh, Bhutan, and the Maldives, gained meaning and popularity, long after the terms 'South-east Asia', 'West Asia' and 'Central Asia' became commonplace. 'South Asia' may indeed be 'an acultural, emotionally empty, territorial concept', as Nandy (2005: 542) puts it, but the very act of defining certain geographical areas as regions works to normalize a particular view of the world. As O Tuathail and Agnew (1992: 194) argue, '[t]o designate a place is not simply to define a location or setting. It is to open up a field of possible taxonomies and trigger a series of narratives, subjects and appropriate foreign-policy responses'. In the case of 'South Asia', the designation of the region brought discourses of fraternity and India's benign civilizational influence, which were insipient during the Nehru era, to the fore. The rendering of 'South Asia' as an arena of particular foreign policy concern, was shaped by a number of important changes and challenges in India's domestic politics, including, Indira Gandhi's growing authoritarianism and the rise to power of her son, Rajiv. Both Indira and Rajiv Gandhi made Sri Lanka a foreign policy priority and chose policy actions that proved imprudent and destructive.

The chapter begins by critiquing the claim that India's policies toward Sri Lanka were the product of an Indian version of the Monroe Doctrine, which has been a common approach to explaining India's policies toward South Asia in the 1980s. I then go on to argue that identity and representation are key to understanding India's behaviour toward its neighbours and, after making some general observations about representations of South Asia in India's foreign policy, I examine the specific issue of India's intervention in Sri Lanka. Finally, I assess the post-intervention phase of foreign policy in the 1990s which gave rise to the 'Gujral doctrine'.

An Indian Monroe doctrine?

In the decades after achieving independence from Britain, successive Sri Lankan governments adopted a variety of discriminatory policies against the Tamil minority including, the use of the language of the Sinhalese majority, Sinhala, as the sole official state language, discriminatory education and employment policies, the abolition of a Constitutional clause protecting minority rights and the instatement of Buddhism as the state religion. From 1977 relations between the Tamil and Sinhalese communities rapidly deteriorated and, following anti-Tamil riots in 1977 and 1981, the Tamil opposition, which had thus far been dominated by the middle-class professional leaders of the Sri Lankan Tamil United Liberation Front (TULF), grew increasingly militant. Emergent groups like the Liberation Tigers of Tamil Eelam (LTTE) and the Eelam Peoples Revolutionary Liberation Front (EPRLF) were led by militant, educated youth who had withstood the worst of the government's discriminatory policies.

One of the legitimating reasons offered for India's intervention centred on the threat posed by the agitation of Sri Lanka's Tamil population to India's large Tamil-speaking population in the state of Tamil Nadu. According to J.N. Dixit (1998: 14), India's High Commissioner to Sri Lanka from 1985 to 1989, Indira Gandhi became 'concerned about Sri Lanka's attitudes and policies' because:

> Sri Lanka's geographical location so near India, and the deep socio-cultural link between Sri Lankan Tamils and Indian Tamils ... compelled India to perceive critical developments in Sri Lanka not purely as the internal affair of a neighbour but as an issue which could affect India's own unity and territorial integrity if India did not respect the sentiments of its own Tamil citizens.
>
> (Dixit 1998: 17)

As Sankaran Krishna (1999: Ch. 3) has argued, however, the idea of an essentialist commonality of Tamil ethnicity between India and Sri Lanka and the notion that ethnic nationalisms are prone toward secessionism are both deeply problematic assumptions given the rather different trajectories taken by Tamil identity in Tamil Nadu and Sri Lanka. Whereas Tamil 'Dravidian' nationalism took shape in the context of campaigns against Brahmanism and Casteism during the colonial era and developed into a potentially secessionist movement in the 1930s, it had lost much of its secessionist character by the early 1960s due to moves by the centre toward greater federal accommodation. In contrast, the Tamil community in Sri Lanka did not focus on their 'Dravidian' Indian roots and, indeed, emphasized their distinctness from Indian Tamils. Anti-Brahmanism and anti-Casteism were not a focus in the Sri Lankan context and post-independence Sri Lanka was dominated by the Westernized Tamil-Sinhala elite which only fragmented in the late 1940s and 1950s when the mobilization of a Sinhala ethnic identity became a political norm.

The claim that Indira Gandhi's government was forced into an intervention because of the threat of a pan-Tamil nationalism to the Indian state is also belied by the reactions of previous governments to the same situation. In 1972, members of the TULF were unsuccessful in their attempts to gain help from the Indian government and Tamil political parties in Tamil Nadu to resolve their problems with the Sri Lankan Government (Krishna 1999: 97). Far from expressing solidarity with their ethnic brethren, on several occasions during the 1970s, the Tamil Nadu government arrested and deported Sri Lankan Tamil militants and, even when anti-Tamil riots escalated in 1977, there were little more than mild protests in Tamil Nadu (Krishna 1999: 94). Moreover, even though the Tamil political movement in Sri Lanka was turning into a secessionist movement led by militant youth, according to Thomas Abraham Sr., India's then-High Commissioner to Sri Lanka, the Janata Prime Minister Moraji Desai was 'not really concerned about the Tamil problem there because, from his point of view, it was not central to the security and well-being of the Indian Republic. He therefore did not want to build the problem too much' (Quoted in Krishna 1999: 106).

Thus, Krishna (1999: 64) argues that the supposed connection between the two nationalisms was used by Indira Gandhi's government as an 'alibi to intervene in Sri Lanka to assert its regional hegemony'. Several other scholars have made similar arguments. Neil Devotta (2003: 367–8), for instance, argues that the new regional power dynamic after 1971 and the pro-Western foreign policy pursued by Sri Lanka's new Prime Minister J.R. Jayewardene in the 1970s and 1980s prompted India to pursue a hegemonic role in South Asia. This was, indeed, another legitimating reason given for India's intervention by J.N. Dixit, who argued that: 'Jayewardene's structuring international equations which could potentially be a strategic challenge to Indian security made India perceive Sri Lankan developments as a critically embryonic regional crisis that called for some decisive action by India' (Dixit 1998: 17). Devotta (2003: 367–8) and several others (Rao 1988: 422; Perkovich 1999: 251) cite the following quote, supposedly made by Indira Gandhi, to prove the existence of an 'Indira doctrine', according to which

> India will neither intervene in the domestic affairs of any states in the region, unless requested to do so, nor tolerate such intervention by an outside power; if external assistance is needed to meet an internal crisis, states should first look within the region for help.[1]

Indira Gandhi, however, made no such statement and the passage above is taken from a think tank report in which it was used to describe Indian policy in South Asia in the 1980s. In fact, Indira Gandhi never 'explicitly enunciated India's regional security preferences' as DeVotta (2003: 368) claims. Rather, the idea of the existence of an Indira Doctrine has its origins in the work of Bhabani Sen Gupta (1983) who argued in 1983 that a regional security doctrine, which he called the 'Indian Doctrine', was emerging under Prime Minister Indira Gandhi. Fifteen years after he suggested the emergence of the Indian Doctrine, however, Sen Gupta came to the conclusion that 'India has neither the power nor the culture, nor the mentality, nor the wherewithal to be a truly hegemonic power' (Rasgotra 1998: 69). This view was echoed by Surjeet Mansingh who argues that 'no Indian version of the Monroe doctrine has functioned in southern Asia. Nor can it function' (Mansingh 1984: 292).

As Mansingh and Sen Gupta suggest, there are a number of reasons why the notion of an Indian Monroe doctrine is flawed. As O Tuathail and Agnew (1992: 196) have argued, 'American involvement with world politics has followed a distinctive cultural logic or set of presuppositions and orientations'. The Monroe Doctrine was initially expounded by James Monroe to prevent further colonization in the Americas. Eventually, however, it became essential to the perpetuation of the myth of the Americas that forms an important facet of US identity. This myth treats the Western Hemisphere as the geographic *tabula rasa* on which the religiously ordained advance of civilization, freedom and progress would be advanced by the descendents of the Christian European settlers. Moreover, Joane Nagel (1998: 251) has argued that both the Monroe Doctrine and the project of westward expansion, known as Manifest Destiny, was tightly interwoven with a 'racialized, imperial masculinity, where adventurous, but civilized white men tame or defeat inferior savage men of colour...'. As we have seen in previous chapters, India's engagement with ideas of civilization, freedom, progress and imperial masculinity have been vastly different, having been affected by being negatively positioned in Western discourses. Thus, simply noting the similarities between India and the US and theorizing from this basis, obscures the fact that India's relations with the world have been conditioned by a different cultural logic particular to its distinct historical experience. That the 'Indira Doctrine' was never clearly enunciated by Indira Gandhi herself marks a fundamental difference from the US's Monroe Doctrine – the principles of which were constantly articulated by American officials in various administrations. Mansingh argues that several elements work against the development of an Indian

Monroe Doctrine. These include the lack of an extensive network of economic levers; the absence of a legitimating theory of racial superiority as the basis of hegemony; India's espousal of nonalignment in place of great power protection and what she calls 'the genius of Indian society' which 'does not appear to lie in political expansionism' (Mansingh 1984: 293).

Krishna's analysis of India's actions in Sri Lanka also notes its lack of expansionist ambitions. He argues that during the Nehru era there was a clear tension between the self-fashioning of India as a non-violent country which was a new and peaceful force in the world and of India as the inheritor of British power in the subcontinent (Krishna 1999: 22). As touched on in the previous chapter, Krishna suggests that after 1971, it was the latter which began to dominate. Yet, he also notes that India's effort to attain regional hegemony was distinctive in that it was not driven by territorial expansion and he concludes that India wanted to be seen as a consensual leader in the region and, therefore, a hegemon in the Gramscian sense (Krishna 1999: 27). While Mansingh points out that, unlike the US, India has not been driven by a theory of racial superiority, Krishna (1999: 28) argues that India's ambitions to consensual leadership were made on the basis of its superior model of nation-building compared to that of its neighbours. In dismissing this 'moralistic conviction' in Indian policy making as mere 'hubris', however, Krishna (1999: 27–8) forecloses the opportunity to analyse this aspect of India's self-representation. His argument that the 1971 war was narrated in India as an event which marked its success in exercising regional hegemony also needs to be clarified for while this was the response of many members of the Indian strategic elite, such as K. Subrahmanyam and J.N. Dixit, the views of this group cannot necessarily be conflated with the views of the political leadership which is ultimately in control of policy decisions (Krishna 1999: 22–3).

As I argued in the last chapter, the government's discourse in the aftermath of 1971 emphasized continuity over change and rejected the idea of India as a regional hegemon. This was because India's self-fashioning as a different sort of nation-state which rejected British geopolitics was much stronger in the Nehru era than Krishna suggests. The reading of Nehru that underpins Krishna's analysis of India's postcolonial identity is similar to that of Partha Chatterjee's in that both view Nehru as a modernist nationalist who, in Krishna's (1999: 14–15), words managed to 'exorcize' the presence of Gandhi by conceding to him the high moral ground while entrenching the 'practical, pragmatic, and powerful enterprise of state building within the logic of realpolitik'. Krishna, like Chatterjee, relies on Nehru's *Autobiography* to substantiate this reading. Yet, as I argued in the first chapter, this text represents Nehru at a particular stage of his intellectual journey during which he was less critical of Western modernity. While some members of the Indian elite viewed postcolonial India as inheriting the British mantle as the regional gendarme, as I argued in Chapter 3, an analysis of Nehru's later writings shows that he was more concerned with fashioning an environment which would facilitate the emergence of a world federation. To this end, he viewed a subcontinental confederation as a natural first step and worked toward this through a politics of friendship which sometimes fell into a discourse of kinship. It was this legacy and the narrative of 'Greater India', in which Indian civilization is seen as playing a mostly benign but influential role in Asia which made possible the construction of an identity that gave rise to foreign policy interests prioritizing, not regional hegemony, but, consensual leadership in South Asia in the 1980s.

Instead of utilizing a Monroe Doctrine analogy to understand India's South Asia policies, or dismissing India's official justifications for its involvement in Sri Lanka's civil war, this chapter takes seriously India's legitimating reasons – which rested on the threats posed by Tamil agitation and foreign interference as well as humanitarian concerns – in order to understand the broader social context that made possible its interventionist policies. As in the 1971 intervention, these legitimating reasons both enabled and constrained India's foreign policy actions.

Representations of South Asia in Indian foreign policy: 1972–1984

South Asia as a space of danger

The period between 1972 and 1977 was a time when the politics of paranoia, which culminated in a short period of authoritarian rule in 1975 that came to be known as 'the Emergency', flourished in India in ways that had important consequences for South Asia policy. This was because this paranoiac politics was not simply internally generated by the dynamics of domestic politics but had significant international dimensions. Consequently, it resulted in the conflation of India's unity and security with that of South Asia's and helped to create what has been described as a 'climate of psychological insecurity' which 'helped the ascendancy of the hawks [such as J.N. Dixit] in the formulation of neighbourhood policies' (Gupta 1990: 712).

By the summer of 1972, Indira Gandhi's slogan *Garibi Hatao* (remove poverty!) had come back to haunt her. Crop failure had led to food scarcity, rising inflation was met with cuts in government expenditure and, consequently, a spate of industrial action spread through the country. Indira Gandhi's response was to further centralize her political authority by funnelling power away from the regional state governments toward the centre. She did so by invoking 'President's Rule', a legacy of the British colonial administration, to run states directly from Delhi and suspend state legislatures to stem opposition to the Congress Party.

The opposition to Indira Gandhi's leadership had grown greater by 1974 after her ruthless suppression of a nation-wide railway strike and the emergence of a movement aimed at non-violent political, economic and social change led by Jayaprakash Narayan, a one-time member of the Congress who retired from mainstream politics in 1957 to devote himself to poverty alleviation at a grass-roots level (Sahgal 1978: 117). Narayan's movement spread through the country by drawing together opposition parties from across the ideological spectrum with the poorer and voice-less sections of the Indian public, like land-less labourers, in a broad moral and political struggle against Indira Gandhi's government. In response, Indira Gandhi alleged that the movement had been instigated and controlled by 'outside forces' and accused Narayan of being backed by the US government through the Central Intelligence Agency (CIA) (Frank 2001: 367). According to Gandhi's advisor, P.N. Dhar (2000: 254), her poor relationship with Richard Nixon and revelations of the CIA's involvement in the overthrow of Salvador Allende in Chile had made her increasingly apprehensive about US intentions in India.

In June 1975 Indira Gandhi was found guilty of electoral malpractice and disqualified from holding public office for six years, a ruling that revitalized the popular movement against her. On the basis of intelligence reports, which indicated CIA involvement in the movement and revealed plans by Narayan for the army and police to mutiny, she declared that '[s]ome drastic emergent action is needed' (Quoted in Frank 2001: 374). On 26 June, after thousands of opposition figures had been imprisoned using colonial-era preventative detention powers, Indira Gandhi (1977: 1) proclaimed Emergency rule, citing a 'deep and widespread conspiracy' to 'negate the very functioning of democracy', and threaten India's unity, stability and economic improvement which 'is bound to encourage dangers from outside' (Gandhi 1977: 2). The official discourse of the Emergency was, therefore, one which pushed to the forefront two interrelated narratives of India's backwardness that emerged during the colonial encounter – that of the fragility of India's unity and India's susceptibility to foreign manipulation.

As noted in previous chapters, in Western narratives, Indian civilization's vulnerability to invasion and conquest derived in part from its inherent disunity. Anti-colonial leaders largely accepted this narrative of backwardness while nonetheless asserting India's civilizational resilience. For M.K Gandhi, unity was to be brought about through a politics of neighbourliness. For Savarkar, a sense of nationalism had been present in the subcontinent for more than five thousand years in the 'Vedic nation' although repeated invasions had impeded its development (Savarkar 1938: 101–2).The creation of a state and society based on the principles of a revived and unifying Hindu nationalism was, therefore, Savarkar's aim. According to Nehru, disunity had been a major cause of India's backwardness and the key source of this disunity was the caste system:

> It was after all our fault that we became backward. Our biggest faults were internal disunity, lack of foresight and our habit of getting involved in petty quarrels and feuds.... The basic thing in India, which ... in my opinion led to our downfall in the last few centuries and weakened us, is our caste system ... Our enemies came and fostered disunity and weakened us by keeping us in separate compartments which prevented the growth of a strong nationalism.
>
> (Nehru 2003: 33)

Nehru also, however, valorized the notion of unity in diversity and his idea of a strong nationalism was an open and democratic internationalist nationalism which would be the basis of 'a collectivism which neither degrades nor enslaves' (Nehru 1982 [1946]: 531).

Whereas unity, democracy and an ethical modernity went hand in hand in Nehru's politics, Indira Gandhi's Emergency created a disjuncture which disrupted, but did not completely erase the discourse of India's postcolonial difference. The Emergency was an attempt to depoliticize India in order to put it on a pure and unadulterated drive toward modernity (Palmer 1977). In other words, it was an attempt to resolve the tension in India's postcolonial identity between mimicry and difference in favour of the former. Indira Gandhi, like Nehru, had struggled with this ambivalence, but the authoritarian traits in her personality and her lack of 'political self-confidence', as Nandy (1980: 119) puts it, made this tension even more acute. Nandy (1980: 119) argues that Indira Gandhi was in power at time when 'almost no one granted the authenticity of the Indian experiment; everyone wanted India to be some other country' and this being the case 'she felt herself pressured by the intellectual atmosphere in the country and in the world to put economic attainments above civil liberties'. Indeed it was a Western scholar that Indira Gandhi (1977: 94) cited to support the Emergency: 'We can no longer afford such slackness or 'softness', as Gunnar Myrdal called it'.[2]

Far from resolving the tensions within India's postcolonial identity, however, the Emergency only intensified them. It brought to prominence Indira Gandhi's son, Sanjay, who with his 'Action Brigade' launched a number of initiatives for a 'new India', including a sterilization drive, predominantly entailing the vasectomies of millions of men who were poor or homeless and were coerced, bribed or forced to undergo the procedure, and a program of urban 'beautification' and regeneration which required the demolition of aesthetically unpleasing slums in Delhi, Bombay, Agra and Varanasi. This resulted in the relocation of tens of thousands of people who were moved at gunpoint and provided with inadequate alternative accommodation (India 1978: Ch. XXI). Indira Gandhi pleaded ignorance of these excesses and according to Dhar, soon grew 'uneasy about its human and political implications' (Dhar 2000: 341). She did not just think of herself as a patriotic daughter of Mother India, but identified with Mother India herself, which made it hard for her to justify smothering India in the 'garb of modernity' in complete disregard for its supposed civilizational legacies like tolerance for plurality. Dhar (2000: 351) argues that ultimately, Indira Gandhi 'was not comfortable with the Emergency, and she wanted to get out of it, somehow, anyhow' for she 'was nostalgic about the way people had reacted to her in the 1971 campaign' – when she became Mother India personified – 'and she longed to hear again the applause of the multitudes' (Dhar 2000: 344).

The climate of insecurity and paranoia that gave rise to the Emergency also affected India's relationship with other countries in the region, which progressively worsened. Take, for instance, the integration of the protectorate of Sikkim into the Indian Union and India's reaction to Nepal's attempts to end their 'special relationship'. In British India's geopolitical reasoning, Sikkim's importance lay in its status as a strategic buffer between India and China. While it was given formal sovereignty under the British, in reality, like the other Princely states it was controlled by a British resident political officer. Upon India's independence, Sikkim was made a protectorate. This meant that India was responsible for Sikkim's defence while the King or Chogyal retained control of internal matters, although the British tradition of instituting a resident political officer in Sikkim was continued. I would argue, however, that this should not be seen as a straightforward acceptance of Britain's geopolitical reasoning, but rather, be viewed in the context of Nehru's vision for a post-sovereign state order which would be brought about through gradual change by nurturing rather than breaking old links. In the first instance, as noted in Chapter 3, this would entail the creation of a confederation in South Asia with countries sharing common defence and economic policies, just as India already had with Sikkim and Nepal.

Nehru, however, was aware of the perceptions of hegemony that arose in such discussions and resorted, often counterproductively, to the language of fraternity in order to build trust. Indira Gandhi also often employed a discourse of fraternity with India's neighbours, but by the 1970s, her suspicions and paranoia about 'the foreign hand' – a discourse which drew on older narratives about India's inherent disunity and vulnerability to invasion and conquest – also coloured her attitudes. By 1973, Sikkim's Chogyal indicated a desire to change the limited nature of his power. At the same time he was also facing demands from the Sikkim Congress Party for greater political representation in his government and this paved the way for India's intervention against the Chogyal who, according to Dhar (2000: 290), fell out of favour with Indira Gandhi because of the American connections and 'anti-Indian moves' of the Chogyal's American-born wife. After the Indian Army intervened to suppress riots against the Chogyal, the Indian government garnered a commitment from him to hold regular elections starting in April 1974. The 1974 election saw the Sikkim Congress win all but one seat in the Sikkim Assembly and in September, India passed a constitutional amendment making Sikkim an associate state of the Indian Union. Faced with being relegated to mere ceremonial status, the Chogyal made a complaint to the UN denying India's right to interfere in Sikkim. In 1975, the Indian army was again sent in to Sikkim, this time to take hold of the Chogyal's palace. Soon after, the Sikkim Assembly voted to abolish the monarchy and join the Indian Union as a full state (Mansingh 1984: 281–2). In Indian discourse, this episode was represented as a victory for democracy and as further evidence of the superiority of India's postcolonial modernity (Dhar 2000: 298). Criticism was deflected by underscoring the moral distinction between India's incorporation of Sikkim into its democracy and Pakistan's annexation of the state of Hunza with '[n]o election. No popular will' (Gandhi 1984a: 727).

Like Sikkim, Nepal's rulers in the 1970s had grown increasingly resentful of India and its insistence on joint consultation regarding matters of security as specified in the 1950 treaty. In response, India agreed to end the activities of its military liaison group and withdraw its military technicians in Nepal but also, however, raised the issue of closing the open border between India and Nepal and delayed negotiations to renew the Trade and Transit Treaty, both of which would have been detrimental to Nepal's economy. Eventually, Nepal's King Mahendra signed the Trade and Transit Treaty without gaining the trade concessions he had demanded or ending the 'special relationship' with India (Mansingh 1984: 284–5). In 1975 when the Trade and Transit Treaty was again up for renewal the new King, Birendra, proposed to make Nepal a 'zone of peace'. India reacted negatively to the proposal and resorted to the strategy it employed previously by stalling negotiations on trade talks and threatening to close the border (Mansingh 1984: 286–8). Once again, the discourse of the 'foreign hand' was prominent in India's interpretation of its deteriorating relations with Nepal. In a speech at a dinner in his honour in Kathmandu, the External Affairs Minister Y.B. Chavan noted that he had '… no hesitation in saying that there are forces whose constant effort it is to sow suspicion and distrust between us. We shall, with our sincerity and vigilance, foil their designs' (Chavan 1976: 38). Thus, the region itself was inscribed as a space of danger. Yet, danger, as David Campbell (1992: 1–2) has argued, is not an objective condition but rather is an 'effect of interpretation' and the very different approach of the Janata government, which was elected after Indira Gandhi lost the election of 1977 that ended the Emergency, lends credence to this argument.

Reinscribing South Asia

After initially postponing the general election for a second time in November 1976, Indira Gandhi reversed her decision two months later and announced that a general election would be held in March 1977, despite being advised by the intelligence agencies that she risked losing an election at that juncture (Frank 2001: 409–10). Indira Gandhi did indeed lose the election to Janata, a broad coalition of opposition parties. The Janata government declared that India's relations with its neighbours had taken a downward spiral under Indira Gandhi and that, therefore, repairing these relations would be a priority of the new government. Foreign policy discourse thus became a site for the revitalized reiteration of India's postcolonial difference and the Emergency was relegated to the status of an aberration in the narrative of India's postcolonial modernity. As the new Prime Minister Morarji Desai explained in a speech in the Lok Sabha after returning from the Commonwealth Prime Ministers' Conference in London in June 1977:

> When questioned on various occasions [about the return to democracy], I pointed out that the tradition of democracy was rooted in the ancient civilization of India. Foreign rule and such aberrations like the period of emergency, were contrary to our values and our national ethos … the Indian people have an inherent moral courage to judge and elect their own rulers without fear.
>
> (Desai 1977a: 95)

Likewise, according to the new External Affairs Minister, Atal Bihari Vajpayee '[a] new India is rediscovering its old personality' (Vajpayee 1977a: 162). In his first speech on foreign affairs in the Lok Sabha, Vajpayee declared the Janata government's commitment to non-alignment and emphasized the importance of not giving the impression of leaning towards a particular bloc as, he implied, Indira Gandhi's government had done. Raju Thomas (1980: 235–6) has argued that initially the Janata defined non-alignment as a Swiss-style neutrality, since it sought to reduce its dependence on the Soviet Union by, for instance, sourcing arms from Western Europe. Yet, this early speech of Vajpayee's reveals an understanding of non-alignment that is much in keeping with Nehru's:

> non-alignment recognises that in today's nuclear world, war or its inevitability must be ruled out ... we reject the need to consign national defence to a committed or dependent military or ideological arrangement. Nonalignment frees a nation from the pressures to borrow foreign models or adopt other ideologies which may be alien to a nation's civilisation or its ethos.
>
> (Vajpayee 1977b: 90)

After highlighting the importance of non-alignment, Vajpayee reiterated that India had 'no history of conquest or expansionism. We have always tried to win the heart and not the body' (Vajpayee 1977b: 90–1). The first priority of his government, Vajpayee said, would be to:

> promote a relationship of co-operation and trust with our immediate neighbours ... If the Indian sub-continent remains free of tensions, it would command unique weight in the counsels of the world. It can be an example of how our ancient heritage can be transformed to modern progress.
>
> (Vajpayee 1977b: 91–2)

Already, in the few months that Janata had been in power,

> the climate for such trust and cooperation with our neighbours[3] has already shown significant improvement. Some old suspicions and irritants have been removed; with sustained diplomacy and reciprocal response we hope we can move steadily forward.
>
> (Vajpayee 1977b: 92)

Vajpayee and Desai undertook visits to the capitals of Pakistan, Bhutan, Sri Lanka, Nepal and Bangladesh reiterating the importance of 'good neighbourliness', 'friendship', 'brotherhood' and 'beneficial bilateralism'. Moreover, according to Vajpayee (1978: 209) 'we have not only professed strict non-interference in the internal affairs of our neighbours, but practised it, often in the face of great temptation to do the contrary'. As a result, 'there is confidence ... that India is today prepared to make its due share of sacrifice to promote the well-being and development of its neighbours...' (Vajpayee 1978: 209). It was during the Janata period that Sri Lanka shifted its foreign policy in a pro-Western and pro-market direction, but this was not a development that particularly concerned

Desai (Krishna 1999: 105). Initiatives taken by his government included an agreement with Bangladesh over a long-running water-sharing dispute, resolving a disagreement with Pakistan over the design of a hydro-electric plant, supporting Pakistan's readmission to the Commonwealth and signing new Trade and Transit Treaties with Nepal. On Nepal, Desai claimed: '[n]o text book on international relations contains an exact parallel to the pattern of relations which exist between our two sovereign nations' for,

> [t]his sub-continent of ours is heir to an ancient civilization with a deep tradition of peace and tolerance. It has no history of conquest or tradition of superiority. It has been the home of many races and many religions. It was only foreign imperialism which vitiated this tradition.
>
> (Desai 1977b: 279)

Thus, 'the subcontinent has the challenge and opportunity to prove to the world that the great tradition of peace of our common civilization thrives even in these troublesome and tension-ridden modern times' (Desai 1977b: 279).

Despite re-invoking a 'tradition of peace' amongst a 'common civilization', Thomas (1980: 230) notes that defence expenditure by the Janata government did not lessen but, in fact, increased. This did not, however, fuel any regional panic and without the discourse of danger on the 'foreign hand' that pervaded Indira Gandhi's rule, there was a general improvement in India's relations with the countries of South Asia during the Janata period and a mostly successful effort to re-anchor India's identity in narratives of civilizational exceptionalism.

Identity politics and the 'foreign hand'

The Janata coalition performed poorly at a domestic level and finally collapsed in August 1979. Despite her comprehensive defeat at the polls in 1977, Indira Gandhi was re-elected as Prime Minister in January 1980, in part, as Emma Tarlo (2003: 43) has argued, by consistently refusing to be cast in the role of dictator that had been assigned to her in the post-Emergency narrative. The 1980 election campaign almost proceeded as if the Emergency had never happened and, as in previous election campaigns, the focus was not on the Congress but on Indira Gandhi as the saviour of India. The politics of suspicion and paranoia that characterized Indira Gandhi's government prior to the Emergency, moreover, was still at the forefront and she argued that she had lost the election in 1977 because she had annoyed the 'administration, which was against us even before' and as a result of 'Western involvement' which helped to spread the Janata's propaganda (Carras 1979: 234).

This fear of the 'foreign hand' was also evident in her response to events in Sri Lanka. As noted earlier, the Janata government refrained from involvement in Sri Lanka's civil conflict when it began to escalate in 1977 and relations between the two countries throughout the 1970s remained mostly conciliatory. Indira Gandhi's response to the Colombo riots of July 1983, however, indicated that South Asia was once again being inscribed as a space of danger and that, now, Sri Lanka would be a focal point of India's attentions. The riots resulted in the deaths of up to 3000 Tamils, the displacement of almost 70 per cent of Colombo's Tamil population to refugee camps, and the flight of more than 160,000 Tamils and much of the Tamil leadership to Tamil Nadu (Krishna 1999: 115–16).

Indira Gandhi's speech at the first meeting of Foreign Ministers for South Asian Regional Cooperation in August 1983 implicitly referred to the situation in Sri Lanka and was a precursor to the way in which India would seek to justify its intervention by blurring the boundaries of Sri Lanka's sovereign authority and legitimizing India as a moral actor. The riots, she said, had caused 'anguish and anxiety' not only to the Tamil population in India but to the entire nation. She had received reassurance from President Jayewardene, however, that the 'situation was coming under control and *our people* would soon be returning to their homes' (Gandhi 1986a: 419) (emphasis added). It was 'clear in every forum and in every possible way that India does not pose any threat to Sri Lanka, nor do we want to interfere in their internal affairs'. Still,

> I pointed out to President that developments in Sri Lanka affect us also. In this matter, India cannot be regarded as just any country. Sri Lanka and India are the two countries who are directly concerned. Any extraneous involvement will complicate matters for both our countries who are directly concerned.... We live in a region where many forces are at work, not all of whom wish India or our neighbours well. Forces of destabilization are at work. Hence we must make every effort to minimize any opportunity for foreign elements to weaken us.
>
> (Gandhi 1986a: 419)

The structure of this speech – first reassuring Sri Lanka that India does not interfere in the internal affairs of others, but citing the close ties between 'the peoples' of India and Sri Lanka and the dangers of 'foreign hands' as the reasons why India could not remain a passive observer – was repeated in many of Indira Gandhi's statements during this period and formed the basis of India's intervention discourse on Sri Lanka.

India began mediating between the TULF and the Sri Lankan government in 1983 with the reluctant agreement of Jayewardene. By 1984, however, there was increasing proof that India's Research and Analysis Wing (RAW) was providing weapons and training to Sri Lanka's Tamil militants in camps in Tamil Nadu (Gupta 1984). Indeed, there is evidence that in April 1984 RAW had helped to organize several militant groups[4] under an umbrella organization called the Eelam National Liberation Front (ENLF). RAW's presumption of control over these militant groups was, however, nothing but a delusion for the leaders of these groups had covertly signed their own pact committing themselves to an independent Tamil state (Krishna 1999: 134).

The purpose of this seemingly contradictory strategy was unclear. Krishna (1999: 126) argues that the policy was undertaken not so much to achieve a prompt resolution of Sri Lanka's problems but rather to keep Sri Lanka in a controlled state of destabilization and achieve a number of the Indian government's ambitions at once. These included, presenting the Congress Party as the defender of Sri Lankan Tamils in order to win votes in Tamil Nadu, preventing Jayewardene from inviting 'foreign influences' into the region and showing other South Asian countries the consequences of alienating India. Krishna's analysis, however, is based on the idea that Indira Gandhi was pursuing a strategy of coercive hegemony in South Asia. To the contrary, I would suggest that her actions in Sri Lanka were the result of a defensive rendering of the region as a space of fear and danger. This perception of South Asia enabled an interventionist policy, but the continued assertion of India's exceptionalism, as a benign civilizational state that rejected coercion, acted as a significant constraint. The result was the covert use of coercion alongside an overt bid to be recognized as a mediator.

Saving Sri Lanka

The 'messiah of modernity'[5]: Rajiv Gandhi and the politics of mediation

Indira Gandhi's death in 1984 brought to power her son, Rajiv, who was even more anxious to have India mediate in Sri Lanka. Rajiv Gandhi came to power with the expressed intention of taking 'India into the twenty-first century' (Quoted in Nigam 2004: 72). While Nehru celebrated the scientists, engineers and architects building India's new cities, nuclear power plants, steel mills and dams and Sanjay Gandhi had his 'Action Brigade' which sought to make India modern through brutal programs of urban beautification and population control, Rajiv Gandhi had his 'computer boys' – a coterie of pragmatic unreflective business executives and technocrats, many of whom were class-mates from the elite Doon School or Cambridge University (Frank 2001: 474). For Rajiv Gandhi and his cronies India's modernity depended on making India efficient by overhauling the bureaucracy of the developmental state, deregulating the economy and appropriating advanced computer technology. They were the embodiment of what Charlotte Hooper (2001: 193) has called, a 'technocratic masculine elite that has the whole globe as its playground'. In the hagiographic words of T.N. Kaul (1995: 172), Rajiv was 'upright, clean, decent and honest'. He had 'a scientific temper and was keen to modernize India through the application of advanced science and technology'. According to his science adviser, M.G.K. Menon, Rajiv Gandhi 'was a man in a hurry' who believed that India's emphasis on self-reliance had slowed down its development and, for that reason, he liberalized the importation of foreign technology and expertise (Quoted in Jayaraman 1991: 431; Gandhi 1987c: 96). According to Gandhi (1987c: 93), India had 'missed one bus with the Industrial Revolution' and 'didn't jump on the second bus on time – and that is the electronic revolution or computer revolution – and now we might have to run behind that bus, catch up to it and jump on to it'. As A.S. Raman (1991: 5–6) writes, Gandhi was 'proud to be known as a little

Messiah of modernity, eager to take his country forward by giant leaps into the twenty first century'. Thus, Rajiv Gandhi's term as Prime Minister was filled with a sense of urgency and this extended into the foreign policy arena as a heightened desire to exercise India's influence by mediating in Sri Lanka.

Just months into his leadership, Rajiv Gandhi dismissed his mother's negotiator, G. Parthasarathi, whose slow and cautious style of diplomacy did not fit well with his approach to politics. Parthasarathi's replacement, Romesh Bhandari, was set to retire in thirteen months and was apparently given the brief of resolving the Sri Lankan conflict in thirty days (Krishna 1999: 133). In an interview, Bhandari revealed that this was part of a larger foreign policy initiative of a 'young prime minister [who] had come in with a massive mandate', who 'was the centre of attraction not only nationally but globally' and who attached the 'highest importance to creating a better climate in the region. Here it was necessary to make our neighbours feel comfortable with a very large country' (Manchanda 1986: 16). With his retirement pending, Bhandari 'tried to do in one year what should normally have taken three years' and 'new initiatives, particularly towards the neighbours, had to be telescoped in a span of twenty days – one night to 38-hour visits to the neighbours' (Manchanda 1986: 16). Rather than constituting a policy shift, however, this was a simply a change in style for '[t]he content of the policy remained the same, it was much more the type of packaging that was different' (Manchanda 1986: 16).

The change in style was also evident in Rajiv Gandhi's attempt to distinguish himself from past governments in his approach to regionalism. 'Fundamentally', he said in a speech in 1985, 'our regional security lies in all the countries in the region building together, not confronting each other. Our security lies in building affection between our people, which is naturally there, building goodwill, warm friendly neighbourliness between our people' (Gandhi 1987c: 54). Accordingly, Gandhi initially attempted to couch the India–Sri Lanka relationship within the broader context of institutionalized regional cooperation. The first in-depth talks with Jaycwardene were conducted on a flight to Dhaka, where Gandhi was making a goodwill visit in the wake of a destructive cyclone and where the first summit for the newly formed regional organization, the South Asian Association for Regional Cooperation (SAARC) was to be held in December. Gandhi had persuaded Jayewardene that the joint visit would symbolize their commitment to regional cooperation (Dixit 1998: 25). Moreover, the first round of talks between the Sri Lankan government and representatives of the Tamil groups took place neither in Sri Lanka nor in India but in Thimpu, the capital of Bhutan under the auspices of the Bhutanese government.

This push for regionalism was a departure from the Nehruvian script as was Rajiv Gandhi's emphasis on state sovereignty in his speeches. Panchsheel was defined as 'where all States are equal, equal in their sovereignty' and national security was to be secured through unity and 'friendly, co-operative relations with our neighbours, while maintaining their sovereignty and equality and working for mutual benefit' (Gandhi 1987c: 51–2). Nonetheless, Rajiv Gandhi, the messiah of modernity still thought it an imperative to mark India's modernity as a distinctly ethical one. Thus, he also spoke against the 'traditional' policy of seeking a balance of power which, 'means confrontation, rivalry and establishes these as basic values and natural conditions for relations between States' and in 'a nuclear age ... translates into a balance of terror', while proclaiming that, '[w] e believe in total equality, brotherhood, mutual cooperation. We do not want an Indian hegemony on the countries around us' (Gandhi 1987c: 50–3).

Thus, Rajiv Gandhi's emphasis on the legal sovereign equality of countries in South Asia was qualified by the continued assertion of South Asia being united by a sense of kinship. Like his mother, therefore, he legitimized India's interest in Sri Lanka on the basis of the supposed ties of ethnicity between Sri Lankan Tamils and Indian Tamils and the influx of Sri Lankan Tamil refugees (Gandhi 1987c: 17, 23, 47). As in 1971, the refugee influx blurred the line between the domestic and the international, and therefore between sovereignty and intervention:

> Sri Lanka in the south is having tremendous internal problems. They are spilling over into India. We now have almost one lakh [100,000] refugees on our soils. Our concern is for the Tamils in Sri Lanka. The concern is not only of people in the south, but is the concern of everyone in India. We have to see that the refugees go back, go back in honour, go back in safety, go back with the security of expecting and getting full freedom to express themselves, to work, to live within the integrity of Sri Lanka.
>
> (Gandhi 1987c: 299–300)

The first of India's mediation efforts, in Thimpu, took place in two rounds, in mid-1985 despite the fact that by this time the fighting between Tamil militants and Sri Lankan security forces had almost escalated into an outright war. With neither side ready to make concessions, however, the Thimpu talks ended in failure. While the Sri Lankan government had only agreed to the talks in an attempt to halt India's assistance to Tamil militants, the Tamil groups thought that agreeing to the talks would ensure India's continued support of them. Apart from the moderate TULF, none of the more militant Tamil groups, who were invited for the first time, sent their senior leadership and consequently, neither did the Sri Lankan government (De Silva 1995: 163).

Although the Thimpu talks failed, it was decided that following further talks in Sri Lanka between Indian representatives and the Tamil and Sri Lankan leadership, Jayewardene and Rajiv Gandhi could announce a peace package at the SAARC summit in November 1986, which was to be held in India. This was despite the Sri Lankan government appearing to be intent on readying itself for a military solution to the conflict and even though India had lost any control it once exercised on the now-dominant Tamil militant group, the LTTE, which had withdrawn from RAW's umbrella organization. According to Dixit, Gandhi and his administration were aware of Jayewardene's lack of commitment to a peaceful solution but, nonetheless, felt that India should persevere (Dixit 1998: 50–1). The discussions in Sri Lanka culminated in a devolution package that still lacked the key Tamil demands for the merger of the Tamil-majority northern and eastern provinces. In a further step to mollify the Sri Lankan government, and in light of India's loss of control over the Tamil militants, the Tamil Nadu government was ordered by Rajiv Gandhi to disarm the Tamil militants based in India in the lead up to the SAARC summit (Gunaratna 1993: 164).

At the SAARC summit, it was the LTTE, rather than the TULF or a combination of militant groups, which was promoted as the chief representative of Sri Lankan Tamils. This constituted a major shift in Indian policy and gave legitimacy to the LTTE's claim of representing the sovereign authority of Sri Lankan Tamils (Krishna 1999: 140). Nonetheless, dissatisfied with the initial negotiations, the LTTE leader Vellupillai Prabhakaran left the summit without even meeting with Jayewardene (Dixit 1998: 59). Not only did India fail to engineer its much longed-for act of reconciliation but Jayewardene's speech at the summit contained a passage referring to India's support for Tamil terrorism and – turning India's rhetoric back on itself – urged a return to the moral principles of peaceful co-existence and non-interference (Dixit 1998: 59).

Even the debacle of SAARC could not shake the Indian government's belief in itself as a mediator. According to Dixit (1998: 62), the Indian government had received intelligence reports that the Sri Lankan government were planning a military assault in the following year and Rajiv Gandhi was anxious to persuade 'the Jayewardene Government to return to the path of reason'. As the bearer of morality and reason, Gandhi yet again sent his negotiators to Colombo. When this failed, Rajiv Gandhi decided on a new policy of putting pressure on the LTTE and the Sri Lankan government for a negotiated resolution that would maintain the territorial integrity of Sri Lanka while committing India as the direct guarantor of any compromises that may be reached (Dixit 1998: 64–5). Meanwhile, the LTTE shifted their base from Tamil Nadu back to Jaffna and reports in Sri Lankan newspapers soon emerged which claimed that they were planning to unilaterally declare an independent Tamil state in the north and east of the country. The Sri Lankan government reacted to this with an increased show of force and in January 1987, an intensified period of fighting began between the Sri Lankan forces and the militant groups led by the LTTE.

Performing humanitarianism: South Asia as a space of desire

India's response to the renewed violence was to threaten to halt its mediation until Sri Lanka stopped its military operations (Quoted in De Silva 1995: 209). After initially rejecting this demand, the Sri Lankan government declared a cease-fire for the New Year and Easter holiday period in April, which ended when the LTTE carried out two attacks on buses killing over 200 civilians (De Silva 1995: 216). The Sri Lankan government's response, 'Operation Liberation' was aimed at gaining control of the Jaffna peninsula to staunch the flow of militants and weapons from Tamil Nadu and militarily weaken the LTTE. At this stage, India's humanitarian discourse was intensified. Rajiv Gandhi made a statement condemning the Sri Lankan government's 'massacre of unarmed non-combatant civilians on this scale' which was 'totally disproportionate to the avowed aim of exterminating the Tamil militant groups' (Gandhi 1987b: 190). The actions were 'a gross violation of every tenet of human rights. The international community must impress upon the Sri Lankan authorities the imperative need for restraint'. Moreover,

> While India was patiently and painstakingly working towards a political solution, it is apparent now that the Sri Lankan Government was buying time for pursuing the military option ... India has done everything to find solutions compatible with the unity of Sri Lanka. But by mercilessly bombing a defenceless people and spreading misery, on the basis of only ethnic difference, Sri Lanka is itself putting its unity and integrity in jeopardy.
>
> (Gandhi 1987b: 190)

After citing humanitarianism as the major legitimating reason for its intervention into Sri Lanka's civil conflict the Indian leadership then sought to convert its humanitarian discourse into foreign policy action. Dixit visited Sri Lanka's Foreign Minister, A.C.S. Hameed, carrying a statement declaring that Sri Lanka's military operations were 'almost genocidal' and that its economic blockade had caused 'extreme hardships' to the people of Jaffna. This being the case, the statement went on to say, India had decided to send 'urgently-needed relief supplies' to Jaffna by sea from Tamil Nadu under the aegis of the Indian Red Cross. The statement emphasized that the convoy was a humanitarian relief operation, that it would not be armed and would be accompanied by Indian and international media. The 'concurrence of the Government of Sri Lanka may kindly be conveyed urgently so that relief can reach the long-suffering citizens of Jaffna without further delay' (India 1987b: 224). In fact, however, the number of journalists invited on the convoy vastly exceeded the number of relief workers.

After some resistance Sri Lanka eventually agreed to receive India's relief supplies in the 'interest of good neighbourly relations' (Gunaratna 1993: 181). It soon issued a retraction, however, stating that it would regard unilateral action by India as a violation of Sri Lanka's independence, sovereignty and territorial integrity (Gunaratna 1993: 181). Not to be denied, Rajiv Gandhi responded by insisting that India would be sending twenty fishing boats to Kalmunai Point off the coast of the Jaffna Peninsula (Gunaratna 1993: 181). When the Indian convoy neared Sri Lanka the next day, it was stopped by the Sri Lankan Navy which informed the convoy that they had been directed to protect Sri Lanka's territorial sovereignty and not allow the boats to enter Sri Lankan waters. India's MEA condemned the Sri Lankan government's prevention 'of relief supplies from reaching the long suffering people of Jaffna' which indicated that the Sri Lankan government 'is determined to continue denying the people of Jaffna their basic human rights'. Moreover,

> The Government and people of India are deeply concerned at the continuing hardships inflicted the Government of Sri Lanka on their Tamil people in defiance of world public opinion. They cannot remain indifferent spectators to the plight of the people of Jaffna, many of whom, have in recent years, fled their homes to seek safety and refuge in India.
>
> (India 1987d: 227)

We see here key shifts in Indian discourse that laid the ground-work for its military intervention. The denial of human rights to 'the people of Jaffna', who are said to have a kinship bond with the people of India, has become the basis for locating the foundation of sovereign authority in the Tamil people and in the 'Government and people of India'. Moreover, the Government and people of India as the representative of 'world public opinion' have also become the community of judgment.

After having its ships turned back to Tamil Nadu, the Indian government made the decision to airdrop relief supplies. The Sri Lankan High Commissioner in New Delhi, Bernard Tilakaratane was informed of the decision shortly before the airdrop was slated to begin and the Indian government released a statement soon thereafter which emphasized India's continuing commitment to providing humanitarian assistance to 'the long suffering and beleaguered people of Jaffna' (India 1987c: 227). The supplies were to be para-dropped over Jaffna and would be 'duly escorted to ensure their defence in case they are attacked while on flight' and accompanied by some of the obviously all-important media contingent (India 1987c: 227). The statement went on to add that the airdrop had to be carried out because, 'the continuing deterioration of the condition of the civilian population of the Jaffna peninsula, which is of legitimate concern to the Government and people of India, has serious implications for peace and security in the area' (India 1987c: 228).

A later press release, put out jointly by the Prime Minister and Opposition leaders was more conciliatory and attempted to situate India's actions in the realm of its civilizational friendship with Sri Lanka:

> It [the airdrop] should be seen against the background of our friendship and good neighbourly relations with Sri Lanka and our consistent wish that the ethnic discord in Sri Lanka be resolved through a political settlement ... India continues to stand for a peaceful solution of the ethnic problem in Sri Lanka within the framework of the unity and territorial integrity of Sri Lanka.
>
> (India 1987a: 228)

Despite the speed with which the decision to carry out the airdrop was made, according to Dixit (1998: 106–7), the action was considered drastic and there was initially some doubt among those consulted[6] by Rajiv Gandhi about whether it should be taken. Ultimately, however, it was decided that Sri Lanka's violence against Tamil civilians had to be stopped and that Sri Lanka's 'defiance of

India's mediatory efforts which it had used as a convenience should be neutralised' (Dixit 1998: 106–7).

The airdrop proceeded without incident but was an event that shocked the Sri Lankan leadership. Foreign Minister Hameed informed Dixit that the airdrop was a violation of Sri Lanka's territorial integrity, that it amounted to interference in its domestic affairs and that it was an attempt to break-up the country (Dixit 1998: 107). Jayewardene accused India of behaving like a bully and wrote the airdrop into a narrative that is deeply imbedded in the discourse of Sinhalese nationalism:

> In the long history of relations between India and the Indian states, we have been invaded 16 times from Indian soil and four times by powers from the Far East and the West ... [T]he Indian invasion of June 4 was the 21st.
>
> (Quoted in Krishna 1999: 152)

The Prime Minister, Ranasinghe Premadasa, and the Minister of Finance and Planning, Ronnie Del Mel, expressed similar sentiments and both tied the airdrop to the narrative of the threat to the Sinhala nation from repeated invasions from South India (Krishna 1999: 152–3). Nonetheless, in the aftermath of the airdrop there was a lull in Sri Lanka's military operations against the Tamil militants in Jaffna. Much to Jayewardene's dismay Sri Lanka received little international sympathy for what it considered to be a violation of its sovereignty (De Silva 1995: 227).[7] With few other options to exercise, submitting to India's mediation with the guarantee that it would underwrite any agreement appeared to Jayewardene to be an attractive choice (De Silva 1995: 225).

The IPKF in Sri Lanka

The negotiation process resumed within two weeks of the airdrop and a draft agreement was prepared at the end of June. After threats by India to withdraw its mediation and give its support to Sri Lankan Tamils, Jayewardene approved the draft agreement in July even though key members of his Cabinet, including Prime Minister Premadasa, remained opposed to it. Obtaining the consent of the LTTE leader Prabhakaran was no easier but eventually Rajiv Gandhi persuaded him to go along with the agreement, even if he did not formally endorse it (Dixit 1998: 150).

Rather than regarding the tenuousness of the Sri Lankan government and LTTE support for the agreement as a reason to slow down the process, Rajiv Gandhi decided that a lasting peace in Sri Lanka would only come about if India was a direct guarantor for the implementation of the agreement. As for the concerns about the LTTE, Gandhi was advised that the Indian and Tamil Nadu governments had enough leverage with the LTTE to gain their acquiescence and that, in any case, India could neutralize the LTTE militarily within two weeks if need be (Dixit 1998: 154–6). At this point, however, a military conflagration was not a serious concern.

The Indo-Sri Lanka Agreement to Establish Peace and Normalcy in Sri Lanka established the desire to 'preserve the unity, sovereignty and territorial integrity of Sri Lanka', recognized Sri Lanka as a multi-ethnic, multi-lingual, plural society and ensured that India 'will underwork and guarantee the resolutions, and co-operate in the implementation of these proposals' (1987: 252–7). This included providing military assistance when the Sri Lankan government requested it. Of all the parties involved in the Agreement it seemed that India was the one that was most satisfied by the outcome. By giving up its unitary conception of statehood, Sri Lanka was not just recognizing India's superior model of nation-building, but was acknowledging India's leadership and guidance. Rajiv Gandhi noted at the post-signing reception, that the Agreement was a 'compact in the cause of brotherhood' that 'consolidates the historic relationship between India and Sri Lanka. It is not mere geographical proximity which binds us. Ours is a relationship of heart and mind...' (Gandhi 1987d: 257–8). He ended his speech by firmly placing India in a paternal role:

> Through this Accord, we resume the journey on which both our countries embarked when Emperor Ashoka, who renounced war and violence, sent his son, Arhat Mahendra, to Sri Lanka with the Buddha's message of non-violence, compassion and justice.
>
> (Gandhi 1987d: 258)

Non-violence, however, was not at the forefront of Jayewardene's mind for, even before the Agreement had been signed, it became clear that he intended to take full advantage of the military provisions in the Agreement, citing the renewed outbreak of violence in Sri Lanka and the strain this placed on Sri Lankan security forces as justification for the deployment of a large Indian Peace-Keeping Force (IPKF) to ensure a cease-fire and surrender of arms by the Tamil militants (Dixit 1998: 169). The day after the Agreement was signed, 6000 Indian troops, less than Jayewardene wanted, arrived in the Jaffna Peninsula. In his announcement in the Indian Parliament Rajiv Gandhi took care to emphasize that the Indian troops had gone to Sri Lanka at the behest of the Sri Lankan government which had invoked India's obligations and commitments under the Agreement (Gandhi 1987a: 252).

Jayewardene himself attempted to uphold Sri Lanka's sovereignty and keep intact the sovereignty/intervention boundary by balancing his call for military assistance from India with requests to the US, Britain and Pakistan for logistical assistance for the Sri Lankan Army. He also insisted on announcing that the IPKF would be under the supreme command of the Sri Lankan government (Dixit 1998: 173–4). This was unconvincing, however, for the Agreement precluded Sri Lankan leaders from involving other countries in direct activities in Sri Lanka, and the only country that responded positively to the request, the US, sought India's authorization before they would commit (De Silva 1995: 249–50). As for the IPKF, Jayewardene assured Rajiv Gandhi that he would not interfere in its operational matters (De Silva 1995: 174).

The IPKF and the Indian government expected the disarming of Tamil militants to happen quickly and planned on being in Sri Lanka no longer than the end of 1987 or the beginning of 1988 (De Silva 1995: 255). In early August, however, Prabhakaran gave a speech condemning the Agreement, which, he said, was made without consulting the representatives of Sri Lankan Tamils and only served India's geopolitical interests. Far from having given up on the idea of a separate state, Prabhakaran had 'unrelenting faith in the proposition that only a separate state of Tamil Eelam can offer a permanent solution to the problem of the people of Tamil Eelam...' and vowed to 'continue to fight for the objective of attaining Tamil Eelam' (Quoted in Gunaratna 1993: 216). Despite this speech, the ceremony to mark the hand-over of arms went ahead as planned in early August as a major media event – the Indian government, as was its wont, had flown in a plane full of Indian and foreign journalists to see the event (Gunaratna 1993: 217). However, the leader of the political wing of the LTTE, Dilip Yogi, attended the ceremony in place of Prabhakaran and, by the middle of August, the LTTE was engaged in fighting with other militant groups[8] while intelligence reports revealed that weapons and ammunition continued to pour into Jaffna (Krishna 1999: 177).

Nonetheless, the Indian government continued its negotiations with the LTTE to obtain cooperation on the Agreement. The document that emerged from the meetings was signed by both LTTE and Indian High Commission representatives and committed the LTTE to cooperating in the implementation of the Agreement and surrendering their remaining arms. (Gunaratna 1993: 233–4). It almost immediately backed away from the agreement, however, and the Sri Lankan Navy intercepted a boat crossing the Palk Straits carrying a group of 17 senior LTTE members as well as arms and ammunition in contravention of the Indo-Lanka Agreement (Gunaratna 1993: 234). While in Sri Lankan custody, 13 men, including Pulendran, one of the LTTE's top leaders, died after swallowing cyanide capsules, apparently on the orders of Prabhakaran (Krishna 1999: 184).

The suicide of his top lieutenants gave Prabhakaran the reason he needed to declare the irrelevance of the Indo-Sri Lanka Agreement and renewed LTTE attacks on civilians and Indian soldiers convinced the Indian army chief General K. Sundarji to order the launch of a ground offensive. This was in contravention of the advice received by the head of the IPKF, Depinder Singh, who warned against the 'hard option' due to the risk of becoming embroiled in a prolonged counter-insurgency operation (Krishna 1999: 185; Gunaratna 1993: 236). According to Dixit, however, 'The feeling in New Delhi was ... that the LTTE had to be neutralized whatever the scale of the operation' and he admits that there was little thought given to the consequences of launching a large-scale military operation (Dixit 1998: 212, 4).

'Operation Pawan', as it was known, began with a plan to destroy the LTTE's operational headquarters and capture the leadership, but was a resounding failure.[9] Prabhakaran and the rest of the LTTE leadership escaped to their forest hideouts and, while there were no casualities among the militants, the IPKF suffered the loss of more than 60 soldiers. Despite this defeat, the IPKF's second plan to subdue the LTTE was even more ambitious than the first – they aimed to capture Jaffna in four days. Two weeks later the IPKF had achieved their mission at the cost of between 2,000 and 5,000 civilian casualties, the death of 262 Indian soldiers and between 700 and 800 LTTE cadres (De Silva 1995: 263; Krishna 1999: 190). According to human rights groups, the death and destruction wreaked on Jaffna went far beyond anything the Sri Lankan Army had ever inflicted (Krishna 1999: 190–1). Moreover, once again, the LTTE leadership and most of its fighters eluded capture. They kept the IPKF, now 50,000 to 60,000 strong, in a counterinsurgency war in the Northern and Eastern Provinces for another two and a half years. During this time, the IPKF inadvertently became directly involved in the administration of the North and Eastern provinces, even while its heavy-handed tactics isolated more and more of the population (De Silva 1995: 294).

The Sri Lankan presidential elections of December 1988 were contested by two main candidates, the Prime Minister R. Premadasa and Sirimavo Bandaranaike, who were both against the Indo-Sri Lankan Agreement and were committed to ousting the IPKF from Sri Lanka as soon as possible (De Silva 1995: 300). Premadasa won the election by a slim margin and promptly informed India that he intended to use his inauguration speech to call for the immediate withdrawal of Indian troops and a review of the Agreement. While Premadasa did not carry through with this threat, it prompted a revision of India's policies in New Delhi. It was decided that while India would not agree to an immediate withdrawal, or to modifying the Agreement extensively, it would be willing to undertake a phased withdrawal beginning in March 1989 (Dixit 1998: 279–81).

In April, Premadasa announced a temporary cease-fire and, in May, his representatives began direct negotiations with the LTTE on the de-induction of the IPKF from Sri Lanka (Gunaratna 1993: 283–8). Evidence later emerged that Premadasa had offered arms and funds to the LTTE to fight the IPKF. In response, RAW attempted to create and arm a new organization, the Tamil National Army (TNA) which was meant to protect the India–friendly Eelam Peoples Revolutionary Liberation Front (EPRLF) government in the Northeast against the LTTE and the Sri Lankan Forces after the IPKF's departure.[10] RAW relied on militant groups opposed to the LTTE to recruit members to the TNA. Invariably these 'recruits' were teenage boys abducted from their families. Unsurprisingly, these child soldiers proved no match for the LTTE and were massacred by the hundreds (De Silva 1995: 317; Krishna 1999: 201–2).

In June, Premadasa announced that he now rejected the previous timetable for the IPKF's departure from Sri Lanka and wanted Indian troops to leave Sri Lanka by the end of July, exactly two years since they arrived (Gunaratna 1993: 289). He then sent the first of what would be a series of acrimonious letters exchanged with Rajiv Gandhi and leaked to the press which implied that the IPKF had destabilized Sri Lanka (Dixit 1998: 371–81). He asked for the Indo-Sri Lankan Agreement of 1987 to be replaced with an Indo-Sri Lanka Friendship Treaty and repeatedly stressed that for the IPKF to remain in Sri Lankan for longer than they were welcome would be considered a gross violation of international law. Repudiating the Indian government's desire for a plural and federal Sri Lankan state, Premadasa emphasized that he would work for a political solution 'within the framework of our Constitution but must also preserve the sovereignty of our people, the unitary character and the territorial integrity of our country' (Quoted in Dixit 1998: 379). In response, Rajiv Gandhi blamed the Sri Lankan government's failure to implement the proposals of the Agreement for the continuation of Tamil militancy and emphasized the need, 'in the spirit of traditional friendship', for a mutually agreed timetable for the withdrawal of the IPKF, keeping in mind the obligations of both countries under the Agreement (Quoted in Dixit 1998: 375).

In the end, neither Premadasa nor Gandhi got their way completely. Eventually, Indian representatives gave up any hope of upholding the Agreement by tying the withdrawal of the IPKF with the effective devolution of powers to the provinces and Premadasa's deadline came and went with Indian troops remaining in Sri Lanka. Instead, both sides eventually agreed to a phased withdrawal to be completed by March 1990. Rajiv Gandhi, who by this time had well and truly tarnished his image as a politically innocent technocrat thanks to a corruption scandal involving the Swedish arms manufacturer, Bofors, was defeated in the general election held in November 1989.[11] The new National Front coalition government of V.P. Singh was eager to extricate Indian troops from Sri Lanka and tried to expedite the process. The last of the Indian troops left Sri Lanka on 24 March, one week before the deadline (De Silva 1995: 319–20).

The Gujral doctrine

While in the 1970s, South Asia was a space of fear and danger and in the 1980s, it was a space of desire, South Asia in the early 1990s was a space of lack, often sharply contrasted to the rise of economic power and the regional cohesiveness of East Asia. In a speech given in May 1992, which reflects the general perception of weakness that followed India's ignominious exit from Sri Lanka, its balance of payments crisis in 1991, and the political flux brought about by the end of the Congress Party's dominance of Indian politics and the rise of coalition governments at the centre, Eduardo Faleiro (1992b: 214), the Minister of State for External Affairs, argued that in contrast to East Asia, South Asia was a region bedevilled by bilateral problems, economic problems and environmental degradation:

> Regional cooperation is now gaining ground practically in all parts of the world and is the wave of the future. We have to face the harsh reality that if our region does not make an effort and fails to be relevant to rest of the world, then it could be by-passed, marginalised and relegated to the periphery for decades to come.
>
> (Faleiro 1992a: 212)

In this context, ASEAN had much to teach South Asia, according to I.K. Gujral (2003: 189), the External Affairs Minister from 1989 to 1990, and the government would give priority to 'South Asian friendship, as doing so would guide the region towards global change'. Normalizing relations with Bangladesh and Nepal and 'removing from the India–Sri Lanka relationship, the abrasive load of the presence of the IPKF in Sri Lanka' were all priorities. Gujral argued that even though renewed fighting between the LTTE and Sri Lankan military was creating concerns about another refugee influx, this was 'Sri Lanka's internal problem and we did not want to intervene' for 'how can any one of us afford to take advantage of domestic problems … of our neighbours?' (Gujral 2003: 189–90).

On this basis, while again serving as External Affairs Minister from 1996 to 1997 and Prime Minister from 1997 to 1998, Gujral formulated and promoted the 'Gujral doctrine', a notion he had first mooted in a speech at Chatham House in 1996:

> The 'Gujral Doctrine', if I may call it so, states that, first, with its neighbours like Sri Lanka, Bangladesh, Bhutan, Maldives and Nepal, India does not ask for reciprocity, but gives and accommodates what it can in good faith and trust. Second, we believe that no South Asian country should allow its territory to be used against the interests of another country of the region. Third, that none should interfere in the internal affairs of another. Fourth, all South Asian countries must respect each other's territorial integrity and sovereignty. And finally, they should settle all their disputes through peaceful bilateral negotiations.
>
> (Gujral 1997: 2833)

While the second, third and fourth points had all been articulated previously as elements of India's South Asia policy it was the principle of non-reciprocity that was noteworthy. Tying his Doctrine closely to the discourse of postcolonial difference, Gujral argued that India's 'cultural journey' could be captured by two words – 'Assimilation and Defiance. We assimilated new technologies, new ideas and new languages. At the same time, we did not get overwhelmed by them. The articulation of the defiance … is the unique character of our freedom struggle' (Gujral 2003: 22). In the long-term, India's foreign policy aimed to 'transform an old world order for the benefit of the world as a whole' for 'we view the entire world as one family (*Vasudativa Kutumbakam*)' (Gujral 2003: 29). Gujral's (2003: 109) narrative of Indian civilization's history followed Nehru's and he explicitly invoked Nehru by referring to his doctrine as 'a new 'Panchsheel'. His doctrine, however, was more reminiscent of Rajagopalchari's politics of friendship, for he argued that,

> [a] close study of history convinced me that whenever necessary and required, India should be prepared to offer unilateral concessions to improve relationships with neighbouring countries … I was no starry-eyed idealist

ignoring the element of reciprocity in international relations, but saw no contradiction in going an extra mile to inspire confidence and generate momentum towards building up new partnerships in South Asia. This approach of accommodation has proven more beneficial than a narrow obsession with mechanical reciprocity.

(Gujral 2003: xviii)

After the damage wrought to India's exceptionalist identity by its involvement in Sri Lanka therefore, the Gujral Doctrine was an attempt to re-anchor postcolonial India in an older framework. During Gujral's tenure as Prime Minister in the United Front government from 1997 to 1998, India signed historic water-sharing treaties with Bangladesh and Nepal and supported the building of a road link between Nepal and Bangladesh – a long-standing Nepali demand. It also offered tariff concessions on hundreds of consumer goods to promote the South Asian Preferential Trade Area (SAPTA), signed an investment promotion agreement with Sri Lanka, unilaterally reduced tariffs and removed non-tariff barriers on tens of products exported from Sri Lanka and offered financial assistance to improve the trade imbalance between India and Sri Lanka (Harshe 2005: 338). With regard to Sri Lanka's civil war, Gujral, like those before him, noted that '[a]s a close neighbour, India cannot but be affected by the conflict in Sri Lanka'. India's desire, however, was 'to be helpful without being obtrusive' (Gujral 1997: 2835). In the case of Pakistan, Gujral offered dialogue and 'unilateral steps to improve the relationship at the people-to-people level. We are also trying to preserve a positive atmosphere, by avoiding polemic and ignoring the occasional hostile rhetoric from across the border' (Gujral 1997: 2833–4). Pakistan, however, was a notable exception in Gujral's Chatham House speech just as it was the exception in Nehru's politics of friendship and Gujral later stated that India's relations with Pakistan did not full under the purview of his doctrine (Noorani 2007).

Conclusion

This chapter has argued that making sense of India's political and military intervention in Sri Lanka's civil war requires an understanding of the broader political and social milieu in which these foreign policy decisions became possible. Specifically, I suggested that Indira Gandhi's foreign policy should be considered in the context of politics of insecurity and paranoia that dominated her time in power. This politics of insecurity drew on narratives of backwardness that pointed to the subcontinent's inherent disunity and vulnerability to invasion and conquest and reflected the developmental strains on the postcolonial state in the 1970s and 1980s. In Indira Gandhi's foreign policy discourse 'South Asia' emerged as a space of danger which created the conditions for confrontational policies toward the countries of the region.

Rajiv Gandhi took foreign policy-making from a climate of insecurity and paranoia to one of over-confidence as South Asia was rendered into a space in which to enact India's rationality, decisiveness, efficiency and consensual leadership in an effort to mark a break from what were seen as the failures of the developmental state. Indian foreign policy toward Sri Lanka became more explicitly interventionist during the 1980s as India rapidly became an official mediator, peace agreement guarantor and peacekeeper in the civil war. The apparently consensual nature of this intervention aimed at reiterating rather than undermining India's dominant state identity as a different sort of nation-state that eschews the domination of others. Thus, while foreign policy in the 1970s needs to be understood in the context of a particular preoccupation with India's failing modernity, foreign policy in the 1980s was driven by a revitalized bid for a successful modernity. Indira Gandhi's pessimism and Rajiv Gandhi's optimism nonetheless produced a politics of interventionism that proved equally destructive.

The end of India's military involvement in Sri Lanka occurred within a rapidly changing political, economic and social context which created a space for the empowerment of new political groups and individuals. One such individual, I.K. Gujral, used the disastrous consequences of India's Sri Lanka policies to introduce an altogether different approach to South Asia that drew on discourses of India's civilizational exceptionalism. Gujral's tenure ended in 1998 with the election of a coalition government led by the Hindu nationalist political party, the BJP. The BJP came to power determined to change India's foreign policy and given the Hindu nationalists' preoccupation with threatening Others, their valorization of military power and their promotion of a Hindu-centric historical narrative of Greater India, the reinscription of the region as a space of danger and, at the same time, a space of desire for the enactment of Indian hegemony was a distinct possibility. As we shall see in the next chapter, however, when in government, the BJP-led coalition claimed that it too had adopted the Gujral doctrine.

7 Foreign policy, identity and the BJP

Correcting the 'emasculation of state power'?[1]

The end of the Congress Party's dominance of Indian politics in the 1990s ushered in a period of unstable coalition governments. The Hindu nationalist BJP, whose electoral fortunes had been on the rise since the 1980s, came to power as the leading member of the National Democratic Alliance (NDA) which formed government in 1998 and stayed in power until 2004 when it was defeated by the United Progressive Alliance led by the Congress. Scholarly opinion has been divided on the role of Hindu nationalist ideology on the BJP-led coalition's foreign policy and the extent to which the NDA brought about a change in direction in Indian foreign policy. Some scholars have argued that despite the BJP's pre-election promises to bring about sweeping change in India's strategic culture, pre-1998 norms constrained its ability to impart its ideological beliefs on foreign policy, though, why this is the case is not made entirely clear in these accounts (Chaulia 2002; Ogden 2010; Chiriyankandath and Wyatt 2005: 211). A few authors have suggested that the BJP was prepared to defy the international community and add a militaristic, aggressive tone to India's global ambitions in a way that other political parties were not and, thus, succeeded in 'communalizing national security' by framing events in Hindu nationalist rhetoric (Ruparelia 2006: 325–7; Vanaik 2002: 324–5, 8–9; Kapur 2006: 206–9). Others view the NDA period as one of significant change, but argue that the NDA was simply developing the policies of previous Congress governments and responding to structural changes associated with the end of the Cold War (Mohan 2003: 260–3; Sridharan 2006: 87).

I argue in this chapter that a discursive analysis of the BJP's foreign policy indicates that a distinctive ethico-political framework did underpin the BJP's attempt to redefine India's identity and foreign policy. This framework was the result of a particular response to colonial modernity and colonial narratives of India's backwardness and aspects of it are shared by sections of the Indian 'strategic elite'. At the same time, the BJP was not unconstrained in its push to remedy what one prominent BJP leader, Jaswant Singh (1999: 13), described as the 'emasculation of state power' for, like previous governments, it had to grapple with the ethico-political project of postcolonial identity initially articulated by Nehru. Indeed, far from ridding India of its postcolonial ambivalence, the BJP's foreign policy discourse reveals an ambivalence of its own, which rests not on a wariness of Western modernity, but on a desire to appropriate Western modernity and at the same time retain a distinctive identity for India which is shaped in opposition to Islam and Muslims, in particular. For this reason, one facet of India's postcolonial difference – its restraint and responsibility – was a key part of the construction of state identity in the BJP's foreign policy discourse, even though this undermined the aggressive and militaristic aspects of Hindu nationalist ideology.

The chapter begins by outlining the rise of the BJP in Indian politics and the views of key figures associated with Hindu nationalism on issues related to foreign policy and international relations. The second part of the chapter focuses on the NDA's decision to carry out nuclear tests in 1998 and the third part analyses its approach to South Asia focusing, in particular, on relations with Pakistan and Bangladesh and the BJP leadership's appropriation of the concept of 'soft power' in its foreign policy discourse.

The BJP and Indian foreign policy

The rise of the BJP

The reasons for the demise of the Congress Party and rise of Hindu nationalism as a force in Indian politics have been much debated. The centralization of political power under Indira Gandhi, corruption, organizational disintegration, and the inability of Congress governments to deliver solutions to entrenched problems like inequality and poverty helped to delegitimize the party and created the space for the emergence of other political actors (Guha 2007; Varshney 1993: 243). The BJP is said to have taken advantage of the communalization of Indian politics by Congress governments which, in the 1980s, sought short-term political gain by taking sides in disputes within and between religious communities, thus undermining the dominant interpretation of Indian secularism that placed the state above the religious divisions in the society (Thakur 1993; Jaffrelot 1996; Varshney 1993). Others have suggested that the BJP's electoral fortunes rose, not because voters began to embrace a Hindu identity politics, but because of its opposition to the Congress's policies on caste-based reservations in educational seats and government jobs. Such policies alienated some upper caste, urban, middle class groups that saw their social, cultural and economic dominance threatened and became receptive to Hindu nationalist discourses. These promised to restore social order, discipline and collective strength by emphasizing notions of national honor, anti-corruption, responsible governance and stability and vaguely committing to policies of economic liberalization (Hansen 1999; Varshney 1993; Jaffrelot 1996: 437–8). It is in this context that the growth in the popularity of the BJP among business executives, administrative officers and former military personnel, a substantial number of whom joined the BJP in 1991, can be understood (Jaffrelot 1996: 433).

One of the administrative officers who joined in 1991 was Brajesh Mishra, a retired diplomat, who later became Prime Minister Atal Behari Vajpayee's national security advisor. Together with Jaswant Singh, another recent BJP member, Mishra was a key individual in the making of the NDA's foreign policy. The appeal of the BJP to the constituency represented by Singh and Mishra is evident in Singh's memoir, *A Call to Honour*. Singh was one of the first ex-military men to join the BJP and served as Minister for External Affairs in the NDA government from 1998 to 2002. He joined the BJP in 1980 and, like Mishra but unlike most BJP leaders, did not have a background in the RSS, the wing of the Hindu nationalist movement that organizes and trains young men, ostensibly for the purpose of providing the strong 'Hindu nation' they wish to create with the disciplined workers and leaders it needs. Singh rejects the term 'Hindu nationalist' as a label for the BJP because of its connotations of intolerance and, instead, uses Savarkar's term, Hindutva, which he defines as 'representing an alternative thought, a self-confident nationalism and pronounced emphasis on civilizational and cultural identity of India as being Hindu, a meritocratic party structure and hierarchy' (Singh 2009a: 405). This alternative thought had 'gathered an (totally undeserved) imagery of extremism' when in reality it is 'profoundly humanist' because at its core lies the 'all-inclusive' concept of 'Sanatan Dharma' which was accommodating of all faiths (Singh 2009a: 89–90). Singh accepts that the BJP has been associated with violence, most notably in Gujarat in 2002 and in Ayodhya in 1992. In Gujarat, the state government of Narendra Modi was implicated in riots that led to the deaths of more than 2000 people, mostly Muslim, while in Ayodhya, the tearing down of the Babri Mosque by Hindu nationalists was accompanied by a similar amount of carnage. He explains this, however, as simply a 'mishandling of events' which was 'regretted' (Singh 2009a: 107).

Sentiments such as these have led to a labelling of Singh, together with Prime Minister Atal Behari Vajpayee, whose decision it was make Singh the External Affairs Minister against the objections of the RSS, as representing the 'moderate' wing of the BJP. Ashok Kapur (2006: 206), for instance, distinguishes between 'soft' and 'hard' Hindutva and argues that while the latter is associated with the RSS and anti-Muslim riots, it had little bearing on foreign policy, which was the domain of 'soft' Hindutva. Yet, as Christophe Jaffrelot (1996: 475) has argued, the differences between 'moderates' and 'hardliners' in the BJP are not over fundamental convictions but, rather, concern the tactics for gaining and holding power. Thus, while Singh 'regretted' the carnage at Ayodhya he also justified it as marking a necessary 'transition from the old to the new' (Quoted in Jaffrelot 1996: 475). Likewise, though Vajpayee initially expressed regret about the events at Ayodhya, calling them 'the party's worst miscalculation', he also described the Babri mosque as a 'symbol of shame' that 'has been erased' and claimed that '[i]n Indonesia, Malaysia, wherever Muslims are living they don't want to live in harmony. They don't mix with the society. They are not interested in living in peace' (Quoted in Popham 1998; Quoted in Bhatt 2002).

Morality and strategic thought

Such views of Islam and Muslims were central to the construction of India's identity in the BJP's foreign policy discourse as was the depiction of Indian traditions of thought as overly idealistic. Like Nehru, Singh argued that India became a subject nation partly because it had missed the industrial revolution. For Singh, however, India's failure to evolve a tradition of 'strategic thought' was the main reason for its backwardness:

> We thought ... 'What does India, well-meaning India, have to fear from any quarter?' To my mind, this was, in turn, both a consequence and a cause. This mentality was the consequence of a failure to evolve an Indian state, and became the cause, in turn, of failing to do so even after Independence.
>
> (Singh 1998)

India's flaws were its 'high-civilizational sense of chivalrous warfare' and its 'belief that our opponents would also fight in the manner to which we subscribed. Invaders down the ages routinely, therefore, outmaneuvered us because we remained wedded to the tactical doctrines of honor...' (Singh 1998). Moreover, India's 'excessive and at times ersatz pacifism, both internal and external, has twisted India's strategic culture into all kinds of absurdities' (Singh 1998). For Singh, India's 'great failing' was the result of 'an accommodative and forgiving Hindu milieu; successive Jain, Buddhist, and later Vaishnav-Bhakti influences resulting in an excessive piety...' (Singh 1999: 13). This is an argument reminiscent of Savarkar who argued that India had proved easy prey to invaders because of the influence of Buddhism and its notions of 'universal brotherhood' and nonviolence which had sapped the 'virility' of the Hindu race leaving it at the mercy of invading 'barbarian hordes' (Savarkar 1938: 28). Having seen the disastrous political consequences of Buddhist expansion, Savarkar argued, the Hindus turned away from the 'mumbos and jumbos of Universal Brotherhood', became 'intensely self-conscious as an organism', and eventually expelled the intruders. Thereafter, a re-militarized India was left 'in an undisturbed possession of independence for centuries on centuries to come' until the 'undisturbed enjoyment of peace and plenty' lulled it into a 'sense of false security and bred a habit of living in the land of dreams' thus again leaving it susceptible to invasion and conquest (Savarkar 1938: 31, 6, 53–4).

According to Singh, overcoming this vulnerability meant that '[w]e have to leaven our idealism with geopolitical realities' (Singh 1998). Unfortunately postcolonial India had only perpetuated the problem, for 'Gandhian pacifism' and nonalignment had 'relegated strategic thinking to an irrelevancy' (Singh 1998). Consequently, 'an unintended consequence of all these influences, spread over many centuries, has been a near total emasculation of the concept of state power' (Singh 1999: 14). Nonetheless, like Savarkar, Singh sees reason for hope in India's history for 'despite the combined influence of such pacifist faiths' there was 'so much else about warfare as an instrument of policy, about the craft of war, about valour and heroism' that remained, as evidenced by the resistance to the Mughal empire which could not spread its reach to the whole of India (Singh 1999: 14).

There is a consistent conflation in Singh's writings between 'confusion' and 'morality' which draws on the work of K. Subrahmanyam, once the doyenne of Indian strategic analysis. Remarking on Nehru's comments on how the 'moral aspect' in foreign policy troubled him, Singh writes:

> This 'moral aspect' was in essence a confusion; it periodically afflicts other nations too, for example, the United States of America. It is a search for the 'moral' in the realm of international affairs, reconciliation then of that 'moral' with the demonstrated reality of the conduct of nations in pursuit of their respective national goals and interests. It is a confusion that arises from not differentiating between individual human morality and ethics, and the reality of national interests. It is also a consequence of not recognising that between high idealism and the hard stone of a pursuit of national goals what will splinter is always this 'moral aspect' ...
>
> Always being 'troubled' by the individual 'moral aspect' resulted in serious long-term consequences, for India and its successive generations, in four ... areas of critical importance: Tibet; Sino-Indian relations; Indo-Pak standoff ... and the nuclear armament question. Ambiguity and a lack of clarity about national purpose on all the four became the national stand.
>
> (Singh 1999: 42–3)

These passages contain a crude articulation of ideas that can be found in some of the work of a diverse group of thinkers, including Hans Morgenthau, Reinhold Niebuhr, E.H. Carr and George Kennan, who have been labelled 'realists' in contemporary IR theory, such as: social action can be dichotomized between 'selfish' and 'moral' actions; individuals can be moral but states cannot; moral action cannot be rational; morality is dangerous. Yet, as several revisionist engagements with post-World War II 'realist' thought have made clear, the dismissal of the moral in the works of some of these thinkers and their interpreters in contemporary IR, obscures the extent to which they all advance a normative vision of what should drive state behaviour (Bell 2008b, Scheuerman 2009; Williams 2005; Campbell 2001: 105–6).

The growing body of scholarship that has challenged the many misleading preconceptions about realism points to the variety of moral considerations which inform the different strands of thought that have been labelled 'realist'. Sean Molloy (2008) argues, for instance, that Morgenthau's tragic understanding of politics led him to an ethics of the lesser evil while for Carr, ethical behaviour in international relations would focus on recognizing the legitimacy of the claims of others. Singh's moral construction of the national interest in *Defending India*, which was written before he entered government, displays a preoccupation with military power and statism that brings him close to espousing a simplistic *realpolitik* form of realism (Bell 2008a: 2). Yet, while he often reiterates a narrative of Indian civilization as preoccupied with morality and portrays this as a liability because it neglects military power, this narrative also serves a vital role in constructing India's identity in a manner that is explicitly counter-poised to Islam and Pakistan and this complicates his professed *real-politik* commitments.

As noted by Strobe Talbot, Jaswant Singh's counterpart in several rounds of talks which began in 1998, Islam fits into Singh's worldview in ways that put it 'inherently at odds with his concept of Hindu civilization':

> in his paean to Hinduism, Jaswant noted how this most polytheistic of the world's great religions included a dizzying array of female goddesses, thus proving itself egalitarian, in contrast to Muslim society, with its proclivity for male chauvinism and misogyny. Hinduism, over the millennia, had proved itself absorptive and hospitable, while Islam was all about conquest and conversion by the sword.
>
> (Talbot 2004: 134)

While Singh admitted that 'there had been 'aberrations, tiny bubbles of irrationality' from time to time' in the form of riots and massacres, he told Talbot that 'India had maintained its 'civilizational essence, its innate rationality, and its ability to absorb shocks'' (Talbot 2004: 119). As for Pakistan, Singh described it as 'the 'avatar' of all that was intolerant, aggressive, and terrorizing about radical Islam. India, by contrast, was the avatar of all that was benign, inclusive, and tolerant in Hinduism – and Hindutva' and the biggest problem in the India–US relationship was 'America's refusal to recognize that the United States and India were on the same side in the war on terrorism – which meant we should be allies against Pakistan' (Talbot 2004: 134, 119). Talbot (2004: 119) argues that this was Singh's variant of Samuel Huntington's (1996) clash of civilizations thesis: 'Jaswant's variant was both ecumenical and Manichean. It posited the need for the Judeo-Christian West, secular India, and moderate Islamic states to make common cause against a single evil of global reach, rooted in radical regimes like Pakistan's and radical groups like al Qaeda'.

Indeed, Singh and some members of the 'strategic elite' regularly tapped into views of Islam and Muslim societies popularized by the likes of Huntington, for whom Islamic societies possess 'consummatory systems' in which the society, the state and authority are all guided by religion while 'Hindu' society possesses an 'instrumental culture' in which 'traditions' are used in such a way that changes associated with modernization appear not to affect existing social institutions (Huntington 1996: 77). K. Subrahmanyam writes in his introduction to Singh's *Defending India*, for instance,

> Professor Huntington is not wholly wrong in talking about the clash of civilizations. It has always been there in history ... While Hindu civilization and culture, irrespective of its many flaws and shortcomings in societal

terms is basically secular and nonexpansionist as it is a non-proselytizing one, Islam was used by the British and cultural and religious chauvinists in a confrontational mode leading to the partition.

(Singh 1999: xiv)

The genealogy of the Indian appropriation of this denigration of Muslims and Islam, which has long had a presence in Western thought, can be traced back to the colonial era (Sardar 1999; Said 1985). For example, Bankim Chandra Chatterjee's efforts to rid Hinduism of its degeneracy and take it back to its 'pure' form, which were outlined in Chapter 2, were underpinned with an obvious hostility toward Islam and Muslims who were seen as the original invaders against whom Hindu authority had to be established before the British could be confronted. Bankim's views were informed by both the biases of the upper caste Hindu Bengali elite at the time as well as the prejudices of European post-Enlightenment culture and were shaped by the need to define Hinduism as a paragon of tolerance and spirituality unlike Islam, which was portrayed as intolerant and unethical (Chatterjee 1986: 77). This strand of thinking was most explicitly picked up by Savarkar, who was dismissive of the idea that British 'divide and rule' policies had produced the split between Hindus and Muslims because 'the solid fact is that the so-called communal questions are but a legacy handed down to us by centuries of a cultural religious and national antagonism' (Savarkar 1949: 26).

Muslims figure prominently in Savarkar's explanation for why an ancient and advanced 'Hindu civilization' succumbed to British rule. Specifically, it was repeated invasions by 'tyrannical Muslims' which took India into a dark age of oppression and persecution (Savarkar 1938: 54–6). Borrowing from Western discourses the image of the bloodthirsty Muslim, Savarkar argued that not just India but many other 'nations and civilizations fell in heaps before the sword of Islam of Peace!!' (Savarkar 1938: 54–5). He wrote of Islam:

> where religion is goaded on by rapine and rapine serves as a hand-maid to religion, the propelling force that is generated by these together is only equalled by the profundity of human misery and devastation they leave behind them in their march.

(Savarkar 1938: 54–5)

In contrast, Hindutva was concerned with love for the mythic land of India, which welcomed everyone who made the choice to love it as Mother and Father (Savarkar 1938: 146; Bakhale 2010).

As we shall see in the remainder of this chapter, the BJP's foreign policy discourse drew on these representations in an attempt to present India as the epitome of restraint and responsibility in contrast to Muslim Pakistan, even while it sought to counter depictions of India and Indians as effeminate and pacifistic.

Hindu nationalism, modernity and nuclear weapons

Perhaps the most controversial foreign policy 'event' of the BJP era was its decision to declare India a nuclear weapons power in May 1998 after carrying out a series of nuclear tests. Scholars who have attempted 'realist' explanations for India's decision to nuclearize have cited the security threats, both real and perceived, posed by Pakistan and China (Malik 1998; Ganguly 1999). Ganguly (1999: 149) has argued, for instance, that 'India's perceptions of external threats and the reactions of the great powers to its security played a *fundamental* role in driving the nuclear program' (emphasis added). Indeed, the threat of the 'Chinese Bomb' has been a factor in Indian debates on nuclear weapons since the 1962 India–China war and China's nuclear tests in 1964 (Krishna 1966). The perception of external threat, however, fails to account for the timing of the nuclear tests in 1998 and the 20 year gap between the 'PNE' and 'Pokharan II'. The tests were conducted at a time when India–China relations had been steadily improving – the two countries signed confidence building accords in 1993 and 1996 and, following this rapprochement, China's diplomatic support and technology transfers to Pakistan decreased (Mistry 2003: 120–1). Moreover, given the reactive nature of Pakistan's military policy, there is little to support the argument that Pakistan would have acquired nuclear weapons regardless of whether India had exercised the nuclear option and, therefore, posed a threat that had to be pre-empted. Further, India's nuclearization was bound to provoke Pakistan into nuclearizing, thus making India's edge in conventional forces irrelevant.

Some scholars have sought to explain India's nuclearization on account of the BJP's Hindu nationalist ideology (Vanaik 2002; Hymans 2002; Hymans 2006; Das 2008). Hymans (2006: 198), for instance, argues that 'Vajpayee, unlike his predecessors, was an oppositional nationalist vis-à-vis Pakistan'. Thus, Pakistan's missile test in April 1998 – which did not cause much of a stir among the strategic elite or the public – 'played into his preexisting tendency to experience a mixture of fear and pride and the letting loose of those emotions proved an explosive psychological cocktail' that led to his decision to conduct nuclear tests. Das (2008) likewise argues that the BJP's articulation of Pakistan as a threat requiring a nuclear deterrent was shaped by its exclusionary Hindu nationalist ideology. Others have dismissed or downplayed the relevance of the BJP's ideology because it was a Congress government that initiated India's nuclear weapons program and it was a Congress leader that gave the go-ahead for India's first nuclear test in 1974 and laid the groundwork for the second test in 1998 (Ganguly 1999: 173; Varadarajan 2004: 337–8). As I have argued in previous chapters, explaining India's relationship with nuclear technology should go beyond a strategic rationale and party political ideology and take into account the broader historical, cultural, and ethico-political context in which foreign policy decisions are made. Yet, the role of the hypermasculine, aggressively modernizing facet of Hindu nationalism that advocates the creation of a militaristic Indian state cannot be minimized in explaining why India took the penultimate step of actually testing nuclear weapons and explicitly declaring itself a nuclear weapons state at that particular juncture in 1998. As Itty Abraham has argued, the decision of the BJP to cross 'the test threshold was symbolically significant as it sought to signal identity with dominant international norms of nuclear meaning' (Abraham 2004: 4999). I will argue, however, that the BJP's appropriation of older discourses on 'nuclear apartheid' and disarmament in the aftermath of the tests, indicate that it was not entirely successful in this respect. My account therefore differs from Abraham, Vanaik, Hymans and Das because I argue that the BJP's nuclear discourse is not as unequivocal as they suggest.

Before examining the 1998 tests and its aftermath, however, it is necessary to consider the developments in nuclear policy during the two decades between India's nuclear explosions. I argue in the next section that India's refusal in 1996 to be party to the CTBT and its use of the language of national security to partly justify its decision indicated hesitant signs of an increased willingness to join the nuclear mainstream. This made the path toward nuclear tests in 1998 easier, though not inevitable.

Beyond the PNE

For Itty Abraham (1998: 164–5) India's inability to confine the signification of the 1974 test to the domain of development meant that, ultimately, it was an event that moved India's nuclear energy establishment and its political leadership 'from a mythic space of non-alignment and peaceful co-existence into an every-day realm of naturalized fear, threat, danger and insecurity'. He suggests that in the years following the 1974 test:

> They began to re-imagine the history of the Indian nuclear programme to fit these 'facts', they began to build long- and short-range rockets and ballistic missiles, and they began to change the state's self-representation.... Ideological sustenance could now be drawn from the dominant discourse of International Relations, the currency and speech of inter-state interaction.
>
> (Abraham 1998: 164–5)

In the years after the 1974 test the nuclear science establishment was subjected to various technology transfer controls as a global non-proliferation regime took effect. Nonetheless, there is indeed evidence that following the test, the nuclear science establishment made a conscious effort to gear the Indian nuclear program toward military development. According to Abraham (1998: 103), this shift began in the late 1950s and early 1960s after the completion of India's first nuclear reactors and was due to the realization that nuclear energy might not be able to deliver the ideological or economic benefits expected of it. The response of the nuclear science establishment, Abraham (1998: 106), argues, 'was to situate atomic energy within another realm of state activity, equally central to the state's ideological mission, equally justified in terms of *raison d'etat*: they decided to build bombs'. Yet, what may have been a relatively easy shift in focus for the scientific establishment was far more difficult for a postcolonial state anchored in a desire fashion a different modernity and this can be seen in the discourse following the 1974 test which did not draw sustenance from 'realism' but continued to try to reiterate an identity based on overcoming backwardness but also demonstrating India's exceptionalism. The nuclear explosion did threaten to upset this balance, however, as we shall see, it did not have the power to change India's self-representation altogether and it is too simplistic to argue, as Khilnani (1999: xii) does, that after 1974 'it was only a matter of time before India would become a nuclear state'.

Thus, while the nuclear science establishment did quietly go about improving the design of India's nuclear device and lobbied for further nuclear tests, they did so without portraying their proposed tests as the beginning of a nuclear weapons program. According to Raja Ramanna and another nuclear scientist, Homi Sethna, Indira Gandhi had little interest in another 'demonstration' despite Pakistan's increasing attempts to develop its nuclear capability. This was contrary to the expectations of American officials that another nuclear test was almost certain to be undertaken after Canada resumed its technology transfers and because an explosion would be a useful diversion from internal unrest (Perkovich 1999: 192–3; 1974b; 1974c).

The Janata coalition which came to power after the Emergency maintained an emphasis on disarmament. While the External Affairs Minister under Janata, Atal Bihari Vajpayee, was a member of the Hindu nationalist Jana Sangh which had long harboured nuclear ambitions for India, his party's views were subordinate to those of the Prime Minister, Morarji Desai, who like Indira Gandhi and Nehru before him, was also Minister for Atomic Energy. Desai considered nuclear weapons development morally abhorrent and financially irresponsible but he was also opposed to signing the NPT and his views about 'peaceful' nuclear explosions fluctuated from opposing them entirely – because as he put it in a debate in the Lok Sabha in July 1977, the 1974 test had been 'misunderstood' and had 'created all these difficulties' – to not ruling them out completely if they were proven necessary for scientific development (1977: 31; Thomas 1980: 238).

According to George Perkovich (1999: 242–3), in late 1982 or early 1983, after Indira Gandhi was returned to power, nuclear scientists Raja Ramanna and V.S. Arunchalam, presented her with the argument that a nuclear test was necessary for India's technological advancement. Once again, however, they were careful to present the test as a scientific experiment rather than the beginning of a nuclear weapons program. According to Perkovich (1999: 243), after initially agreeing to the test, Gandhi quickly changed her mind. The reasons for this are unknown and the allegation that American pressure was involved remains unsubstantiated. K. Subrahmanyam (1998), a prominent member of the pro-bomb lobby, has claimed that Indira Gandhi's son and successor as Prime Minister, Rajiv Gandhi, approved the beginning of a nuclear weapons program in 1988 after the failure of the nuclear weapon states to heed his calls for disarmament – which included an 'Action Plan' to eliminate nuclear weapons by 2010 and a proposal for a nuclear weapon-free Asia. By his own admission, however,

Subrahmanyam had not been in contact with Gandhi since 1985 following a meeting in which the latter complained that the former's briefings never focused on the possibility of signing the NPT (Perkovich 1999: 276). Moreover, whatever the truth of Subrahmanyam's claim, there is no evidence that Rajiv Gandhi contemplated marking this shift with a nuclear test or considered revising his opinions on the evils of the policy of nuclear deterrence, which he once described as 'the ultimate expression of the philosophy of terrorism holding humanity hostage to the presumed security needs of a few' (India 1988b: 282).

When the threat from China was once again raised following a short skirmish in 1987 along the India–China border, Rajiv Gandhi responded by denying that this changed his position on nuclear weapons: 'We have lived with the Chinese bomb for several years without feeling that we must produce our own' (Quoted in Perkovich 1999: 290). The government also faced pressure to nuclearize when reports emerged of further developments in Pakistan's nuclear program following the claims made by the Pakistani nuclear scientist A.Q. Khan. Rajiv Gandhi, however, would only give a commitment to revaluating the government's position if Pakistan developed a nuclear bomb but reiterated that the 'costs of going nuclear, not just money cost, but all the other costs, are much too heavy and we would like to do anything to prevent ourselves going nuclear' (Gandhi 1990: 461). Privately, according to a close advisor, although the Pakistani threat was taken seriously, 'we didn't feel we had to best them' (Quoted in Perkovich 1999: 283). Moreover, even though in 1988 there were continued advances in the design of nuclear devices, to the extent that they could be turned into weapons if desired, Perkovich (1999: 295) notes that the scientists involved did not view their activities as constituting a nuclear weapons program.

Similar sentiments to those held by Rajiv Gandhi about nuclear weapons were expressed by Narasimha Rao when he was External Affairs Minister in 1982. Addressing the UN General Assembly's special session on disarmament Rao said: '[n]uclear war doctrines are, in essence, doctrines of terrorism practised by nation States' (India 1988b: 213). By 1995, however, Rao was Prime Minister and the nuclear scientific establishment was again pushing for nuclear tests in order to improve and demonstrate their technological innovations. Like Indira Gandhi before him, Rao apparently agreed to the tests only to rescind his permission. Despite claims that this was due to American pressure, according to K. Subrahmanyam (2004: 593), Rao explained his change of heart to him as being due to a lack of consensus among his economic, administrative and scientific advisors. Clearly, even in 1995 when India's nuclear weapons program was at an advanced stage, the impetus to cross the nuclear test threshold and risk stripping India's nuclear program completely free of its peaceful associations still did not exist.

In 1996, another one of Nehru's visions, a global agreement to end nuclear testing, became a potential reality in the Comprehensive Nuclear Test-Ban Treaty (CTBT). The CTBT obliged signatories to undertake 'not to carry out any nuclear weapon test explosion or any other nuclear explosion, and to prohibit and prevent any such nuclear explosion at any place under its jurisdiction or control'. Further, signatories were required to 'refrain from causing, encouraging, or in any way participating in the carrying out of any nuclear weapon test explosion or any other nuclear explosion' (1968). After India blocked consensus on the treaty at the Conference on Disarmament, the CTBT was taken to the UN General Assembly where it was passed with just India, Bhutan and Libya voting against it. India's position at the CTBT negotiations was consistent with its position thirty years ago at the talks for an NPT – objections to global hierarchy and coercion were central to its arguments. When India refused to rule out blocking the CTBT, for instance, the Minister of External Affairs, I.K. Gujral, recalled being subjected to rude and patronizing behaviour from the US Secretary of State Warren Christopher. 'This is frequently the way you Americans treat Indians' Gujral told Perkovich in an interview, 'unless we do something to make you stop and pay attention, you patronize us' (Perkovich 1999: 382–3).

India did indeed try to 'do something' to make the US 'pay attention' – during the CTBT negotiations India's chief negotiator, Arundhati Ghose, introduced into her speeches the language of national security (Ghose 1996). Ghose (1997: 239) argued that the treaty did not meet India's requirement that it be secured in a framework of global disarmament and include a time-bound framework for the elimination of all nuclear weapons. Moreover, India wanted a truly comprehensive test-ban that would prevent the continued refinement of existing nuclear weapons through laboratory testing. Instead, the treaty was anchored in a framework of non-proliferation and India's concerns were not taken seriously:

> It appeared that the United States was neither interested in India's concerns nor receptive to the Indian proposals that reflected these concerns. The United States appeared to be mainly interested in bringing Russia and China within a control regime ... The United Kingdom and France clearly viewed the CTBT as a pure non-proliferation measure aimed at non-nuclear states. They would not even consider qualitative capping of their weapons development through this Treaty.
>
> (Ghose 1997)

Thus, India's decision not to sign the treaty was based on '...its approach towards nuclear disarmament, its perception of a potential threat from the existence of nuclear weapons, its strategic circumstances and, above all, the unanimous rejection by the Indian Parliament of what was seen as an unequal, dangerous and coercive treaty' (Ghose 1997: 239). The gesture toward the dominant vocabulary of International Relations in the reference to 'strategic circumstances' clearly differentiated India's position from that taken during the NPT negotiations. Trivedi and Husain both raised the issue of security in their statements during the NPT negotiations as did Indira Gandhi. Yet, it was clear that security was conceived of in terms of economic development and the inherent dangers posed by nuclear weapons to all countries rather than as the search for military security in an anarchical world filled with states driven to maximize their power. Even though Ghose breaks with this to an extent it is important to note that she fails to elaborate on what these strategic circumstances are, and that this point is furtively sandwiched between references to traditional concerns about disarmament, the dangers posed to the world in general from existing stockpiles, and discrimination. In highlighting that India is 'above all' against an unequal and coercive treaty Ghose was still keen to emphasize the continuity of India's postcolonial difference as a country driven by its commitment to a non-colonial global order more than the imperatives of geopolitical self-interest.

Nonetheless, the appearance of the language of strategy in a discourse that was previously free of it suggests a significant shift. Strands of thinking that promote a coercive international relations have always been present in India and usually come to the fore after times of crises, as can be seen in the debates following China's nuclearization. Despite brief surges of popularity, such thinking remained necessarily marginalized in a country that sought to anchor its identity in the repudiation of the violent and dehumanizing elements of modernity. In 1996, however, India's postcolonial identity was more open to challenge. After the assassination of Rajiv Gandhi in 1989, India was led by a series of weak coalition governments and the period between May and June in 1996, when the negotiations for a CTBT were at a crucial stage, was a time of leadership flux at the level of the Office of the Prime Minister and at the Ministry of External Affairs. Gujral's defensiveness, as noted above, might also be understood in the context of the heightened challenge posed to the constitutive component of India's postcolonial identity – autonomy and freedom from coercion – by the program of neoliberal economic reforms which was introduced by the Rao government in 1991 and prompted accusations that India was once again succumbing to foreign pressure and selling out to a neo-colonial order (Varadarajan 2004: 336).

Moreover, a vocal pro-bomb lobby had come into existence by the mid-1990s and included the BJP and a group of analysts – among them K. Subramanyam and Raja Mohan – and government officials who, as David Cortright and Amitabh Mattoo (1996: 550) put it, used 'the idiom of Western strategic thought to support their arguments in favour of India crossing the nuclear threshold' and have the 'doctrine of nuclear deterrence' as 'an integral part of their world view'. One of these officials was an arms control advisor, Rakesh Sood, on whose advice Ghose had relied during the CTBT negotiations (Perkovich 1999: 379). According to Perkovich (1999: 379), Sood believed that 'the United States and others would pay more attention to Realpolitik presentations than to traditional moralism, whether or not India actually had a clear national security strategy'. Sood (2002) later went on to be India's Permanent Representative to the Conference on Disarmament where he gave speeches advocating a 'step-by-step process towards a legally-binding instrument prohibiting the use or threat of use of nuclear weapons' so by no means was there an outright transformation in the discursive representation of India's foreign policy. Nonetheless, the fact that Sood felt compelled to articulate India's position in the terms of national security is telling of the strength of the language of *realpolitik* in international relations, despite the end of the Cold War and the supposed rise of human rights norms and ethical foreign policies. The election of the BJP, which had long advocated *realpolitik* and nuclear weapons, added another important element in India's slide toward the 1998 nuclear tests.

Hindu nationalism and nuclear technology

As a number of authors have noted, an 'anxious masculinity', which builds on the gendered discourses of early Indian leaders like Bankim Chandra Chatterjee, Vivekananda and Aurobindo Ghose, permeates Hindu nationalist ideology (Kishwar 1998; Anand 2007). As Sikata Bannerjee (2006) and Runa Das (2006) have argued, moreover, this 'anxious masculinity' has important ramifications for Indian women, given that it reinforces patriarchal gender roles in which women are victims in need of protection and valorizes restrictive models of femininity associated with the 'heroic mother, chaste wife and celibate warrior'. My interest here, however, is on the way Hindu nationalist gender codings were employed in an attempt to transform India's state identity during the NDA era.

To trace the genealogy of these gender codings and their relation to violence and nuclear weapons, we must again consider the convictions of V.D. Savarkar. For Savarkar, the goal of (1949: 302, 201) Hindutva was to 'Hinduise all politics and militarise Hinduism' and he urged 'all Hindus to get themselves re-animated and re-born into a martial race' by re-learning the 'manly lessons' taught by figures in the Sanskrit epics the *Mahabharata* and the *Ramayana*, Manu, Rama and Krishna who, for him, epitomized masculine Hinduism. Like Nehru, Savarkar believed that 'science would lead all material progress and would annihilate superstition' (Quoted in Corbridge 1999: 227). When he exhorted a group of high school students in 1953 to bring 'the secret and science of the atom bomb to India and make it a mighty nation', however, he had in mind a more militaristic vision than Nehru's dream of nuclear energy driving India's economic development (Quoted in Corbridge 1999: 227).

Savarkar followed the early nationalist leaders in attributing India's subjugation at the hands of the British to the degeneration of a once strong and masculine Hinduism based on martial valour, courage, physical strength and organizational efficiency (Banerjee 2006: 67). Savarkar was a mentor to the Mahatma Gandhi's assassin, Nathuram Godse, who declared at his trial:

> the teachings of absolute *ahimsa* (non-violence) as advocated by Gandhiji would ultimately result in the emasculation of the Hindu community and thus make the country incapable of resisting the aggression or inroads of other communities, especially the Muslims.
>
> (Quoted in Veer 1994: 96)

According to Godse, it was Gandhi and his feminine, devotional brand of Hinduism that was responsible for the partition of India, which both he and Savarkar referred to as the 'vivisection of the Motherland': 'Gandhiji failed in his duty as the Father of the Nation. He has proved to be the Father of Pakistan. I as a dutiful son of Mother India thought it my duty to put an end to the life of the so-called Father of the Nation who had played a very prominent part in bringing about vivisection of the country – our Motherland' (Quoted in Nandy 1980: 83). In killing Gandhi – who, because of his 'old superstitious beliefs such as the power of the soul, the inner voice, the fast, the prayer and the purity of mind', had failed in his duty as father of the nation to defend the Mother – Godse thought he would be ensuring that India would be 'practical, able to retaliate, and would be powerful with the armed forces' (Quoted in Nandy 1980: 91). Thus, 'the nation would be free to follow the course founded on reason which I consider to be necessary for sound nation-building' (Quoted in Nandy 1980: 91).

Like Godse, Savarkar needed to masculinize the Motherland in order to put it on the correct path to modern nationhood. Indeed, Savarkar's interchangeable and inconsistent uses of the terms 'motherland' and 'fatherland' in *Hindutva* indicates his unease with the feminine. Unlike Nehru's ambivalence to the feminine, which was partly resolved with an incorporation of Mother India's wisdom and morality into his vision of Indian modernity, Savarkar's gender identity crisis is resolved when the beleaguered motherland in need of protection from her loyal sons or masculinized daughters like the Rani of Jhansi[2] transforms into a disciplinarian fatherland that tolerates no ambiguity in his children. For instance, writing about the need for Indian Muslims and Christians to embrace Hindutva or forever be positioned outside the nation, Savarkar declared:

> Ye, who by race, by blood, by culture, by nationality possess almost all the essentials of Hindutva and had been forcibly snatched out of our ancestral home by the hand of violence – ye, have only to render wholehearted love to our common Mother and recognise her not only as Fatherland (*Pitribhu*) but even as a Holyland (*Punyabhu*); and ye would be most welcome to the Hindu fold.
>
> (Savarkar 1938: 146)

The transformation of the motherland into the fatherland was not, however, the destabilizing move that it was for Nehru. This is because the Hindu nationalist conception of Indian identity is one in which the masculine is already immanent in the feminine Mother India. Modernity is not a masculine, Western garb that must be put on because all the values that it signifies – instrumental reason, rationality, a 'scientific temper' – can be found in the glorious past of 'Hindu civilization'.

It was within this framework that the BJP's nuclear policy was formulated and this was why Hindu nationalist organizations have never expressed the kinds of reservations about nuclear technology held by past Indian governments. For M.S. Golwalkar, the second leader of the RSS, the development of a nuclear bomb was deemed essential and the BJP's earlier incarnation, the Jana Sangh, was one of the most vocal advocates of India going nuclear after the 1962 war with China (Chiriyankandath and Wyatt 2005: 203). According K.S. Sudarshan, the general secretary of the RSS in 1998, the organization's support for the production of a nuclear bomb was based on the understanding that: '[o]ur history has proved that we are a heroic, intelligent race capable of becoming world leaders. But the one deficiency that we had was of weapons, good weapons. Our stature among world nations will go up only if we possess good weapons like other countries' (Quoted in Muralidharan and Ramakrishnan 1998).

In the lead-up to the 1998 election which propelled the BJP into political power, the exercise of the nuclear option was foremost in the minds of those in the leadership who would later shape India's foreign policy. As well as pledging to 'give India a role and position in world affairs commensurate with its size and capability', the election manifesto stated that a BJP government would '[r]e-evaluate the country's nuclear policy and exercise the option to induct nuclear weapons' (BJP 1998a, 1998b). Brajesh Mishra was vocal in his opinion that India's security environment left it no option but to 'go nuclear' (Perkovich 1999: 405). Jaswant Singh (1998), speaking at a conference in the United States in May 1997 on the future of nuclear weapons, bemoaned the fact that in 1974 'India demonstrated an ability, but disclaimed the intent' and argued that

> Had we straight thereafter conducted a series of other such tests and established clearly our ability, then it would have been easier to cope with all the confusion of subsequent years, these current international pressures, and all the other difficulties of today. Instead, we went into a nuclear trance; pretense replaced policy.
>
> (Singh 1998)

The BJP's views on nuclear weapons were buttressed by certain members of India's strategic elite, who also bear the influence of an 'anxious masculinity'. Just as the Hindu nationalist leader, Bal Thackeray (1998) argued that India needed to test nuclear weapons because 'we have to prove that we are not eunuchs', the strategic analyst, Brahma Chellaney responded to calls for India to sign the CTBT and a treaty banning unsafeguarded fissile material production by arguing that these were 'self-castration measures' that would turn India into a 'nuclear eunuch' (Quoted in Perkovich 1999: 458). Chellaney further criticized India's nuclear policy of restraint as being the equivalent of 'chronic impotence' (Quoted in Perkovich 1999: 458). Neither of these references to 'eunuchs' can be made sense of without taking into account the homology between sexual and political dominance that was made in colonial discourse and the hypermasculine response to this from some members of the Indian elite which was discussed in Chapter 2. This further indicates that it would be a mistake to distinguish, as Cohen (2001: 45) does, between 'realist' and Hindu nationalist views on the basis that the latter has a 'culture-driven' view of the world while the former does not. Rather, what the similarities between the positions of K. Subrahmanyam and Jaswant Singh and Bal Thackeray and Brahma Chellaney indicate is that Hindu nationalism shares with a certain prominent strand of realism in India an ethico-political vision which rests on a valorization of a hypermasculine approach to power and violence and generates a desire for a state identity that is structured on an opposition to threatening and inferior Others.

The 1998 nuclear tests

The BJP's election platform also promised to carry out a comprehensive strategic defence review and to establish 'a National Security Council to constantly analyze security, political and economic threats and render continuous advice to the Government' (BJP 1998b). Among those appointed to the task-force which would prepare recommendations for the constitution of the Council were Jaswant Singh, Jasjit Singh – a prominent member of the 'strategic elite', and K.C. Pant who, as we saw in Chapter 5, urged the government in 1966 to give up its 'nuclear celibacy', and had recently resigned from the Congress Party to join the BJP. Yet there is evidence that that the BJP leadership made the decision to conduct nuclear tests in late March, prior to the formation of this task-force in early April (Perkovich 1999: 411–12). Apart from Prime Minister Atal Bihari Vajpayee and his deputy L.K. Advani, the only other political figure involved in the decision to test was an RSS officer, Rajendra Singh (Corbridge 1999: 241). Like the Defence Minister, George Fernandes – the leader of the socialist Samata Party which had joined the BJP's NDA coalition – Jaswant Singh was under the impression that a decision on the nuclear option would be made after the strategic defence review. Indeed, both Fernandes and Singh were only told of the tests after the fact. The journalist Christopher Kremmer (2006) quotes an unnamed Western diplomat's account of Singh's reaction to the phone call informing him of the nuclear tests in the following way: '(Jaswant Singh) brought us into a tight group around him, and said, '[y]ou won't believe this – India has just tested. Only five people knew. I have to go on TV tonight. This is dumb, dumb, dumb'. The three chiefs of services were also kept uninformed of the decision until the day prior to the explosion. This clearly raises doubts about the argument that 'strategic considerations' rather than the BJP's Hindu nationalist ideology were behind the decision to test nuclear weapons. The absence of military leaders and high level ministers in the decision-making process is reminiscent of the 1974 'demonstration' and hints at more continuity between the BJP and previous Indian governments than the likes of Jaswant Singh – who came to office with the expressed intent of making India 'strategically minded' – would like to admit. How then, did the post-test foreign policy discourse of the BJP government compare with that following the 1974 nuclear test?

The first statement about the 1998 nuclear tests was made by Prime Minister Vajpayee on the evening of 11 May announcing the underground explosion of a fission device, a low yield device and a thermonuclear device and congratulating the scientists and engineers on their achievements. Confirmation that these tests were intended as part of a nuclear *weapons* program was given shortly afterwards by Brajesh Mishra, who stated that '[t]hese tests have established that India has a proven capability for a weaponized nuclear programme' (Muralidharan and

Cherian 1998). Another departure was Mishra's comments implying that there was now a greater willingness to sign the CTBT.

Two days later, on 13 May, two more explosions of low yield devices were carried out. The same day a letter to US President Bill Clinton from Vajpayee explaining the rationale behind the tests was leaked to the *New York Times*. As in 1974 when Indira Gandhi's first explanation for India's nuclear test was made to an American newsmagazine rather than the Indian public, Vajpayee's first extensive comments on the 1998 tests were made to a foreign audience. In the letter, Vajpayee expressed his deepening concern 'at the deteriorating security environment, specially the nuclear environment, faced by India for some years past' (1998b: 14). It later emerged that this was one of eight identical letters prepared for the Group of Eight countries prior to the test. Clearly, the Vajpayee government had prepared for the test in anticipation of presenting to the world a new India, driven solely by *realpolitik* self-interest. Yet almost immediately after the tests had been conducted the government began to retreat from the position taken in the letter. A contradictory press release on 15 May addressing the UN Security Council statement rebuking the tests, states, '[t]he tests which our scientists carried out are not directed against any country' but then goes on to make reference to China and Pakistan, without naming them:

> It is because of the continuing threat posed to India by the deployment, overtly and covertly, of nuclear weapons *in the lands and seas adjoining us* that we have been forced to carry out these tests, so that we can retain a credible option to develop these weapons, should they be needed for the security of India's people.
>
> (India 1998c) (Emphasis added)

We also see in this statement, however, the re-emergence of older discourses – those of disarmament and discrimination. The UN Security Council's position on India's tests, the statement said, was unacceptable because:

> India is a responsible member of the international community, and has consistently supported the United Nations. We were among the first to propose, and continue to promote, the goal of general and complete disarmament, and the elimination of all nuclear weapons. To this end, we have made a series of concrete proposals for the consideration of the international community, and the nuclear weapon states in particular. Every one of these has been thwarted and distorted for their own purposes by the nuclear weapons states.
>
> (India 1998c)

Similar sentiments were expressed in Vajpayee's interview with an Indian newsmagazine on 25 May in his first attempt to explain the rationale behind the tests to a domestic audience. Vajpayee (1998b) explained the timing of the tests as simply delivering on an election promise and said that India had just responded to the 'stark global and regional reality' that it lives surrounded by nuclear weapons. He highlighted the significance of the tests by declaring that 'India is now a nuclear weapons state' although '[o]urs will never be weapons of aggression' (Vajpayee 1998b). Further explaining this Vajpayee said:

> India has never considered military might as the ultimate measure of national strength. It is a necessary component of overall national strength. I would, therefore, say that the greatest meaning of the tests is that they have given India shakti, they have given India strength, they have given India self-confidence.
>
> (Vajpayee 1998b)

Here Vajpayee seems to be attempting to put to rest the ghost of Gandhi and his identification of strength with non-violence and moral courage while resuscitating the spirit of Aurobindo Ghose and his exhortation to worship the mother as Shakti. Yet, when asked whether his government's nuclear policy constituted a radical departure from that of previous governments Vajpayee replied in the negative: 'My Government's policy is consistent with the nuclear disarmament policy that successive governments have followed'. Moreover, he distanced his government from previous indications that India would now be more willing to sign the CTBT, stating that '[t]here is no question of India accepting any treaty that is discriminatory in character'.

Vajpayee's subsequent statement in the Indian Parliament on 29 May also cited strategic insecurity as a rationale for 'going nuclear' while still attempting to assert continuity rather than a dramatic departure from the conception of India's postcolonial identity that was constructed in the foreign policy discourse of previous governments. The tests, Vajpayee said, '...are a continuation of the policies set into motion that put this country on the path of self-reliance and independence of thought and action'. Thus,

> The present decision and future actions will continue to reflect a commitment to sensibilities and obligations of an ancient civilization, a sense of responsibility and restraint, but a restraint born of the assurance of action, not of doubts or apprehension.
>
> (Vajpayee 1998a)

This statement is repeated in the paper submitted to the Parliament as an accompaniment to Vajpayee's statement with the addition of a passage from the Bhagavad Gita: 'Action is a process to reach a goal; action may reflect tumult but when measured and focused, will yield its objective of stability and peace' (India 1998b). In this paper, India's 'restraint' was again depicted as its defining difference: 'This is where our approach to nuclear weapons is different from others. This difference is the cornerstone of our nuclear doctrine. It is marked by restraint and striving for the total elimination of all weapons of mass destruction' (India 1998b). Likewise, India's 'restraint', and Pakistan's lack of it, framed Vajpayee's response to Pakistan's retaliatory nuclear tests on 28 May. In another speech to the Indian Parliament on 29 May, Vajpayee described Pakistan as obsessed with India and irrationally insecure even though India was committed to friendship based on justice and mutual respect and had never sought to take advantage of its size to dominate Pakistan. He went on to offer Pakistan a no-first-use-agreement and a voluntary moratorium on further testing (India 1998b). In highlighting India's restraint in this way, Vajpayee (1998a) sought to encompass the discourse of India's postcolonial difference based on civilizational morality into a Hindu nationalist conception of masculine strength based on physical or military power – in this case described as 'the assurance of action'.

In the months after the 1998 nuclear tests various other continuities in India's nuclear discourse became apparent. Running through all of Vajpayee's statements after the nuclear tests was another key component of India's postcolonial identity – the celebration of its techno-scientific prowess. Reiterating a thirty-year old argument Jaswant Singh made the Indian government's case for the tests in the pages of *Foreign Affairs* in an article entitled 'Against Nuclear Apartheid'.[3] The draft nuclear doctrine released in August, 1999 clearly sought to display a hard-headed clarity in India's strategic intentions and yet it also contained a section devoted to disarmament (National Security Advisory Board 1999). Thus, while the BJP may have begun its term in office determined to discipline the meanings attached to the nuclear program, its inability to do so indicates that ambivalence continues to define India's postcolonial modernity.

The BJP and South Asia

India and Pakistan

After the tensions generated by the nuclear tests and the BJP's election manifesto to 'take active steps to persuade Pakistan to abandon its present policy of hostile interference in our internal affairs by supporting insurgent and terrorist groups' and to assert 'India's sovereignty over the whole of Jammu and Kashmir, including the areas under foreign occupations', a heightening of tensions with Pakistan under the NDA government may have been expected (BJP 1998a). Indeed, shortly after the nuclear tests, BJP leaders made several statements that appeared to indicate a more belligerent policy toward Pakistan and the issue of Kashmir would be pursued by the NDA. L.K. Advani, for instance, said that 'Islamabad should realise the change in the geo-strategic situation in the region and roll back its anti-India policy, especially with regard to Kashmir...' (1998a). Advani and various other BJP figures also claimed that India was now ready to pursue a policy of 'hot pursuit' whereby insurgents would now be pursued across the Line of Control (LoC) into Pakistan Occupied Kashmir (Ahmad 1998). An examination of India's relations with Pakistan during the NDA era, however, reveals a more complex picture.

The Lahore Declaration

Despite the belligerent statements directed at Pakistan by some in the BJP, Vajpayee sought a conciliatory approach akin to that taken in his earlier stint as Minister for External Affairs in the Janata coalition in the late 1970s when he abandoned his party's vocal declarations of wanting to unite India and Pakistan in favour of assertions that 'India would rejoice in the progress and prosperity of Pakistan' (Quoted in Chaulia 2002: 224). In February 1999 Vajpayee became the first Prime Minister in forty years to visit Pakistan by inaugurating a newly established bus route between New Delhi to Lahore, in a move designed to show that: 'Pokharan[4] and peace are the two sides of one coin. Our bus initiative to Lahore has greatly blunted the false image of the BJP being an anti-Muslim party' (Quoted in Gupta 1999). While in Pakistan, Vajpayee made a speech which invoked India and Pakistan's shared history and culture, quoting lines from the eleventh century poet Mas'ud bin S'ad bin Salman's paean to the city of Lahore. Over the objections of some of his colleagues Vajpayee also sought to repudiate the Hindu nationalist tendency to delegitimize the existence of Pakistan by visiting the Minar-e-Pakistan, the monument where the Muslim League in 1940 issued a declaration in support of the establishment of a state for Muslims (Philipose 1999). The jointly authored Lahore Declaration pledged to undertake consultations on a number of issues including Kashmir and nuclear issues, to abide by the principles of coexistence and implement the Simla agreement 'in letter and spirit' (1999b).

Vajpayee's motivation for pursuing this 'bus diplomacy', as it came to be called, has been attributed to his desire to be seen as a statesman and to leave a lasting legacy (Kumar 1999: 168). The pursuit of diplomacy with Pakistan could also be seen, however, as a way to attempt to overcome the negative impact on India's self-identity caused by the 1998 nuclear tests, for despite the BJP's claims that the tests had given India strength and self-confidence, the reactions of the 'international community' constituted a significant challenge to that aspect of India's identity that highlighted its restraint and responsibility particularly in relation to Pakistan. For instance, in response to Advani's claims that India's had 'brought about a qualitatively new state in Indo-Pakistani relations' to which Pakistan should react by revising its aggressive stance on Kashmir, the US State Department spokesman James Rubin said that with such statements, 'India is foolishly and dangerously increasing tensions with its neighbours' (Quoted in Kinzer 1998). Whatever Vajpayee's motivations for pursuing the Lahore Declaration, however, the conciliatory climate did not last long.

The Kargil war

In May 1999, Pakistani soldiers crossed the LoC in the Kargil sector of Kashmir, provoking a low-level war in which the Indian Army succeeded in pushing the infiltrators back to the LoC.[5] The LoC was established in 1972 as a de facto border by the Simla agreement. As touched on in Chapter 5, the Simla agreement was not just a symbol of India's military victory over Pakistan but an endorsement of India's rejection of the two-nation theory and its foreign policies of peaceful coexistence and nonalignment. For Pakistan on the other hand, the LoC and the Simla agreement were symbols of India's expansionism and aggression and it had long accused India of wanting to coerce it into converting the LoC into an international border and of violating the LoC on numerous occasions. One of these alleged violations, India's operations in Siachen, which Pakistan claims is illegally occupied by India, became the basis of Pakistan's post-facto justification for its actions in Kargil, which it sought to portray as an extension of Siachen (Tellis *et al.* 2002: 43–4).

Kargil was India's first televised war and sections of the Indian media depicted India as being at the front line of Islamic terrorism (Tellis *et al.* 2002: Ch.2). Yet, despite the media frenzy and calls by former army generals, BJP/RSS apparatchiks and strategic analysts like Bharat Karnad for India to respond to the incursion by implementing a policy of 'hot pursuit' into the Pakistan side of the LoC, the Indian government publicly disavowed the option of crossing the LoC (Deshpande 1999; Karnad 1999; Chaulia 2002: 224; Tellis *et al.* 2002: 25). While some, such as Sumit Ganguly and Devin Hagerty (Ganguly and Hagerty 2005; Ganguly 2008), have claimed that India was deterred from undertaking an aggressive approach in the Kargil war by Pakistan's nuclear weapons, S. Paul Kapur (2008: 79) has argued, on the basis of interviews with key figures such as Fernandes and Vajpayee, that '[t]actical and diplomatic calculations … rather than Pakistani nuclear weapons, were primarily responsible for the Indian refusal to cross the LoC during the Kargil conflict'. According to Vajpayee, '[w]e never thought atomic weapons would be used, even if we had decided to cross the LoC' (Quoted in Kapur 2008: 79). Tactically, the army leadership did not think it necessary for India to cross the LoC to fulfil their military objectives and, diplomatically, the political leadership wanted to cultivate a reputation for restraint (Kapur 2008: 78). As G. Parthasarathy, India's High Commissioner to Pakistan during the Kargil war put it, refraining from crossing the LoC would result in 'political gains with the world community' and allowed India to 'keep the high moral ground' while getting the world 'to accept that this was Pakistan's fault' (Quoted in Kapur 2008: 78). Jaswant Singh's account of the Kargil war is at variance with that of his colleagues for he suggests that the decision not to cross the LoC, despite the tactical advantages it would have conferred, was taken because of the presence of nuclear weapons (Singh 2009a: 227). Singh's aim, however, is not to make the case for nuclear deterrence but to highlight, in contrast to Pakistan, India's restraint and responsibility. His concluding comments on Kargil focus on the approval given to India's restrained handling of the conflict by Strobe Talbott, who expressed his admiration that India had 'held fast to the moral high ground throughout the crisis, in the face of enormous provocation' and Madeleine Albright, who congratulated him on 'a masterly handling of the Kargil crisis', (Singh 2009a: 229). Thus, whether or not nuclear weapons played a role in India's decision not to cross the LoC during the Kargil war, a concern with preserving India's self-image of restraint and responsibility was clearly a factor.

In the immediate aftermath of the Kargil war, a fundamentally altered discourse on how the NDA government should deal with Pakistan was not evident. In an interview in June 1999, Singh (1999a) called Kargil 'an aberration' which did not call into question the government's policy of instigating peace initiatives with its neighbours and George Fernandes attempted to absolve Vajpayee's interlocutor, Pakistani Prime Minister Nawaz Sharif, who was subsequently ousted in a military coup, of any wrongdoing and instead pinned the blame on the Pakistan Army: 'the Pakistan Army has hatched a conspiracy to push in infiltrators, and the Nawaz Sharif Government did not have a major role' (Quoted in Swami 1999).[6] According to Ashley Tellis, however,

> [w]ell-placed interlocutors in the Prime Minister's Office, Ministry of Defence, and Ministry of External Affairs explained that one of the most important changes in the Indian mindset precipitated by Kargil is that those who formerly were proponents of engaging Pakistan have been silenced or no longer support this position.
>
> (Tellis *et al.* 2002: 18)

This became clear during the second major incident between India and Pakistan during the NDA's tenure in 2001–2002.

Troop deployment in 2001–2002

On 13 December, 2001 armed gun-men attacked the Indian parliament and succeeded in killing several security personnel. The Indian government accused two groups, Lashkar-e-Taiba, and Jaish-e-Mohammed, which it has long claimed are extensively supported by Pakistan, were responsible for the attack. Consequently, India launched Operation Parakram, described as a strategy of 'coercive pressure' by Brajesh Mishra (Kapur 2008: 81). Parakram involved the deployment of 500, 000 troops on the Indian side of the LoC and a threat by India to carry out a limited conventional war against Pakistan unless key demands, including closing militant training camps on Pakistani territory and stopping the infiltration of militants into Indian territory, were met. Pakistan responded with its own deployment of troops, resulting in the amassment of one million soldiers in a stand-off along the LoC. India's representation of the attack on its parliament as an India–Pakistan crisis took advantage of the 11 September attacks on New York and Washington and the declaration of a 'war on terror' by the then-President, George W. Bush. Indeed, the attack on the Indian parliament provided the opportunity to bring India's foreign policy into line with long-held Hindu nationalist tenets about Pakistan. India's new Minister for External Affairs, Yashwant Sinha, for instance, branded Pakistan a 'rogue state', a 'sham democracy', a proliferator of nuclear technology, an exporter of terrorism and a trafficker of drugs: 'While Bush may have the idea that there are three members of the axis of evil (North Korea, Iran and Iraq), one may conclude that one has been left out: Pakistan' (Quoted in Doyle 2002).

According to Advani, the attack was the work of 'Pakistani terrorists' and it had occurred because:

> Pakistan – itself a product of the indefensible Two-Nation Theory, itself a theocratic State with an extremely tenuous tradition of democracy – is unable to reconcile itself with the reality of a secular, democratic, self-confident and steadily progressing India, whose standing in the international community is getting inexorably higher with the passage of time.
>
> (Advani 2001)

This passage is an indicator of the importance of the language of secularism and, therefore, a key part of the postcolonial identity produced during the Nehru era, in Hindu nationalist discourse for 'secularism' clearly distinguishes India from Pakistan while delegitimizing the latter. Hindu nationalist discourse, however, differentiates the BJP's secularism from the Congress's by claiming that the latter's constitutional provisions for the rights of minorities and its alleged denigration of Hindu traditions amounts 'pseudo-secularism' while its 'genuine secularism' draws on the innate tolerance of Hinduism: 'Indian secularism has its roots in religion—in the Hindu view that all roads lead to God, as enunciated in the Vedic dictum '*Ekam Sat Vipraha Bahudha Vadanti*' (Truth is One; the wise interpret it differently)' (Advani 2010). In this way, the BJP is able to appropriate the language of secularism while still promoting a Hindu majoritarianism.

India began withdrawing its troops from the LoC at the end of 2002 leading to a de-escalation of tensions. As in 1999, India's failure to attack Pakistan in 2001–2002, despite having the intelligence capacity and military capability to strike insurgent training camps across the LoC, has been attributed to the presence of nuclear weapons (Ganguly and Kraig 2005). Ganguly and Kraig (Ganguly and Kraig 2005) argue, that India's actions, or lack thereof, in 2001–2002 show the limits of coercive diplomacy in a context in which nuclear weapons are present, because India failed to achieve its objectives of stopping the infiltration of insurgents across the LoC and compelling Pakistan to hand over individuals wanted for insurgent acts in India. Yet, reports of the conversations that took place within the political leadership during this time and the comments of key actors in interviews afterward indicate that India's goals appeared to be more modest than Ganguly and Kraig claim, as they centred on stopping attacks in the immediate future on the scale of the attack on the Parliament, gaining a commitment from Pakistan to stop cross-border infiltration, consolidating its relationship with the US and reinforcing its reputation for restraint and responsibility. Media reports from 14 December cite senior officials from the Prime Minister's Office revealing that L.K. Advani and some of his colleagues in the BJP were aggressively lobbying for the Indian Army to employ a 'hot pursuit' strategy to destroy training camps in Pakistan-controlled Kashmir (Shankar Sahay 2001c). According to the BJP's parliamentary spokesman Vijay Kumar Malhotra:

If the terrorist attack in Parliament yesterday is sending the message that India is a soft state, we certainly want the government to take to hot pursuit so that their camps in PoK can be destroyed. That will teach them a lesson and also underscore that the government's might cannot be challenged in so defiant a fashion.

(Shankar Sahay 2001c)

Advani was opposed, however, by Jaswant Singh, who argued that India was a partner in the 'war against terrorism' with the US, and had to undertake consultations before any such step could be undertaken (Shankar Sahay 2001c). The prospect of limited strikes against training camps in Pakistani Kashmir was again raised in May when a public bus was attacked inside an army camp near Jammu resulting in the deaths of 22 people. Following the incident, letters were despatched by Vajpayee to the heads of governments of the US, UK, Russia and France warning of an escalation (Gupta 2002). Ultimately, however, Vajpayee stated in interviews that 'America gave us the assurance that something will be done by Pakistan about cross-border terrorism' and '[t]hat was an important factor' in India's decision not to escalate the conflict (Quoted in Kapur 2008: 82, 2002c). The measures taken by Pakistan included the banning of Lashkar-e-Taiba and Jaish-e-Mohammed, and a speech by President Musharaff committing his government to preventing Pakistan's territory from being used by militant groups targeting India. There was also a discernable decrease in cross-border infiltration and a promise from Musharaff, brokered by the US Deputy Secretary of State Richard Armitage in June, to end the infiltration permanently. According to Brajesh Mishra, this convinced the Indian government that the 'coercive pressure was working' (Quoted in Kapur 2008: 81). George Fernandes has claimed that India 'stayed mobilized to make the point that another attack would result in an immediate response' and since '[n]o further attacks happened' there was 'no reason to attack' (Quoted in Kapur 2008: 82).

Jaswant Singh (Singh 2009a: 341–5) is insistent in his memoir, written several years after the BJP lost government, that despite Western 'scaremongering' and 'offensively patronizing' concerns, the events of 2001–2002 had 'no nuclear dimension' for India had always exercised 'great restraint' and 'continued to go its own way, at its own pace and with no nuclear fears in its mind or in its heart'. India's nuclear weapons were a 'deterrent, not for war-fighting' and India was committed to

striving for peace with Pakistan through persuasion, not compulsion, through a transformation of their mindset, an abandonment by Pakistan of this path of a perpetual and induced hostility for India, adopted early by them as an essential ingredient of separate nationhood.

(Singh 2009a: 348)

In Singh's (2009a: 348–9) interpretation, which reiterates a discourse of India's civilizational exceptionalism, the 'US experience [with terrorism] has led that country into excessive and a gross militarization', India had exercised 'patience, a finely tuned sense of "strategic restraint"' which was the legacy of its 'absolutely unconquerable attributes. It has unmatched resilience, we will absorb shocks'.

India and Bangladesh

In 2001, India found itself in another military confrontation, albeit on a smaller scale than anything involving Pakistan. In mid-April, the Bangladesh Rifles (BDR) took over the Indian-controlled village of Pyrdiwah, along a disputed part of the India–Bangladesh border. The ensuing clashes on various other sites along the border between the BDR and India's Border Security Force (BSF) resulted in the deaths of personnel from both sides. Due to the porous nature of the India–Bangladesh border and the established historical and cultural relationship between West Bengal and Bangladesh, the issue of unauthorized migration from Bangladesh in India has long been a political issue. The idea of a border fence was proposed by Indira Gandhi in the 1980s and despite objections from Bangladesh, construction began in the late 1990s (Harshe 1999: 1102). The skirmish of 2001 was notable, however, because it involved the deaths of security personnel and came after a decade of concerted effort on behalf of the BJP to turn the issue of migration into one of national security. A 1992 resolution from the BJP National Executive stated that 15 million migrants from Bangladesh had crossed the border illegally into India and claimed that the influx constituted a

> serious strain on the national economy, a severe stress on the national society and, withal, a serious threat to the stability and security of the country. And yet the Congress takes no action to stem this flood or push back illegal immigrants, because it views them as its vote bank.
>
> (Quoted in Gillan 2002: 77)

In 1993, BJP posters in Delhi issued a 'declaration of war' against Bangladeshi migrants, and another resolution instructed party workers to expel Bangladeshi migrants from Indian cities if the Congress government did not address the issue' (Gillan 2002: 78–9). In 1997 the newly elected Shiv Sena-BJP coalition government in the state of Maharashtra announced that 'Bangladeshis who do not vacate the city on their own will be thrown out' (Quoted in Gillan 2002: 78–9). The BJP's 1998 election manifesto repeated the claims of the 1992 resolution and pledged to take more 'stringent measures' to intercept and turn back infiltrators, to fence the border 'urgently', intensify border patrolling and to 'initiate steps to detect illegal infiltrators' including establishing a national register of citizens (BJP 1998b). The BJP's agitation on the issue of migration from Bangladesh was also distinctive in its presentation of the issue as one of a 'crisis' and its explicit focus on the religious identity of the migrants – Hindu migrants were characterized as victims and refugees while Muslim migrants were labelled 'infiltrators'. This was achieved through the selective and exaggerated use of official statistics which are, in any case, subject to inaccuracies given the difficulty of obtaining information on 'illegal' immigrants residing in India (Gillan 2002: 83–4).

Yet, when there was an opportunity to bring this 'crisis' to a head, following the clash between Bangladeshi and Indian border forces in 2001, it is significant that the BJP leadership retreated from its belligerent rhetoric. Advani remained publically silent on the incident and Jaswant Singh vetoed proposals to reinforce BSF troops because he was 'against annoying the friendly neighbour' (Gokhale 2001). Singh's statement on the clash in the Lok Sabha stressed that 'strong ties of friendship exist between the two countries', that 'acts of criminal adventurism should not be permitted to affect these ties' and that 'the Bangladesh prime minister has expressed regret and said her government would fully investigate the issue' (Quoted in Shankar Sahay 2001a). Although the BJP leadership's handling of the incident elicited strong criticism from members of the BJP parliamentary party and other Hindu nationalist organizations like the VHP and the Bajrang Dal, who argued that India should be prepared to 'retaliate even if it means war' and accused the BJP leadership of a 'soft reaction' which placed 'their image' before 'national interests', the situation was finally pacified with the signing of a pact in June between the Bangladeshi and Indian governments to resolve the problem of the un-demarcated sections of the border (2001a; 2001b; Shankar Sahay 2001b).

After the 11 September 2001 attacks in the US by Al Qaeda operatives and, in the same year, the election of a coalition government in Bangladesh that included several Islamist parties, BJP leaders including Advani and the new Minister for External Affairs, Yashwant Sinha, pointed to Bangladesh as a centre of Islamist militant activity (2002b; 2002a; Singh 2009b; Jones 2009; Wright 2002). It has been argued that the BJP fashioned India's state identity along Hindu nationalist lines and, by adopting an international discourse on 'Islamic terror' during its time in power, rendered Bangladesh into a threat to India (Singh 2009b). I would suggest, however, that the NDA's foreign policy/identity discourse was rather more ambivalent than a narrow focus on its representation of Bangladesh and 'illegal' immigration would indicate. The BJP leadership's discourse on South Asia was also concerned with a desire to demonstrate a self-image of restraint and responsibility and in the later years of the NDA's tenure this resulted in the government officially adopting the Gujral Doctrine as its policy on South Asia which it linked with the notion of 'soft power'.

Soft power

Whereas in the 1980s, an interventionist policy was considered essential and non-intervention became unimaginable, in 2000 the opposite was true. In the years that followed the withdrawal of the IPKF from Sri Lanka, successive Indian governments, including the NDA, strenuously avoided becoming entangled in Sri Lanka's civil conflict. This was the case even as Norway became involved in facilitating talks between the LTTE and the government and even after Sri Lanka requested urgent military assistance in May 2000 when it appeared that the LTTE were on the verge of capturing the Jaffna peninsula and, with it, 20,000 to 30,000 Sri Lankan troops (India 2001: 2918). In this instance, the BJP-led government ruled out any kind of military intervention, gave promises of humanitarian assistance and emphasized the need for a politically negotiated settlement. They remained steadfast in this position even when Sri Lanka began requesting military aid from Israel, Pakistan and China and when the United States sent parts of its Fifth Fleet near Sri Lanka in a show of support for the government (DeVotta 2003: 366). As the records of the debate in the Indian Parliament show, moreover, there was cross-party support for the government's policy (See Bhasin 2001: 2919–25).

Neil DeVotta (2003: 367) has argued that even though India remained committed to keeping other powers out of the region and still sought to be recognized as the undisputed regional hegemon, domestic challenges, particularly the insurgencies in the Northeast of India and in Kashmir, have left it militarily over-extended and therefore unable to display its 'hegemonic prowess in the region as it did in the 1980s'. I have argued, however, that India's military intervention in Sri Lanka in the 1980s was the result of its desire to be seen as a responsible political mediator to buttress its credentials as a benign leader rather than a domineering hegemon. Moreover, an examination of the foreign policy discourse in 2000 gives the picture of an India that was not unable but was unwilling to undertake the kind of intervention it carried out in 1987 because of the consequences of its earlier intervention. Jaswant Singh, for instance, stated that given India's previous experience 'military intervention in Northern Sri Lanka is not an option that we are even contemplating' (India 2001: 2924).

The fear of the 'foreign hand' in the region, which had played a significant role in Indira and Rajiv Gandhi's foreign policy discourses, was notably absent in 2000. Speaking in 2003 the Minister for External Affairs, Yashwant Sinha linked the BJP coalition government's policy with that of the Janata government's in the late 1970s which he identified as a precursor to the Gujral Doctrine:

> ...India remains committed to the good neighbourhood policy of Mr Vajpayee. India remains committed to the Gujral Doctrine and today, I would like to say that we are prepared to move further ahead also in the direction of peace, friendship and prosperity with all our neighbours.
>
> (Sinha 2003a)

He went on in the speech to support the idea of a South Asian Union, which would replace the existing ineffective regional organizations (Sinha 2003a). In speeches in 2004, Sinha (2004b) argued that the countries of South Asia had 'a unique opportunity to define international relations on the ethic of plurality and equality, consensus and cooperation, compassion and co-existence' and Vajpayee (2004) invoked the idea of South Asian kinship: 'The bonds of religion, language, ethnicity and culture which hold us together as a South Asian family are far more enduring than the relatively recent barriers of political prejudice we have erected'. Likewise for Sinha:

> We approach our neighbours in a spirit of fraternity. We will always be willing to give much more than we receive. We will continue to extend our hands in friendship even in the face of repeated rebuffs from our interlocutors.
>
> (Sinha 2003b)

In another speech, Sinha (2004a) expressed this politics of fraternity as 'soft power'. Speaking on the topic of 'what it takes to be a world power', he said:

> Any quest for power is ... immediately identified with violence, genocide, hegemony and imperialism...
>
> It is important therefore that India distances itself from the conventional idea of power, as the ability of a nation to bend other nations to its will through coercive use of force. It is also essential to make clear at the very outset that India approaches the notion of power with an alternate vision and a deep consciousness of its responsibilities. There can be no other way for India.
>
> ...
>
> What constitutes Power as far as the nations of the world are concerned? How does India perform in terms of various attributes of power? Academics divide power into two general categories – hard power and soft power. Hard power consists of elements such as military strength, economic resources and technological capacity. Soft power comprises culture, values, social cohesion, the quality of diplomacy and governance.
>
> (Sinha 2004a)

In his book *Soft Power*, Joseph Nye (2004: ix) complains that when the then-Secretary of Defence, Donald Rumsfeld was asked at a conference in 2003 what he thought about soft power, Rumsfeld replied that he did not know the term meant. As I have tried to show, India has always implicitly prioritized something akin to 'soft power' in its enactment of foreign policy/identity discourses. It is perhaps unsurprising, then, that unlike American officials, once the phrase 'soft power' came into common use in academic parlance, Indian officials were quick to engage with it. In his speech, Sinha went on to note that while India had many achievements in terms of hard power, in the realm of soft power:

> India's influence has spread far and wide since ancient times on the strength of our culture, religion and philosophy. As the land of Gandhi and as a nation that won its independence through a struggle unique in the annals of history, India has an international image that few others can claim.
>
> (Sinha 2004a)

Not only South Asia but also Asia, in general, was entered into India's foreign policy discourse as the repository for the benign influence of Indian civilization in a manner reminiscent of the discourse on a 'Greater India' which was elaborated on in Chapter 3. Significantly, however, Sinha eschews the more Hindu-centric Greater India narratives articulated by his Hindu nationalist forebear, Savarkar, and members of Greater India society in favour of narratives more reminiscent of Nehru:

> If you look at the geography of this continent [Asia], you will find, India is at the heart of it. Not merely must we be geographically in the center of things, but in our engagement also, we must be in the center of things.
>
> India never went out with its sword to these countries. We never went out as conquerors or as colonizers. We went out with our civilizational values, with our culture, with our religion and in friendship and in amity. That is in the historical character of the Indian nation and I do not think that historical character can be altered by contemporary or future events.
>
> (Sinha 2003c)

Conclusion

The BJP entered into political office with the aim of transforming Indian foreign policy and identity in order to bring it into line with Hindu nationalist tenets of masculinity, military power and 'rationality'. This chapter has argued, however, that an analysis of the BJP's foreign policy discourse and practices reveals a clear disjuncture between the party's pre-election and post-election commitments. On the issue of nuclear weapons, for instance, while the NDA carried out a long-standing BJP pledge to undertake nuclear tests in 1998 shortly after its election, but, as Bharat Karnad (2009), an enthusiastic supporter of the BJP's professed ambition for making India more 'realist' puts it, 'rather than have open-ended testing of higher yield weapon designs and hydrogen warheads for various missiles with different nose-cone geometries eventuating in a proven thermonuclear deterrent', the government announced a voluntary moratorium on further tests, re-affirmed its commitment to disarmament and retreated from its initial justification for the tests which centred on the threats from Pakistan and China. Karnad (2002a) is also of the opinion that an 'Indian Monroe Doctrine' is necessary in order 'to reclaim the strategic concept bequeathed by the British Raj of turning the Indian Ocean into an Indian lake' but finds that '[a]las, if its record in office is any guide, the BJP coalition government does not seem to have the mettle for so consequential an enterprise'. Indeed, while on the one hand, the BJP represented both Pakistan and Bangladesh as threats during various times during its tenure, this was countered by a conciliatory or restrained approach during crises and it eventually adopted both the Gujral Doctrine and the language of 'soft power' during its latter years in government.

The BJP's inability to please hyper-realists of the likes of Karnad by failing to diverge significantly from established foreign policy discourses and renderings of

India's state identity can be understood, I have argued, by taking into account the Hindu nationalist negotiation of modernity and the colonial encounter, which has significantly been shaped through a representation of the Muslim Other. Overcoming 'Hindu weakness' through the celebration of hyper-masculinity and the defence of the motherland/fatherland were important themes in Hindu nationalist discourse but they coexisted with those on 'rapacious' and 'tyrannical' Muslims which were contrasted in the BJP's discourse with India's sense of restraint and responsibility. Reiterating rather than diverging from established discourses of state identity thus served Hindu nationalist interests.

8   Conclusion

This book has argued that foreign policy has been a key site for the production of India's postcolonial identity. A reconceptualization of Indian foreign policy as postcoloniality was therefore suggested, and this has entailed a focus on the co-constitution of foreign policy, ethics and identity. I have argued that the politics of negotiating the colonial encounter continued to inform India's foreign policy in the postcolonial era and that successive governments have grappled in various ways with the ethico-political project established by India's first Prime Minister Jawaharlal Nehru. Nehru established foreign policy as a key arena for the enactment of a postcolonial identity underpinned by a desire to both embrace and repudiate 'Western' modernity. A perception of India's backwardness was a feature of the negotiation of the colonial encounter by a number of Indian leaders. For Nehru, who drew on colonial narratives of India's past, India had succumbed to colonial rule because of its technological and scientific backwardness, since it had isolated itself from the rest of the world and as a result of its vulnerability to invasion and its political disunity. Adopting certain aspects of modernity, like science and technology, was therefore vital. Nehru, however, was also a critic of modernity and what he saw as the tendency, in modernity's Western manifestation, toward violence and domination. He was convinced, however, that India, with its civilizational traits of restraint, wisdom, resilience and tolerance would be able to fashion a uniquely ethical modernity.

The idea of India as a civilization has therefore imparted to India's postcolonial identity a sense of what I have referred to as 'exceptionalism'. Daniel Bell (1975: 197) has written of 'American exceptionalism' in a way that partly resonates with India's sense of civilizational exceptionalism. Bell argued that American exceptionalism, among other things, encompassed the idea that 'the United States, in becoming a world power, a paramount power, a hegemonic power, would, because it was democratic, be different in the exercise of that power than previous world empires'. Whereas the US located its exceptionalism in its lack of 'history', however, central to Indian exceptionalism has been the particularity of its history as an ancient civilization, which gives India the capacity to produce a better, more ethical modernity.

In analysing Nehru's international thought in Chapters 2, 3 and 4, and treating him as a normative thinker whose ideas were informed by a particular experience of modernity and his position as an anti-colonial nationalist leader, this book has sought to contribute to the 'decolonization' of the discipline of IR. As a number of scholars have noted, in general, even critical approaches to IR that engage with Marxism, cosmopolitanism, postmodernism and feminism generally fail to give due regard to the histories and thought associated with anti-colonial struggles and the politics of the colonial past and, consequently, IR has 'distanced itself from the processes that helped shape the future of more than two-thirds of the world's peoples' (Darby 2006b: 20).[1] As I argued in the first three chapters, Nehru's international thought has a distinctive intellectual history which was informed by Buddhism, Marxism, and the thought of Gandhi and Tagore. His focus on psychology and emotion in his interpretation of international politics and his desire to develop an 'internationalist nationalism', has not only helped to shape India's postcolonial present but has resonance with recent theoretical debates in IR on the roles of trauma, memory and humiliation in the behaviour of state and non-state actors (See Bleiker and Hutchison 2008; Fattah and Fierke 2009; Steele 2007; Bell 2006).

In exploring the gendered nature of foreign policy/identity discourses I have argued that the politics of colonial masculinity and the nationalist rendering of India as 'Bharat Mata' or Mother India has had relevance beyond the consolidation of colonial rule, nationalist sloganeering or the creation of hegemonic gender norms in Indian society. Rather, just as the representation of India as Mother emerged as an important anti-colonial resource in colonial Bengal which allowed the colonial intelligentsia to 'accommodate the public image of the foreign rulers into an unmistakable indigenous sign that would mark a colonial Bengali man as distinct from the alien rulers' (Bagchi 1990: WS 65), the sign of Mother India circulated in Nehru's writings, in particular, as a marker of India's distinctiveness as an ancient civilization with an inclination to prioritize ethics and morality. The ethico-political project that Nehru placed at the heart of his construction of India's postcolonial identity, and which his foreign policy discourse helped to constitute, was thus grounded in a feminized semiotic that imparted a unique intertwining of gender and ethics to India's state identity.

I have sought to show that a focus on Nehru's ethico-political project and on other anti-colonial negotiations of the colonial encounter, in general, is necessary because successive Indian governments have continued to grapple and engage with these. Analysing foreign policy as postcoloniality helps to give a fuller and more complete understanding than conventional models of foreign policy analysis which have a difficult time explaining certain aspects of India's foreign policy behaviour. For instance, as my examination of India's nuclear policies over several chapters indicates, without taking into account India's broader postcolonial social imaginary it is difficult to explain why India waited 24 years after its first nuclear test to conduct another test and why on both occasions – rather than highlighting the military and security implications of the tests – it emphasized scientific advances and characterized its nuclear program as being unique in terms of its restraint and its commitment to total nuclear disarmament. Furthermore, understanding the cultural context of the gendered language that accompanies discussions of India's nuclear policies is only possible by taking into account anti-colonial negotiations of discourses of colonial masculinity and native effeminacy. Similarly, considering the narratives of civilizational exceptionalism and backwardness in India's postcolonial social imaginary is necessary for comprehending the nature and timing of India's involvement in Sri Lanka's civil war and its unwillingness to pursue a more extensive military campaign against Pakistan in 1971. As I argued in Chapter 4, moreover, understanding how India came to engage in a discourse of friendship with China, rather than adopt the anti-communist stance of other democratic states requires an examination of the anti-colonial rejection of imperial geopolitics. Making sense of how India eventually went to war with China in 1962 over two remote pieces of territory, on the other hand, requires a focus on the negotiation of the emotions related to the colonial experience and anti-colonial struggle such as honour, humiliation and betrayal.

In analysing foreign policy as postcoloniality, the book has also sought to explore the interlinked nature of domestic, regional and international politics. As Chapters 2 and 5 argued, India's promotion of nuclear disarmament, its reluctance to endorse nuclear non-proliferation treaties and its 'peaceful nuclear explosion' in 1974 can only be understood by considering domestic debates about science, progress and violence. Likewise, India's declaration of itself as a nuclear weapons power in 1998, which was examined in Chapter 7, needs to be understood in terms of the shifts in electoral politics and the space this created for heightened domestic contestations over the character of modern India and the world it inhabits. As Chapters 5 and 6 argued, moreover, the rendering of South Asia into a space of danger under Indira Gandhi needs to be considered in the context of her growing authoritarianism, the developmental strains on the postcolonial state and the politics of the Cold War. The region's transformation, under Rajiv Gandhi, into a space in which to enact India's leadership should be viewed in the context of the delegitimization of the old developmental state and the emergence of a new leadership determined to overhaul existing models of economic and political behavior.

There now appears to be a growing consensus on India's status as a rising great power. Its credentials include having one of the highest growth rates in the world, an increasing share of world trade, greater political influence thanks to its role in institutions such as the Group of 20 (G20) and the ability to change global norms, as evidenced by the recently concluded India–US agreement on civilian nuclear cooperation and the decision of the Nuclear Suppliers Group to sell India uranium despite its unwillingness to sign the NPT. Yet, the rise of India has not generated the geopolitical 'hyperbole' that has accompanied the rise of China, with claims of a 'China threat' from Western and Japanese commentators and counter-claims from Chinese officials and commentators that it is committed to a 'peaceful rise' and 'peaceful development' (Callahan 2005: 701, Glaser and Medeiros 2007). Nonetheless, there is now an emerging, predominantly American, 'rise of India' discourse and distinctive responses to this from Indian policymakers. The 'rise of India' represents India as 'the un-China' (Elliot 2006). According to one journalist:

[o]ne Asian giant is run by a Communist Party that increasingly appeals to nationalism as a way of legitimating its power. The other is the largest democracy the world has ever seen ... democrats are easier to talk to than communist apparatchiks

(Elliot 2006)

Likewise, for the former US ambassador to India, David Mulford, who was part of an administration, under George W. Bush, which pledged 'to help India become a major world power in the twenty-first century' (Tellis 2005: 1),

[t]he US–India relationship is based on our shared common values. We are multiethnic democracies committed to the rule of law and freedom of speech and religion ... there is no fundamental conflict or disagreement between the United States and India on any important regional or global issues.

(Quoted in Walker 2006: 24)

Similarly, according to Martin Walker:

While retaining its rich and historic cultures, India is thoroughly familiar with these core values and determinants of the American civic system. And as a religiously tolerant, multi-ethnic democracy with commercial, legal, and educational systems developed during the British Raj, India is – like the English language itself – familiar and reassuring to Americans.

(Walker 2006: 29–30)

The production of India as the un-China is something that Indian policy-makers have taken heed of. According to Manmohan Singh, '[u]nlike China's rise, the rise of India does not cause any apprehensions' for, '[t]he world takes a benign view of India. They want us to succeed' and '[w]e should take advantage of it. This benign mood cannot last' (2010b). The normative distinction between China and India, moreover, is something that Singh has promoted:

there is no doubt that the Chinese growth performance is superior to Indian performance. But I've always believed that there are other values which are important than the growth of the gross domestic product. I think the respect for fundamental human rights, the respect for the rule of law, the respect for multicultural, multi-ethnic, multi-religious rights, I think those have values also.

(2010b)

Yet, this does not make India a 'budding ally' of the US, as Robert Kaplan (2009: 24) has claimed, for there are limits to the extent of identification with the US, and Western liberal democracies, in general, that Indian policy-makers are willing to pursue. India's stance at the climate change negotiations in Copenhagen in 2009 is a case in point. In the lead-up to Copenhagen it emerged that the

Environment Minister Jairam Ramesh wanted India to disassociate itself from the Group of 77 (G77), its stance on equity and development and the maintenance of the Kyoto Protocol, in favour of an Australian proposal which was backed by the US and would abandon the Kyoto Protocol, in order to embed India in the G20 (Sethi 2009). He found little domestic support, however, for what would have amounted to a major shift in India's foreign policy and, at Copenhagen, India entered into a coalition with Brazil, South Africa and China (BASIC) and has been insistent that the coalition will continue to align with the G77 (2010a).

Furthermore, while commentators like Zenia Dormandy (2007: 117–18) and Martin Walker (2006: 28) tend to attribute India's rise to economic liberalization policies adopted in 1991,[2] India's embrace of neo-liberalism has been partial and tentative and significant differences between the US and India have emerged in WTO talks on trade liberalization. According to India's current Prime Minister, Manmohan Singh, for instance, 'I am not unambiguously attached to reforms. I feel that India has to compete with the rest of the world on its own strength. I am not enamoured of India copying the western consumption style' (2006b). Invoking the vocabulary of anti-colonial nationalism, Singh went on to argue, 'you must understand the relevance of swadeshi [self-reliance] in today's context', he went on to note, for,

> Swadeshi brings with it the positive message of self-reliance. After all, what did Gandhiji say about swadeshi? He said I want to build a house that is open on all four sides. I want to absorb all that is good and reject all that is not consistent with our cultural, social and economic heritage.
>
> (2006b)

Furthermore, while Indian policy-makers have highlighted commonalities in values with the US, they have gone further in institutionalizing a normative element in India's relationships with the other non-Western democracies of South Africa and Brazil. The IBSA (India–Brazil–South Africa) forum, which was co-founded by the BJP-led government in 2003, has been described by Singh as 'a strong moral force in today's unsettled world' and has been represented as a key component of India's negotiation its rise as a great power (Singh 2010). The IBSA forum promotes the reform of the multilateral trading system and international institutions to include greater Southern representation, the expansion of South-South trade, dialogue and development aid and is said to have a 'vast potential for shaping the debate on global issues ... so that globalization becomes a positive force for the benefit of the developing countries' (Shashank 2004).

As I touched on in the introductory chapter, moreover, Indian policy-makers have responded to the discourse on India's rise by questioning dominant notions of power and drawing on older identity discourses that celebrate India's civilizational restraint, wisdom and influence over others. While Sonia Gandhi is 'uneasy with the very word "Superpower"' (Gandhi 2006), for Manmohan

Singh, global interdependence means that 'power as traditionally understood may become less relevant in international affairs and the concept of a super power as we generally understand it, even less so' (Singh 2006a). Singh went on in this speech to reiterate many of the narratives of backwardness and exceptionalism that I have explored in this book. He noted that, 'size does give us a certain weight in global affairs and this will get recognized across the world. We will be seen as a growth engine', however, 'this has to be tempered by the realization that the ultimate goal is to work for rule based rather than power based relationships' (Singh 2006a). This was an approach that was:

> in line with our history, culture and civilization. For centuries, we have lived in peace with the world around us, traveling to distant lands as traders, teachers and scholars. Rarely has the world seen armies sailing out of India as conquerors. The Indian influence across much of Asia has been one of culture, language, religion, ideas and values, not of bloody conquest. We have always been respected for our traditional export knowledge! Does that not also make India a 'global superpower', though not in the traditional sense! Can this not be the power we seek in the next century?
>
> (Singh 2006a)

It was 'our neglect of modern science and technology and our inability to harness it for growth that made us miss the industrial revolution' but India was now,

> at an inflexion point in world history. Once again, advances in science and technology, particularly in IT and connectivity, are making enormous changes in the way we organize our lives, our industries, our economies and our institutions ... If we have to realize our destiny and once again be counted among the great nations of the world, we have to ensure that we do not miss this new wave of industrialisation.
>
> (Singh 2006a)

What this speech indicates is that the changes in India's material resources and structural environment have not led to any dramatic breaks in its self-representation. Understanding the colonial encounter and its negotiation by Indian leaders therefore remains vital to understanding the identity which underpins its foreign policy interests. How might India's sense of backwardness and exceptionalism influence its choices as a great power? How might they shape India's approach to global governance, its ability and willingness to exercise leadership and its relationships with other powers? These are all pertinent questions to ask of a rising India in a transforming world order.

Notes

1 Introduction

1 Exceptions include Muppidi (1999, 2004), Krishna (1999), Abraham (1998).
2 See Hardt and Negri's (2000) (theorization of the relationship between colonialism, modernity and Eurocentrism. On the pervasive Eurocentrism of knowledge production and representations of non-Europeans as the Other, see Said (1995) and Young (1990).
3 See Bowden (2009) on the historical evolution of the concept of 'civilization' and the 'standard of civilization'. See Jahn (2000) on 'the state of nature' as a key category of Western political thought, its impact on Europe's relations with non-Europeans and on the discipline of International Relations. See Anghie (2004) on the idea of the 'civilizing mission' as central to the imperial and colonial projects and to the development of international law and the sovereignty doctrine.
4 I follow Romila Thapar (2002) in dividing eighteenth and nineteenth century Western scholarship on India into three groupings: the Orientalists, the Utilitarians and the Romantics.
5 The colonial encounter provoked a number of different responses among Indians and I do not wish to suggest that the accounts discussed here were the only important ones. Anti-colonial resistance to the British, rather than being the seamless nationalist account that has been given official sanction, was in fact comprised of various nineteenth century struggles by peasants, soldiers and civil servants, none of which took the defence of 'Indian civilization' as their driving motivation. The focus in this book however, is on elite forms of nationalist resistance and many of these engaged with the idea of an 'Indian civilization'.
6 See for instance, Darby (1997) (1998) (2006a), Krishna (2001), Chowdhry and Nair (2002), Grovogui (2001) (1996), Beier (2005), Persaud (1997), Ling, (2002), Muppidi (2004) (1999), Paolini (1999), Inayatullah and Blaney (2004).
7 This study builds on the work of several scholars, in particular, Krishna (1999), Muppidi (2004) and Abraham (1998), who also draw on postcolonial theory in their analysis of specific issues in Indian foreign policy, although the scope of my analysis, which traverses several decades and issues, is broader and my particular arguments concerning the ethico-political basis of India's postcolonial identity are different.
8 Pant cites Morgenthau's reductionist, abstract notion of the national interest as defined by power and universally valid to make his argument. However, although he did not focus on it, Morgenthau's understanding of the national interest was significantly more complicated, for he argued that while the 'idea of interest is indeed of the essence of politics and is unaffected by circumstances of time and place', the 'kind of interest determining political action in a particular period of history depends upon the political and cultural context within which foreign policy is formulated'. See Morgenthau (1967: 8–9).

2 Nuclear technology, disarmament and the ambivalence of postcolonial identity

1 I am grateful to Revathi Krishnaswamy for clarifying this point in a personal correspondence.
2 While my focus here is Gandhi because of his relationship with Nehru, Gandhi was not the only figure in colonial India to advance conceptions of alternative sciences and technologies. See Nandy (1995).

3 Rejecting the 'fear complex': constructing an international politics of friendship

1 Ashoka's edicts were: (i) individualistic transcendentalism, (ii) nonviolent pacifism, (iii) religious pluralism with an educational emphasis, (iv) compassionate welfare paternalism, and (v) reliance on a powerful central authority to affirm the rights of individuals over claims of intermediate groups. See Thurman (1988).
2 It is not clear which countries Nehru meant by South East Asia. He does, however, omit China, which he places in a separate category with the Far East.
3 A grouping formed in 1954 in response to the Indo-China war which was seen as the product of neo-colonial interference.
4 Sri Lanka was called Ceylon until 1972.
5 The Sri Lankan nationalist movement was largely engaged in a legalistic form of agitation and ultimately achieved its independence as a result of India's independence movement.
6 The 'Rajaji formula' was never explicitly articulated in public but private letters suggest that it would have involved placing the Kashmir Valley in UN trusteeship while keeping 'Azad' Kashmir in Pakistani hands and Jammu under Indian control. See Guha (2007: 356).

4 From friendship to 'betrayal': the India–China war

1 A corruption of the word which appears in the *Rig Veda* as *arya* and in the *Zend Avesta* as *airiia*.
2 From the Sanskrit term *Tiravitam* which refers to the South and, in Vaisnava literature, as the language spoken there.
3 See Edney (1997) for an examination of the role of map-making and surveying in producing India as an object that could be controlled. This process began with the maps produced by James Rennell for the East India Company and continued to the end of the Great Trigonometrical Survey under George Everest.
4 The phrase 'the Great Game' was, however, apparently not Kipling's own invention but was borrowed from the writings of a chess-playing Bengal cavalry officer called Arthur Connelly. See Alan Sandison's explanatory notes in Kipling (1987).
5 Sumathi Ramaswamy (2002: 166–7) emphasizes that little is still known about the extent to which the colonial effort to disseminate cartographic literacy was internalized by ordinary Indians.
6 Correspondence between the Prime Ministers on border issues had begun in December 1958.
7 The missing party had been captured by the Chinese the day before the shooting incident on the 20 October 1959.
8 Among the reasons speculated on for China's unilateral cease-fire are the rhetorical and military support offered by Western countries to India as the war progressed, the oncoming winter weather, China's attempt to further humiliate India by showing magnanimity. See Mullik (1971: 457–9).
9 Burma, Cambodia, Ghana, Indonesia and the United Arab Republic (Egypt).

10 By 1966 the size of the military had been doubled and defence spending was trebled. See Brown (2003: 330).

5 Interventions and explosions: wither an ethical modernity?

1 The full extent of Nixon's hostility to India and his tilt toward Pakistan can be discerned in the United States Government's recently declassified Documents on South Asia, 1969–1972, some of which are available online: www.state.gov/r/pa/ho/frus/nixon/e7.
2 See also the FRUS documents www.state.gov/r/pa/ho/frus/nixon/e7.
3 See for instance, the speeches of India's Foreign Minister Swaran Singh in the UN from 12 December.
4 India, unlike other democracies, does not follow the thirty-year rule in regard to diplomatic records.

6 India in South Asia: danger, desire, friendship and fraternity

1 DeVotta takes this quote from an article by P. Venkateshwar Rao (1988) who, in turn, cites an article by R.V.R. Chandrasekhar Rao (1985: 63). Rao attributes the quote to the International Institute of Strategic Studies' *Strategic Survey: 1983–84.*
2 In his *Asian Drama: An Inquiry into the Poverty of Nations* Gunnar Myrdal argued that India was a 'soft state' unable to maintain the discipline needed to modernize and develop and that an authoritarian regime may have more success.
3 Which Vajpayee specifies elsewhere as Pakistan, Bangladesh, Nepal, Sri Lanka and Bhutan.
4 Tamil Eelam Liberation Organisation (TELO), Eelam Revolutionary Organisation (EROS), and Eelam Peoples Revolutionary Liberation Front (EPRLF).
5 The phrase is borrowed from Raman (1991: 5).
6 The Cabinet Committee on Political Affairs, the Intelligence agencies, the Service Chiefs and the Foreign Office were all extensively consulted (Dixit 1998: 106).
7 The US and Britain maintained a studied ambiguity, neither condemning nor approving of India's actions. Indeed, Jayewardene was advised by most Western states to work with India rather than seek a confrontation. See Krishna (1999: 155). Although other South Asian countries did raise objections to India's actions, the prohibition on bringing bilateral issues into the ambit of SAARC left Sri Lanka with little option but to come to terms with India's intervention.
8 It was alleged that RAW was involved in arming the LTTE's rivals in order to weaken it and its opposition to the Agreement but this is a claim that is impossible to confirm.
9 The LTTE were well aware of the planned attack and knew the details of the IPKF's operational strategy. Moreover, the IPKF had little knowledge of the territory on which they were fighting and possessed only the most basic maps, some of which were produced in the colonial era (Krishna 1999: 188–9).
10 The EPRLF had been elected to head the provincial council established under the provisions of the Agreement but the win had little credibility given the reality of the LTTE's control of the North and the violence and intimidation that accompanied the election.
11 One and a half years later, Rajiv Gandhi was assassinated by an LTTE suicide bomber at an election rally in Tamil Nadu.

7 Foreign policy, identity and the BJP: correcting the 'emasculation of state power'?

1 This phrase is Jaswant Singh's (1999: 13).
2 The Rani of Jhansi was a near-legendary figure who died fighting the British in the

rebellion of 1857. Savarkar portrays her as a heroic mother defending her son's inheritance by giving up her femininity and fighting to the death dressed as a masculine warrior.

3 For a detailed examination of the BJP's use of the discourse of 'nuclear apartheid' see Biswas (2001).

4 This was a reference to India's nuclear tests which were conducted at Pokhran in Rajasthan.

5 For a good account of the probable reasons for Pakistan's actions, the perceptions on both sides and the possible consequences of Kargil see Tellis, Fair and Medby (2002). For a collection of essays on various aspects of the Kargil war see Krishna and Chari (2001).

6 The issue of Nawaz Sharif's knowledge of the Kargil incursion is still a matter of controversy. Sharif himself claims that he had no knowledge of the Pakistan army's plans and blames its head, General Pervez Musharraf. Musharraf however, claims that Sharif was fully appraised on the situation (2009) (2006a).

8 Conclusion

1 For other recent moves to 'decolonize' IR see Gruffydd Jones (2006), Shani (2007), Hobson (2007), Shilliam (2011), Grovogui (2006), Chowdhry and Nair (2002), Acharya and Buzan (2010).

2 c.f. Rodrik and Subramaniam (2004), Kohli (2007), Saraswati (2008).

Bibliography

Abraham, I. (1995) 'Towards a Reflexive South Asian Security Studies', in Weinbaum, M.G. and Kumar, C. (eds) *South Asian Approaches the Millennium: Reexamining National Security*, Boulder: Westview Press.

Abraham, I. (1998) *The Making of the Indian Atomic Bomb: Science, Secrecy and the Postcolonial State*, London: Zed Books.

Abraham, I. (2004) 'Notes Toward a Global Nuclear History', *Economic and Political Weekly*, 39: 4997–5005.

Abraham, I. (2008) 'From Bandung to NAM: Non-alignment and Indian Foreign Policy, 1947–65', *Commonwealth and Comparative Politics*, 46: 195–219.

Acharya, A. (2005) *'Why Is There No NATO in Asia?' The Normative Origins of Asian Multilateralism*, Working Paper. Cambridge, MA: Weatherhead Center for International Affairs.

Acharya, A. and Buzan, B. (eds.) (2010) *Non-Western International Relations Theory: Perspectives On and Beyond Asia*, New York: Routledge.

Advani, L.K. (2001) 'Parliament statement: 18 December', *Outlook*, Online. Available: www.outlookindia.com/article.aspx?214064 (Accessed 4 June 2010).

Advani, L.K. (2010) *Secularism vs. Pseudo Secularism*, Lal Krishna Advani, Online. Available: www.lkadvani.in/eng/content/view/381/349/ (Accessed 6 June 2010).

Ahmad, A. (1998) 'Subcontinental crisis'. *Frontline*, Online. Available: www.thehindu.com/fline/fl1512/15120220.htm (Accessed 23 May 2010).

Ali, D. (1998) 'Recognizing Europe in India: Colonial Master Narratives and the Writing of Indian History', in Cox, J. and Stromquist, S. (eds.) *Contesting the Master Narrative: Essays in Social History.* Iowa City: Iowa Press.

Anand, D. (2007) 'Anxious Sexualities: Masculinity, Nationalism and Violence', *British Journal of Politics and International Relations*, 9: 257–69.

Anghie, A. (2004) *Imperialism, Sovereignty and the Making of International Law*, Cambridge: Cambridge University Press.

Arendt, H. (1958) *The Human Condition*, Chicago: University of Chicago Press.

Arendt, H. (1963) *On Revolution*, New York: Viking Press.

Arnold, D. (2004) 'Race, place and bodily difference in early nineteenth-century India', *Historical Research*, 77: 254–73.

Ayoob, M. and Subrahmanyam, K. (1972) *The Liberation War*, New Delhi: S. Chand and Co.

Bagchi, J. (1990) 'Representing Nationalism: Ideology of Motherhood in Colonial Bengal', *Economic and Political Weekly*, 24: WS 65–71.

Bahuguna, H.N. (1972) 'Shri Bahuguna's Speech', *Foreign Affairs Record*, XVIII: 379.

Bajpai, K. (1998) 'India: Modified Structuralism', in Alagappa, M. (ed.) *Asian Security Practice*, Stanford, Ca: Stanford University Press.

Bajpai, K. (2003) 'Indian Conceptions of Order and Justice: Nehruvian, Gandhian, Hindutva and Neo-liberal', in Foot, R., Gaddis, J.L. and Hurrell, A. (eds) *Order and Justice in International Relations*, New York: Oxford.

Bakhale, J. (2010) 'Country First? Vinayak Damodar Savarkar (1883–1966) and the Writing of Essentials of Hindutva', *Public Culture*, 22: 149–86.

Banerjee, P. (2007) 'Chinese Indians in Fire: Refractions of Ethnicity, Gender, Sexuality and Citizenship in Post-colonial India's Memories of the Sino-Indian War', *China Report*, 43: 437–63.

Banerjee, S. (1994) 'National Identity and Foreign Policy', in Choudhry, N.K. and Mansur, S. (eds) *The Indira-Rajiv Years: The Indian Economy and Polity 1966–1991*, Toronto: University of Toronto.

Banerjee, S. (2006) 'Armed Masculinity, Hindu Nationalism and Female Political Participation in India: Heroic Mothers, Chaste Wives and Celibate Warriors', *International Feminist Journal of Politics*, 8: 62–83.

Bangladesh Documents, vol. 2 (1971) New Delhi: Publications Division, Ministry of Information and Broadcasting.

Bayly, S. (1999) *Caste, Society and Politics in India from the Eighteenth Century to the Modern Age*, Cambridge: Cambridge University Press.

Bayly, S. (2004) 'Imagining 'Greater India: French and Indian Visions of Colonialism in the Indic Mode', *Modern Asian Studies*, 38: 703–44.

BBC (2002a) 'Bangladesh denies al-Qaeda claim', *BBC*, Online. Available: http//news. bbc.co.uk/2/hi/south_asia/2437901.stm (Accessed 22 June 2010).

BBC (2002b) 'Dhaka rejects Indian al-Qaeda claims', *BBC*, Online. Available: http:// news.bbc.co.uk/2/hi/south_asia/2522783.stm (Accessed 22 June 2010).

Behera, N.C. (2006) *Demystifying Kashmir*, Washington DC: Brookings Institution Press.

Beier, J.M. (2005) *International Relations in Uncommon Places: Indigeneity, Cosmology, and the Limits of International Theory*, New York: Palgrave Macmillan.

Bell, D. (1975) 'The End of American Exceptionalism', *Public Interest*, 41: 193–224.

Bell, D. (ed.) (2006) *Memory, Trauma and World Politics: Reflections on the Relationship Between Past and Present*, New York: Palgrave Macmillan.

Bell, D. (ed.) (2008a) 'Introduction: Under an Empty Sky – Realism and Political Theory', *Political Thought and International Relations: Variations on a Realist Theme*, Oxford: Oxford University Press.

Bell, D. (ed.) (2008b) *Political Thought and International Relations: Variations on a Realist Theme* Oxford: Oxford University Press.

Berenskoetter, F. (2007) 'Friends, There Are No Friends? An Intimate Reframing of the International', *Millennium*, 35: 647–76.

Bhabha, H.K. (1994) *The Location of Culture*, London: Routledge.

Bhagavan, M. (2008) 'A New Hope: India, the United Nations and the Making of the Universal Declaration of Human Rights', *Modern Asian Studies*, 44: 311–47.

Bhasin, A.S. (ed.) (2001) *India–Sri Lanka: Relations and Sri Lanka's Ethnic Conflict Documents – 1947–2000*, New Delhi: India Research Press.

Bhatt, C. (2000) 'The Lore of the Homeland: Hindu Nationalism and Indigenist "Neoracism"', in Back, L. and Solomos, J. (eds.) *Theories of Race and Racism: A Reader*, London and New York: Routledge.

Bhatt, C. (2001) *Hindu Nationalism: Origins, Ideologies and Modern Myths*, Oxford and New York: Berg.

Bhatt, S. (2002) 'Muslims don't want to live in harmony, says Vajpayee', *Rediff*, Online. Available: www.rediff.com/news/2002/apr/12bhatt.htm (Accessed 28 May 2010).

Bially Mattern, J. (2005) 'Why 'Soft Power' Isn't So Soft:: Representational Force and the Sociolinguistic Construction of Attraction in World Politics', *Millennium: Journal of International Studies*, 33: 583–612.

Bilgrami, A. (2003) 'Gandhi, the Philosopher', *Economic and Political Weekly*, 38: 4159–65.

Biswas, S. (2001) '"Nuclear apartheid" as Political Position: Race as a Postcolonial Resource?', *Alternatives: Global, Local, Political*, 26: 485–521.

BJP (1998a) *BJP Election Manifesto 1998: Chapter 7 – Our Foreign Policy*, BJP, Online. Available: www.bjp.org/content/view/2631/376/ (Accessed 13 May 2010).

BJP (1998b) *BJP Election Manifesto 1998: Chapter 8 – Our Nation's Security*, BJP, Online. Available: www.bjp.org/content/view/2631/376/ (Accessed 13 May 2010).

Bleiker, R. and Hutchison, E. (2008) 'Fear No More: Emotions and World Politics', *Review of International Studies*, 34: 115–35.

Boquerat, G. (2005) 'India's Committment to Peaceful Coexistence and the Settlement of the Indochina War', *Cold War History*, 5: 211–34.

Bose, S. (2002) 'Space and Time on the Indian Ocean Rim: Theory and History', in Bayly, C.A. and Fawaz, L. (eds.) *Modernity and Culture: From the Mediterranean to the Indian Ocean*, New York: Columbia University Press.

Bose, S. (2006) *A Hundred Horizons: The Indian Ocean in the Age of Global Empire*, Delhi: Permanent Black.

Bowden, B. (2009) *The Empire of Civilization: The Evolution of an Imperial Idea*, Chicago: University of Chicago Press.

Brecher, M. (1968) *India and World Politics: Krishna Menon's View of the World*, London: Oxford University Press.

Brimnes, N. (2002) 'Globalization and Indian Civilisation: Questionable Continuities', in Mozaffari, M. (ed.) *Globalization and Civilizations*, London: Routledge.

Brown, J.M. (2003) *Nehru: A Political Life*, New Haven: Yale University Press.

Bulley, D. (2009) *Ethics as Foreign Policy: Britain, the EU, and the Other*, London: Routledge.

Burke, R. (2006) '"The Compelling Dialogue of Freedom": Human Rights at the Bandung Conference', *Human Rights Quarterly* 28: 947–65.

Burke, R. (2010) *Decolonization and the Evolution of International Rights*, Philedelphia: University of Pennsylvania Press.

Callahan, W.A. (2004) 'National Insecurities: Humiliation, Salvation, and Chinese Nationalism', *Alternatives: Global, Local, Political*, 29: 199–218.

Callahan, W.A. (2005) 'How to understand China: the dangers and opportunities of being a rising power', *Review of International Studies*, 31: 701–14.

Campbell, D. (1992) *Writing Security: United States Foreign Policy and the Politics of Identity*, Manchester: Manchester University Press.

Campbell, D. (2001) 'Justice and international order: The case of Bosnia and Kosovo', in Coicaud, J.-M. and Warner, D. (eds) *Ethics and International Affairs: Extent and Limits*, Tokyo: United Nations University Press.

Carras, M.C. (1979) *Indira Gandhi: In the Crucibe of Leadership – A Political Biography*, Boston: Beacon Press.

Castoriadis, C. (1998) *The Imaginary Institution of Society*, Cambridge, Mass.: MIT Pree.

Chakrabarty, D. (2000) *Provincializing Europe: Postcolonial Thought and Historical Difference*, Princeton: Princeton University Press.

Chakrabarty, D. (2005) 'Legacies of Bandung: Decolonisation and the Politics of Culture', *Economic and Political Weekly*, 40: 4812–18.

Chakravarti, U. (1990) 'Whatever Happened to the Vedic *Dasi*? Orientalism, Nationalism and a Script for the Past', in Sangari, K. and Vaid, S. (eds) *Recasting Women: Essays in Indian Colonial History*, New Bruswick: Rutgers University Press.

Chandler, D. (2003) 'Rhetoric without responsibility: the attraction of "ethical" foreign policy', *British Journal of Politics and International Relations*, 5: 295–316.

Chandrasekhar Rao, R.V.R. (1973) 'The Breznev Plan and the Indo-Soviet Treaty: Expectations and Frustrations', *Economic and Political Weekly*, 8: 2059–65.

Chandrasekhar Rao, R.V.R. (1985) 'Regional Cooperation in South Asia', *The Round Table*, 1: 53–64.

Chatterjee, P. (1986) *Nationalist Thought and the Colonial World: A Derivative Discourse*, London: Zed Books.

Chatterjee, P. (1993) *The Nation and its Fragments: Colonial and Postcolonial Histories*, Princeton, NJ: Princeton University Press.

Chaulia, S.S. (2002) 'BJP, India's Foreign Policy and the 'Realist Alternative' to the Nehruvian Tradition', *International Politics*, 39: 215–34.

Chavan, Y.B. (1976) 'Speech by the Foreign Minister at Dinner in His Honour at Kathmandu', *Foreign Affairs Record*, XXII: 37–8.

Chiba, S. (1995) 'Hannah Arendt on Love and the Political: Love, Friendship, and Citizenship', *The Review of Politics*, 57: 505–5.

Chiriyankandath, J. and Wyatt, A. (2005) 'The NDA and Indian Foreign Policy', in Adeney, K. and Saez, L. (eds) *Coalition Politics and Hindu Nationalism*, London: Routledge.

Chowdhry, G. and Nair, S. (eds) (2002) *Power, Postcolonialism and International Relations: Reading Race, Gender and Class*, London: Routledge.

Chowdhury-Sengupta, I. (1995) 'The Effeminate and the Masculine: Nationalism and the Concept of Race', in Robb, P. (ed.) *South Asia and the Concept of Race*, Delhi: Oxford University Press.

CNN (1998) 'Indian nuclear test sparks concerns of arms race', *CNN*, Online. Available: www.cnn.com/WORLD/asiapcf/9805/12/india.nuclear.on/ (Accessed 27 October 2005).

CNN (2002) 'Vajpayee: Pakistan pledges helped avert war' *CNN*, Online. Available: http://archives.cnn.com/2002/WORLD/asiapcf/south/06/17/india.pakistan/index.html (Accessed 10 June 2010).

Cohen, S.P. (2001) *India: Emerging Power*, Washington, DC: Brookings Institution Press.

Cohn, C. (1987) 'Sex and Death in the Rational World of Defense Intellectuals', *Signs: Journal of Women in Culture and Society*, 12: 687–718.

Corbridge, S. (1999) ' "The Militarization of All Hindudom?" The Bharatiya Janata Party, the Bomb, and the Political Spaces of Hindu Nationalism', *Economy and Society*, 28: 222–55.

Cortright, D. and Mattoo, A. (1996) 'Public Opinion and Nuclear Weapons Policy in India', *Asian Survey*, 36: 545–60.

Crawford, N.C. (2000) 'The Passion of World Politics: Proposition on Emotion and Emotional Relationships', *International Security*, 24: 116–56.

Crocker, W. (1966) *Nehru: A Contemporary's Estimate*, London: George Allen and Unwin.

Curzon, G.N.C. and Raleigh, T. (1906) *Lord Curzon in India: Being a Selection from his*

Speeches as Viceroy and Governor-General of India 1898–1905, Macmillan's Colonial Library. London: Macmillan.

Darby, P. (ed.) (1997) *At the Edge of International Relations: Postcolonialism, Gender and Dependency*, London: Pinter.

Darby, P. (ed.) (1998) *The Fiction of Imperialism: Reading Between International Relations and Postcolonialism*, London: Cassell.

Darby, P. (ed.) (2006a) *Postcolonizing the International: Working To Change the Way We Are*, Honolulu: University of Hawai'i Press.

Darby, P. (ed.) (2006b) 'Reworking Knowledge Conventions', in Darby, P. (ed.) *Postcolonizing the International: Working To Change the Way We Are*, Honolulu: University of Hawai'i Press.

Das, R. (2002) 'Engendering Post-Colonial Nuclear Policies through the Lens of Hindutva: Rethinking the Security Paradigm of India', *Comparative Studies of South Asia, Africa and the Middle East*, 22: 76–89.

Das, R. (2006) 'Encountering Hindutva, Interrogating Religious Nationalism and (En)gendering a Hindu Patriarchy in India's Nuclear Policies: Ordering, Bordering and Othering', *International Feminist Journal of Politics*, 8: 370–93.

Das, R. (2008) 'State, Identity, and Representations of Danger: Competing World Views on Indian Nuclearisation', *Commonwealth and Comparative Politics*, 46: 2–28.

Dawson, W.H. (1923) 'Forward Policy and Reaction 1874–1885', in Ward, A.W. and Gooch, G.P. (eds) *The Cambridge History of British Foreign Policy 1783–1919*, Cambridge: Cambridge University Press.

De Silva, K.M. (1995) *Regional Powers and Small State Security: India and Sri Lanka 1977–1990*, Washington, DC: Woodrow Wilson Center Press.

Deccan Chronicle (2010) 'BASIC countries support Copenhagen Accord', *Deccan Chronicle*, Online. Available: www.deccanchronicle.com/international/basic-countries-support-copenhagen-accord-346 (Accessed 6 August 2010).

Desai, M. (1977a) 'Prime Minister's Speech in Lok Sabha', *Foreign Affairs Record*, XXIII: 95–8.

Desai, M. (1977b) 'Shri Morarji Desai Speech', *Foreign Affairs Record*, XXIII: 278–80.

Deshpande, A. (1999) 'Options in Kargil: Half-Forward Policy', *Economic and Political Weekly*, 34: 1978.

Devji, F.F. (2005) 'A Practice of Prejudice: Gandhi's Politics of Friendship', in Mayaram, S., Pandian, M.S.S. and Skaria, A. (eds) *Subaltern Studies XII: Muslims, Dalits, and the Fabrications of History*, Delhi: Permanent Black and Ravi Dayal.

DeVotta, N. (2003) 'Is India Over-Extended? When Domestic Disorder Precludes Regional Intervention', *Contemporary South Asia*, 12: 365–80.

Dhar, P.N. (2000) *Indira Gandhi, The Emergency and Indian Democracy*, New Delhi: Oxford University Press.

Di Lodovico, A.M., Lewis, W.W., Palmade, V. and Sankhe, S. (2001) 'India – From Emerging to Surging', *McKinsey Quarterly*.

Diez, T. (2004) 'Europe's Others and the Return of Geopolitics', *Cambridge Review of International Affairs*, 17: 319–35.

Diez, T. (2005) 'Constructing the Self and Changing Others: Reconsidering "Normative Power Europe"', *Millennium – Journal of International Studies*, 33: 613–36.

Dirks, N.B. (1987) *The Hollow Crown: Ethnohistory of an Indian Kingdom*, Cambridge: Cambridge University Press.

Dixit, J.N. (1998) *Assignment Colombo*, Delhi: Konark Publishers.

Dixit, J.N. (2004) *Makers of India's Foreign Policy: Raja Ram Mohun Roy to Yashwant Sinha*, New Delhi: HarperCollins.

Dormandy, X. (2007) 'Is India, or Will it Be, a Responsible International Stakeholder?', *The Washington Quarterly*, 30: 117–30.

Doty, R.L. (1993) 'Foreign Policy as Social Construction: A Post-Positivist Analysis of U.S. Counterinsurgency Policy in the Philippines', *International Studies Quarterly*, 37: 297–320.

Doyle, L. (2002) 'India says Pakistan is a rogue nation that supports terror', *Independent*, Online. Available: www.independent.co.uk/news/world/asia/india-says-pakistan-is-a-rogue-nation-that-supports-terror-610668.html (Accessed 12 December).

Dutt, S. (1956) 'Cable of the Foreign Secretary of the Indian Ministry of External Affairs to the Indian Ambassader in Moscow K.P.S. Menon', in Bhasin, A.S. (ed.) *Nepal–India, Nepal–China Relations – Documents: 1947–June 2005*, New Delhi: Geetika Publishers.

Economic Times (2006) 'Refarmer Manmohan', *Economic Times*, Online. Available: http://timesofindia.indiatimes.com/home/specials/Refarmer-Manmohan/articleshow/1701290.cms#ixzz10ryeDfN0 (Accessed 29 September 2010).

Edney, M.H. (1997) *Mapping an Empire: The Geographical Construction of British India 1765–1843*, Chicago: University of Chicago Press.

Elliot, M. (2006). 'India Awakens', *Time*.18 June, Online. Available: www.time.com/time/magazine/article/0,9171,1205374,00.html (Accessed 18 March 2010).

Faleiro, E. (1992a) 'Changing World Order', *Foreign Affairs Record*, XXXVIII: 211–14.

Faleiro, E. (1992b) 'South Asia as a Dynamic Partner', *Foreign Affairs Record*, XXXVIII: 214–17.

Fattah, K. and Fierke, K.M. (2009) 'A Clash of Emotions: The Politics of Humiliation and Political Violence in the Middle East', *European Journal of International Relations*, 15: 67–93.

Fifield, R.H. (1958) 'The Five Principles of Peaceful Co-Existence', *American Journal of International Law*, 52: 504–10.

Fonteyne, J.L. (1973–1974) 'The Customary International Law Doctrine of Humanitarian Intervention: Its Current Validity Under the UN Charter', *California Western International Law Journal*, 4: 203–470.

Foreign Affairs (2006) 'The Rise of India', *Foreign Affairs*, 85.

Foreign Relations of the United States (1971a) 'Document 138. Conversation Among President Nixon, the President's Assistant for National Security Affairs (Kissinger), the Indian Foreign Minister (Singh), and the Assistant Secretary of State for Near Eastern and South Asian Affairs (Sisco), Washington, June 16, 1971, 2:58–3:41 p.m.', *Foreign Relations of the United States 1969–1976: Volume E-7 – Documents on South Asia 1962–1972*. Online. Available: www.state.gov/r/pa/ho/frus/nixon/e7/48523.htm (accessed 23 September 2006).

Foreign Relations of the United States (1971b) 'Document 171. 'Conversation Between President Nixon and his Assistant for National Security Affairs (Kissinger), Washington, December 9, 1971, 5:57–6:34 p.m' *Foreign Relations of the United States 1969–1976: Volume E-7 – Documents on South Asia 1962–1972*. Online. Available: www.state.gov/r/pa/ho/frus/nixon/e7/48541.htm (accessed 23 September 2006).

Foreign Relations of the United States (1971c) 'Document 138. 'Conversation Among President Nixon, the President's Assistant for National Security Affairs (Kissinger), the Indian Foreign Minister (Singh), and the Assistant Secretary of State for Near Eastern and South Asian Affairs (Sisco), Washington, June 16, 1971, 2:58–3:41 p.m.', *Foreign*

Relations of the United States 1969–1976: Volume E-7 – Documents on South Asia 1962–1972, Online. Available: www.state.gov/r/pa/ho/frus/nixon/e7/48523.htm (Accessed 23 September 2006).

Foreign Relations of the United States (1974a) 'Document 162. Telegram TOSEC 794/104621 From the Department of State to the Mission to the International Atomic Energy Agency, May 18, 1974, 2238Z', *Foreign Relations of the United States 1969–1976: Volume E-8 – Documents on South Asia* 1973–1976. Online. Available: www.state.gov/r/pa/ho/frus/nixon/e8/96787.htm (Accessed 23 September 2009).

Foreign Relations of the United States (1974b) 'Document 208. Interagency Memorandum DCI/NIO 1686, Washington, July 18, 1975', *Foreign Relations of the United States 1969–1976: Volume E-8 – Documents on South Asia 1973–1976*. Online. Available: www.state.gov/r/pa/ho/frus/nixon/e8/97055.htm (Accessed 23 September 2009).

Foreign Relations of the United States (1974c) 'Document 229 Interagency Intelligence Memorandum 76–021, Washington, May 1976', *Foreign Relations of the United States 1969–1976: Volume E-8 – Documents on South Asia 1973–1976.* Online. Available: www.state.gov/r/pa/ho/frus/nixon/e8/97083.htm (Accessed 23 September 2009).

Foucault, M. (1984a) 'Truth and Power', in Rabinow, P. (ed.) *The Foucault Reader: An Introduction to Foucault's Thought*, New York: Pantheon.

Foucault, M. (1984b) 'What Is an Author?', in Rabinow, P. (ed.) *The Foucault Reader: An Introduction to Foucault's Thought*, New York: Pantheon.

Fox, R.G. (1996) 'Gandhi and Feminized Nationalism in India', in Williams, B.F. (ed.) *Women Out of Place: The Gender of Agency and the Race of Nationality*, New York: Routledge.

Franck, T.M. and Rodley, N.S. (1973) 'After Bangladesh: The Law of Humanitarian Intervention by Military Force', *American Journal of International Law*, 67: 275–305.

Frank, K. (2001) *Indira: The Life of Indira Nehru Gandhi*, London: HarperCollins.

Gandhi, I. (1966) 'Prime Minister's Speech at Dinner in Honour of the Prime Minister of Nepal', *Foreign Affairs Record*, XII: 111–12.

Gandhi, I. (1971a) 'Prime Minister's Statement on Hijacking of Indian Airlines Plane', *Foreign Affairs Record*, XVII: 34–5.

Gandhi, I. (1971b) 'Text of the Prime Minister's Intervention During the Debate in Lok Sabha on March 27, 1971', in Singh, S.K., Gupta, S., Kumar, S., Shukla, H.C., Nevrekar, V.V. and Basu, D.K. (eds) *Bangladesh Documents*, vol. 1, New Delhi: Publications Division, Ministry of Information and Broadcasting.

Gandhi, I. (1971c) *The Years of Challenge: Selected Speeches of Indira Gandhi, January 1966–August 1969*, vol. 1, New Delhi: Publications Division, Ministry of Information and Broadcasting, Government of India.

Gandhi, I. (1972) *India and Bangla Desh: Selected Speeches and Statements, March to December 1971*, New Delhi: Orient Longman.

Gandhi, I. (1975a) *India: The Speeches and Reminiscences of Indira Gandhi, Prime Minister of India*, London: Hodder and Stoughton.

Gandhi, I. (1975b) *The Years of Endeavour: Selected Speeches of Indira Gandhi, August 1969–August 1972*, vol. 2, New Delhi: Publications Division, Ministry of Information and Broadcasting, Government of India.

Gandhi, I. (1977) *Democracy and Discipline: Speeches of Shrimati Indira Gandhi*, New Delhi: Ministry of Information and Broadcasting, Government of India.

Gandhi, I. (1984a) *Selected Speeches and Writings of Indira Gandhi, September 1972– March 1977*, vol. 3, New Delhi: Publications Division, Ministry of Information and Broadcasting, Government of India.

Gandhi, I. (1986a) *Selected Speeches and Writings 1982–1984*, vol. 5, New Delhi: Publications Division, Ministry of Information and Broadcasting, Government of India.

Gandhi, L. (1996–1997) 'Concerning Violence: The Limits and Circulations of Gandhian 'Ahimsa' or Passive Resistance', *Cultural Critique*: 105–47.

Gandhi, M.K. (1938) *Hind Swaraj or Indian Home Rule*, Ahmedabad: Navajivan Press.

Gandhi, M.K. (1942) 'Appendix V: Resolution Passed By All-India Congress Committee', *The Collected Works of Mahatma Gandhi*, vol. 83, New Delhi: Publications Division, Ministry of Information and Broadcasting, Government of India.

Gandhi, M.K. (1986b) 'Science and Civilization', in Iyer, R. (ed.) *The Moral and Political Writings of Mahatma Gandhi*, vol. I, Oxford: Clarendon Press.

Gandhi, M.K. (1999a) 'Congress report on the Punjab disorders ', *The Collected Works of Mahatma Gandhi*, vol. 20, New Delhi: Publications Division, Ministry of Information and Broadcasting, Government of India.

Gandhi, M.K. (1999b) 'Cow Protection (Young India, 4–8–1920)', *The Collected Works of Mahatma Gandhi*, vol. 21, New Delhi: Publications Division, Ministry of Information and Broadcasting, Government of India.

Gandhi, M.K. (1999c) 'Hind Swaraj', *The Collected Works of Mahatma Gandhi*, vol. 10, New Delhi: Publications Division, Ministry of Information and Broadcasting, Government of India.

Gandhi, M.K. (1999d) 'His Will Be Done (Harijan, 6–5–1933)', *The Collected Works of Mahatma Gandhi*, vol. 61, New Delhi: Publications Division, Ministry of Information and Broadcasting, Government of India.

Gandhi, M.K. (1999e) 'The Indian Franchise (December 16, 1895)', *The Collected Works of Mahatma Gandhi*, vol. 1, New Delhi: Publications Division, Ministry of Information and Broadcasting, Government of India.

Gandhi, M.K. (1999f) 'Interview to Chinese Delegation (November 6, 1947)', *The Collected Works of Mahatma Gandhi*, vol. 97, New Delhi: Publications Division, Ministry of Information and Broadcasting, Government of India.

Gandhi, M.K. (1999g) 'Notes (Harijan 10–11–1933)', *The Collected Works of Mahatma Gandhi*, vol. 62, New Delhi: Publications Division, Ministry of Information and Broadcasting, Government of India.

Gandhi, M.K. (1999h) 'Question Box, December 10, 1947 (Harijan, 21–12–1947)', *The Collected Works of Mahatma Gandhi*, vol. 98, New Delhi: Publications Division, Ministry of Information and Broadcasting, Government of India.

Gandhi, M.K. (1999i) 'Some Rules of Satyagraha (Young India, 27–2–1930)', *The Collected Works of Mahatma Gandhi*, vol. 48, New Delhi: Publications Division, Ministry of Information and Broadcasting, Government of India.

Gandhi, M.K. (1999j) 'Speech at AICC Meeting, August 8, 1942 (Mahatma, vol. VI, pp. 154–64)', *The Collected Works of Mahatma Gandhi*, vol. 83, New Delhi: Publications Division, Ministry of Information and Broadcasting, Government of India.

Gandhi, M.K. (1999k) 'Speech at Gandhi Seva Sangh meeting (March 28 1938)', *The Collected Works of Mahatma Gandhi*, vol. 73, New Delhi: Publications Division, Ministry of Information and Broadcasting, Government of India.

Gandhi, M.K. (1999l) 'Speech at public meeting, Tinnevelly, October 7, 1927', *The Collected Works of Mahatma Gandhi*, vol. 40, New Delhi: Publications Division, Ministry of Information and Broadcasting, Government of India.

Gandhi, M.K. (1999m) 'Talk with a Sikh friend, January 13, 1948 (Harijan, 18–1–1948)', *The Collected Works of Mahatma Gandhi*, vol. 98, New Delhi: Publications Division, Ministry of Information and Broadcasting, Government of India.

Gandhi, M.K. (1999n) 'To the women of India (Young India 10–4–1930)', *The Collected Works of Mahatma Gandhi*, vol. 49, New Delhi: Publications Division, Ministry of Information and Broadcasting, Government of India.

Gandhi, M.K. (1999o) 'To the women of India (Young India, 11–8–1921)', *The Collected Works of Mahatma Gandhi*, vol. 24, New Delhi: Publications Division, Ministry of Information and Broadcasting, Government of India.

Gandhi, R. (1984) *The Rajaji Story: 1937–1972*, Bombay: Bharatiya Vidya Bhavan.

Gandhi, R. (1987a) 'Prime Minister's Statement on Agreement', *Foreign Affairs Record*, XXXIII: 250–2.

Gandhi, R. (1987b) 'Prime Minister's Statement on Sri Lanka', *Foreign Affairs Record*, XXXIII: 190–1.

Gandhi, R. (1987c) *Rajiv Gandhi: Selected Speeches and Writings, 1984–85*, vol. 1, New Delhi: Publications Division, Ministry of Information and Broadcasting, Government of India.

Gandhi, R. (1987d) 'Shri Rajiv Gandhi's Remarks at the Colombo Reception', *Foreign Affairs Record*, XXXIII: 257–8.

Gandhi, R. (1990) *Selected Speeches and Writings*, vol. 3, New Delhi: Publications Division, Ministry of Information and Broadcasting.

Gandhi, S. (2006) 'Text of Inaugral Address by Sonia Gandhi', *Hindustan Times*, Online. Available: www.hindustantimes.com/news/specials/leadership2006/coverage_17110603. shtml (Accessed 17 November 2006).

Ganguly, S. (1999) 'India's Pathway to Pokhran II: The Prospects and Sources of New Delhi's Nuclear Weapons Program', *International Security,* 23: 148–77.

Ganguly, S. and Hagerty, D.T. (2005) *Fearful Symmetry: India–Pakistan Crises in the Shadow of Nuclear Weapons*, New Delhi: Oxford University Press.

Ganguly, S. and Kraig, M.R. (2005) 'The 2001–2002 Indo-Pakistani Crisis: Exposing the Limits of Coercive Diplomacy', *Security Studies*, 14: 290–324.

Ganguly, S. (1999) 'India's Pathway to Pokhran II: The Prospects and Sources of New Delhi's Nuclear Weapons Program', *International Security*, 23: 148–77.

Ganguly, S. (2003/04) 'India's Foreign Policy Grows Up', *World Policy Journal*, 20: 41–6.

Ganguly, S. (2008) 'Nuclear Stability in South Asia', *International Security*, 33: 45–70.

Ghose, A. (1996) *Statement made by Ms. Arundhati Ghose, Ambassador/Permanent Representative of India to UN in the Plenary Meeting of the Conference On Disarmament, Geneva on June 20, 1996*, Embassy of India – Washington DC, Online. Available: www.indianembassy.org/policy/CTBT/ctbt_cd_june_20_96.htm (Accessed August 3 2008).

Ghose, A. (1997) 'Negotiating the CTBT: India's Security Concerns and Nuclear Disarmament', *Journal of International Affairs*, 51: 239.

Gillan, M. (2002) 'Refugees or infiltrators? The Bharatiya Janata Party and "illegal" migration from Bangladesh', *Asian Studies Review*, 26: 73–95.

Glaser, B.S. and Medeiros, E.S. (2007) 'The Changing Ecology of Foreign Policy-Making in China: The Ascension and Demise of the Theory of "Peaceful Rise"', *China Quarterly*, 190: 291–310.

Gokhale, N.A. (2001) 'Home-Made Fiasco', *Outlook*, Online. Available: www.outlookindia.com/article.aspx?211529 (Accessed 22 June 2010).

Gopal, S. (1984) *Jawaharlal Nehru: A Biography*, vol. 3, London: Jonathan Cape.

Grovogui, S.N. (1996) *Sovereigns, Quasi Sovereigns, and Africans: Race and Self Determination in International Law*, Minneapolis: University of Minnesota Press.

Grovogui, S.N. (2001) 'Come to Africa: A Hermeneutics of Race in International Theory', *Alternatives: Global, Local, Political*, 26: 425–47.

Grovogui, S.N. (2003) 'Postcoloniality in Global South Foreign Policy: A Perspective', in Braveboy-Wagner, J.A. (ed.) *The Foreign Policies of the Global South: Rethinking Conceptual Frameworks*, Boulder, Co.: Rienner.

Grovogui, S.N. (2006) *Beyond Eurocentrism and Anarchy: Memories of International Order and Institutions*, New York: Palgrave Macmillan.

Gruffydd Jones, B. (ed.) (2006) *Decolonizing International Relations*, Lanham: Rowman and Littlefield.

Guha, R. (2007) *India After Gandhi: The History of the World's Largest Democracy*, London: Picador.

Gujral, I.K. (1997) 'Speech of the Indian Minister for External Affairs Inder Kumar Gujral, at the Bandaranaike Center for International Studies: 'Aspects of India's Foreign Policy,' Colombo, January 20, 1997', in Bhasin, A.S. (ed.) *India–Sri Lanka: Relations and Sri Lanka's Ethnic Conflict Documents – 1947–2000*, vol. V, New Delhi: India Research Press.

Gujral, I.K. (2003) *Continuity and Change: India's Foreign Policy*, New Delhi: Macmillan.

Gunaratna, R. (1993) *Indian Intervention in Sri Lanka: The Role of India's Intelligence Agencies*, Colombo: South Asian Network on Conflict Research.

Gupta, A. (1990) 'A Brahmanic Framework of Power in South Asia?', *Economic and Political Weekly*, 25: 711–14.

Gupta, A. (1999) 'Mellow BJP to cobble brand new front', *Indian Express*, 3 May, Online. Available: www.expressindia.com/news/ie/daily/19990503/ipo03002.html (Accessed 23 May 2010).

Gupta, S. (1984) 'Sri Lanka's Rebels: An Ominous Presence in Tamil Nadu.' *India Today*, 31 March: 84–94.

Gupta, S. (2002) 'When India Came Close To War', *India Today*, Online. Available: www.india-today.com/itoday/20021223/cover.shtml (Accessed 10 June 2010).

Hagerty, D.T. (1991) 'India's Regional Security Doctrine', *Asian Survey*, 31: 351–63.

Haider, Z. (2009) 'A Revisit to the Indian Role in the Bangladesh Liberation War', *Journal of Asian and African Studies*, 44: 537–51.

Hamilton, B. (1996) 'Continental Drift: Prester John's Progress Through the Indies', in Beckingham, C.F. and Hamilton, B. (eds) *Prester John, the Mongols and the Ten Lost Tribes*, Aldershot: Variorum.

Hansen, T.B. (1999) *The Saffron Wave: Democracy and Hindu Nationalism*, Princeton, NJ: Princeton University Press.

Hardiman, D. (2003) *Gandhi: In His Time and Ours*, New Delhi: Permanent Black.

Hardt, M. and Negri, A. (2000) *Empire*, Cambridge: Harvard University Press.

Harootunian, H.D. (1999) 'Postcoloniality's unconscious/area studies' desire', *Postcolonial Studies*, 2: 127–47.

Harshe, R. (1999) 'South Asian Regional Co-operation: Problems and Prospects', *Economic and Political Weekly*, 34: 1100–5.

Harshe, R. (2005) 'South Asian Regional Cooperation: Problems and Prospects', in Harshe, R. and Seethi, K.M. (eds) *Engaging with the World: Critical Reflections on India's Foreign Policy*, New Delhi: Orient Longman.

Heehs, P. (1993) *The Bomb in Bengal: The Rise of Revolutionary Terrorism in India 1900–1910*, Oxford: Oxford University Press.

Hegel, G.W.F. (1956) *The Philosophy of History*, New York: Dover Publications.

Hilali, A.Z. (2001) 'India's Strategic Thinking and its National Security Policy', *Asian Survey*, 41: 737–7364.

Hobson, J.M. (2007) 'Is critical theory always for the white West and for Western imperialism? Beyond Westphilian towards a post-racist critical IR', *Review of International Studies*, 33: 91–116.

Hoffmann, S.A. (1990) *India and the China Crisis*, Berkeley: University of California Press.

Hoffmann, S.A. (2006) 'Rethinking the Linkage between Tibet and China–India Border Conflict: A Realist Approach', *Journal of Cold War Studies*, 8: 165–94.

Hooper, C. (2001) *Manly States: Masculinities, International Relations and Gender Politics*, New York: Columbia University Press.

Huntington, S.P. (1996) *The Clash of Civilizations and the Remaking of World Order*, New York: Simon and Schuster.

Husain, A. (1968) 'Statement by the Indian Representative (Husain) to the First Committee of the General Assembly: Nonproliferation of Nuclear Weapons, May 14, 1968', *Documents on Disarmament, 1968*, Washington DC: United States Arms Control and Disarmament Agency.

Hymans, J.E.C. (2002) 'Why Do States Acquire Nuclear Weapons? Comparing the Cases of India and France', in Sardesi, D.R. and Thomas, R.G.C. (eds) *Nuclear India in the Twenty-First Century*, New York: Palgrave Macmillan.

Hymans, J.E.C. (2006) *The Psychology of Nuclear Proliferation: Identity, Emotions, and Foreign Policy*, Cambridge: Cambridge University Press.

Hymans, J.E.C. (2009) 'India's Soft Power and Vulnerability', *India Review*, 8: 234–65.

Inayatullah, N. and Blaney, D.L. (2004) *International Relations and the Problem of Difference*, New York: Routledge.

Inden, R. (1990) *Imagining India*, Oxford: Basil Blackwell.

India, Government of and Sri Lanka, Government of (1987) 'Indo-Sri Lanka Agreement to Establish Peace and Normalcy in Sri Lanka', *Foreign Affairs Record*, XXXIII: 252–7.

India, Government of (1954–1959) *Notes, Memoranda and Letters Exchanged and Agreements Signed Between the Governments of India and China: White Paper No. I*, New Delhi: Ministry of External Affairs.

India, Government of (1959) *Notes, Memoranda and Letters Exchanged Between the Governments of India and China and a Note on the Historical Background of the Himalayan Frontier of India: White Paper No. II*, New Delhi: Ministry of External Affairs.

India, Government of (1959–1960) *Notes, Memoranda and Letters Exchanged Between the Governments of India and China: White Paper No. III*, New Delhi: Ministry of External Affairs.

India, Government of (1962) *China's Betrayal of India*, Delhi: Publications Division, Ministry of Information and Broadcasting.

India, Government of (1963) *Notes, Memoranda and Letters Exchanged Between the Governments of India and China and a Note on the Historical Background of the Himalayan Frontier of India: White Paper No. VIII*, New Delhi: Ministry of External Affairs.

India, Government of (1974) 'Statement by the Indian Atomic Energy Commission on Nuclear Explosion, May 18, 1974', *Documents on Disarmament 1974*, Washington DC: United States Arms Control and Disarmament Agency.

India, Government of (1978) *Shah Commission of Inquiry*, vol. 3, New Delhi: Controller of Publications.

India, Government of (1987a) 'Government and Opposition Leaders' Statement on Sri Lanka', *Foreign Affairs Record*, XXXIII: 228.

India, Government of (1987b) 'Government of India's Messages to Colombo', *Foreign Affairs Record*, XXXIII: 224–5.

India, Government of (1987c) 'Refusal of Sri Lanka to Allow Humanitarian Supplies – Statement of Official Spokesman', *Foreign Affairs Record*, XXXIII: 227–8.

India, Government of (1987d) 'Return of Relief Convoy to Rameshwaram – Statement of Official Spokesman', *Foreign Affairs Record*, XXXIII: 227.

India, Government of (1988a) *Disarmament: India's Initiatives*, New Delhi: External Publicity Division.

India, Government of (1988b) *India and Disarmament: An Anthology of Selected Writings and Speeches*, New Delhi: External Publicity Division.

India, Government of (1998a) 'The Indian Memorial Submitted to the International Court of Justice on Status of Nuclear Weapons in International Law', *Seminar*: 71–4.

India, Government of (1998b) *Paper laid on the table of the House on 'Evolution of India's Nuclear Policy', May 27, 1998*, Embassy of India – Washington DC, Online. Available: www.indianembassy.org/pic/nuclearpolicy.htm (Accessed 25 May 2006).

India, Government of (1998c) *Press Release issued in New Delhi on UN Security Council Resolution on India's nuclear tests*, Embassy of India – Washington DC, Online. Available: www.indianembassy.org/pic/PR_1998/May98/prmay1598.htm (Accessed 20 May 2006).

India, Government of (2001) 'Statement of the Indian Minister for External Affairs Jaswant Singh in the *Rajya Sabha* on the 'Situation in Sri Lanka', New Delhi, May 4, 2000', in Bhasin, A.S. (ed.) *India–Sri Lanka: Relations and Sri Lanka's Ethnic Conflict Documents – 1947–2000*, vol. V, New Delhi: India Research Press.

Indian and Foreign Review (1974a) 'India's Peaceful Nuclear Experiment', *Indian and Foreign Review*, 11: 8.

Indian and Foreign Review (1974b) 'India Not 'Nuclear Weapons' Country: Mrs Gandhi's Interview With U.S. Newsmagazine', *Indian and Foreign Review*, 11: 7.

Indian Embassy (1999) *Interview with Minister of External Affairs, Shri Jaswant Singh*, Embassy of India – Washington DC, Online. Available: www.indianembassy.org/new/NewDelhiPressFile/Jaswant_Singh_June_01_1999.htm (Accessed 26 February 2007).

Jaffrelot, C. (1996) *Hindu Nationalist Movement and Indian Politics: 1925 to the 1990s*, London: Hurst and Co.

Jaffrelot, C. (2003) 'India's Look East Policy: An Asianist Strategy in Perspective', *Asian Review*, 2: 35–68.

Jahn, B. (2000) *The Cultural Construction of International Relations: The Invention of the State of Nature*, New York: Palgrave.

Jalal, A. (1985) *The Sole Spoksman: Jinnah, the Muslim League and the Demand for Pakistan*, Cambridge: Cambridge University Press.

Jalal, A. (1998) 'Exploding Communalism: The Politics of Muslim Identity in South Asia', in Bose, S. and Jalal, A. (eds) *Nationalism, Democracy and Development: State and Politics in India*, Delhi: Oxford University Press.

Jayaraman, K.S. 1991. 'Scientist will miss Gandhi', *Nature*, 351: 431.

Jepperson, R., Wendt, A. and Katzenstein, P. (1996) 'Norms, Identity and Culture in National Security', in Katzenstein, P. (ed.) *The Culture of National Security*, New York: Columbia University Press.

Jones, R. (1788a) 'The Second Anniversary Discourse [1785]', *Asiatic Researches*, 1: 405–14.

Jones, R. (1788b) 'The Third Anniversary Discourse [1786]', *Asiatic Researches*, 1: 415–31.

Jones, R. (1790) 'The Sixth Anniversary Discourse [1789]', *Asiatic Researches*, 2: 43–66.

Jones, R. (1970) *The Letters of Sir William Jones*, Oxford: Oxford University Press.

Jones, R. (2009) 'Geopolitical boundary narratives, the global war on terror and border fencing in India', *Transactions of the Institute of British Geographers*, 34: 290–304.

Kaplan, R.D. (2009) 'Center Stage for the Twenty-first Century: Power Plays in the Indian Ocean', *Foreign Affairs*, 88: 16–32.

Kapur, A. (2006) *India: From Regional to World Power*, New York: Routledge.

Kapur, S.P. (2002) Vajpayee: Pakistan pledges helped avert war' *CNN*, Online. Available: http://archives.cnn.com/2002/WORLD/asiapcf/south/06/17/india.pakistan/index. html (Accessed 10 June 2010).

Kapur, S.P. (2008) 'Ten Year of Instability in a Nuclear South Asia', *International Security*, 33: 71–94.

Karnad, B. (1999) 'Using LoC to India's Advantage', *Economic and Political Weekly*, 34: 1869–70.

Karnad, B. (2002a) 'India First', *Seminar*, 519, Online. Available: www.india-seminar. com/2002/519/519bharatkarnad.htm (Accessed 1 November 2009).

Karnad, B. (2002b) *Nuclear Weapons and Indian Security: The Realist Foundations of Strategy*, New Delhi: Macmillan.

Karnad, B. (2009) Habit of free-riding. *Seminar*, Online. 599. Available: www.india-sem-inar.com/2009/599/599_bharat_karnad.htm (Accessed 1 November 2009).

Kaul, T.N. (1995) *My Years Through Raj to Swaraj*, New Delhi: Vikas Publishing.

Kaviraj, S. (1986) 'Indira Gandhi and Indian Politics', *Economic and Political Weekly*, XXI: 1697–708.

Keenleyside, T.A. (1982) 'Nationalist Indian Attitudes Towards Asia: A Troublesome Legacy for Post-Independence Indian Foreign Policy', *Pacific Affairs*, 55: 210–30.

Khilnani, S. (1999) *The Idea of India*, New York: Farra, Straus and Giroux.

Kinzer, S. (1998) 'Restraint by Pakistan is eroding, leader says' *New York Times*, Online. Available: www.nytimes.com/1998/05/24/world/restraint-by-pakistan-is-eroding-leader-says.html?pagewanted=print (Accessed 25 May 2010).

Kipling, R. (1987) *Kim*, Oxford: Oxford University Press.

Kishwar, M. (1998) BJP's Wargasm. *Manushi*, Online. Available: www.indiatogether.in/manushi/issue106/wargasm.htm (Accessed 23 May 2010).

Kissinger, H. (1979) *White House Years*, Boston: Little, Brown & Co.

Kohli, A. (2007) 'State, Business and Economic Growth in India', *Studies in Comparative International Development*, 42: 87–114.

Kremmer, C. (2006) *Inhaling the Mahatma*, Pymble, NSW: HarperCollins.

Krishna, A. and Chari, P.R. (eds) (2001) *Kargil: The Tables Turned*, New Delhi: Manohar.

Krishna, G. (1984) 'India and the International Order: Retreat From Idealism', in Bull, H. and Watson, A. (eds) *The Expansion of International Society*, Oxford: Clarendon Press.

Krishna, R. (1966) 'India and the Bomb', in Shah, A.B. (ed.) *India's Defence and Foreign Policies*, Bombay: Manaktalas.

Krishna, S. (1999) *Postcolonial Insecurities: India, Sri Lanka, and the Question of Nationhood*, Minneapolis: University of Minnesota Press.

Krishna, S. (2001) 'Race, Amnesia, and the Education of International Relations', *Alternatives: Global, Local, Political*, 26: 401–23.

Krishnaswamy, R. (1998) *Effeminism: The Economy of Colonial Desire*, Ann Arbor: University of Michigan Press.

Kumar, S. (1975) 'The Evolution of India's Policy Towards Bangladesh in 1971', *Asian Survey*, 15: 488–98.

Kumar, S. (1999) 'Indo-Pak bus diplomacy', *Strategic Analysis*, 23: 167–70.

Laffey, M. (2000) 'Locating Identity: Performativity, Foreign Policy and State Action', *Review of International Studies*, 26: 429–44.

Lahore Summit: February 20–21 1999, (1999) Stimpson Centre, Online. Available: www.stimson.org/southasia/?sn=sa20020109215 (Accessed 23 May 2010).

Lal, V. (2003) 'Provincializing the West: World History from the Perspective of Indian History', in Stuchtey, B. and Fuchs, E. (eds) *Writing World History 1800–2000*, Oxford: Oxford University Press.

Lamb, A. (1960) *Britain and Chinese Central Asia: The Road to Lhasa 1767 to 1905*, London: Routledge and Kegan Paul.

Lamb, A. (1964) *The China–India Border: The Origins of the Disputed Boundaries*, London: Oxford University Press.

Lamb, A. (1966a) *The McMahon Line: A Study in the Relations between India, China and Tibet, 1904 to 1914*, vol. 2, London: Routledge and Kegan Paul.

Lamb, A. (1966b) *The McMahon Line: A Study in the Relations between India, China and Tibet, 1904 to 1914*, vol. 1, London: Rouledge and Kegan Paul.

Le Goff, J. (1980) *Time, Work, and Culture in the Middle Ages*, Chicago: University of Chicago Press.

Lebow, R.N. (2006) 'Fear, interest and honour: outlines of a theory of International Relations', *International Affairs*, 82: 431–48.

Ling, L.H.M. (2002) *Postcolonial International Relations: Conquest and Desire between Asia and the West*, New York: Palgrave.

Lok Sabha Debates, vol. IX (1962) New Delhi: Lok Sabha Secretariat.

Lok Sabha Debates, vol. XII (1963) New Delhi: Lok Sabha Secretariat.

Lok Sabha Debates, vol. XXIX (1964) New Delhi: Lok Sabha Secretariat.

Lok Sabha Debates, vol. IV (1977) New Delhi: Lok Sabha Secretariat.

Lyotard, J.F. (1989) *The Postmodern Condition: A Report on Knowledge*, Minneapolis: University of Minnesota Press.

Macaulay, T.B. (1870) *Critical and Historical Essays, Contributed to the Edinburgh Review*, London: Longmans, Green, Reader, and Dyer.

Mackinder, H.J. (1951) *The Scope and Methods of Geography and The Geographical Pivot of History*, London: The Royal Geographical Society.

Mackinder, H.J. (1962) *Democratic Ideals and Reality*, New York: W.W. Norton and Company.

Mahajan, S. (2002) *British Foreign Policy: The Role of India*, London: Routledge.

Majeed, J. (2007) *Autobiography, Travel and Post-national Identity: Gandhi, Nehru and Iqbal*, New York: Palgrave Macmillan.

Malik, J.M. (1998) 'India Goes Nuclear: Rationale, Benefits, Cost, and Implications', *Contemporary South Asia*, 20.

Manchanda, R. 1986. 'A Foreign Affair – Interview/Romesh Bhandari'. *Illustrated Weekly*, 13 April: 16–17.

Manners, I. (2002) 'Normative Power Europe: A Contradiction in Terms?', *Journal of Common Market Studies*, 40: 235–58.

Mansingh, S. (1984) *India's Search for Power: Indira Gandhi's Foreign Policy 1966–1982*, New Delhi: Sage.

Marwah, O. (1979) 'India's Military Intervention in East Pakistan, 1971–1972', *Modern Asian Studies*, 13: 549–80.

Maxwell, N. (1972) *India's China War*, Harmondsworth: Pelican Books.

Maxwell, N. (2006) 'Settlements and Disputes: China's Approach to Territorial Issues', *Economic and Political Weekly*, 41: 3873–81.

McClintock, A. (1992) 'The Angel of Progress: Pitfalls of the Term "Postcolonialism"', *Social Text*, 31/32: 84–98.

Mehta, V. (1970) *Portrait of India*, New York: Farrar, Straus and Giroux.

Metcalf, T.R. (1994) *Ideologies of the Raj*, Cambridge: Cambridge University Press.

Mill, J. (1848a) *The History of British India*, vol. 2, London: James Madden.

Mill, J. (1848b) *The History of British India*, vol. 5, London: James Madden.

Mill, J. (1848c) *The History of British India*, vol. 1, London: James Madden.

Mill, J. (1975) *The History of British India*, (abridged) Chicago: University of Chicago Press.

Mirchandani, G.G. (1968) *India's Nuclear Dilemma*, New Delhi: Popular Book Services.

Mishra, B.C. (1974) 'Statement by the Indian Representative (Mishra) to the Conference of the Committee on Disarmament [Extract]: Nuclear Explosion, May 23, 1974', *Documents on Disarmament 1974*, Washington DC: United States Arms Control and Disarmament Agency.

Mistry, D. (2003) 'The Unrealized Promise of International Institutions: The Test Ban Treaty and India's Nuclear Breakout', *Security Studies*, 12: 116–51.

Mitra, S.K. (2001) 'War and peace in South Asia: a revisionist view of India–Pakistan relations', *Contemporary South Asia*, 10: 361–79.

Mitzen, J. (2006) 'Ontological Security in World Politics: State Identity and the Security Dilemma', *European Journal of International Relations*, 12: 341–70.

Mohan, C.R. (2003) *Crossing the Rubicon: The Making of India's New Foreign Policy*, New Delhi: Penguin Books.

Mohan, C.R. (2007) 'Balancing Interests and Values: India's Struggle with Democracy Promotion', *The Washington Quarterly*, 30: 99–115.

Molloy, S. (2008) 'Hans J. Morgenthau Versus E.H. Carr: Conflicting Conceptions of Ethics in Realism', in Bell, D. (ed.) *Political Thought and International Relations: Variations on a Realist Theme*, Oxford: Oxford University Press.

Morgenthau, H.J. (1967) *Politics Among Nations: the Struggle for Power and Peace*, New York: Alfred A. Knopf.

Morphet, S. (2004) 'Multilateralism and the Non-Aligned Movement: What is the Global South Doing and Where is it Going?', *Global Governance*, 10: 517–37.

Mosley, L. (1961) *The Last Days of the British Raj*, London: Weidenfeld and Nicolson.

Mullik, B.N. (1971) *My Years With Nehru: The Chinese Betrayal*, Bombay: Allied Publishers.

Mullik, B.N. (1972) *My Years With Nehru 1948–1964*, New Delhi: Allied Publishers.

Muppidi, H. (1999) 'Postcoloniality and the Production of International Insecurity: The Persistent Puzzle of U.S.-Indian Relations', in Weldes, J., Laffey, M., Gusterson, H. and Duvall, R. (eds) *Cultures of Insecurity: States, Communities and the Production of Danger*, Minneapolis: University of Minnesota Press.

Muppidi, H. (2004) *The Politics of the Global*, Minneapolis: University of Minnesota Press.

Muralidharan, S. and Cherian, J. (1998) 'The BJP's Bombs', *Frontline*, Online. Available: www.flonnet.com/fl1511/15110040.htm (Accessed 4 June 2005).

Muralidharan, S. and Ramakrishnan, V. (1998) 'Political Echoes', *Frontline*, Online. Available: www.hinduonnet.com/fline/fl1511/15110180.htm (Accessed 5 June 2005).

Nagel, J. (1998) 'Masculinity and Nationalism: Gender and Sexuality in the Making of Nations', *Ethnic and Racial Studies*, 21: 242–69.

Nandy, A. (1974) 'Between Two Gandhis: Psychopolitical Aspects of the Nuclearization of India', *Asian Survey*, 14: 966–70.

Nandy, A. (1980) *At The Edge of Psychology: Essays in Politics and Culture*, New Delhi: Oxford University Press.

Nandy, A. (1983) *The Intimate Enemy: Loss and Recovery of Self Under Colonialism*, Delhi: Oxford University Press.

Nandy, A. (1987) *Traditions, Tyranny and Utopias: Essays in the Politics of Awareness*, Delhi: Oxford University Press.

Nandy, A. (1988) *Introduction: Science as a Reason of State in Science, Hegemony and Violence*, Tokyo: United Nations University, Online. Available: www.unu.edu/unu-press/unupbooks/uu05se/uu05ee00.htm (Accessed 20 April 2006).

Nandy, A. (1995) *Alternative Sciences: Creativity and Authenticity in Two Indian Scientists*, Delhi: Oxford University Press.

Nandy, A. (1997) 'The Fantastic India–Pakistan Battle', *Futures*, 29: 909–18.

Nandy, A. (2005) 'The idea of South Asia: a personal note on post-Bandung blues', *Inter-Asia Cultural Studies*, 6: 541–5.

Nandy, A. (2006) 'Nationalism, Genuine and Spurious: Mourning Two Early Post-Nationalist Strains', *Economic and Political Weekly*: 3500–4.

Narlikar, A. (2006) 'Peculiar chauvinism or strategic calculation? Explaining the negotiating strategy of a rising India', *International Affairs*, 82: 59–76.

Nath, K. (2008) *Dinner Address – Kamal Nath*, The International Institute for Strategic Studies, Online. Available: www.iiss.org/conferences/iiss-citi-india-global-forum/igf-plenary-sessions-2008/opening-remarks-and-dinner-address/dinner-address-kamal-nath/?locale=en (Accessed 24 December 2010).

National Security Advisory Board. (1999) *Draft Report of National Security Advisory Board on Indian Nuclear Doctrine*, Government of India, Online. Available: www.indianembassy.org/policy/CTBT/nuclear_doctrine_aug_17_1999.html (Accessed 25 May 2006).

Nayar, B.R. and Paul, T.V. (2004) *India in the World Order: Searching for Major Power Status*, Cambridge: Cambridge University Press.

Nehru, J. (1942 [1936]) *Jawaharlal Nehru: An Autobiography (With Musings on Recent Events in India)*, London: John Lane, Bodley Head.

Nehru, J. (1949) 'Letter from the Indian Prime Minister Jawaharlal Nehru to the Indian Ambassador in Nepal Chandreshwar Prasad Narain Singh', in Bhasin, A.S. (ed.) *Nepal–India, Nepal–China Relations – Documents: 1947–June 2005*, vol. 1, New Delhi: Geetika Publishers.

Nehru, J. (1956) 'Cable of the Indian Prime Minister Jawaharlal Nehru to the Indian Ambassador in Nepal Bhagwan Sahay', in Bhasin, A.S. (ed.) *Nepal–India, Nepal–China Relations – Documents: 1947–June 2005*, New Delhi: Geetika Publishers.

Nehru, J. (1961) *India's Foreign Policy: Selected Speeches, September 1946–April 1961*, Delhi: Publications Division, Ministry of Information and Broadcasting, Government of India.

Nehru, J. (1965) *Nehru: The First Sixty Years*, vol. 1, London: Bodley Head.

Nehru, J. (1972) *Selected Works of Jawaharlal Nehru*, vol. 3, *First Series*. New Delhi: Orient Longman.

Nehru, J. (1973) *Selected Works of Jawaharlal Nehru*, vol. 5, *First Series*. New Delhi: Orient Longman.

Nehru, J. (1974) *Selected Works of Jawaharlal Nehru*, vol. 6, *First Series*. New Delhi: Orient Longman.

Nehru, J. (1980) *Jawaharlal Nehru: An Autobiography*, New Delhi: Jawaharlal Nehru Memorial Fund.

Nehru, J. (1981) *Selected Works of Jawaharlal Nehru*, vol. 14, *First Series*. New Delhi: Orient Longman.

Nehru, J. (1982 [1946]) *The Discovery of India*, Calcutta: Signet Press.

Nehru, J. (1984a) *Selected Works of Jawaharlal Nehru*, vol. 1, *Second Series*. New Delhi: Jawaharlal Nehru Memorial Fund.

Nehru, J. (1984b) *Selected Works of Jawaharlal Nehru*, vol. 2, *Second Series*. New Delhi: Jawaharlal Nehru Memorial Fund.

Nehru, J. (1986) *Selected Works of Jawaharlal Nehru*, vol. 4, *Second Series*. New Delhi: Jawaharlal Nehru Memorial Fund.

Nehru, J. (1987) *Selected Works of Jawaharlal Nehru*, vol. 5, *Second Series*. New Delhi: Jawaharlal Nehru Memorial Fund.

Nehru, J. (1988) *Selected Works of Jawaharlal Nehru*, vol. 7, *Second Series*. New Delhi: Jawaharlal Nehru Memorial Fund.

Nehru, J. (1993) *Selected Works of Jawaharlal Nehru*, vol. 15, *Series Two*. New Delhi: Jawaharlal Nehru Memorial Fund.

Nehru, J. (1994) *Selected Works of Jawaharlal Nehru*, vol. 16, *Second Series*. New Delhi: Jawaharlal Nehru Memorial Fund.

Nehru, J. (1996 [1934–1935]) *Glimpses of World History: Being Further Letters to His Daughter Written in Prison, and Containing a Rambling Account of History for Young People*, New York: Jawaharlal Nehru Memorial Fund.

Nehru, J. (1996) *Glimpses of World History: Being Further Letters to His Daughter Written in Prison, and Containing a Rambling Account of History for Young People*, New York: Jawaharlal Nehru Memorial Fund.

Nehru, J. (1999a) *Selected Works of Jawaharlal Nehru*, vol. 24, *Series Two*. New Delhi: Jawaharlal Nehru Memorial Fund.

Nehru, J. (1999b) *Selected Works of Jawaharlal Nehru*, vol. 25, *Second Series*. New Delhi: Jawaharlal Nehru Memorial Fund.

Nehru, J. (2001a) *Selected Works of Jawaharlal Nehru*, vol. 28, *Second Series*. New Delhi: Jawaharlal Nehru Memorial Fund.

Nehru, J. (2001b) *Selected Works of Jawaharlal Nehru*, vol. 29, *Second Series*. New Delhi: Jawaharlal Nehru Memorial Fund.

Nehru, J. (2002 [1946]) *The Discovery of India*, New Delhi: Jawaharlal Nehru Memorial Fund.

Nehru, J. (2003) *Selected Works of Jawaharlal Nehru*, vol. 32, *Second Series*. New Delhi: Jawaharlal Nehru Memorial Fund.

Nehru, J. (2005) *Selected Works of Jawaharlal Nehru*, vol. 36, *Second Series*. New Delhi: Jawaharlal Nehru Memorial Fund.

Nigam, A. (2004) 'Imagining the Global Nation: Time and Hegemony', *Economic and Political Weekly*, 39: 72–9.

Noorani, A.G. (1967) 'India's Quest for a Nuclear Guarantee', *Asian Survey*, 7: 490–502.

Noorani, A.G. (2004) 'Nehru and the Cold Wars'. *Frontline*, Online. Available: http://hindu.com/fline/fl2104/stories/20040227000407600.htm (Accessed 13 June 2010).

Noorani, A.G. (2007) 'An insider's view'. *Frontline*, Online. Available: www.hinduonnet.com/fline/fl2408/stories/20070504000105900.htm (Accessed 10 June 2010).

Nye, J. (2004) *Soft Power: The Means to Success in World Politics*, New York: Public Affairs.

O Tuathail, G. (1994) 'Problematizing Geopolitics: Survey, Statemanship and Strategy', *Transactions of the Institute of British Geographers*, 19: 259–72.

O Tuathail, G. (1996) *Critical Geopolitics: The Politics of Writing Global Space*, Minneapolis: University of Minnesota Press.

O Tuathail, G. and Agnew, J. (1992) 'Geopolitics and Discourse: Practical Geopolitical Reasoning in American Foreign Policy', *Political Geography*, 11: 190–204.

Observer (1998) 'Advani asks Pakistan to roll back anti-India policy', *Observer*, 19 May.

Odysseos, L. and Petito, F. (eds) (2007) *The International Political Thought of Carl Schmitt: Terror, Liberal War and the Crisis of Global Order*, London: Routledge.

Ogden, C. (2010) 'Norms, Indian Foreign Policy and the 1998–2004 National Democratic Alliance', *The Round Table*, 99: 303–15.

Palit, D.K. (1972) *The Lightning Campaign*, New Delhi: Thomson Press (India).

Palmer, N.D. (1977) 'Indian in 1976: The Politics of Depoliticization', *Asian Survey*, 17: 160–80.

Pant, H. (2009) 'A Rising India's Search for a Foreign Policy', *Orbis*, 53: 250–64.

Paolini, A.J. (1999) *Navigating Modernity: Postcolonialism, Identity, and International Relations*, Boulder: Lynne Rienner Publishers.

Perkovich, G. (1999) *India's Nuclear Bomb: The Impact on Global Proliferation*, Berkeley: University of California Press.

Persaud, R.B. (1997) 'Frantz Fanon, Race and World Order', in Gill, S. and Mittelman, J.H. (eds) *Innovation and Transformation in International Studies*, Cambridge: Cambridge University Press.

Philip, K. (2003) *Civilising Natures: Race, Resources and Modernity in Colonial India*, New Delhi: Orient Longman.

Philipose, P. (1999) 'The symbol of Pakistan', *Indian Express*, Online. Available: www.indianexpress.com/res/web/pIe/ie/daily/19990222/ige22062.html (Accessed 23 May 2010).

Popham, P. (1998) 'BJP chief in limbo as "ally" pulls out of pact' *Independent*, Online. Available: www.independent.co.uk/news/bjp-chief-in-limbo-as-ally-pulls-out-of-pact-1150125.html?cmp=ilc-n (Accessed 28 May 2010).

Prakash, G. (1999) *Another Reason: Science and the Imagination of Modern India*, Princeton, NJ: Princeton University Press.

Prasad, J. (2006) *Statement by Mr Jayant Prasad, Permanent Representative of India, at the Conference on Disarmament on nuclear disarmament – March 2, 2006*, Ministry of External Affairs, Government of India, Online. Available: http://meaindia.nic.in/mystart.php?id=515110923 (Accessed 10 May 2006).

Raghavan, S. (2010) *War and Peace in Modern India: Strategic History of the Nehru Years*, New Delhi: Permanent Black.

Raman, A.S. (1991) 'Rajiv Gandhi: The End of an Era', *Contemporary Review*, 259: 4–6.

Ramana, M.V. (2003) 'La Trahison des Clercs: Scientists and India's Nuclear Bomb', in Ramana, M.V. and Reddy, C.R. (eds) *Prisoners of the Nuclear Dream*, New Delhi: Orient Longman.

Ramanna, R. (1991) *Years of Pilgrimage*, New Delhi: Viking.

Ramaswamy, S. (2002) 'Visualising India's Geo-body: Globes, Maps, Bodyscapes', *Contributions to Indian Sociology*, 36: 151–89.

Rana, A.P. (1969) 'The Intellectual Dimensions of India's Nonalignment', *Journal of Asian Studies*, 28: 299–312.

Rao, P.V. (1988) 'Ethnic Conflict in Sri Lanka: India's Role and Perception', *Asian Survey*, 28: 419–36.

Rasgotra, M. (ed.) (1998) *Rajiv Gandhi's India: A Golden Jubilee Retrospective*, New Delhi: UBSPD.

Ray, S. (2000) *En-Gendering India: Woman and Nation in Colonial and Postcolonial Narratives*, Durham: Duke University Press.

Rediff (2001b) 'Sangh flays govt's 'soft' stance on Bangladesh', *Rediff*, Online. Available: http://imworld.rediff.com/news/2001/apr/23bang2.htm (Accessed 22 June 2010).

Rediff (2001a) 'BJP MPs criticise handling of Bangladeshi intrusion', *Rediff*, Online. Available: http://imworld.rediff.com/news/2001/apr/24bang.htm (Accessed 22 June 2010).

Risley, H.H. (1999) *The People of India*, New Delhi: Asian Educational Services.

Rodrik, D. and Subramaniam, A. (2004) *From 'Hindu Growth' to Productivity Surge: The Mystery of the Indian Growth Transition*, IMF Working Paper. WP/04/77.

Roosa, J. (1995) 'Orientalism, Political Economy, and the Canonization of Indian Civilization', in Federici, S. (ed.) *Enduring Western Civilization: The Construction of the Concept of Western Civilization and its 'Others'*, Westport, CT: Praeger.

Roy, S. (2007) *Beyond Belief: India and Politics of Postcolonial Nationalism*, New Delhi: Permanent Black.

Ruparelia, S. (2006) 'Rethinking Institutional Theories of Political Moderation: The Case of Hindu Nationalism in India, 1996–2004', *Comparative Politics*, 38: 317–36.

Sahgal, N. (1978) *Indira Gandhi's Emergence and Style*, New Delhi: Vikas Publishing House.

Said, E.W. (1985) 'Orientalism Reconsidered' in Barker, F (ed.), *Europe and Its Others: proceedings of the Essex Conference on the Sociology of Literature 1984*, Colchester: University of Essex.

Said, E.W. (1995) *Orientalism: Western Conceptions of the Orient*, London: Penguin Books.

Saklani, A. (1999) 'Colonialism and Early Nationalist Links between India and China', *China Report*, 35: 259–70.

Saraswati, J. (2008) 'The Indian IT Industy and Neoliberalism: the irony of a mythology', *Third World Quarterly*, 29: 1139–52.

Sardar, Z. (1999) *Orientalism*, Buckingham: Open University Press.

Sarkar, T. (2001) *Hindu Wife, Hindu Nation: Community, Religion and Cultural Nationalism*, London: Hurst and Company.

Saunders, H.H. and Hoskinson, S.M. (1972) *Memorandum From Harold Saunders and Samuel Hoskinson of the National Security Council Staff to the President's Assistant for National Security Affairs (Kissinger), Washington, April 24, 1972 on India's Postwar Foriegn Policy*, US Department of State, Online. Available: www.state.gov/documents/organization/48034.pdf (Accessed 24 September 2006).

Savarkar, V.D. (1938) *Hindutva*, New Delhi: The Central Hindu Yuvak Sabha.

Savarkar, V.D. (1949) *Hindu Rashtra Darshan: A Collection of the Presidential Speeches delivered from the Hindu Mahasabha Platform*, Bombay: Laxman Ganesh Khare.

Scheuerman, W.E. (2009) *Hans Morgenthau: Realism and Beyond*, Cambridge: Polity Press.

Schlegel, F. (1889) *The Aesthetic and Miscellaneous Works of Friedrich von Schlegel*. Translated by Millington, E.J., London: George Bell & Sons.

Scott, D. (1999) *Refashioning Futures: Criticism After Postcoloniality*, Princeton, NJ: Princeton University Press.

Sen Gupta, B. (1983) 'The Indian Doctrine', *India Today*, 31 August: 14–15.

Sen, S. (1971a) 'Statement by Mr Samar Sen, Representative of India December 6 1971', in Singh, S.K., Gupta, S., Kumar, S., Shukla, H.C., Nevrekar, V.V. and Basu, D.K. (eds) *Bangladesh Documents*, vol. 2, New Delhi: Publications Division, Ministry of Information and Broadcasting.

Sen, S. (1971b) 'Statement by Samar Sen, Permanent Representative of India', in Singh, S.K., Gupta, S., Kumar, S., Shukla, H.C., Nevrekar, V.V. and Basu, D.K. (eds) *Bangladesh Documents*, vol. 2, New Delhi: Publications Division, Ministry of Information and Broadcasting.

Sen, S. (1971c) 'Statement by Samar Sen, Permanent Representative of India December 4, 1971', in Singh, S.K., Gupta, S., Kumar, S., Shukla, H.C., Nevrekar, V.V. and Basu, D.K. (eds) *Bangladesh Documents*, vol. 2, New Delhi: Publications Division, Ministry of Information and Broadcasting.

Sethi, N. (2009) Jairam for major shift at climate talks. *Times of India*, Online. Available: http://timesofindia.indiatimes.com/articleshow/5136979.cms?prtpage=1 (Accessed 19 October 2009).

Shahi, A. (1971) 'Statement by Mr. Agha Shahi, Representative of Pakistan December 4, 1971 ', in Singh, S.K., Gupta, S., Kumar, S., Shukla, H.C., Nevrekar, V.V. and Basu, D.K. (eds) *Bangladesh Documents*, vol. 2, New Delhi: Publications Division, Ministry of Information and Broadcasting.

Shani, G. (2007) ' "Provincializing" critical theory: Islam, Sikhism and international relations theory', *Cambridge Review of International Affairs*, 20: 417–33.

Shankar Sahay, T. (2001a) ' "Criminal adventurism" must not go unpunished: Jaswant' *Rediff*, Online. Available: http://imworld.rediff.com/news/2001/apr/23ls1.htm (Accessed 22 June 2010).

Shankar Sahay, T. (2001b) 'Delhi, Dhaka sign pact to end border row', *Rediff*, Online. Available: http://imworld.rediff.com/news/2001/jun/13bang.htm (Accessed 22 June 2010).

Shankar Sahay, T. (2001c) 'Jaswant opposes Advani's "hot pursuit" ', *Rediff*, Online. Available: www.rediff.com/news/pat2001.htm (Accessed 23 May 2010).

Shashank. (2004) *On the meeting of IBSA Dialogue Forum by Foreign Secretary Shri Shashank*, Ministry of External Affairs, Online. Available: www.mea.gov.in/mystart.php?id=53037624 (Accessed 29 September 2010).

Shilliam, R. (ed.) (2011) *International Relations and Non-Western Thought: Imperialism, Colonialism and Investigations of Global Modernity*, London: Routledge.

Singh, J. (1998) *What Constitutes National Security in a Changing World Order?: India's Strategic Thought*, Centre for the Advanced Study of India, Online. Available: www.sas.upenn.edu/casi/ (Accessed 31 August 2005).

Singh, J. (1999) *Defending India*, Houndmills: Macmillan Press.

Singh, J. (2009) *A Call to Honour: In Service of Emergent India*, New Delhi: Rupa & Co.

Singh, M. (2006a) *PM's speech at the HT Leadership Summit – 'India: The Next Global Superpower?' – November 17, 2006*, Prime Minister's Office, Online. Available: http://pmindia.nic.in/speech/content4print.asp?id=449 (Accessed 16 January 2010).

Singh, M. (2006b) 'Suo-motu Statement on Civil Nuclear Energy Cooperation with the United States', *Hindu*, Online. Available: www.hindu.com/thehindu/nic/suomotuu.htm (Accessed 2 May 2006).

Singh, M. (2010) *PM's address at the Plenary Session of the IBSA Summit, April 15*, Prime Minister's Office, Online. Available: http://pmindia.nic.in/visits/content.asp?id=329 (Accessed 30 September 2010).

Singh, S. (1966) 'Sardar Swaran Singh's Reply: Debate on Tashkent', *Foreign Affairs Record*, XII: 53–9.

Singh, S. (1971) 'External Affairs Minister's Reply to Lok Sabha Debate', *Foreign Affairs Record*, XVII: 97–103.

Singh, S. (1974) 'Statement by the Indian External Affairs Minister (Singh) on Nuclear Explosion, May 21, 1974', *Documents on Disarmament, 1974*, Washington DC: United States Arms Control and Disarmament Agency.

Singh, S. (2009b) '"Border Crossings and Islamic Terrorists": Representing Bangladesh in Indian Foreign Policy During the BJP Era', *India Review*, 8: 144–62.

Sinha, M. (1995) *Colonial Masculinity: the Manly Englishman and the Effeminate Bengali*, Manchester: Manchester University Press.

Sinha, Y. (2003a) *Inaugral Address by Mr Yashwant Sinha, Hon'ble Member for External Affairs At the Seminar on South Asian Cooperation organised by the South Asian Centre for Policy Studies, Dhaka*, Indian Embassy – Moscow, Online. Available: www.indianembassy.ru/docs-htm/en/en_hp_win_official_direct_t003.htm   (Accessed 27 September 2006).

Sinha, Y. (2003b) *Keynote Address by Shri Yashwant Sinha on Inauguration of the South Asia Forum*: Ministry of External Affairs, Online. Available: www.mea.gov.in/mystart. php?id=53016843 (Accessed 26 February 2007).

Sinha, Y. (2003c) *Remarks by Shri Yashwant Sinha External Affairs Minister on occasion of release of Book 'Rediscovering Asia, Evolution of India's Look East policy' by Prakash Nanda*, Ministry of External Affairs, Online. Available: www.mea.gov.in/ mystart.php?id=53017299 (Accessed 26 February 2007).

Sinha, Y. (2004a) *Address by Shri Yashwant Sinha External Affairs Minister of India at India Today Conclave 2004, Building an Indian Century Session on 'Geopolitics: What it takes to be a world power'*, Ministry of External Affairs, Online. Available: www. mea.gov.in/mystart.php?id=53017655 (Accessed 20 September 2006).

Sinha, Y. (2004b) *Speech by H.E. Mr Yashwant Sinha, External Affairs Minister of India at Woodrow Wilson Centre, Washington D.C. 'After the SAARC Summit: Vision for South Asia'*, Indian Embassy – Moscow, Online. Available: www.indianembassy.ru/ en/en_hp_win_official_direct.html (Accessed 20 September 2006).

Sisson, R. and Rose, L. (1990) *War and Secession: Pakistan, India and the Creation of Bangladesh*, Berkeley: University of California Press.

Skaria, A. (2002) 'Gandhi's Politics: Liberalism and the Question of the Ashram', *The South Atlantic Quarterly*, 101: 955–86.

Skaria, A. (2006) 'Only One Word, Properly Altered: Gandhi and the Question of the Prostitute', *Economic and Political Weekly*, 41: 5065–72.

Smith, V.A. (1924) *The Early History of India: From 600 B.C. to the Muhammadan Conquest, Including the Invasion of Alexander the Great*, Oxford: Clarendon Press.

Snow, E. (1963) *The Other Side of the River: Red China Today*, London: Victor Gollancz.

Sood, R. (2002) *L.51: Convention on the Prohibition of the Use of Nuclear Weapons. Statement by H.E. Mr. Rakesh Sood, Ambassador, Permanent Representative to the Conference on Disarmament October 17, 2002*. United Nations, Online. Available: http://secint04.un.org/india/ind920.pdf (Accessed 22 July 2008).

Spivak, G.C. (2001) 'The Burden of English', in Castle, G. (ed.) *Postcolonial Discourses: An Anthology*, Oxford: Blackwell Publishing.

Sridharan, K. (2006) 'Explaining the Phenomenon of Change in Indian Foreign Policy Under the National Democratic Alliance Government', *Contemporary South Asia*, 15: 75–91.

Srinivasan, V. (2009) *Gandhi's Conscience Keeper: C. Rajagopalchari and Indian Politics*, Ranikhet: Permanent Black.

Steele, B.J. (2007) *Ontological security in International Relatons*, London: Routledge.

Steele, B.J. (2008) ' "Ideals that were really never in our possession": Torture, Honor and US Identity', *International Relations*, 22: 243–61.

Subrahmanyam, K. (1998) 'India's Nuclear Policy–1964–98', in Singh, J. (ed.) *Nuclear India*, New Delhi: Knowledge World.

Subrahmanyam, K. (2004) 'Narasimha Rao and the Bomb', *Strategic Analysis*, 28: 593–5.

Swami, P. (1999) 'The Bungle in Kargil', *Frontline*, Online. Available: www.flonnet. com/fl1613/16130040.htm (Accessed 3 June 2006).

Tagore, R. (2002) *Nationalism*, New Delhi: Rupa and Co.

Talbot, S. (2004) *Engaging India: Diplomacy, Democracy, and the Bomb*, Washington DC: Brookings Institution Press.

Tarlo, E. (2003) *Unsettling Memories: Narratives of the Emergency in Delhi*, New Delhi: Permanent Black.

Tellis, A.J.(2005) *Policy Brief: South Asian Seesaw: A New U.S. Policy on the Subcontinent*, Washington: The Carnegie Endowment for International Peace.

Tellis, A.J., Fair, C.C. and Medby, J.J. (2002) *Limited Conflicts Under the Nuclear Umbrella: Indian and Pakistani Lessons from the Kargil Crisis*, Santa Monica, CA: RAND.

Thackeray, B. (1998) 'Indian nuclear test sparks concerns of arms race', *CNN*, Online. Available: www.cnn.com/WORLD/asiapcf/9805/12/india.nuclear.on/ (Accessed 27 October 2005).

Thaindian News (2009) 'Sharif's 'kept in dark' over Kargil claims 'an absolute lie': Musharraf', *Thaindian News*, Online. Available: www.thaindian.com/.../sharifs-kept-in-dark-over-kargil-claims-an-absolute-lie-musharraf_100210105.html (Accessed 23 May 2010).

Thakur, R. (1993) 'Ayodhya and the Politics of India's Secularism: A Double-Standards Discourse', *Asian Survey*, 33: 645–64.

Thapar, R. (1989) 'Imagined Religious Communities? Ancient History and the Modern Search for a Hindu Identity', *Modern Asian Studies*, 23: 209–31.

Thapar, R. (2002) *The Penguin History of Early India: From the Origins to AD 1300*, New Delhi: Penguin Books India.

Thomas, R.G.C. (1980) 'Indian Defense Policy: Continuity and Change Under the Janata Government', *Pacific Affairs*, 53: 223–44.

Thurman, R.A.F. (1988) 'Social and Cultural Rights in Buddhism', in Rouner, L.S. (ed.) *Human Rights and the World's Religions*, Notre Dame, Ind.: Notre Dame Press.

Time (1971) 'Bangladesh: Out of War, a Nation Is Born'. Online. Available: www.yacht-ingnet.com/time/magazine/article/0,9171,878969,00.html (accessed 20 December 2008).

Times of India (2006) 'Nawaz blames Musharraf for Kargil', *Times of India* 28 May.

Times of India (2010) 'World has benign view of India's rise: PM Manmohan Singh', *Times of India*, Online. Available: http://timesofindia.indiatimes.com/india/World-has-benign-view-of-Indias-rise-PM-Manmohan-Singh/articleshow/5825572.cms (Accessed 17 April 2010).

Trautmann, T.R. (1997) *Aryans and British India*, Berkely: University of California Press.

Treaty on the Non-proliferation of Weapons (1968) Arms Control Association. Online. Available: www.armscontrol.org/documents/npt.asp (accessed 13 June 2006).

Trivedi, V.C. (1967) 'Statement by the Indian Representative (Trivedi) to the Eighteen Nation Disarmament Committee: Nonproliferation of Nuclear Weapons, May 23', *Documents on Disarmament 1967*, Washington DC: United States Arms Control and Disarmament Agency.

Uebel, M. (2000) 'Imperial Fetishism: Prester John Among the Natives', in Cohen, J.J. (ed.) *The Postcolonial Middle Ages*, New York: St. Martin's Press.

UN General Assembly. (2005) *2005 World Summit Outcome*, Online. Available: www. who.int/hiv/universalaccess2010/worldsummit.pdf (Accessed 20 December 2009).

UN Security Council (1971) *UN Security Council Official Records, Twenty-sixth year, Supplement for October, November and December 1971*, New York: United Nations.

United States Arms Control and Disarmament Agency (1974) *Documents on Disarmament 1974*. Washington DC: United States Arms Control and Disarmament Agency.

Unno, T. (1988) 'Personal Rights and Contemporary Buddhism', in Rouner, L.S. (ed.) *Human Rights and the World's Religions*, Notre Dame, Ind.: Notre Dame Press.

Vajpayee, A.B. (1977a) 'Shri Vajpayee's Address at Council of Foreign Relations', *Foreign Affairs Record*, XXIII.

Vajpayee, A.B. (1977b) 'Shri Vajpayee's Speech in Lok Sabha', *Foreign Affairs Record*, XIII: 89–94.

Vajpayee, A.B. (1978) 'Shri Vajpayee's Speech at Seminar on "Continuity and Change in India's Foreign Policy"', *Foreign Affairs Record*, XXIV: 207–13.

Vajpayee, A.B. (1998a) *Suo Motu Statement by Prime Minister Atal Bihari Vajpayee in the Indian Parliament on May 27, 1998*, Embassy of India – Washington DC, Online. Available: www.indianembassy.org/pic/pm-parliament.htm (Accessed 30 August 2005).

Vajpayee, A.B. (1998b) 'We have shown them that we mean business', *India Today*, Online. Available: www.india-today.com/itoday/25051998/vajint.html (Accessed 30 August 2005).

Vajpayee, A.B. (2004) *Prime Minister's statement at the 12th SAARC Summit*, Ministry of External Affairs, Online. Available: www.mea.gov.in/mystart.php?id=53017466 (Accessed 20 September 2006).

Vajpayee, B.V. (1998) 'Nuclear Anxiety; Indian's Letter to Clinton On the Nuclear Testing', *New York Times*, 13 May.

van der Veer, P. (1994) *Religious Nationalism: Hindus and Muslims in India*, Berkeley: University of California Press.

Van Hollen, C. (1980) 'The Tilt Policy Revisited: Nixon-Kissinger Geopolitics and South Asia', *Asian Survey*, 20: 339–61.

Vanaik, A. (2002) 'Making India Strong: The BJP-Led Government's Foreign Policy Perspectives', *South Asia*, 25: 321–41.

Varadarajan, L. (2004) 'Constructivism, identity and neoliberal (in)security', *Review of International Studies*, 30: 319–41.

Varshney, A. (1993) 'Contested Meanings: India's National Identity, Hindu Nationalism, and the Politics of Anxiety', *Daedalus*, 122: 227–61.

von Schlegel, F. (1889) *The Aesthetic and Miscellaneous Works of Friedrich von Schlegel*, London: George Bell & Sons.

Walker, M. (2006) 'India's Path to Greatness', *Wilson Quarterly*, 30: 22–30.

Waltz, K.N. (1979) *Theory of International Politics*, Reading: Addison Wesley Publishing Company.

Weber, C. (1998) 'Performative States', *Millennium*, 27: 77–95.

Weber, C. (1999) *Faking It: U.S. Hegemony in a Post-Phallic Era*, Minneapolis: University of Minnesota Press.

Weldes, J. (1999) *Constructing National Interests: The United States and the Cuban Missile Crisis*, Minneapolis and London: University of Minnesota Press.

Wendt, A. (1992) 'Anarchy is what States Make of it: The Social Construction of Power Politics', *International Organization*, 46: 391–425.

Wendt, A. (1999) *Social Theory of International Politics*, Cambridge: Cambridge University Press.

Wheeler, N.J. and Dunn, T. (1998) 'Good International Citizenship: A Third Way for British Foreign Policy', *International Affairs*, 74: 847–70.

Wheeler, N.J. (2000) *Saving Strangers: Humanitarian Intervention in International Society*, Oxford: Oxford University Press.

Williams, M.C. (2005) *The Realist Tradition and the Limits of International Relations*, Cambridge: Cambridge University Press.

Wright, D. (2002) 'Bangladesh and the BJP', *South Asia: Journal of South Asian Studies*, 25: 381–93.

Young, R.J.C. (1990) *White Mythologies: Writing History and the West*, London: Routledge.

Young, R.J.C. (2001) *Postcolonialism: An Historical Introduction*, Oxford: Blackwell.

Zachariah, B. (2004) *Nehru*, London: Routledge.

Index